THE FAMILY Handyman®

BEST TIPS & PROJECTS

THE FAMILY Handyman®

BEST TIPS & PROJECTS

by The Editors of *The Family Handyman* magazine

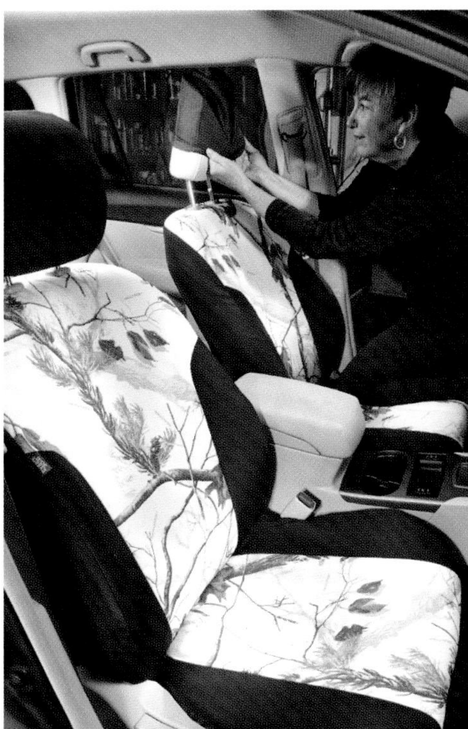

THE FAMILY HANDYMAN BEST TIPS & PROJECTS
(See page 288 for complete staff listing.)
Editor in Chief: Ken Collier
Project Editor: Teresa Marrone
Contributing Designers: BatScanner Productions, LLC
Contributing Copy Editors: Donna Bierbach, Peggy Parker
Indexing: Stephanie Reymann

Vice President, Group Publisher: Russell S. Ellis

The Reader's Digest Association, Inc.
President & Chief Executive Officer: Bonnie Kintzer

Warning: All do-it-yourself activities involve a degree of risk. Skills, materials, tools, and site conditions vary widely. Although the editors have made every effort to ensure accuracy, the reader remains responsible for the selection and use of tools, materials, and methods. Always obey local codes and laws, follow manufacturer's operating instructions, and observe safety precautions.

ISBN 978-1-62145-255-3

Address any comments about *The Family Handyman Best Tips & Projects* to:
Editor, Best Tips & Projects
2915 Commers Drive, Suite 700
Eagan, MN 55121

To order additional copies of *The Family Handyman Best Tips & Projects,* call 1-800-344-2560.

For more Reader's Digest products and information, visit our Web site at rd.com.
For more about *The Family Handyman* magazine, visit familyhandyman.com.

Printed in China
1 3 5 7 9 10 8 6 4 2

SAFETY FIRST—ALWAYS!

Tackling home improvement projects and repairs can be endlessly rewarding. But as most of us know, with the rewards come risks. DIYers use chain saws, climb ladders and tear into walls that can contain big and hazardous surprises.

The good news is, armed with the right knowledge, tools and procedures, homeowners can minimize risk. As you go about your projects and repairs, stay alert for these hazards:

Aluminum wiring

Aluminum wiring, installed in about 7 million homes between 1965 and 1973, requires special techniques and materials to make safe connections. This wiring is dull gray, not the dull orange characteristic of copper. Hire a licensed electrician certified to work with it. For more information go to cpsc.gov and search for "aluminum wiring."

Spontaneous combustion

Rags saturated with oil finishes like Danish oil and linseed oil, and oil-based paints and stains can spontaneously combust if left bunched up. Always dry them outdoors, spread out loosely. When the oil has thoroughly dried, you can safely throw them in the trash.

Vision and hearing protection

Safety glasses or goggles should be worn whenever you're working on DIY projects that involve chemicals, dust and anything that could shatter or chip off and hit your eye. Sounds louder than 80 decibels (dB) are considered potentially dangerous. Sound levels from a lawn mower can be 90 dB, and shop tools and chain saws can be 90 to 100 dB.

Lead paint

If your home was built before 1979, it may contain lead paint, which is a serious health hazard, especially for children six and under. Take precautions when you scrape or remove it. Contact your public health department for detailed safety information or call (800) 424-LEAD (5323) to receive an information pamphlet. Or visit epa.gov/lead.

Buried utilities

A few days before you dig in your yard, have your underground water, gas and electrical lines marked. Just call 811 or go to call811.com.

Smoke and carbon monoxide (CO) alarms

Almost two-thirds of home fire deaths from 2003 to 2006 resulted from fires in homes with missing or nonworking smoke alarms. Test your smoke alarms every month, replace batteries as necessary and replace units that are more than 10 years old. As you make your home more energy-efficient and airtight, existing ducts and chimneys can't always successfully vent combustion gases, including potentially deadly carbon monoxide (CO). Install a UL-listed CO detector, and test your CO and smoke alarms at the same time.

Five-gallon buckets and window covering cords

Since 1984, more than 275 children have drowned in 5-gallon buckets. Always store them upside down and store ones containing liquid with the covers securely snapped.

According to Parents for Window Blind Safety, over 560 children have been seriously injured or killed in the United States in the past few decades after becoming entangled in looped window treatment cords. For more information, visit pfwbs.org or cpsc.gov.

Working up high

If you have to get up on your roof to do a repair or installation, always install roof brackets and wear a roof harness.

Asbestos

Texture sprayed on ceilings before 1978, adhesives and tiles for vinyl and asphalt floors before 1980, and vermiculite insulation (with gray granules) all may contain asbestos. Other building materials, made between 1940 and 1980, could also contain asbestos. If you suspect that materials you're removing or working around contain asbestos, contact your health department or visit epa.gov/asbestos for information.

For additional information about home safety, visit mysafehome.org.
This site offers helpful information about dozens of home safety issues.

Contents

INTERIOR PROJECTS, REPAIRS & REMODELING

Home Care & Repair 10
Triple Your Closet Space 14
Patching a Wall 23
20 Secret Hiding Places 26
Tips for Trapping Mice 31
Handy Hints 34
Fastening to Concrete and Masonry... 39
Taping Drywall 44
5 Steps to a Secure Home 48

Special Section: PAINT LIKE A PRO 52

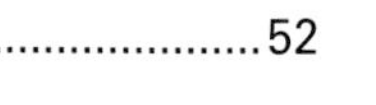

ELECTRICAL & HIGH-TECH

Home Care & Repair 64
Great Goofs 67
Fishing Wire 68
Working with PVC Conduit 72
Get Faster and Better Wi-Fi in Your Home 76
Handy Hints 78
Great Goofs 79

Special Section: ADDING OUTLETS 80

PLUMBING, HEATING & APPLIANCES

Home Care & Repair 88
Working with PEX 90
Can You Count on Your Sump Pump? 94
Great Goofs 97
Air Conditioner Repairs 98
Choose a Faucet You'll Love 102
Great Goofs 105
Installing Faucets 106

WOODWORKING & WORKSHOP PROJECTS & TIPS

Hide-the-Mess Lockers 110
Advanced Trim Tips 114
Top 10 Tips for Gluing Wood 120
Tips for Tighter Miters 124
Table Saw Helpers 128
Ken's Favorite Shop Tips 131
Sharpening Knives and Tools 136
Driving Screws 140
A Classic Workbench 143
Building Face-Frame Cabinets 148
Master the Reciprocating Saw 152
Finish a Tabletop 156
Handy Hints 160
Hardware Organizer 164
10 Simple Woodworking Jigs 167
Get Creative with Tools 172

Special Section: WORK SMARTER 176

5

EXTERIOR REPAIRS & IMPROVEMENTS

Home Care & Repair 184
How to Roof a House 187
Great Goofs 195
Exterior Spray Painting 196
Tips for Reviving a Wood Deck 200

Special Section: DEALING WITH OLD MAN WINTER 203

6

OUTDOOR STRUCTURES, LANDSCAPING & GARDENING

Home Care & Repair 210
Avoid the Top 4 Fertilizer Blunders .. 212
Deck a Patio 216
Mark's Mini Shed 221
Handy Hints 228
North Woods Bench 232
Roof Under a Deck 236

7

VEHICLES & GARAGES

Car Care & Repair 240
Replace Your Car's Seat Covers 242
Replace a Serpentine Belt 246
Roll On a Truck Bed Liner 249
Pro Tips for Detailing a Motorcycle .. 252
Advanced Garage Door Repairs 255
Great Goofs 261
Don't Just Polish—Rejuvenate! 262
Spray-On Paint Protection 265
Great Goofs 267
Refinish Wheels & Wheel Covers 268
Great Goofs 271
Small-Engine Gas Tips 272
Handy Hints 274
Motor Oil Smarts 277
Handy Hints 281

Great Goofs Bonus Section: BE CAREFUL! 282

Index 284
Acknowledgments 288

1 Interior Projects, Repairs & Remodeling

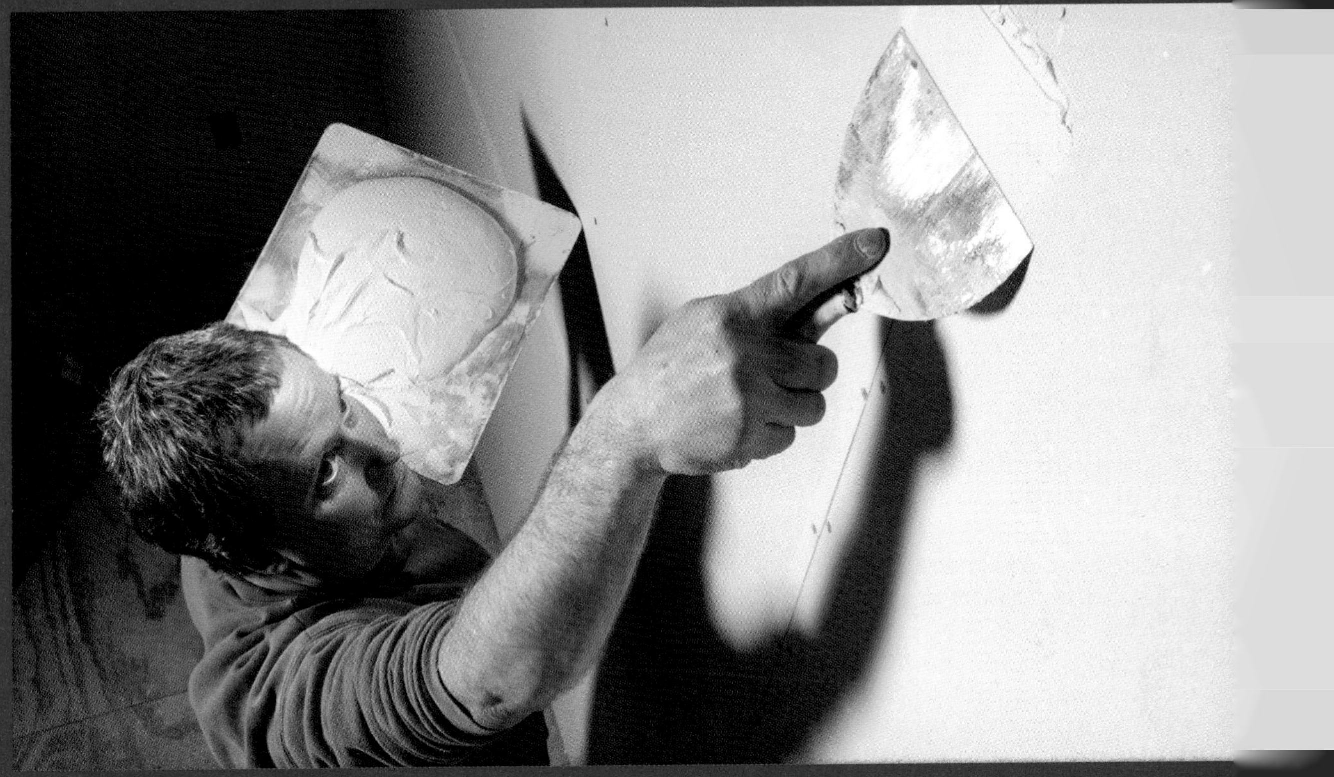

IN THIS CHAPTER

Home Care & Repair 10
Replace a sink strainer, repair a broken-out hinge, pre-level your doorjambs and more

Triple Your Closet Space 14

Patching a Wall 23

20 Secret Hiding Places 26

Tips for Trapping Mice 31

Handy Hints 34
Ladder-free lightbulb changes, install flooring in tight spots, souped-up litter box and more

Fastening to Concrete and Masonry 39

Taping Drywall 44

5 Steps to a Secure Home 48

REPLACE A SINK STRAINER

Kitchen sink basket strainers/drain assemblies work great when they're new. But with daily use and cleaning, the chrome or painted finish starts to wear off. The basket-strainer stopper may also start leaking. Once that happens, you can forget about soaking pots and pans overnight. You might think that the solution is to buy a new basket strainer. Good luck finding one that fits and seals. You can buy a "universal" replacement that'll work as a strainer. But it usually doesn't seal well because it's not an exact fit. So your best option is to replace the entire drain assembly.

You can replace the drain assembly yourself, but it's much easier with two people. You'll save about $100 in labor. The hardest part of the job involves removing the old drain locknut. If your locknut comes off easily, you can finish the entire job in less than an hour. However, a drain locknut that's corroded is tougher to deal with. We'll show you two quick ways to conquer stubborn locknuts. And we'll offer some tips on shopping for a new, longer-lasting basket strainer/drain assembly. Let's get started.

Remove the drainpipes

Place a bowl under the P-trap. Then use slip-joint pliers to loosen the compression nuts at the drain tailpiece and both nuts on the trap. Completely unscrew the tailpiece nut and swing the P-trap out slightly. Now unscrew the trap nuts completely, then remove and drain the entire trap and tailpiece assembly to give yourself more working space.

Loosen and remove the drain locknut

Crawl under the sink and check for corrosion on the large drain locknut. If it's corroded, spray all around the nut with rust-penetrating oil and allow it to soak for at least 15 minutes. Then have a friend hold the drain so you can loosen the locknut (**Photo 1**). Loosen the locknut with a hammer and chisel (**Photo 2**). If the locknut won't loosen or the entire drain spins and your helper can't hold it, cut it off (**Photo 3**).

If you don't have either a helper or a rotary cutoff tool and you've tried but can't loosen the locknut yourself, there's still another option to try. Head to the home center or hardware store and fork over about $25 for a sink drain wrench to loosen the nut and a plug wrench to help hold the drain (**Photo 4**). Once you get the locknut off, pull the entire drain up and out of the sink.

Clean the sink flange and install the new drain

Scrape off the plumber's putty or silicone from around the drain flange in the basin and under the sink. If the old drain was caulked with silicone, use silicone remover to clean it. Then apply a fresh bead of silicone around the flange in the basin and insert the new drain. Next, install the new O-ring and locknut in the order shown in **Photo 5**. Tighten the locknut until the rubber O-ring compresses slightly. Then reassemble the trap and tailpiece and attach it to the new sink drain. Clean off any excess silicone in the basin with a paper towel. Then clean off the O-ring and locknut.

Test for leaks by filling the sink with water and releasing it while you check the pipes under the sink.

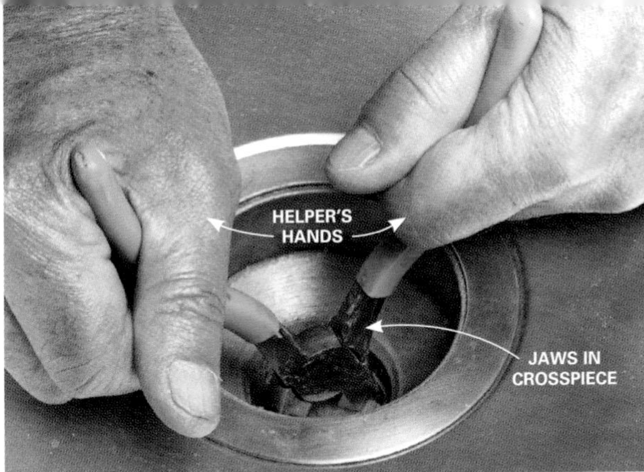

1 Hold the drain to loosen the locknut. Jam needle-nose pliers into the crosspiece section at the bottom of the drain. Have your friend spread the pliers and hold it tightly in the drain to prevent it from turning while you loosen the locknut.

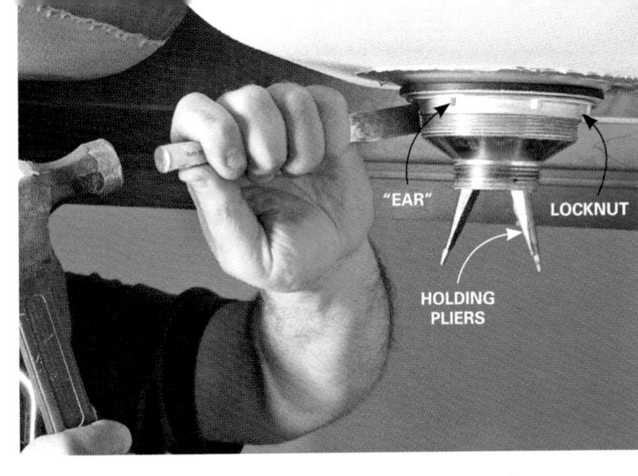

2 Loosen the locknut. Place the chisel tip against a locknut "ear." Then smack the chisel with a hammer. Move the chisel to the next ear and repeat until the nut spins by hand.

3 Drastic measures for stuck nuts. If all else fails, chuck a metal cutoff wheel into a rotary tool and cut the locknut. Cut until you reach the cardboard ring above the nut. Don't cut into the sink. If the nut still doesn't spin, fit your chisel into the cut area and smack it with a hammer to crack it open. Wear eye protection.

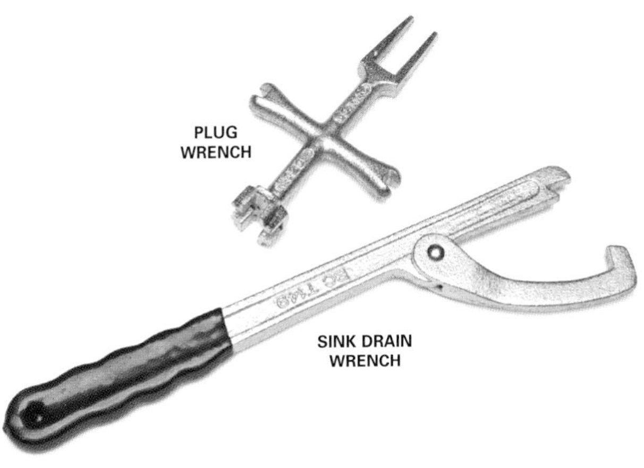

4 No helper? No problem! You can buy these tools for about $25 at any home center. Loosen the locknut with the sink drain wrench while you hold the drain with pliers and the plug wrench.

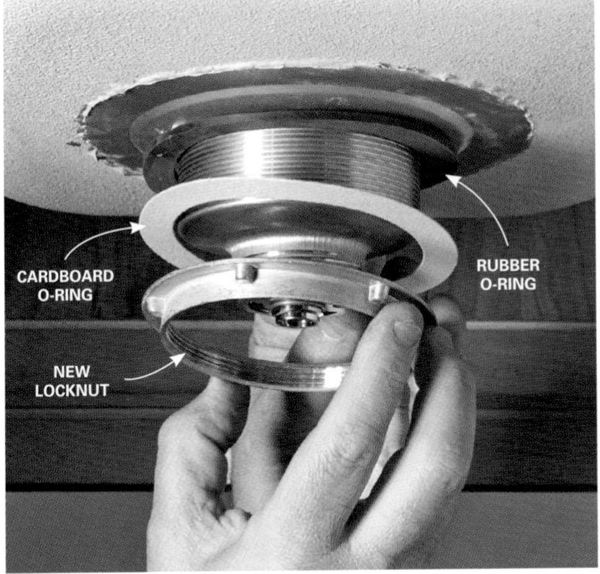

5 Install the new strainer. Slide the rubber O-ring on first. Then add the cardboard O-ring and the locknut. Tighten the nut until it starts compressing the rubber O-ring.

Buying tips

You'll have to spend at least $50 to get a high-quality strainer/drain assembly with a durable finish and a reliable stopper mechanism. The best strainers have either a spin-lock or a twist-and-drop style stopper. The spin-lock stopper doesn't have any parts that can wear, but screwing it in and out can be annoying. The twist-and-drop style is easier to use but requires occasional O-ring replacement.

Avoid push-in style strainers that have a non-replaceable neoprene stopper or a plastic knob. The plastic parts break and can lose their sealing ability if exposed to boiling water.

Spin-lock stopper | **Twist-and-drop stopper** | **Push-in stopper**

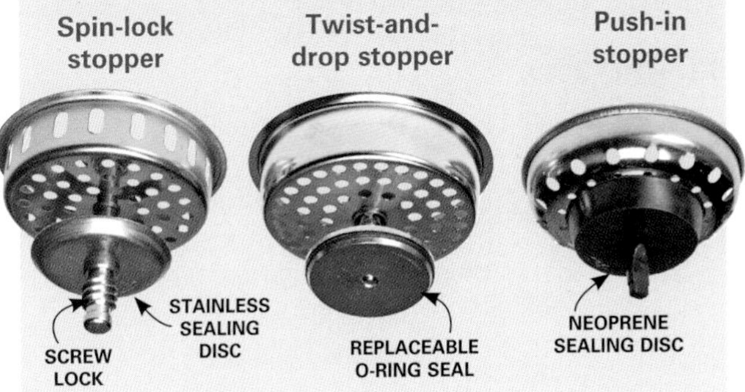

REPAIR YOUR OFFICE CHAIR

When casters roll around long enough in dust, dirt and hair, they stop rolling and start skidding. And that's how your floors get scratched up or your carpet gets wear tracks. Sometimes you can bring casters back from the dead by cleaning and lubricating them. So try that first. Just spray household degreaser/cleaner right onto the roller axles. Then spin the wheels to loosen them up. If that helps, rinse off the cleaner, blow them dry with compressed air, and then lubricate them. If cleaning doesn't help, you'll have to replace them. Here's how.

Most office chairs use a twin-wheel grip-ring style caster. The grip ring compresses and snaps into a groove in the socket. The easiest way to remove a grip-ring caster is with a flat bar (**Photo 1**). Before you buy replacements, measure the width and height of the stem. The most common widths are 3/8 in. and 7/16 in. There's only a 1/16-in. difference between the two, so measure carefully! If you try to fit a 7/16-in. stem into a 3/8-in. socket, you'll crack the socket.

Next, measure the wheel diameter. If you want the chair to push back easier or roll over small items on the floor rather than get stuck, buy a caster with a larger wheel. Buy a urethane tread caster for wood (and composite), tile or vinyl floors. But if the chair needs to roll on carpet, buy a hard rubber or nylon tread caster.

To install the caster, tilt it into the socket to compress the grip ring (**Photo 2**). If you can't get it started, apply a drop of oil to the ring. If the caster only goes in halfway, tap it with a mallet (**Photo 3**).

Casters are available online; search "replacement casters" for sources.

1 Pop out the old caster. Slip the angled end of a flat bar under the caster and pop the caster out of its socket in one quick motion. If it doesn't come out all the way, grab it again and pry it the rest of the way.

2 Start the new caster at an angle. Rotate the open end of the grip ring so it's facing up. Then tilt the caster stem into the socket until the ring gap starts to close. Straighten it up and push it home.

3 Tap it in. Position a small block of wood directly over the caster stem. Then tap it with a mallet until the stem pops all the way into the socket.

ERASE SCRATCHES ON PLASTIC

When we moved into our house there were dull areas on the black plastic door of the microwave. A closer look revealed that the dullness was not dirt or smudges but fine scratches where someone had used an abrasive cleaning product. I happened to have a swirl remover product intended for automobile paint. I followed the instructions for "hand application," and the results were amazing. Just be careful about using it on a surface that has text printed on the plastic because it will remove the printing.

Don Confarotta, Field Editor

BAKING SODA—THE ALL-AROUND ODOR ABSORBER

The best thing to make bad smells go away is baking soda. People think about it for their freezer or refrigerator, but it's good for much more than that. You can sprinkle it on carpet, work it in a bit and vacuum it up. For other items, like mattresses, cushions and clothing, dampen the fabric and gently rub with baking soda, then wipe off/rinse with cold water.

PRE-LEVEL YOUR DOORJAMBS

If your floors are going to be carpeted, you don't have to worry about a gap under one of the doorjamb sides. In fact, most trim installers raise the doors so they don't drag on the carpet. This is done by resting the jambs on 3/8-in.-thick shims, or temporary scraps of trim. That raises the whole door so it completely clears the carpet. But if the jambs have to fit tight to tile, wood or vinyl floors, you'll have to cut them to fit an out-of-level floor. The two photos below show how.

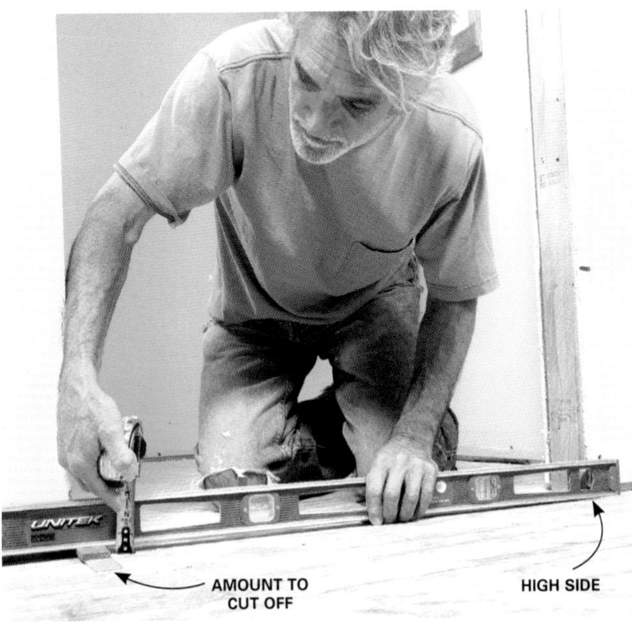

1 Check the opening. Lay a level across the opening and shim under one end until the bubble is centered. Measure the thickness of the shims.

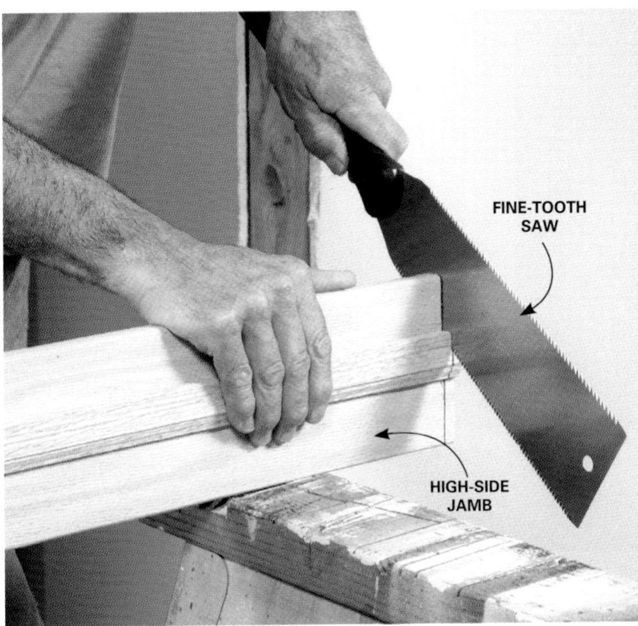

2 Trim the bottom of the jamb. Transfer the measurement to the appropriate jamb and draw a cutting line with a square. Saw along the line to trim the jamb. Now when you set the door in the opening, the top of the jamb will be level.

REPAIR A BROKEN-OUT HINGE

It doesn't take much of a blow to break hinge screws out of a particleboard door. If the screws just stripped and pulled out cleanly, you could fill the hole with toothpicks and wood glue, then reinstall the screws. But if the surrounding particleboard has broken away, it's quicker to fill the void with gap-filling glue (Loctite Go2 Glue is one choice).

Start by removing the hinge and preparing the damaged area (**Photo 1**). Apply petroleum jelly to the movable portions of the hinge to protect them from the glue. Then scuff the cup portion of the hinge with sandpaper where it will contact the adhesive. If you're using polyurethane adhesive, dampen the hinge with water to activate the glue. Apply glue to the damaged area and immediately install the hinge and screws (**Photo 2**). Secure the hinge with weights or clamps until the glue dries. Then reinstall the door.

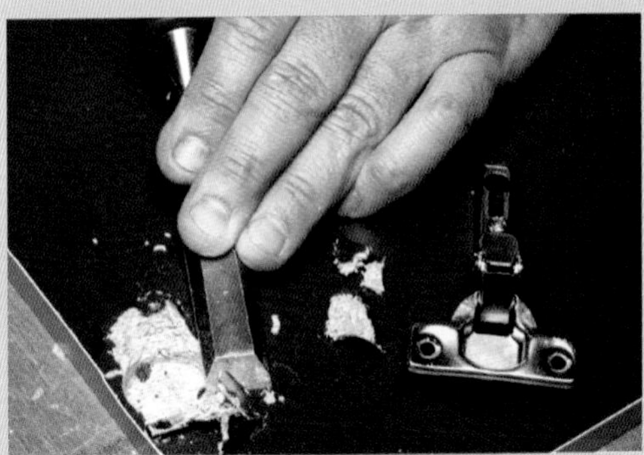

1 Prep the damaged area. Chisel out the damaged wood and enlarge the area slightly to give the adhesive more area to grip. Remove all loose chips and blow off any remaining dust.

2 Fill the void with glue. Squeeze in enough glue to fill the broken-out screw holes and coat the cup area. Then press the cup into the opening until the glue oozes out. Drop the screws into the hinge holes and tighten the ones that still have some wood to bite into.

TRIPLE YOUR **CLOSET SPACE**

Add extra clothes storage space to any room with these attractive cabinets

by **Jeff Gorton, Associate Editor**

It seems like no matter how much closet space you have, there's never quite enough. But building attractive clothes cabinets like these allows you to expand storage into your bedroom or a spare room and gain the extra space you need. You can build one storage tower or connect several together. Each tower consists of a drawer base, a wall cabinet with doors, and two side panels with holes for adjustable shelves. We'll show you how to build the cabinets and assemble the towers. And we'll also include details for adding a clothes hamper drawer, a pullout pants-hanging rack and shoe storage between the two towers.

Even though the style is simple, building these cabinets requires close attention to detail and accurate cuts. If you can cut plywood precisely and have the patience to carefully assemble the parts, you shouldn't have any trouble building this project.

We used 3/4-in. maple plywood for everything but the drawers and the backs of the cabinets. For these we used good-quality shop-grade plywood. We spent about $50 per sheet for the maple plywood. You could substitute less expensive plywood for the cabinet boxes to save a little money.

What it takes

TIME: Two or three weekends

COST: $400 per tower

SKILL LEVEL: Intermediate to advanced

TOOLS: Standard carpentry tools plus a table saw, miter saw, compressor and pin nailer, and a 35-mm Forstner bit

Tons of storage for all your clothes

Jeff's closet solution

I live in a 100-year-old house with a few very small, overflowing closets. But we do have an extra room that's only for guests. I figured this would be a perfect place for more storage. So I designed

this clothes-organizing system to fit along one wall of the extra room. And if we need more storage space, I can always build another tower.

Left: The large, deep drawers hold sweaters and other bulky items. Full-extension ball-bearing slides allow easy access.

The shoe shelves can store shoes, purses and hats, or small baskets for socks and underwear.

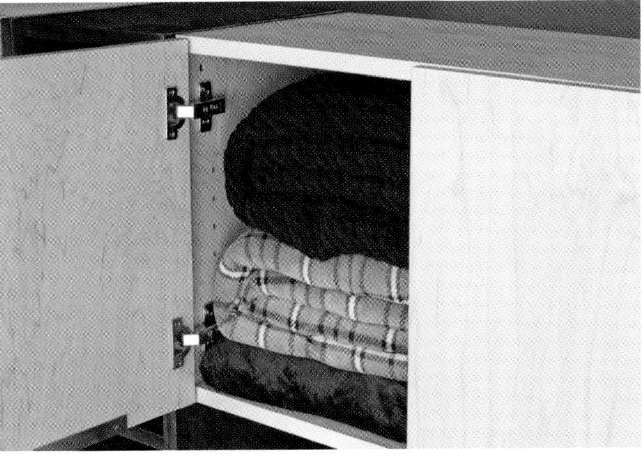

The wall cabinet has space for extra bedding or off-season clothes.

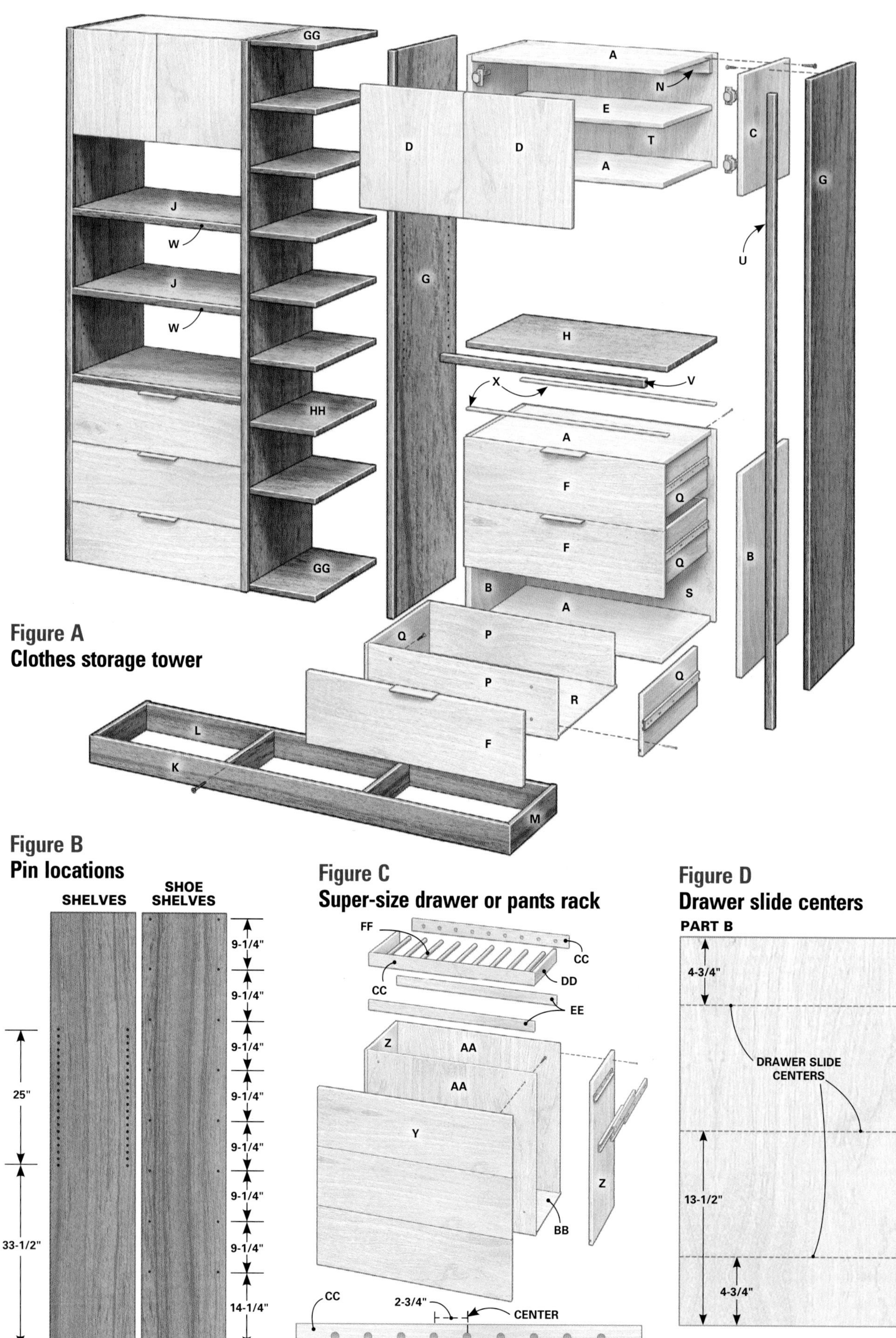

Figure A
Clothes storage tower

Figure B
Pin locations

Figure C
Super-size drawer or pants rack

Figure D
Drawer slide centers

Cut and prepare the plywood

The most important step in the building process is cutting the parts accurately. Use the Cutting List and **Figure E** (p. 22) as a guide. Our plywood was a full 3/4 in. thick, and the sizes shown are for 3/4-in. plywood. If yours is slightly thinner, cut the shelves, doors and drawer parts after you've assembled the cabinet boxes so you can adjust the fit.

A stationary table saw with an accurate fence and outfeed tables would be ideal for this job. But you can get great results with a portable table saw too. You'll need a top-quality blade designed to crosscut plywood. We splurged on a 90-tooth 10-inch blade ($60) and were amazed at the glass-smooth, splinter-free cuts we got.

After all the parts are cut, separate out the uprights and shelves that receive solid wood nosing. Then cover the raw plywood edges of the remaining 3/4-in. plywood parts with edge-banding veneer. For the cabinet boxes, you only need to cover the front edges. On the doors and drawer fronts, you'll want to cover all four edges.

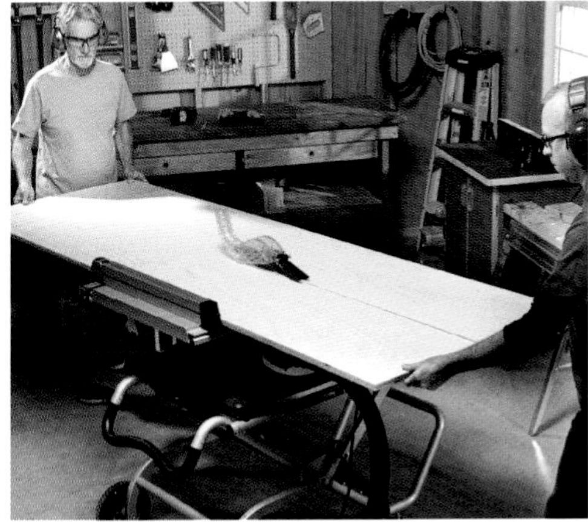

1 Rip the plywood. Round up a helper and rip the plywood sheets into strips according to Figure E on p. 22. Choose the best-looking plywood for the tall end panels because these are the most visible.

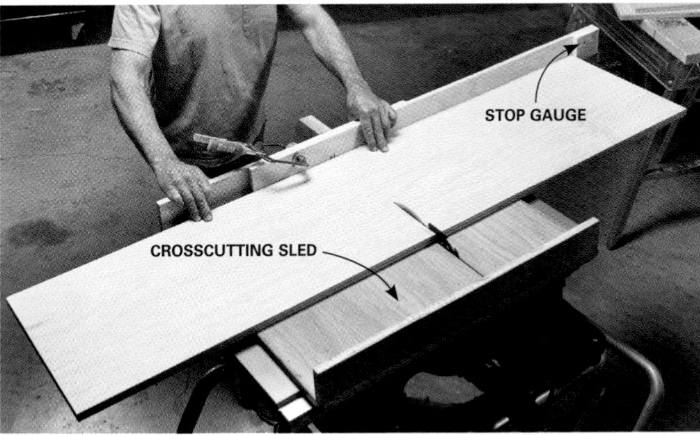

2 Crosscut the plywood. A crosscutting sled is the best tool for accurately cutting the plywood strips to length. Take the time to build a sled if you don't have one. Clamp a stop to the crosscutting sled to cut same-size parts accurately.

MATERIALS LIST
(for one tower)

ITEM	QTY.
4' x 8' x 3/4" maple plywood	3*
4' x 8' x 1/2" shop-grade plywood	1
4' x 8' x 1/4" shop-grade plywood	1
3/4" x 5-1/2" x 8' maple board	1
13/16" maple veneer edge banding	75 ln. ft.
16" full-extension drawer slides	3 pairs
Blum 120-degree clip-top hinges (B071T5550)	4
Blum frameless 0mm screw-on mounting plates (B173H710)	4
1/4" shelf pins	12
Screws, nails, wood glue, drawer and door pulls, finishing supplies	
Optional drawer slide for super-size drawer: KV 8505 16" file-cabinet drawer slide	1
Optional hamper for super-size drawer: Rubbermaid Configurations Hampers	2

**Leftover materials can be used to make a drawer front for the super-size laundry drawer and the shoe shelves.*

We purchased the Blum hardware and the file-cabinet drawer slide from wwhardware.com.

3 Cover the raw plywood edges. Finish the edges of the cabinet parts and the shoe shelves with edge banding. Self-adhesive edge banding is shown here, but iron-on edge banding also works. Center the edge banding and press or iron it on according to the manufacturer's instructions.

4 Trim the ends. Place the banded edge down on the work surface and use a sharp utility knife to trim the ends flush.

5 Trim the edges. Use a veneer edge trimmer to slice off the excess edge banding along the sides. A double-edge trimmer like this one ($20) trims both edges at once. Single-edge trimmers cost about $9 and work well. It just takes a little longer. Use sandpaper to remove any overhanging edge banding to create a perfectly flush edge.

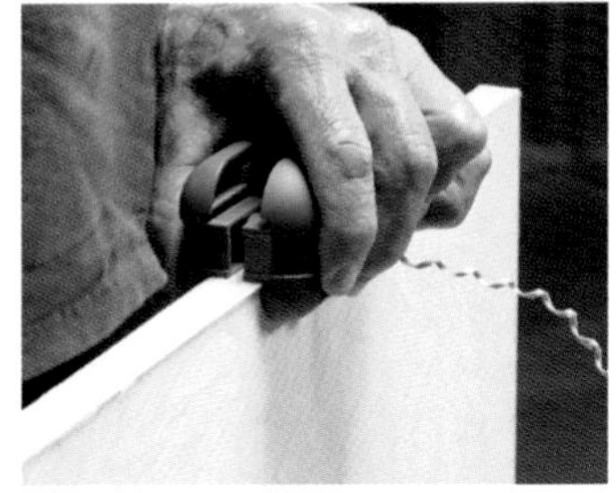

Build the cabinet boxes

The cabinets are simple plywood boxes with drawers or doors added. The key to accuracy is to make sure that the edges of the plywood remain perfectly aligned as you assemble the boxes and that the cabinet box is square. Photos 6 – 8 show how.

6 Install the slides first. It's easier to attach slides to the cabinet sides before the cabinet is assembled. Draw lines to indicate the center of the slides. Then center the screw holes on the line and attach the slide with the included screws.

7 Nail, then screw parts. To prevent the plywood from sliding around when you're drilling pilot holes, tack the parts first with a brad nailer. Then drill countersink pilot holes and connect the parts with screws.

8 Attach the back. If you're careful to cut the back perfectly square, you can use it to square the cabinet. Apply a bead of glue and set the back onto the cabinet. Make sure one edge of the back is flush with one side of the cabinet box and fasten it with 1-in. nails. Adjust the cabinet box until the other sides align, then partially drive a nail to hold it. Check the cabinet for square, then finish nailing on the back.

Super-size drawer

Replacing three drawers with one huge drawer allows you to hang pants or store two clothes hampers. The big drawer is just a deeper version of the small drawers. But to keep it from sagging, we mounted the drawer on file-cabinet drawer slides instead. To simulate three drawers, we grooved a single sheet of plywood by running it through the table saw with the blade raised 1/4 in., and used this for the drawer front. To convert the drawer for pants storage, just build the dowel rack and rest it on cleats.

Super-size laundry drawer
Figure C (p. 16) shows the parts for the deep drawer. Center the cabinet part of the file-drawer slide 4-3/4 in. from the top of the cabinet, and the drawer part of the slide 1 in. down from the top of the drawer. Finish by mounting the grooved drawer front.

Pullout pants rack
Use **Figure C** (p. 16) as a guide to build this rack from 2-in. strips of plywood and 5/8-in. dowels. Screw cleats to the front and back of the drawer, 2-1/4 in. from the top, to support the rack.

Build the drawers

The most critical part of the drawer-building process is to make sure the finished drawer is between 1 in. and 1-1/16 in. narrower than the inside dimensions of the cabinet to allow for the drawer slides. To determine the exact dimensions of the front and back of the drawers (parts P), measure between the cabinet sides and subtract twice the thickness of the drawer plywood. Then subtract another 1-1/16 in. Photos 9 – 14 show how to build and install the drawers.

9 Groove the drawer parts. Set your table saw fence at 1/2 in. and raise the blade 1/4 in. above the table. Cut a groove in the drawer sides and fronts. Move the fence away from the blade about 1/16 in. and make a second pass to widen the groove. Check the fit of the drawer bottom plywood. It should be snug but not too tight. You may need a third pass. After the grooves are cut, rip the backs to width.

10 Build the drawer boxes. Glue and nail the sides to the front and back. Use glue sparingly to avoid squeeze-out mess. Use 1-1/4-in. nails and aim carefully to prevent them from shooting out the sides. Make sure the grooves line up—it's easy to get a part upside down.

11 Slide in the bottom. Check the fit of the drawer bottom and trim the width a little if needed. Don't force the plywood or it may push the drawer sides apart.

12 Nail the drawer bottom. Measure diagonally to make sure the drawer is square. Then drive 1-in. nails through the drawer bottom into the drawer back to hold it in place.

13 Attach the drawer slide. Draw a line 3-3/4 in. from the top edge of the drawer. Center the drawer slide on the line, keeping the front edge lined up with the front of the drawer. Attach it with two screws. Add the remaining screws later to secure the drawer slide in place after making any adjustment.

14 Install the drawer fronts. Mount each drawer front with hot-melt glue, then pull it out and secure it with four screws driven from inside the drawer. Set the bottom door flush with the bottom of the cabinet. Then use two stacks of two pennies as spacers between the drawer fronts. The top drawer should be 1/8 in. below the top of the cabinet.

Hang the doors with Euro hinges

This type of cabinet construction is perfect for Euro-style hinges. You simply mount a plate to the cabinet and drill a 35-mm (1-3/8-in.) recess in the door to accept the hinge. The Blum 120-degree clip hinges we're using are adjustable up and down, in and out, and side to side, making final door fitting a breeze. Photos 15 – 21 show how to install the hinges and hang the doors.

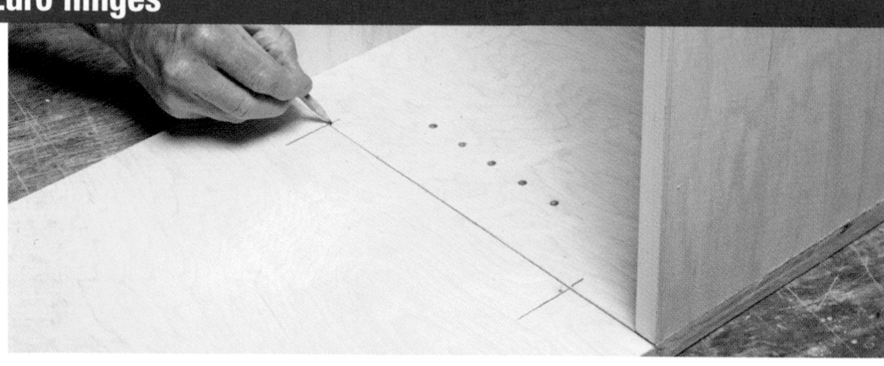

15 **Mark the hinge locations.** Mark the hinge position on the doors, 3 in. from the top and bottom. Then align the door with the cabinet and transfer the marks to the cabinet side.

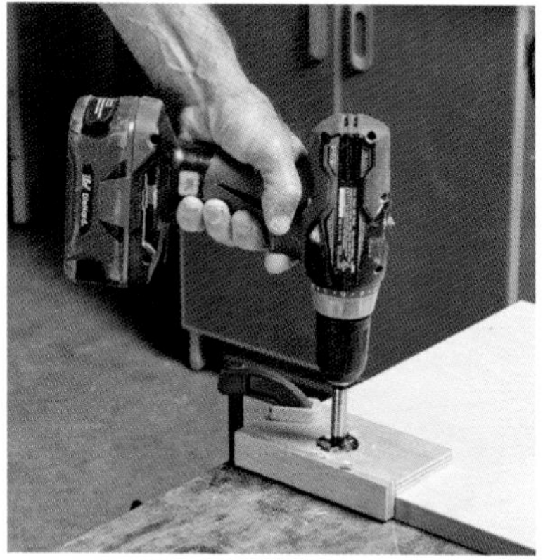

16 **Start the hinge holes.** We built this plywood jig as a guide for starting the hinge holes. You can also buy a jig, or simply mark the center of the hinge and use a center punch to create a starting hole. For these Blum hinges, the center of the hole is 7/8 in. from the edge of the door. Start drilling the hole with the 35-mm (or 1-3/8-in.) Forstner-style bit.

17 **Complete the hinge hole.** Remove the guide so you can judge how deep to drill. With most bits you can drill until the top of the bit is flush with the surface. The recess should be 1/2 in. deep. Drill a hole in a scrap first to check the depth before drilling a door.

18 **Mount the hinge.** Press the hinge into the recess and align it with a square. Use a self-centering bit to drill pilot holes for the hinge screws. Then attach the hinge with the screws provided.

19 **Mark for the hinge plates.** Draw lines 1-7/16 in. from the front of the cabinet to locate the center of the hinge plates. If you're using a different hinge, check the instructions to find the correct distance.

20 **Attach the hinge plates.** Center the hinge plates on the marks and line up the center of the screw holes with the second mark. Drill pilot holes with a self-centering bit and attach the plates with the screws.

21 **Hang the door.** Clip the hinges to the plates to hang the doors. Don't bother to adjust the hinges until after the cabinet is mounted to the wall.

Build the side panels

The side panels have 1-in.-wide solid wood edging on one side and shelf-pin holes on one face. If you'll be adding shoe shelves between two towers as shown in the photo on the opening page, then drill holes for these shelf pins too. Be careful to attach the nosing to the correct edge of each panel. Since the shelf-pin holes are not an equal distance from top and bottom, the two sides are not interchangeable, but are mirror images.

22 Drill the shelf-pin holes. We're using a store-bought jig, but you can also use a length of 1/4-in. pegboard as a template for drilling the holes. Mount a stop on your 1/4-in. drill bit to drill the holes 3/8 in. deep.

23 Glue and nail the nosing. Spread a bead of glue along the plywood edge. Align the wood edging flush to the inside edge of the panel and attach it with 1-1/4-in. nails.

Install the cabinets in your room

After all the cabinets and side panels are built, you'll want to stain and varnish or paint them before installing them in your room. Remove all the drawers, doors and hardware to make finishing easier. Carefully sand all the parts. We used a random orbital sander and 120-grit sandpaper. Then we stained the side panel and shelves and finally brushed two coats of polyurethane on all the parts. After the finish dries, reinstall the hardware and carry the cabinets, side panels and base into your room. Mark the studs in the location where you'll install the cabinets. Photos 24 – 27 show the installation steps.

24 Level the base. Installing the towers is easier if you start out with a level base. If your floor isn't level, slide shims under the base to level it. Then screw it to the studs. Cut off the shims and cover the gap with molding if necessary. You can make your own molding by ripping 3/8-in.-wide strips from 3/4-in. maple, or buy base-shoe molding.

25 Assemble the towers. Arrange the cabinets and side panels on the floor. We built simple 2x4 supports to hold the cabinets and side panels in place while we screwed them together. Drill holes through the cabinet sides a few inches from each corner. Then carefully line up the panels so the tops and bottoms are flush with the cabinets, and attach them with 1-1/4-in. screws.

26 Attach the towers to the wall. Transfer the stud locations to the inside of the cabinet and drive 2-1/2-in. screws into the studs to secure the towers. Use the 12-in.-wide shoe shelves as spacers at the top and bottom to position the second tower.

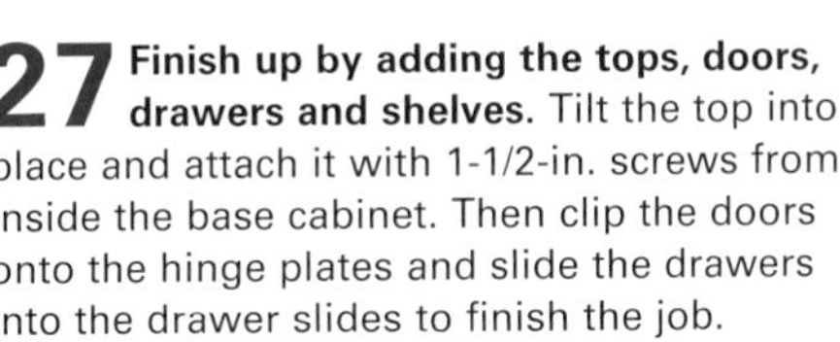

27 Finish up by adding the tops, doors, drawers and shelves. Tilt the top into place and attach it with 1-1/2-in. screws from inside the base cabinet. Then clip the doors onto the hinge plates and slide the drawers into the drawer slides to finish the job.

Figure E
Plywood cutting diagrams

1/4" PLYWOOD

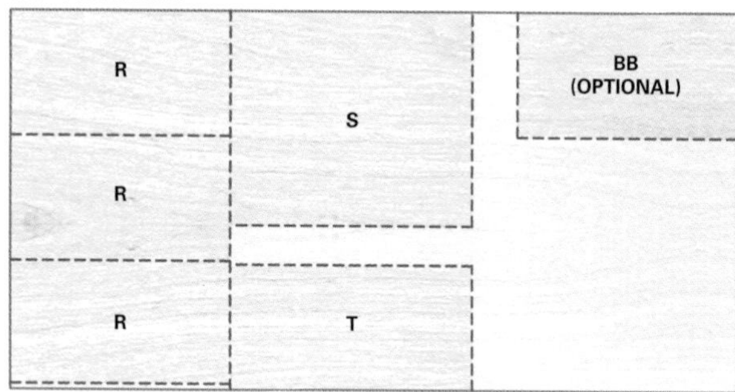

3/4" PLYWOOD

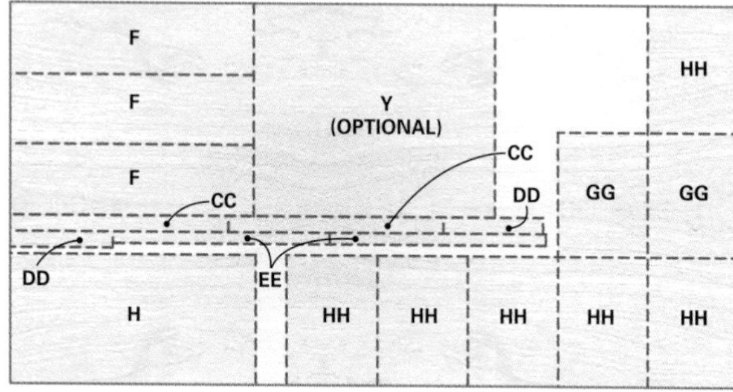

3/4" PLYWOOD

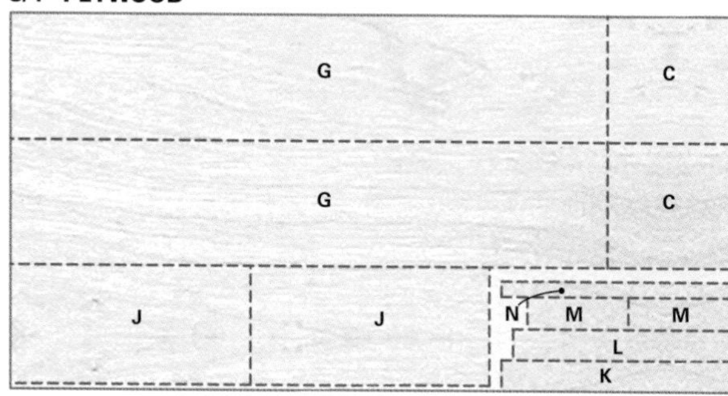

3/4" PLYWOOD

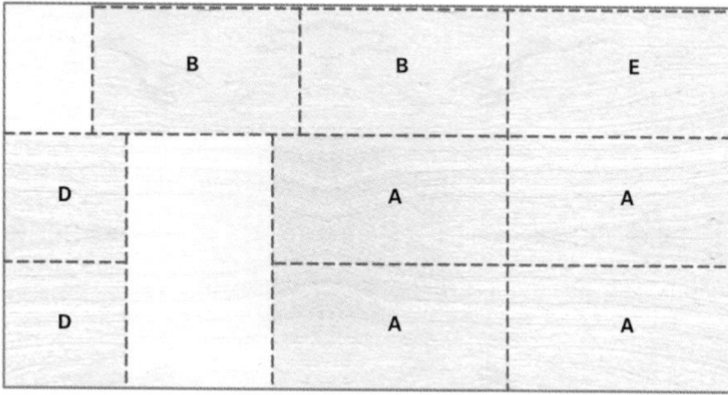

1/2" PLYWOOD

AA (OPTIONAL)	AA (OPTIONAL)	Q	P
		Q	P
		Q	P
		Q	P
Z (OPTIONAL)	Z (OPTIONAL)	Q	P
		Q	P

CUTTING LIST

KEY	DIMENSIONS	QTY.	NAME
3/4" maple plywood			
A	15-7/8" x 30-1/2"	4	Cabinet tops and bottoms
B	15-7/8" x 27"	2	Lower cabinet sides
C	15-7/8" x 16"	2	Upper cabinet sides
D	15-3/4" x 15-7/8"	2	Upper cabinet doors
E	15-7/8" x 30-3/8"	1	Upper cabinet shelf
F	8-7/8" x 31-3/4"	3	Lower cabinet drawer fronts
G	16-1/8" x 79-3/4"	2	Side panels
H	16-1/8" x 32"	1	Lower cabinet top
J	15-1/4" x 31-7/8"	2	Shelves
K	4" x 30-1/2"	1	Base front (extend as needed for two towers)
L	4" x 29"	1	Base back
M	4" x 13-1/2"	2	Base sides
N	2" x 30-1/2"	1	Upper cabinet hanging strip
1/2" shop-grade plywood			
P	7-1/2" x 28-1/2"	6*	Drawer fronts and backs (cut backs to fit)
Q	7-1/2" x 15-3/4"	6	Drawer sides
1/4" shop-grade plywood			
R	15-1/2" x 29"	3	Drawer bottoms
S	27" x 32"	1	Lower cabinet back
T	16" x 32"	1	Upper cabinet back
3/4" solid maple			
U	1" x 79-3/4"	2	Side panel edging
V	1" x 32"	1	Lower cabinet top edging
W	1" x 31-7/8"	2	Shelf edging
X	1/4" x 32"	2	Spacers
OPTIONAL LARGE DRAWER			
3/4" maple plywood			
Y	26-7/8" x 31-3/4"	1	Grooved drawer front
1/2" shop-grade plywood			
Z	15-3/4" x 25"	2	Drawer sides
AA	28-1/2" x 25" *	2	Drawer front and back (cut back to fit)
1/4" shop-grade plywood			
BB	15-1/2" x 29"	1	Drawer bottom
OPTIONAL PANTS RACK			
3/4" maple plywood			
CC	2" x 28-3/8"	2	Front and back
DD	2" x 13-1/8"	2	Sides
EE	1-1/2" x 28-1/2"	2	Cleats
5/8" dowels			
FF	13-7/8"	9	Dowels
OPTIONAL SHOE SHELVES			
GG	16" x 12"	2	Top and bottom shelves
HH	16" x 11-7/8"	7	Middle shelves

** Adjust size to compensate for plywood thickness*

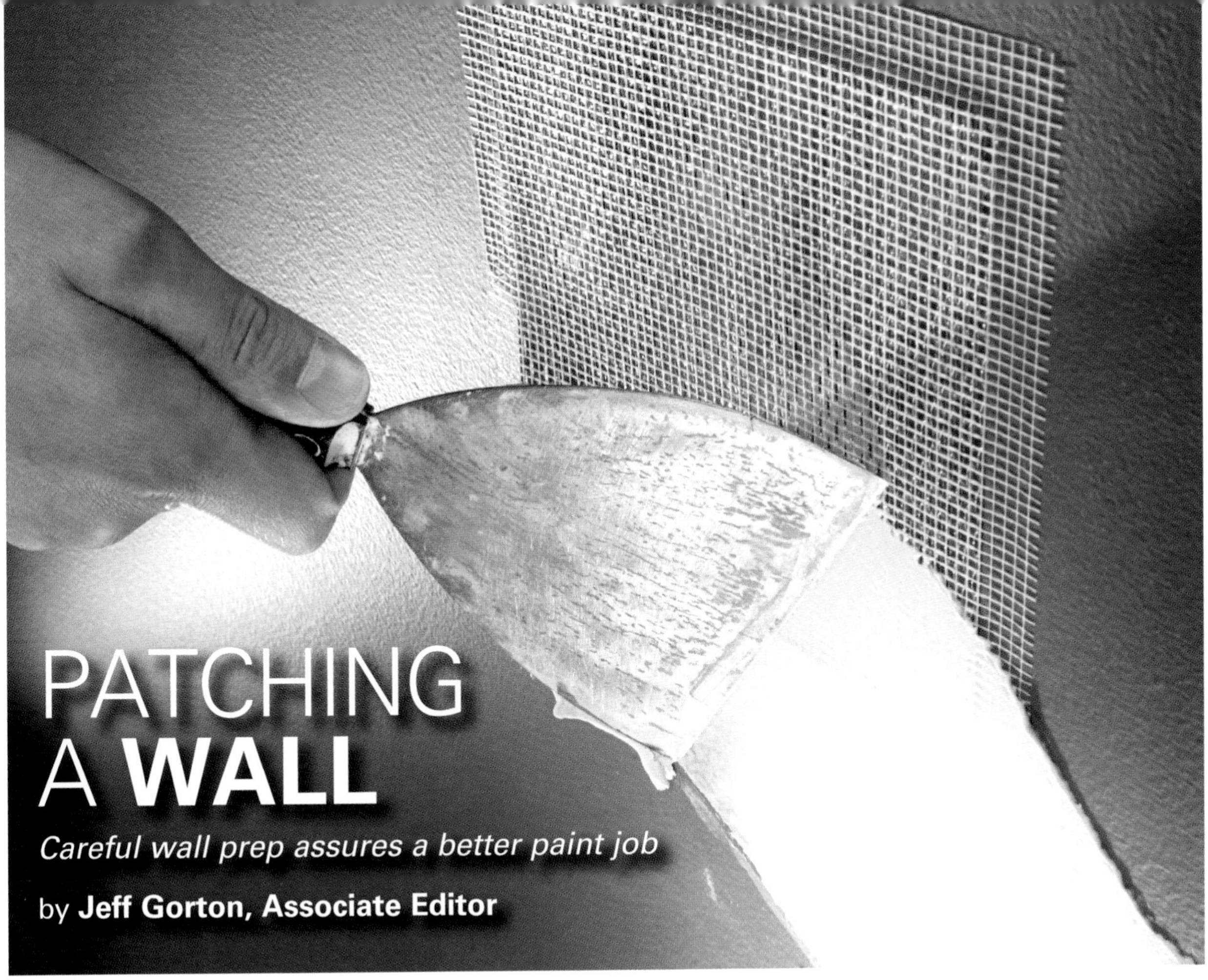

PATCHING A WALL

Careful wall prep assures a better paint job

by **Jeff Gorton, Associate Editor**

Preparing walls for paint inevitably involves patching. It's one of the most important steps. But sometimes it takes more than just a can of spackling and a small putty knife to get good results. We'll show you some wall patching tips and products that will help you speed up the job and avoid problems.

Cover cracks with repair spray

Stress cracks usually show up around window and door openings. The cracks are the result of framing movement and are hard to fix permanently. But using spray-on crack repair is a good way to at least extend the life of your repair. The spray forms a flexible membrane over the crack that can stretch and relax as the building moves.

If the crack is open, fill it first with patching compound. Then follow the instructions on the can to cover the crack with the crack-repair spray. Let it dry and cover it with paint to finish the repair. Crack-repair spray is sold at hardware stores, paint stores or online for about $4 a can.

Use stick-on patches for midsize holes

There are all kinds of ways to patch doorknob-size holes. But the quickest and easiest is to use one of these stick-on mesh patches. They're available in a few different sizes for $2 to $4 each at paint stores, hardware stores and home centers. To use the patch, just clean the wall surface and sand it to give the surface a little "tooth." Then stick the patch over the hole and cover it with two or three thin layers of joint compound. You can speed up the process by using setting-type compound for the first coat.

Use self-priming filler

Patches made with traditional patching materials need to be primed with a sealing-type primer before painting. Otherwise the patched areas could show through the finished paint job as foggy spots. But if you patch with a self-priming patching material, you can avoid this extra step. There are several brands; just look for the words "self-priming" or "with primer" on the container.

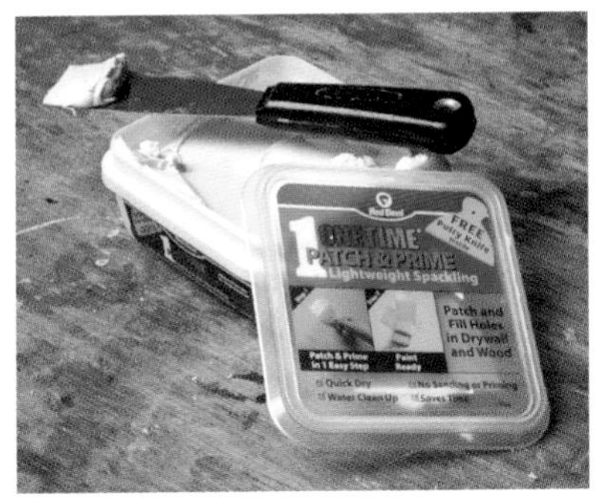

Use setting compound for big holes

It's fine to fill screw holes and other small wall dings with patching compound, but for dime-size and larger repairs, and for holes that are deep, it's best to use a joint compound that sets up by a chemical reaction. These are available in powder form with setting times ranging from five to 90 minutes.

The reaction starts when you mix in the water, and the compound hardens in the specified time. The five-minute version is nice because you can buy the powder in a convenient 5-lb. box, and the compound hardens quickly, so you can apply another coat right away. Remember, setting-type compounds are harder to sand than regular patching materials, so make sure to strike them off flush to the surface when you fill the hole. You'll find setting-type compounds wherever drywall taping supplies are sold.

Seal exposed drywall paper before patching

When you peel off old adhesive or self-sticking picture hangers, you often tear off the top layer of drywall paper, leaving fuzzy brown paper exposed. If you try to patch over this without sealing it first, the water in the patching material will cause the paper to bubble and create an even bigger problem. The key to patching torn drywall paper is to seal it first with an oil- or shellac-based sealer (KILZ Original and BIN are two brands). These are available in spray cans or liquid that you can brush on. Don't use a water-based product or you'll likely have the same bubbling problem. After the sealer dries, sand the area lightly to remove the hardened paper fuzz. Then cover it with patching compound as you would for any other wall repair.

Make a dent for the patching compound

When you remove a nail, drywall anchor or picture hanger, there is usually a little ridge of old paint or drywall sticking out that's hard to cover with patching material. The solution is to make a dent over the hole, and then fill the dent. Most good-quality putty knives have a rounded hard plastic or brass end on the handle that works perfectly for making the dent. The rounded end of a screwdriver handle or the handle of a utility knife will also work. Press the handle against the hole and twist it slightly while applying pressure to dent the surface, or if you have good aim, use your denting tool like a hammer.

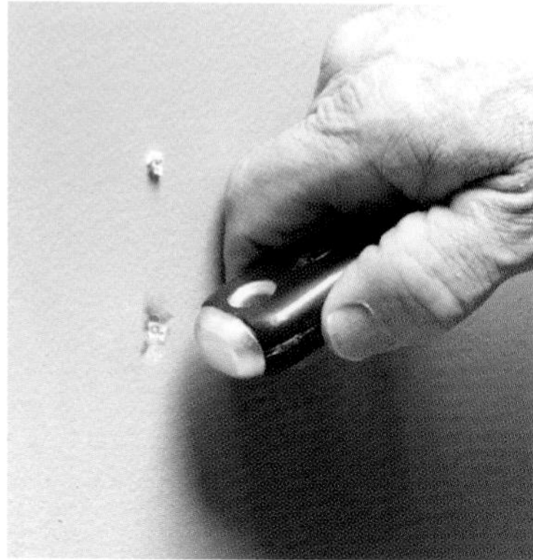

Skim-coat areas with lots of dings or holes

In areas with a lot of dents and holes, like in the mudroom where boots, hockey sticks and golf club bags leave their marks, don't try to fill every dent individually. Instead get a wider taping knife—a 6-in.-wide putty knife will do—and simply skim the entire area with joint compound. For the best results, use "topping" or "all-purpose" joint compound.

Mix a tablespoon or two of water into three or four cups of the joint compound to make it easier to spread. Then put a few cups into a drywall pan and use your 6-in. knife to spread it. Spread a thin coat of joint compound over the area. Then scrape it off, leaving just enough to fill the recesses and holes. You may have to apply two or three coats to completely fill holes, but the thin layers dry quickly and are easy to apply. Sand the wall after the final coat dries.

Fill a row of holes with one swipe

Professional drywall tapers always fill a row of screw holes with one long stripe of joint compound, rather than filling every screw hole separately. In addition to being faster, this method disguises the screw holes better and makes it easier to sand the patch. Instead of sanding around each hole, you can just sand the whole stripe.

You can take advantage of this tip whenever you're filling a series of holes that are lined up and close together, like the holes left from a shelf standard or a row of pictures. Use a 6-in.-wide putty knife and apply the compound as shown in the two photos.

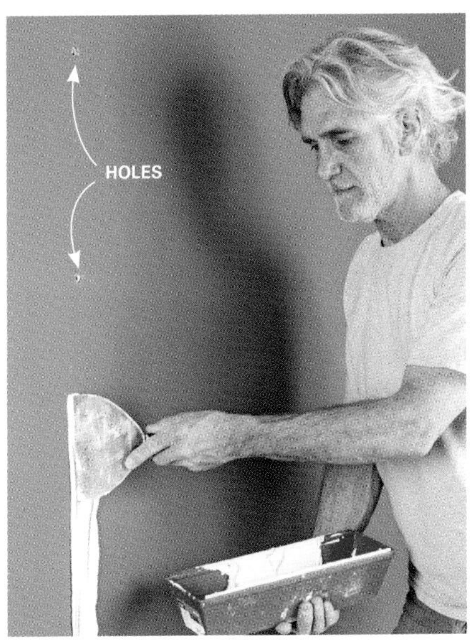

1 Fill the holes. Use a 5- or 6-in.-wide putty knife and apply the compound with the knife held parallel to the line of holes.

2 Remove the excess. Turn your knife so the blade is perpendicular to the stripe of joint compound and remove the excess. To completely fill the holes, you'll probably need to apply another coat after this one dries.

You can spray on wall texture

Orange peel texture on walls or ceilings is nice for hiding defects and adding interest, but it can be a real pain if you have to make a big patch. Luckily you can buy spray-on orange peel patch that will allow you to match the texture of the patch without hiring a pro. You can buy the patching material in a few different versions: regular, quick-drying and pro. The pro version gives you the most control over the spray pattern.

Make sure to practice spraying the texture onto a scrap of drywall or cardboard to fine-tune your technique before you spray it on the wall patch. Let the test piece dry before you decide whether you need to adjust the nozzle for a coarser or finer texture. Remember, you can always add another coat if there's not enough texture after the first coat dries.

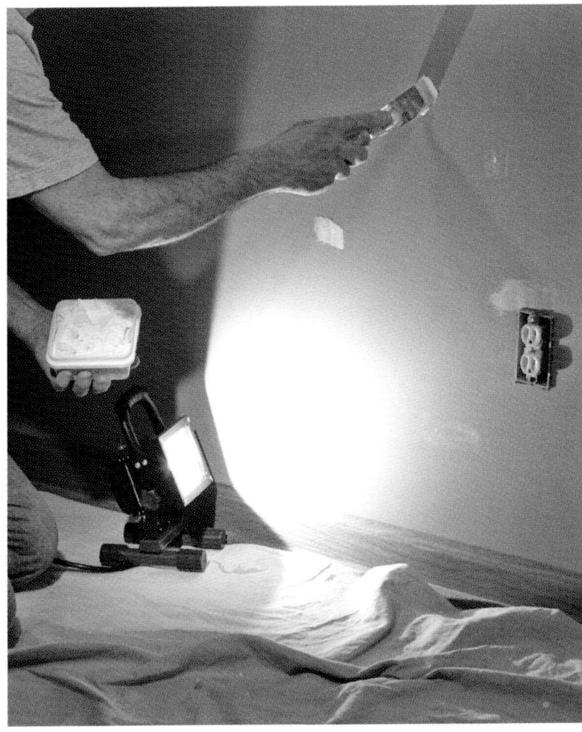

Use a raking light when patching walls

When you're preparing your walls for paint, position a bright light so that the beam rakes across the wall as shown here. This will accentuate any defects, making them easier to see and fix, and will alert you to patches that need more fill or additional sanding. If your walls look smooth in raking light, you can be sure they'll look awesome when you're done painting.

20 SECRET **HIDING PLACES**

Clever ways to hide your valuables

by **Travis Larson, Senior Editor**

Got some real valuables to hide? Frankly, the best advice is to get a safe-deposit box at your bank. But that's not very fun. Plus, it's a hassle if you need to get to your valuables often or quickly. Here are a bunch of clever, simple ways to hide those items from all but the smartest, most determined crooks.

The old hollowed-out book trick

We've all seen the hollowed-out book, but there's not much room in one of those. Instead, use several books with a plywood box attached to the back. If you have a band saw for cutting out the pages, great. If not, you can use a jigsaw. (After all, books are just a form of wood.)

If the sides of the books will be visible, fold back the covers of the books on the left and right sides of the assembly before cutting. Build a plywood box to fit the opening and glue the book parts to the box with construction adhesive. The disadvantage? You can see inside the box on low shelves, so you need to display it so the opening is above eye level.

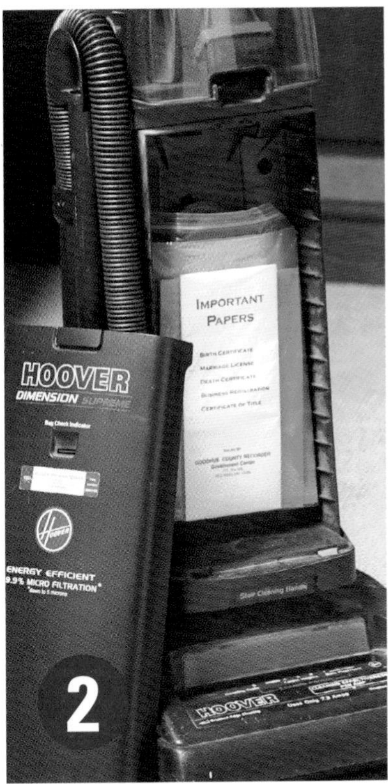

Right out in the open

It doesn't have to be an old vacuum cleaner. Any common household item that has a cavity will work. Think old printers, computer towers, children's toys, etc. (Just be sure family members know about it so your valuables don't get donated or tossed!) For easy access, choose an item that opens instantly, like a vacuum cleaner bag compartment. For more security, choose an item with a cover that screws shut.

Air-return stash

Cut out a stud space opening to fit a return air grille. Cut off the grille screws and glue just the heads in place. Run four drywall screws into the corners of the opening so they fit just inside the rim of the grille. Then glue rare earth magnets to the back of the grille so they line up with the screw heads.

Buried treasure

Roll up some cash, stick it in a medicine bottle or any other watertight container, and bury it in a potted plant. For quicker access and to keep dirt from getting under your fingernails, place a stone or pine cone over it. Not many burglars are going to be excavating around your houseplants.

MORE
HIDING PLACES

5

False-bottom drawer

Pick a deep drawer so the depth change won't be obvious. Cut 1/4-in. plywood 1/16 in. smaller than the drawer opening and rest it on a couple of wood strips that are hot-glued to the drawer sides. Then hot-glue some item you'd expect to find in that drawer to the bottom so you have a handle to lift the false bottom and reveal the booty.

6

Cabinet hidey-hole

Between almost every pair of upper cabinets, there's a 1/2-in. gap. Take advantage of that gap by hanging a big envelope containing cash, papers or anything flat. Hang the cash with binder clips that are too wide to fall through the crack.

7

Toe-kick hideaway

There's a huge 4-in.-tall cavity under all those kitchen cabinets behind the toe-kicks. It takes a few carpentry skills, but you can pull the toe-kicks free and make them removable. Most are 1/4-in. plywood held in place with 1-in. brads, and they're pretty easy to pull off. If you have a secondary 3/4-in. toe-kick, you'll have to cut it out at both ends. An oscillating tool works well for that task.

Stick both halves of round hook-and-loop self-adhesive tape to the toe-kick. Then push the toe-kick into place. The adhesive will stick to the cabinet base and leave half of the hook-and-loop tape in place when you pull it free. You can store approximately $2.4 million in gold bullion under two average-size cabinets—provided the floor is strong enough to support it.

8

Counterfeit containers

Go online and type in "secret hiding places" and you'll be amazed by how many brand-name phony containers are available. Comet, Coca-Cola, Bush Beans—whatever. But you can craft a homemade version too. This mayonnaise jar had its interior spray-painted with cream-colored paint for plastic.

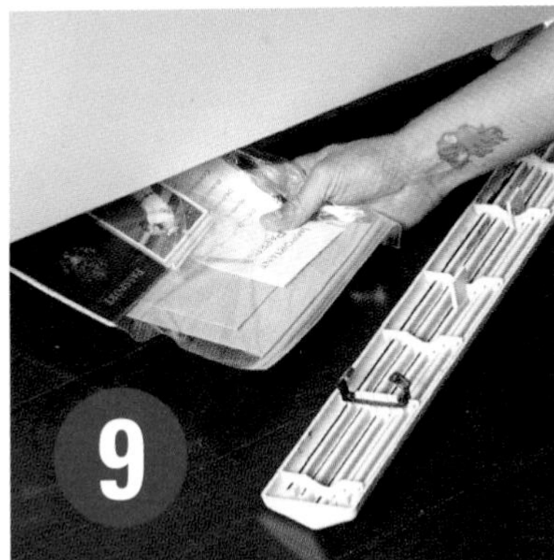

9

The appliance caper

Fridges and dishwashers have a snap-off grille in the front, and there's a lot of secret storage space under there. Ask yourself this: How many burglars think about cleaning your refrigerator coils? But before you stuff treasures under a fridge, look to see where the coils are. On some models, added objects might block the airflow. That will make the fridge work harder and could even damage it.

Our Field Editors weigh in

We received lots of tips from our Field Editors about their hiding spots—and we promised not to include their names or addresses. Here are their favorites:

10. "Drill a hole in the top of any interior door. Size it to fit a cylinder such as an old film container or a cigar tube. Roll up some bills and keep them there."
Editor's Note: If you want to do this trick on a hollow-core door, you have to stick close to the outside edges. Look at the door from the top and you'll see how wide the solid internal frame is.

11. "Which paint can contains the loot?"

12. "It took some effort, but I freed a tread from the oak stairs to the second story and attached a piano hinge to the back. It's almost invisible."

13. "Whenever I build a piece of furniture, I build in a stash spot. The last project I built was a dresser, and when I assembled it, I put a 1/4-in. sheet of plywood just above the top drawers and installed a piano hinge on the top. That's where we keep everything we care about."

14. "Believe it or not, I put our passports and a bit of cash underneath the shroud that covers the garage door opener."

15. "I put in a fake PVC pipe complete with a cleanout plug in my basement. Unscrew the plug and there are the goods."

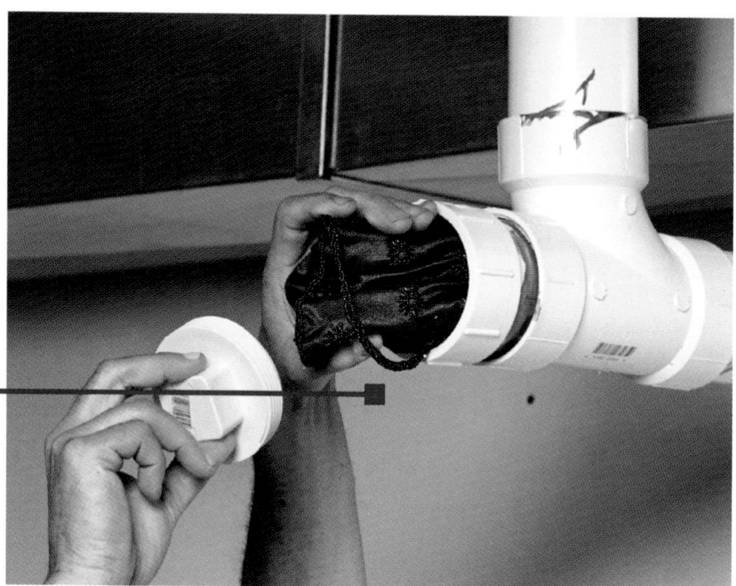

16. "How many thieves are going to go through the dozens of pockets in your closet? I put cash in the pockets of my old pants and suit coats." Just be sure the clothes don't get donated!

17. "I think the key is to use lots of hiding places. It's stupid to put all your eggs in one basket. I keep hundred-dollar bills between pages in books, tape an envelope behind my headboard and put cash behind the false panel in my dishwasher."

18. "No burglar worth his salt looks in a kid's room for valuables. It's just full of useless junk. So find somewhere in there where the kid won't find it either."

19. "My secret stash is taped on the underside of drawers in the kitchen."

20

Hide a key in plain sight

Say you want to hide a key—other than under the rug or over the door. How about mounting a phony plastic LB fitting? Screw it to the wall and run a bit of 1/2-in. conduit to the ground so it looks official. Cut the head off the bottom screw and glue it in place. That's it. Swing the cover aside and there's the key.

TIPS FOR **TRAPPING MICE**

Here's how to deal with the little varmints!

by **Travis Larson, Senior Editor**

I've lived in my house for 33 years, 31 of those mostly mouse-free. But two years ago, I had a serious infestation. They were everywhere! I got busy doing a whole lot of research and then I got to work. I trapped 54 mice in one month, and I've seen very few since. I concluded early on that the good, old-fashioned spring trap was the best choice for me.

However, my trapping method might not be everyone's cup of tea. It can be downright grizzly and entails some dirty work from time to time. If trapping isn't for you, learn about alternatives by searching online for "humane rodent control."

Buy and set lots of traps

Anywhere you see mouse droppings is a primo place to set traps.And the more traps you set, the more mice you'll catch—period. So don't think you'll place a few traps around the house and take care of your mouse problem. The kitchen is often the worst room, so that's a good place to start. Buy ordinary Victor traps (a pack of four costs about $6). Before you go to bed every night (mice come out only at night), bait and set at least six traps.

Peanut butter is my bait of choice

Many baits work well, but good ol' peanut butter has succeeded for me. (By the way, cheese is one of the least effective.) Here's a tip. Mark the top of the peanut butter bait jar and let your family know what it's for. Think about it: You're baiting the traps with peanut butter and then in the morning Junior might be spreading his toast with contaminated peanut butter. I always use plastic knives and throw them away when I'm through rebaiting and resetting traps. Better yet, keep the bait jar out of the kitchen.

Pet food is a problem—and an opportunity

My wife found a cache of cat food under the cushions of the couch in the basement. We were amazed that 3-in.-long animals hauled those food nuggets one at a time down 10 ft. of stairs (100 total feet) to stash them away. So I set three traps next to the cat dish (the cat wasn't interested in peanut butter—or catching mice), and caught eight mice in one week. Dogs love peanut butter just as much as mice do. So if you don't want Rex to get his tongue caught in a trap, let him sleep in your bedroom and keep the door closed. But near Rex's dish is an excellent place to put traps.

Look for the pathways

A mouse is like Tarzan when it comes to climbing. In fact, a mouse can jump up to 8 in. and climb up electrical cords to get to other places. So if you find droppings in high places, look low and put your traps there.

My mouse-trapping philosophy

I know most people don't relish killing animals—even mice—but for me, it was the best choice. Here's my take on some other options:

1. Live traps. Mice, by nature, build nests and store food. So you trap them this fall and let them go outside where they start their life anew, right? Well, that's not how it works. They have no food stored away and no nest to live in, and they'll most likely die of starvation and/or exposure.

2. Poison. Most poisons are ingested and cause dehydration or blood coagulation. It's not a painless death.

3. Live with the disease-carrying creatures. However, as they run around your floors, countertops, plates with leftovers and your pet's food dishes, they're leaving a trail of waste behind them.

4. Sticky mouse traps. So then what? They're not dead and you have to either kill them with your shoe or throw them into the trashcan where they'll die a slow, miserable death from thirst.

All this mouse-killing business isn't for the faint-of-heart. Sometimes, my method of dealing with mice means they don't get killed right away. And sometimes they suffer. But if you have a mouse problem and ignore it, you're putting your family's health at risk.

Under cabinets

The spaces under cabinets are like a freeway for mice. Pull out your bottom drawers and look for droppings. Put traps down there on the floor, replace the drawers and check the traps every morning.

Look for feeding areas

Just like pet dishes, there are other sources of food. I have to admit that the stovetop in my shop isn't as clean as the stove in the house. So when I found mouse scat there, I put some traps there. And caught five mice on the countertop nearby.

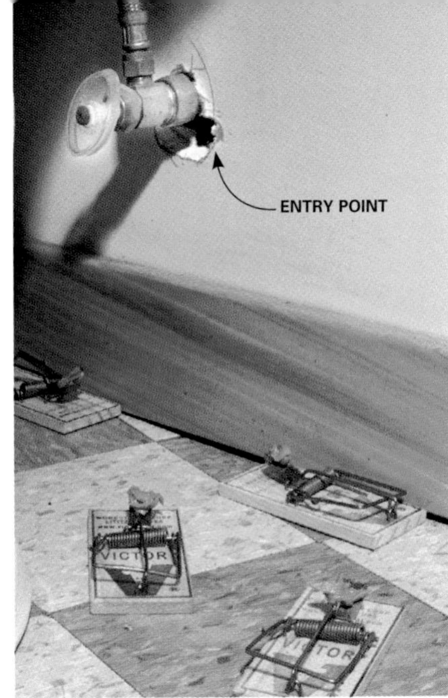

Look for wall penetrations

Mice love to live inside walls where they're safe and warm. Look around to see where plumbing or anything else penetrates drywall or plaster and put traps just below it. That's where they'll come in at night to feed.

Keep 'em out!

When the temperature starts dropping, mice are looking for a warm, dry place with food and good nesting conditions. In other words, they want to live inside your house. They enter through the smallest imaginable holes and cracks. Young ones can worm their way through a 1/4-in. opening. Take a very close look around the outside of your house, and then caulk, plug or do whatever it takes to close every entry point you can find.

Worn weather stripping under doors can be a perfect, easy entry point for mice looking for a warm place to winter. Replacing it is usually as simple as taking the door off the hinges and slipping a new weather strip into the slots. Take the old weather stripping to the home center to find a match.

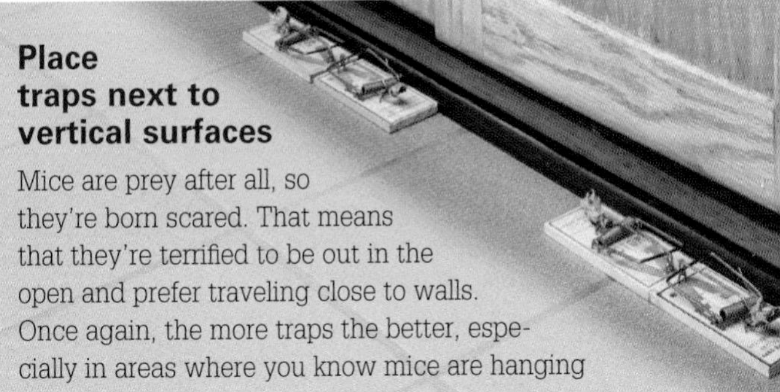

Place traps next to vertical surfaces

Mice are prey after all, so they're born scared. That means that they're terrified to be out in the open and prefer traveling close to walls. Once again, the more traps the better, especially in areas where you know mice are hanging out—usually where there's food.

HandyHints®

FROM OUR READERS

LADDER-FREE LIGHTBULB CHANGES

The walls in my shop are more than 12 ft. high. I love the space, except when it comes to changing lightbulbs. Last Father's Day, I asked one of my kids for a lightbulb changer on a pole. I wasn't sure that it would work (that's why I didn't spend my own money on it), but I've already changed a half-dozen lightbulbs. I love this thing! My son picked it up for about $20 at a home center.

—Mark Petersen, Contributing Editor

FAST FIX FOR STICKING DRAWERS

The drawers in our dining room buffet stick badly. To remedy the problem, I grabbed a candle from one of the drawers and rubbed it along the bottom of the drawer and along the wood runner. Now they slide like new and almost as smoothly as our kitchen drawers with the fancy drawer glides.

—Red Danske

READY REFERENCE

I save all my back issues of *The Family Handyman* magazine and love the projects and repair tips. The trouble is, I'm not always ready to do the project when the issue arrives. To make my favorite articles easy to find at a later date, I put a stick-on label on the cover and then add notes for easy reference when the time comes to do the job.

—Willie Schreiber

GIFT WRAP RACK

I wrap lots of gifts, but I don't like the clutter of all those rolls of gift wrap in the closet. I decided to make a rack to organize them. I glued a bunch of 30-in.-long pieces of 3-in. PVC waste pipe with all-purpose PVC glue. The rack is perfect for storing all the rolls and ribbons. I leave it set up on a table in the basement.

—Donna M. Courie

STAY ON THE PAGE

I was looking around the kitchen for something to prop my new cookbook open. As I was getting a mixing spoon out of the drawer, I noticed a Chip Clip clamp. The next time I was at the grocery store, I picked up a couple extras—just in case the first one is clipped to a bag the next time I'm cooking!

—Jenny Holte

DUST CATCHER

As an art gallery owner, I hang a lot of paintings and photos, which means drilling lots of holes for wall anchors, which means lots of dust on the floor. I catch it all with a Post-it note that I fold in the middle and stick to the wall just under where I plan to drill. It catches all the dust, keeping it off the floor and any furniture below.

—Tim Benton

GET YOUR FIRST ROW OF TILE PERFECTLY LEVEL

Tubs and shower bases aren't always level, so starting your first row of tile against them could throw off your whole job. Instead, make level marks on the wall, line up the ends of a straight board with the marks and screw the board to the wall. Rest the first row of tile on the board for a perfectly level tile job. The distance from the top of the shower or tub to the top of the board should be less than the width of a tile. That way you can custom-cut the tiles to accommodate an out-of-level tub or shower and keep consistent grout lines.

INSTALLING FLOORING IN TIGHT SPOTS

When I was installing wood flooring in the cramped corners of a closet, I found it tough to hold the last edge and corner pieces to glue them in. Then it dawned on me to use duct tape to make a little "handle" for the plank to pull the pieces together. That way I can stick the tape onto the adjoining plank to act as a clamp while the glue dries. Double efficient!

—Bryce Wunder

HandyHints®

SOUPED-UP LITTER BOX

To make litter box cleanup just a bit more pleasant, I keep the cleaning supplies in a handy spot—on the litter box shroud. I bought some adhesive-backed hooks and stuck them to the side of the shroud. I bought the whisk and dustpan at a sporting goods store (they're made for cleaning small tents).

—Mr. Arthur Harshman

CHLORINATE A STINKY DRAIN

Every few months, our kitchen sink develops a foul smell. We use the sink every day, so I know a dry trap isn't the problem. Whatever the cause, a cup of bleach kills the stink … until the next time.

—Gary Wentz, Senior Editor

SOFTEN OLD MASKING TAPE

I'm surely not the only one who has grabbed an old roll of masking tape and spent the next 15 minutes trying to peel off even an inch or two before it tore jaggedly on the roll. To end this frustration, I put the roll in the microwave for about 10 seconds. It softens the adhesive just enough to peel the tape nicely off the roll.

—Charles Crowley

A STURDIER GROCERY BAG

Cloth grocery bags are great—except for the flimsy piece of plastic at the bottom of the bag. I wanted to find something that would hold up better. I cut a piece of pegboard to size and used it instead. The pegboard is lightweight and the holes help keep the bags dry. All the baggers at the grocery store remember me because of my special bags, which hold heavier items and are easier to pack.

—Mike Tate

SHOE SOLUTION

We have a strict policy at our house about removing your shoes before entering the house. (It works most of the time.) Once we implemented the rule, the next problem was the clutter of shoes blocking the door. While I was looking at the coatrack in the entry, it dawned on me that I could do the same for shoes, so I built another one and hung it close to the floor.

—Jimmy Keen

HINGE FACE-LIFT

Awhile back we remodeled our kitchen and decided to replace our chrome fixtures with new ones that had a copper finish. This meant new matching knobs for the doors and drawers as well. When it came to the hinges, it was difficult to find new ones that fit the old mounting holes, and the choices were expensive. We decided that painting the hinges metallic copper would work since they weren't handled every day and wouldn't show wear. We removed the hinges, rubbed them with steel wool and sprayed them with metallic paint and a clear coat. The hinges look great, at a fraction of the cost of new.

—Dennis Badertscher

HOUSEPLANT POT LINER

I have several houseplants in pots around the house and had soil leaking out of the bottom of the pot when I watered. When I was discarding the coffee filter, I had a great idea. Works there—why not in the potted plants! Now, when I repot the plants, I set a filter on the bottom of the pot and then fill the pot with dirt! No more wet soil leaking out.

—Tom Horner

SPRAY TUBE HOLSTER

I used to constantly lose the plastic spray tubes on cans of lubricant. On a new can, the tube is taped to the side, but after a few uses, the tape gets loose or torn or falls off. My solution was to attach a plastic drinking straw to the side of the can to house the tube. I just cut the straw so it was slightly shorter than the spray tube, hot-glued the straw to the can and then glued the bottom of the straw shut. Works like a charm!

—Jim Kucharik

HandyHints®

LEVEL A ROW OF PICTURES

Getting a row of pictures to line up at the top can be tricky, especially if the hanging wires are different lengths. Here's a tip from a professional picture hanger. Hook a tape measure to the wire and pull it tight (**Photo 1**). Measure to the top of the picture frame. On the wall, measure down from a level line and mark this distance at the centerline of your new picture location. Align the hook of the picture hanger with the mark and nail it to the wall (**Photo 2**). Repeat this process for all of the pictures, and their tops will be perfectly aligned.

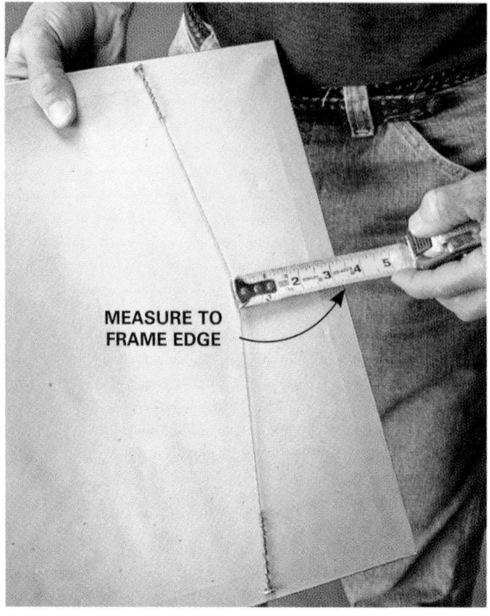

1 Measure from the wire. Measure the distance from the stretched wire to the top of the picture frame.

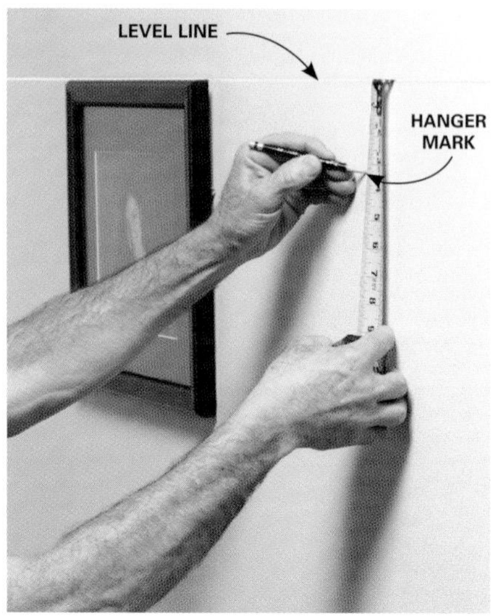

2 Mark for the picture hanger. Measure down from the level line and mark for the location of the picture-hanging hook.

JAR CLEANING WITH BBs

I've gone to auctions for years and have collected lots of antique jars and bottles. Often they've been stained inside, and they used to be really tough to get clean. Not anymore! I just put a little soapy water in the bottle and add a few tablespoons of BBs. After a bit of soaking and several shakes, the bottles come clean. I've also used the same method to clean peanut butter and jam jars. By rinsing and drying the BBs afterward, I can reuse them. Just remember to keep them out of the sink and away from small children and pets!

—Connie DeHaven

FIND SWITCHES IN THE DARK

Our house was built in the days of gas lighting. When electricians installed the retrofit electrical system, they put light switches where it was convenient for them, not where the rest of us expect switches to be. To make life easier, I gave the misplaced switches a dab of glow-in-the-dark paint. Now our guests don't have to grope around in the dark anymore. A 7-oz. can of Rust-Oleum glow-in-the-dark paint costs less than $10 at home centers.

—Gary Wentz,
Senior Editor

FASTENING TO CONCRETE AND MASONRY

Specialized know-how for basement remodeling, updating and repair projects

by **Mark Petersen, Contributing Editor**

Whether you're doing framing, plumbing or electrical work or just hanging shelves, eventually you're going to tackle a project that requires fastening to bricks, blocks or solid concrete. There are dozens of specialty masonry fasteners on the market to help you finish those projects. Here, I'll show you which fasteners I prefer for various projects and share some tips for quick, easy and long-lasting fastening solutions.

MEET AN EXPERT

Mark Petersen is a contributing editor at *TFH*. He spent 20 years in construction, first as a siding guy, then as a general contractor.

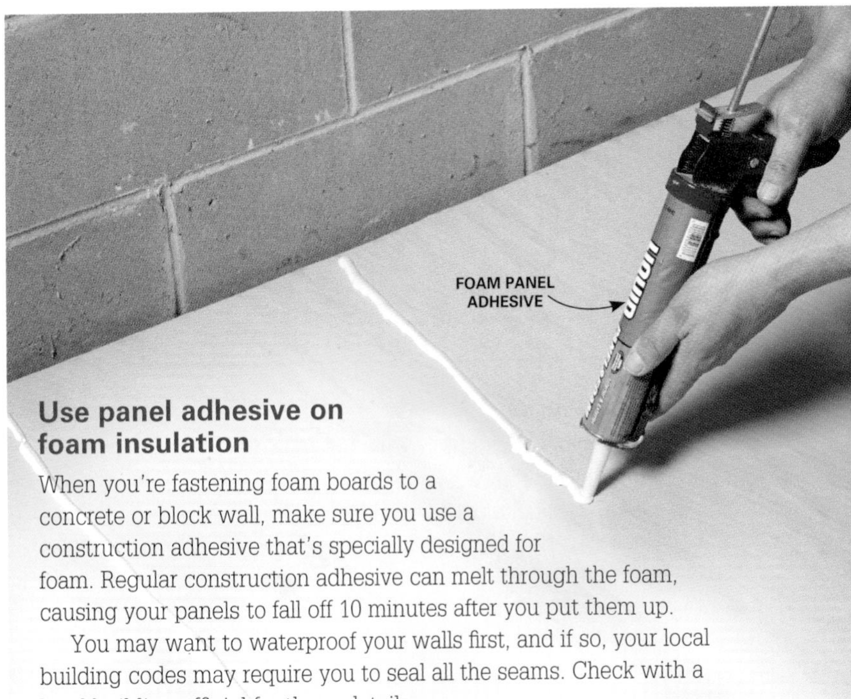

Use panel adhesive on foam insulation

When you're fastening foam boards to a concrete or block wall, make sure you use a construction adhesive that's specially designed for foam. Regular construction adhesive can melt through the foam, causing your panels to fall off 10 minutes after you put them up.

You may want to waterproof your walls first, and if so, your local building codes may require you to seal all the seams. Check with a local building official for those details.

What you should know about concrete screws

Using concrete screws is fast and easy—you just drill a hole and screw them in the same as a wood screw. They work great for light- to medium-duty tasks like fastening shelving brackets, plumbing straps, electrical boxes and furring strips. Concrete screws don't work well on old, crumbling concrete. And they lose much, if not all, of their holding power when they're removed and reused in the same hole, so if you do have to pull one out, try to drill a new hole in another location.

Hex vs. flathead

Hex-head screws are less likely to strip out, so I always use them when the screw head can sit proud of the surface, as it can on sill plates and plumbing straps. Flathead screws are the way to go when the screw head needs to be flush, such as with furring strips that will be clad with drywall or plywood.

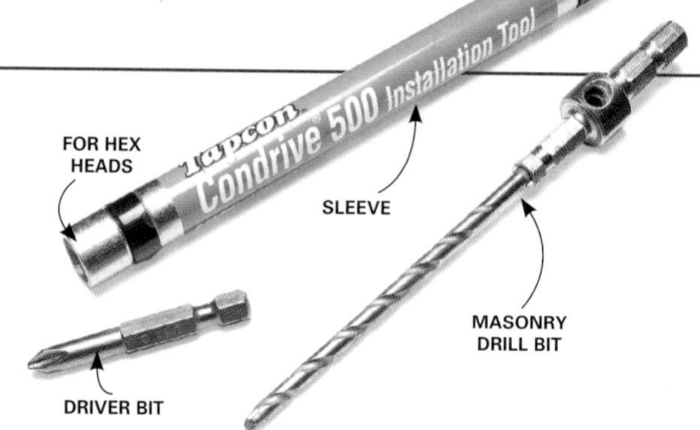

Speed up the process

Installing concrete screws is even faster with a drill bit/ driver combination set like this one. The drill bit is covered by the removable sleeve that contains the driver. That way you don't need to have two drills on hand, or to keep switching between drill bit and driver. A combination set costs about $25 at home centers.

Drill 1/4 in. deeper

Set the depth gauge on your drill so the hole is 1/4 in. deeper than the length of the screw, keeping in mind the thickness of the material you're working with. If your drill doesn't have a depth gauge, wrap a little tape around the bit so you'll know when to stop. Always drill the proper diameter hole. The container the screws come in will indicate which size bit to use. A bit is included in some larger containers.

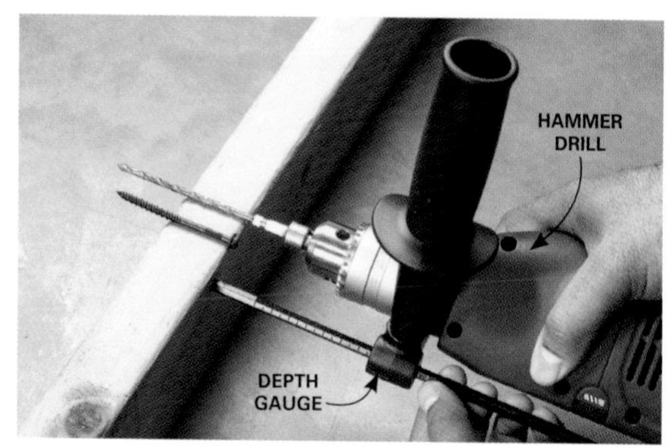

Fasten bottom plates with a powder-actuated tool

I've found the fastest way to attach bottom plates to a slab is with a powder-actuated tool (PAT). Most residential-grade PATs are powered by .22 caliber blank cartridges, which drive in nail-like fasteners. I place the fasteners about 5 ft. apart and within 6 in. of the end of a wall. I also add a little construction adhesive for more holding power.

The PATs that require a hammer blow to fire the load cost about $25 at home centers, and those that have a trigger, like the tool shown, cost about $90. Buy 2-1/2-in. fasteners so they will penetrate the concrete about 1 in. to 1-1/4 in. Wear safety glasses as well as hearing protection—these suckers are loud. For more information on PATs, search "powder actuated tools" at familyhandyman.com.

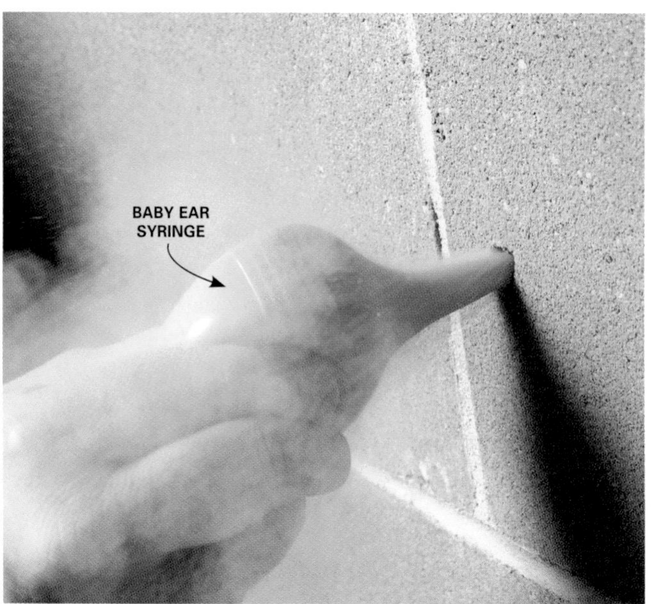

Blow out the dust

If drilling dust is left in the hole, it can prevent the fasteners from being driven all the way in. So remove it with a vacuum or blower. A baby's ear syringe (about $5 at any drugstore) works great for this and doesn't take up much room in a toolbox. Just shove it into the hole and puff out the dust.

Don't drill too close to edges

Two mistakes you really want to avoid are busting off a chunk of a concrete stair step and cracking the corner of a patio slab. To avoid these disasters, don't drill any closer than 4 in. from the edge. If there's no other option, turn off the hammering action on the drill. Also, avoid wedge-type anchors. They exert a huge amount of outward pressure, which could literally "wedge" the concrete apart.

Drill right through the wood

Masonry drill bits will also plow through wood, so don't be afraid to drill right through the wood and into the wall or slab. That makes it a lot easier to get the furring strip, or whatever you're working with, exactly where you want it. I drill one hole and install that fastener first. (You'll have better luck holding the board in place if you drill the first hole toward the middle.) Then I go back and drill the rest of the holes and install those fasteners.

Pound on the nut

I use wedge anchors for heavy-duty projects. To install them, all you need to do is drill a hole, tap them in and then tighten the nut. Don't tap directly on the bolt or you could damage the threads, making the nut nearly impossible to remove and reinstall. Loosen the nut so it extends slightly beyond the bolt to protect the threads, and then tap on the nut instead.

Minimize masonry fastening

Fastening to masonry isn't all that difficult, but fastening to wood is easier; that's why we attach drywall to furring strips instead of directly to concrete walls. For projects that require a bunch of fasteners, like a column of shelving, install strips of pressure-treated wood with a couple of fasteners, and attach the shelf brackets to that. You'll save the expense and drudgery of all those extra masonry fasteners.

Hydraulic cement prevents cracking

When you're fastening posts, poles, large bolts or rebar to concrete, drill an oversize hole and fill it with hydraulic cement. Hydraulic cement creates an extremely strong and weatherproof bond. It also holds up to repeated movement, which is why professional metal railing installers use it to anchor posts.

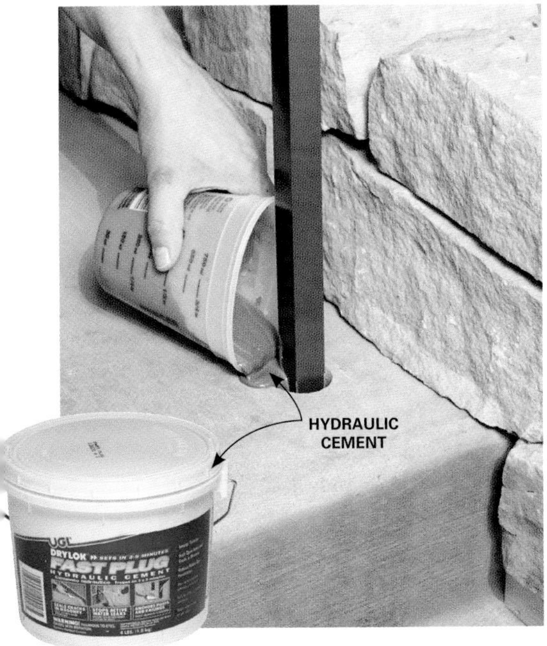

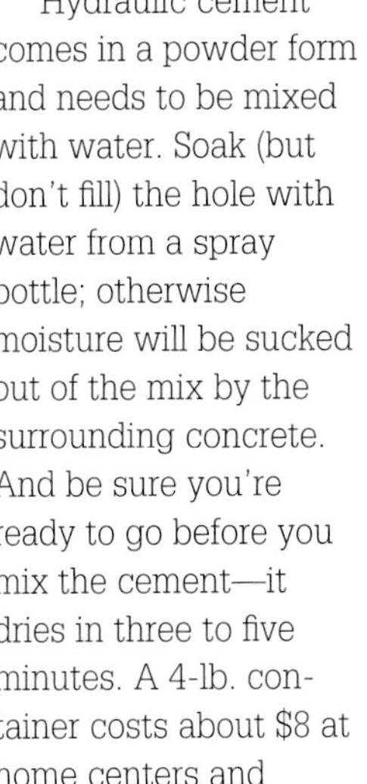

Hydraulic cement comes in a powder form and needs to be mixed with water. Soak (but don't fill) the hole with water from a spray bottle; otherwise moisture will be sucked out of the mix by the surrounding concrete. And be sure you're ready to go before you mix the cement—it dries in three to five minutes. A 4-lb. container costs about $8 at home centers and hardware stores.

Don't drill into brick

Whenever I install a lightweight item like a downspout on brick, I drill into the mortar joints instead of the brick face. The brick is more likely to crack, and if the item ever needs to be moved, patching a hole in gray mortar is a lot easier than trying to match the color of the brick. And I always install plastic anchors because metal anchors are more likely to crack the mortar when they expand.

TAPING DRYWALL

This three-day process assures a top-quality job

by **Mark Petersen, Contributing Editor**

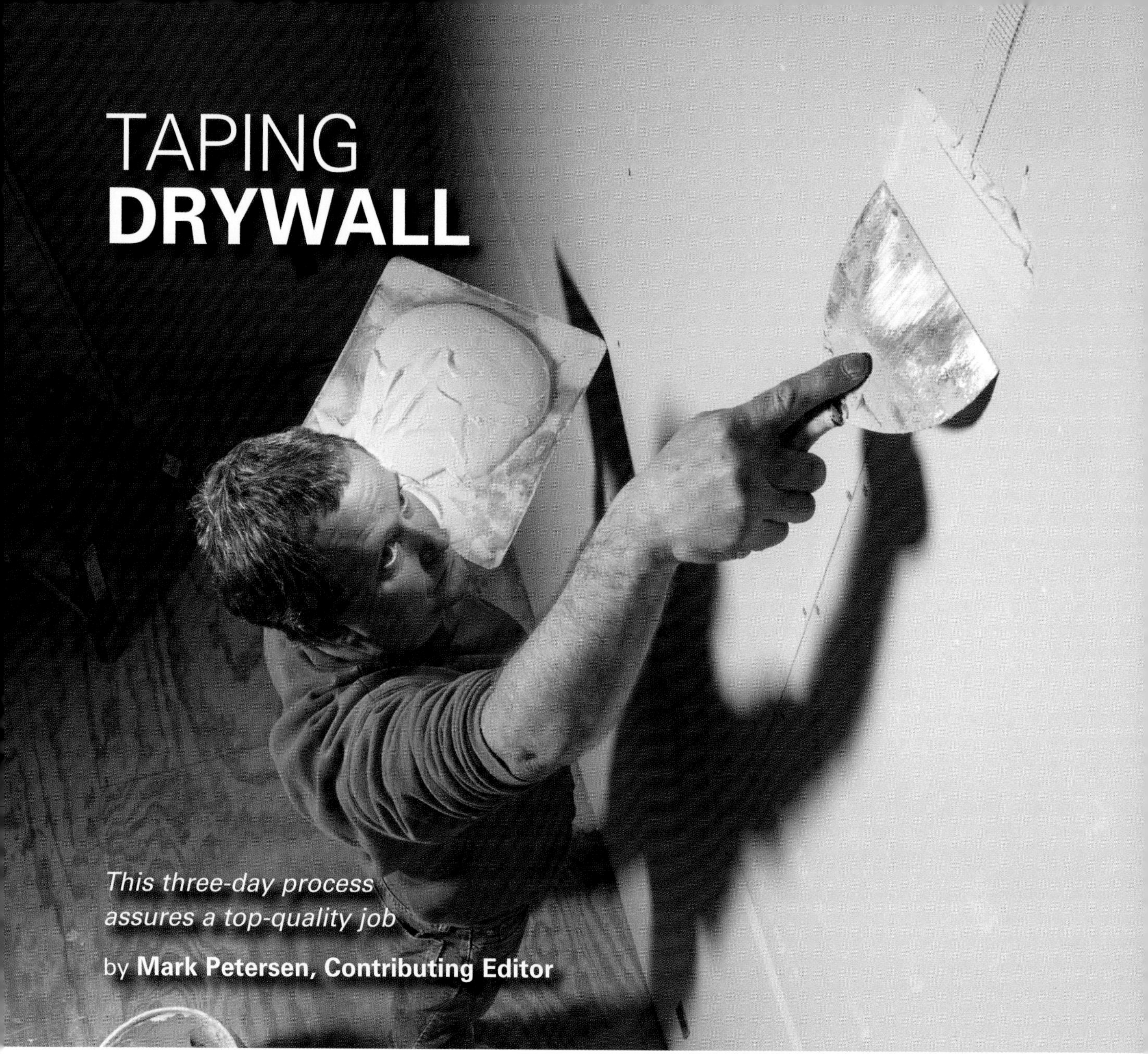

Drywall taping is one of the most important jobs on any construction project. A skilled taper can hide a lot of mistakes left behind by less-than-perfect framing and drywall hanging. But a poor taping job can make trim carpentry and painting much more challenging than it should be. A quality outcome requires the proper tools and materials (a steady hand doesn't hurt either). We asked pro taper Scott Pauly to show us his three-day, step-by-step taping routine. He gave us some great tips that will help you end up with smooth walls and crisp corners.

MEET AN EXPERT

Scott Pauly started his drywall career as a teenager when his mother said he could have his own bedroom in the basement if he hung and taped the drywall himself. Since then he's slung more mud than an aging politician.

Mud management

Scott's tools are caked with mud, but he works mostly on new homes where water is usually unavailable. He also burns through most of his tools in months, not years, so he focuses only on keeping the edges clean—a must for smooth mud lines. Here are some tips for managing your mud.

- Scrape and wipe out the bucket sides to remove mud before it dries and crumbles into the good mud.
- Clean lids after opening new buckets for the same reason.
- Never return unused mud to the bucket. Throw it away.
- Keep a wet rag or sponge on hand to clean tools and buckets with.
- Add a little water to the top of your mud at the end of the day to keep a crust from forming.

Day 1

Tack on corner bead

Scott installs the outside corner beads with a staple gun that shoots 1-in., 18-gauge staples with a 1/4-in. crown. Drywall nails will also do the job, but using a staple gun frees up one hand to get the bead exactly where you want it before tacking it into place. Outside corners take a lot of abuse, so make sure the corner beads are securely fastened to the framing. Nail or staple each side of the bead every 10 to 12 in. A staple gun like this one costs about $100.

Roll out the fiber mesh

Installing fiber mesh saves time because it's self-adhering. And unlike paper tape, fiber mesh allows mud to pass right through it, so you don't need to fill cracks and gaps in the drywall before you install the tape. All you need to do is roll it onto the wall and trim it off with a 6-in. taping knife. Tape over all the joints, large gaps, holes larger than 1/8 in., and both sides of the outside corner beads. On inside corners, only areas with a gap larger than 1/8 in. need mesh. The rest of the inside corners will get covered on Day 2 with paper tape.

Mix up the setting compound

Setting compound shrinks less than regular joint compound, and it dries rock hard. This makes it ideal for Day 1, which is all about filling the big holes and gaps. But setting compound doesn't sand nearly as easily as joint compound, so thinner coats are better. It comes in powder form, and the number on the bag indicates how many minutes it takes to set up. The bigger the job, the longer the working time you'll want. Use a mixing paddle bit in a 1/2-in. drill. Keep a bucket of water standing by so you can clean the paddle right away. Setting compound sets up like concrete—even under water!

Cover the tape and fill the gaps

Cover all the tape with setting compound using a 6-in. taping knife. Apply enough mud to fill the gaps under the tape, but remember, setting compound is much harder than the two coats of joint compound you're going to apply the next two days, so you want to end up with just a thin coat covering the tape. If you sand through the joint compound into the setting compound, the result could be noticeably different textures on the two surfaces.

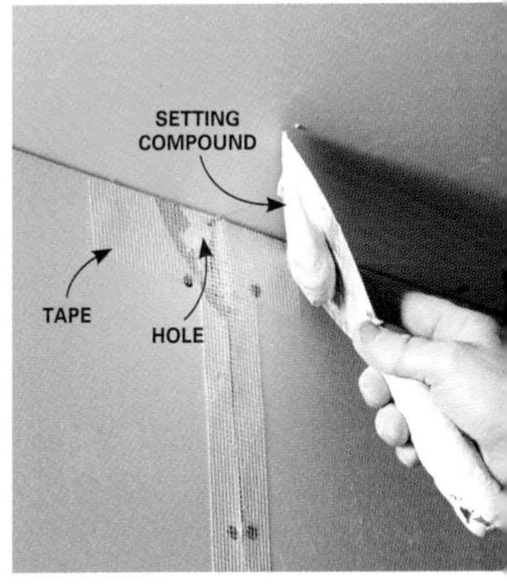

Day 1 tools

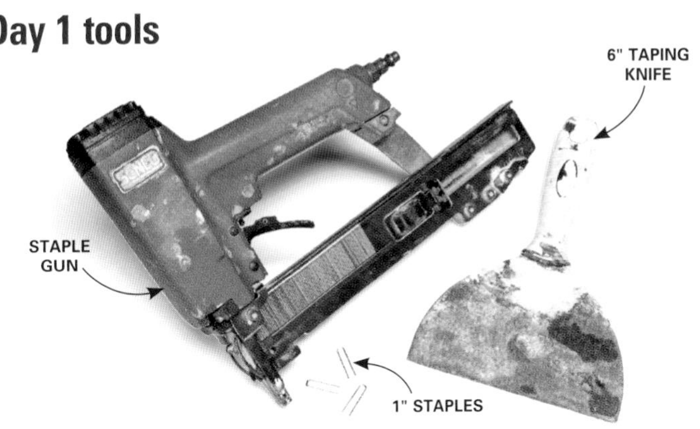

Day 2

Coat the butt joints with a knife

Use a lightweight joint compound on Day 2. Knock off any crumbs or ridges left over from the day before with a clean 6-in. taping knife—Scott always has one in his back pocket. Spread a thin coat of joint compound on the butt joints with a 14-in. taping knife.

Coat the tapered joints with a trowel

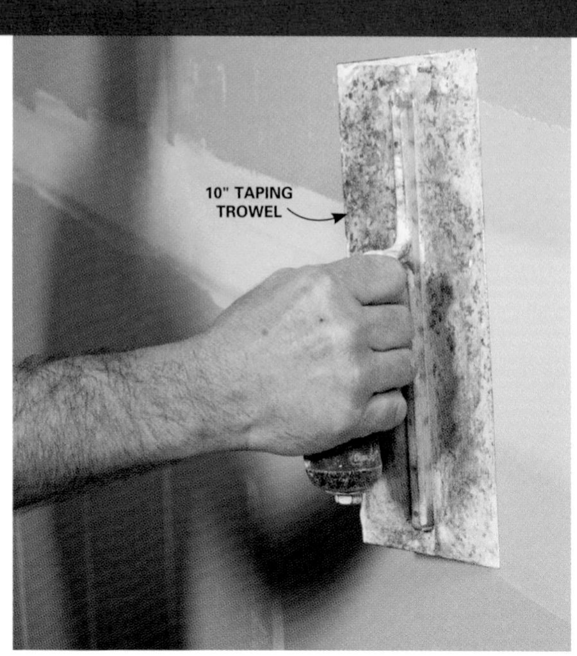

Each of the long sides of drywall is tapered to allow room for the mud. The goal is to fill this recessed area with mud so the wall ends up smooth. Taping knives are flat but flexible. If you press one too hard against a tapered joint in the wall, it could bend into the recess, and you could squeeze too much mud out, creating a trough. Taping trowels have a little bend in them, so when you press them against the wall, they flatten out to form a straight bridge across the tapered joint. Scott uses a 10-in. trowel on Day 2. Be careful when you buy one: A taping trowel might look like a concrete trowel but it's not—a concrete trowel is bent in the opposite direction.

Tape the inside corners

Paper tape is more flexible than fiber mesh and has a crease in it, which makes it easier to push into the corners. Scott uses a banjo to install paper tape on all the inside corners. He holds the tape secure with one hand as he moves the banjo along the corner. Once a long section of tape is pulled out, he pushes it into the corner with a corner trowel.

If you don't own a banjo, lay down a thin coat of mud and push the tape into the mud. Make sure there's mud under every square inch of the tape or you'll end up with bubbles. Banjos do a great job of applying the proper amount of mud to the tape, but regular joint compound will have to be watered down when you're using one. This will require about 1 cup of water for every gallon of mud, but it depends on the moisture content of the mud you're working with, so just keep adding a little water until it's roughly the consistency of yogurt. You can buy a mid-quality banjo for about $100.

Top-coat the corner tape

A banjo applies mud only on the bottom of the tape, so once the tape is laid down, it will need to be top-coated. Scott uses a corner trowel. Corner trowels can be tricky to work with—the secret (as with much of taping) is to not lay down too much mud. This is especially true where inside corners meet the ceiling and floor. Too much mud will round out the corners, making it difficult to install trim and moldings. Start at the top of an inside corner an inch or so down from the ceiling because a lot of mud will ooze out the top side of the trowel when you first press it to the walls. Then go back for another pass and smooth out the excess left behind.

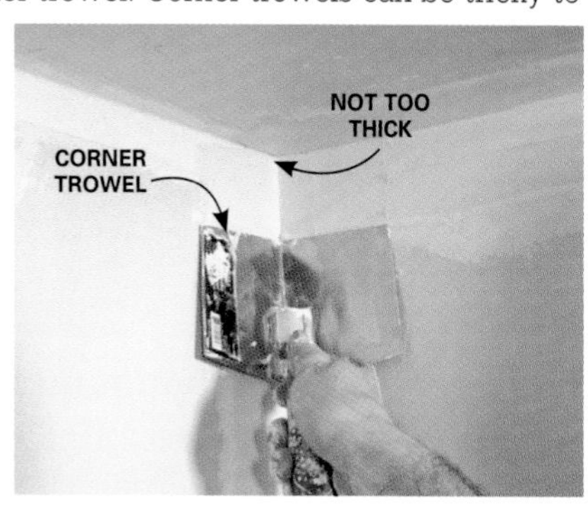

Once the tape has been covered, Scott goes back with his 6-in. knife and cleans up each side of the tape. This step takes skill and practice. An easier (but more time-consuming) method is to top-coat one side of the tape, and do the other side after the first side has dried.

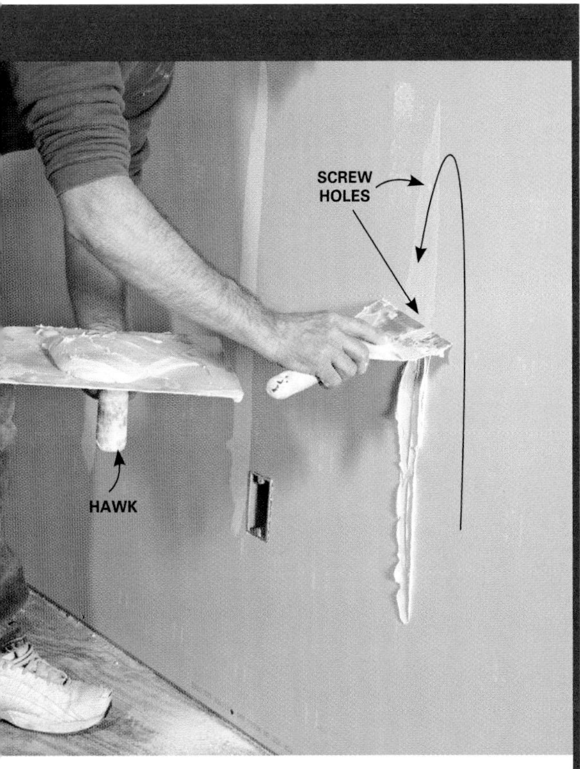

Fill the screw holes

Make two passes over every screw hole with a 6-in. taping knife. Hit all the screws that line up vertically in the field of each panel of drywall at the same time. To eliminate voids, each pass should come from a different direction. One efficient method is to lay out a thick coat in an upward motion, and then come back down, scraping off the excess as you go. Don't forget about the screws on the ceiling. Save yourself a lot of walking around by covering all the joints, corners and screw holes in one area of a room at a time. It's time to set up some fans and call it a day.

Day 2 tools

Day 3

Make your own topping compound

The same lightweight joint compound you used on Day 2 will also work for your final coat on Day 3, but topping compound works better. Topping compound is easier to sand and doesn't leave behind as many tiny air pockets. You could buy a bucket of topping compound or you could make your own. Scott pours about 1/2 cup of dish soap (any brand will do) into a 4-1/2 gallon pail of lightweight joint compound. He's found that this concoction works every bit as well and is cheaper and a lot more convenient.

Cover everything one more time

Scott applies the final coat on the inside corners the same way he did on Day 2, laying down the mud with a corner trowel and smoothing each side with a 6-in. knife. He covers all the recessed joints with a 12-in. trowel (2 in. larger than the one used on Day 2). The farther the mud is feathered out, the less noticeable the joint will be, especially on butt joints. That's why after Scott lays down a layer of mud on the butt joints with his 14-in. knife, he immediately follows with a monster 2-ft. knife—no need to add more mud on the second pass. That's it. You're done. Now set up some fans so you can move on to sanding.

Day 3 tools

5 STEPS TO A **SECURE HOME**

Simple upgrades pay off big in added security

by **Rick Muscoplat, Contributing Editor**

Most crooks avoid challenges. They just want a quick, easy score. That's good news for you—it means that small, simple security upgrades are a major deterrent. If you make your home just a little harder to break into, the vast majority of burglars will bypass you and move on to easier pickings.

1 Strengthen windows

The factory latches on double-hung windows are no match for a burglar with a pry bar. But crooks can't get past inexpensive pin locks (about $2 each). You can install a pin in just a few minutes per window (photo right).

Time: 10 minutes per window
Cost: $2 to $5 per window

Pry bars work on casement or sliding windows too. But the pin lock we show here won't work with them. Find casement and sliding window locks for about $5 per window at home centers.

Secure double-hung windows
Add a lock pin to prevent the sash from being pried up. Drill a hole to lock the window closed, and a second hole a few inches up to lock the window partly open for ventilation.

2 Secure sliding patio doors

There are two ways a burglar can easily get past sliding patio doors: by prying the door up and off the bottom track and by prying against the jamb and breaking the latch. To prevent latch breakage, some homeowners lay a long stick (like a broom handle) in the lower track. But a crook can easily move the stick with a coat hanger.

The best solution is to install a tension-fit drop-down security bar (aka "charley bar") and snap latch (Photo 1). They're ugly, but they work and send a strong signal to crooks that you've fortified your home. To prevent the crook from prying the door up, install anti-jacking screws (Photo 2).

Time: 1 hour
Cost: About $20

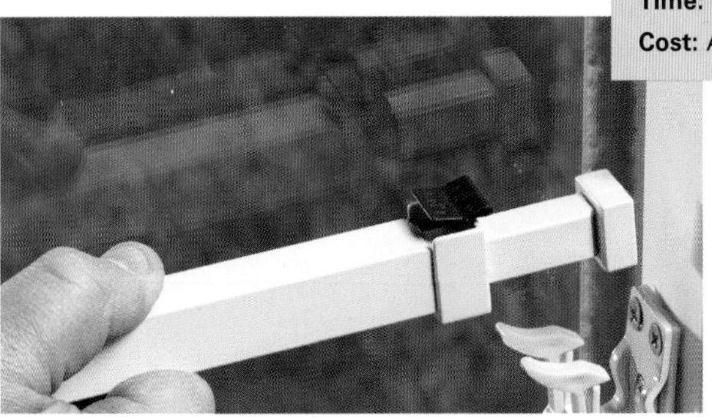

1 Install a security bar. Secure the pivoting end of the security bar to the door frame at mid-height, so it's easy to operate and the crooks can see it. Then install the locking latch on the sliding door. Lower the bar and extend it so it wedges against the sliding door.

2 Install anti-jacking screws. Drive two 3-in.-long screws through the top track and into the header above the sliding door or window. Leave enough clearance to allow the sliding door or window to move, but not enough to allow a burglar to raise the door off the track.

3 Reinforce your exterior doors

Time: 1 hour
Cost: $25 to $105

Burglars can open most entry doors with a few kicks or body blows. Even with a dead bolt, the blow shatters the doorjamb and splits the door itself (even steel doors). You can dramatically increase the strength of your doorjamb by installing longer strike plate screws that anchor into the stud behind the jamb (**Photo 1**).

The first step would be to take out one of the existing screws. If it's shorter than 3 in., replace it. For even greater doorjamb security, consider installing a 6-in.-long heavy-duty strike plate (about $10). This is a much bigger job because you have to mortise a larger opening and drive in six 3-in. screws. However, if your entry door butts up to a sidelight and you can't install long screws, buy and install a 48-in.-long doorjamb reinforcement plate (one choice we found is the StrikeMaster II 55724; about $80 online).

Next, prevent door splitting with a door edge guard. Measure the door thickness and dead bolt lock backset before you head to the home center. Then buy a guard (about $13) to fit around your door and dead bolt. Installing the guard takes about 15 minutes (**Photo 2**).

1 Strengthen the doorjamb. Remove the puny 3/4-in. screws from the strike plate. Drill pilot holes into the framing behind the jamb. Then drive in 3-in. screws to anchor the strike plate to the framing.

2 Install an edge guard. It will keep the door from splitting from a sudden blow. Simply remove the dead bolt and screw on the guard.

Understand your foes

Most burglaries occur on weekdays between 10 a.m. and 5 p.m. The perpetrators are usually substance abusers in their twenties looking for easy-to-pawn items to raise quick cash. They look for homes that appear unoccupied during the day, are dark at night, and display signs of wealth (such as immaculate landscaping, expensive cars and fancy decks). They prefer homes that are secluded or shielded by fences or shrubbery. And they always prefer breaking in through a ground-level side window or back door.

Most burglars don't pick locks or break glass. That takes too long, makes noise and risks personal injury. Instead, they simply kick in a door (even doors with a dead bolt) or pry open a window or sliding patio door. In many cases, they take advantage of a homeowner's carelessness by climbing in through an open window or unlocked door (window screens and storm doors offer no protection). Burglars tend to shy away from homes with dogs, and homes with an alarm system.

Once inside, burglars head right to the master bedroom looking for gold jewelry, cash, furs and guns. Next, they scoop up prescription drugs from the bathroom and finish up with laptops, tablets and smartphones. Then they hightail it out.

Your job is to make your home less target-worthy, frustrate their attempts to break in and limit your losses if they do manage to get inside.

4 Light up the night

A well-lit home is your best protection against in-home assault and burglary. Light up all the vulnerable areas of your house and yard with dusk-to-dawn lighting.

It costs less than $2 per month to run four low-wattage CFL or LED floodlights all night long. If you have a motion sensor floodlight, swap in a photocell for just $10 (**Figure A**). Or, buy a ready-to-install dusk-to-dawn floodlight fixture for about $25 at any home center. Screw in cold-weather outdoor-rated floodlights and aim them at areas around your doors and windows, the garage and toward the alley.

Time: 1 hour
Cost: $30

Figure A
Convert a motion sensor to dusk-to-dawn

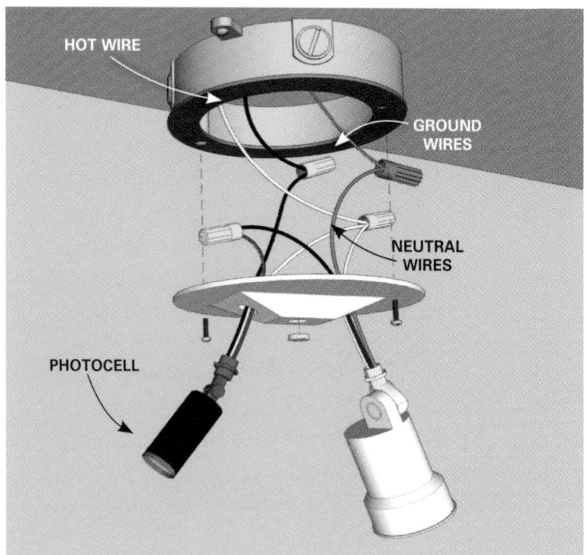

Turn off the power and double-check with a voltage sniffer. Then swap out the motion sensor with a photoelectric cell. Connect all the white neutral wires together. Then connect the black wire from the photocell to the black hot wire. Connect the red wire from the photocell to the light.

5 Add video surveillance, real or fake

Burglars are increasingly aware that they're being watched, so a video camera can be a deterrent as long as the crooks believe it's real. A real video camera with good resolution costs about $400. However, you can get the same deterrent value by modifying a fake $15 camera so it looks real (**photo below**). Find fake cameras at home centers and online stores. Skip the smoked glass "dome" style and get a more traditional-looking unit. Mount it near the vulnerable doors and windows, but don't activate the red flashing light—real cameras don't have lights.

Time: 1 hour
Cost: $15

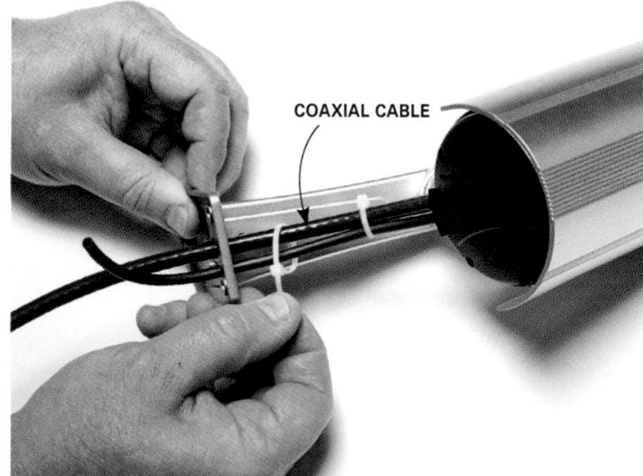

Make a fake camera look real
Real cameras have coaxial cables, so zip-tie coaxial cable to the fake power cable that came with the camera. Drill a second hole in the mounting bracket and hot-glue the cable into place.

Alarm systems are easier to install than you think

Police interviews with burglars prove that alarm systems are a deterrent. If burglars are convinced your home has a real alarm system, they'll move on to a more vulnerable target rather than take a risk at your home.

You can buy a professional grade wireless alarm system for about $200 from many online sources (homesecuritystore.com is one). Installing professional alarm hardware is easy, but programming the system can be a challenge.

For more information on installin g a professional security system, go to familyhandyman.com and search for "security system."

If you don't want to tackle the programming or can't find a supplier who will program it for you, skip the professional gear and buy a consumer-style DIY wireless alarm instead (one example is the Iris system starter kit; $300 at Lowe's). Starter kits come with a control unit, arming station, motion sensor and a few door/window sensors (photo above). But plan on buying enough extra sensors to install on each ground-level door and window.

Mount the arming station in a location where a burglar can see it from the most likely entry door or window. Then mount the sensors, connect the control box to power and your Internet router and program the system from your home computer. The system notifies you of a break-in or system failure with text messages and phone calls.

Time: Half a day
Cost: $200 and up

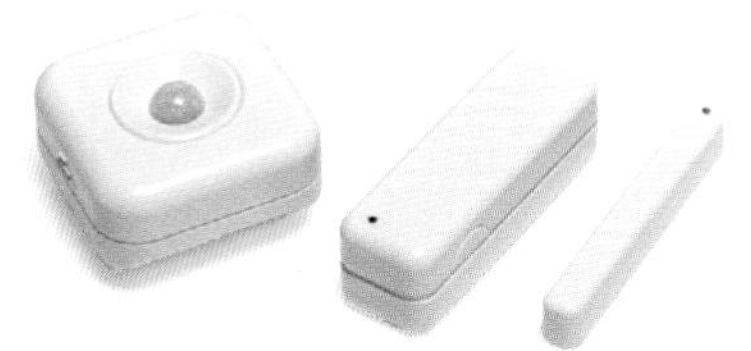
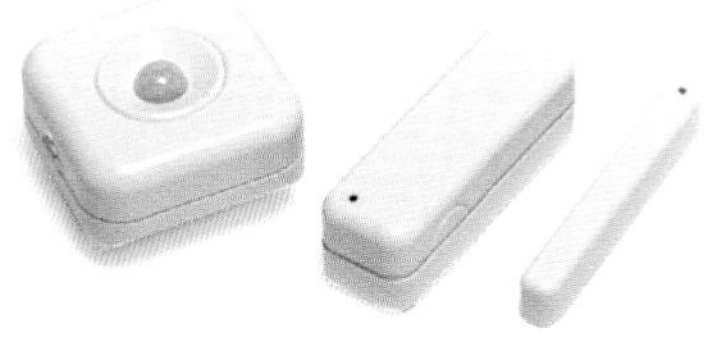

Wireless systems are simple
A battery-powered wireless DIY alarm system requires no wiring. Just plug the control box into your Internet router, mount the sensors and arming station, and program the unit with your computer.

Advertise your alarm
Stick yard signs by your front and back doors. Then plaster stickers on all the ground-floor windows.

Cut your losses if they do get in

- Immediately file a fraud alert with credit bureaus and contact your bank and credit card companies.
- Inspect your checkbook for missing checks—close the account if any are missing.
- Don't keep cash in your bedroom.
- Get a nice-looking jewelry box and fill it with your less expensive jewelry. Keep your valuable jewelry elsewhere.
- Keep guns locked in a safe.
- If you haven't taken steps to secure your home since the burglary, do it now! Burglars often come back about six weeks later to get the brand new items you bought with the insurance proceeds.

SPECIAL SECTION Paint Like a Pro

SOLUTIONS FOR OLD PAINT

There could be the makings of a minimalist masterpiece in your garage. If you have old, nearly empty cans of paint that have been in storage for a couple years, chances are you'll never use them. Just take old rosin or kraft paper that you've used to protect flooring and dump the paint over the paper out in the yard. The paint will dry into a flexible mat, and then you can either frame your art and hang it in your living room or roll it up and toss it into the trash.

—Mac Wentz

WIPE OFF GOOFS

Even pros occasionally get paint where they don't want it. One method of cleaning up goofs is to wrap a damp rag around a putty knife. Make sure the cloth is only one layer thick for the most accurate cleanup. Then carefully slide the putty knife along your goof to wipe it off. You have to do this right away, though. Once the paint starts to dry, you'll have to use more aggressive measures.

CEILING-PAINTING TIPS

Ceilings present some unique painting challenges. They're usually much larger than any single room wall and are often illuminated with raking light that accentuates even the smallest flaw in the paint. Add to that the challenge of working overhead and things can get messy in a hurry. Here are some tips to help you get a perfect job.

- **Use a stain-blocking primer to cover flaws.** Roof leaks, overflowing sinks, tobacco smoke and spills can all leave ceiling stains or dinginess that is impossible to conceal with plain paint. So cover the stain with a coat of stain-blocking primer before painting. White pigmented shellac is a favorite primer of many pros. If you're painting over a ceiling that's yellow from smoke, roll a coat of shellac over the entire ceiling before painting with latex.
- **Buy special ceiling paint.** While there are exceptions, in general you'll get the best results with paint that's formulated for a ceiling application. For a ceiling, you want paint that doesn't spatter, dries slowly, and is flat instead of glossy. Most ceiling paints are formulated with these qualities. And you can have ceiling paint tinted if you want a color other than "ceiling white."
- **Cut in before you roll.** This allows you to cover most of the brush marks with the roller. For best results, carefully brush paint along the edge of a 10-ft. section of the ceiling and then roll that section. The cut-in section will remain wet until you roll, so it blends in better. (For more information on cutting in, see pp. 58 – 59.)
- **Roll gently on textured ceilings.** If the texture has been painted over already, it's probably safe to paint again. But don't go back and forth with the roller, as this may pull the texture from the ceiling. If the ceiling needs another coat of paint, wait for the first coat to dry completely, then roll another coat *perpendicular to the first one* using the same careful technique.

  If the texture has never been painted, the water in the paint could loosen the texture, causing it to fall off in sheets. Before painting the full ceiling, do a test in a closet or other inconspicuous area. If the texture loosens, painting the full ceiling is risky. Finally, keep in mind that spray painting is less likely to loosen the texture, whether or not it's been painted before.

PAINT A **PANEL DOOR** PERFECTLY

How to master this tricky painting task

by **Gary Wentz, Senior Editor**

Paneled doors are the ultimate painter's challenge. A large area broken up by shaped surfaces is just plain tough to cover before the paint becomes sticky and unworkable. And since doors are a prominent feature, ugly mistakes like brush marks or drips are noticeable. Even though I had painted dozens of them over the years, I still felt a twinge of anxiety whenever I saw "paint door" on my to-do list. So I set out to find easier ways to get better results. I tried different tools, used different paints and watched professional painters. Here's what I learned.

Before you start

The actual work involved in painting a door typically amounts to three to five hours, depending on the condition of the door and how fussy you are. But add in the drying time and it's a full-day project. So if you're painting a door you can't live without—like a bathroom or exterior door—get started first thing in the morning so it can be back in service by day's end.

While you're picking a paint color, also think about sheen: With a flat finish, scuff marks and handprints are hard to wipe away. High gloss is easy to clean but accentuates every little flaw, so your prep and paint job have to be perfect. Satin and semigloss are good compromise choices. Also check the operation of the door. If it rubs against the jamb or drags on the carpet, now's the time to sand or plane the edges. If you have several doors that need painting, start with the least prominent one. It's better to make learning mistakes on the inside of a closet door than on your entry door.

What it takes

TIME: Three to five hours per door

COST: $15 to $40 per door

SKILL LEVEL: Beginner to advanced

TOOLS: High-quality brush and rollers, powerful lighting, shop vacuum, sanding supplies, possibly a random-orbital sander

1 Remove all the hardware. Slice through paint buildup around hinges and latches. Otherwise, you might splinter surrounding wood as you remove hardware.

2 Sand it smooth. On flat areas, level out old runs and brush marks with a hard sanding block. For the shaped profiles, you'll need a combination of sanding pads, sponges and scraps of sandpaper.

SPECIAL SECTION
PAINT LIKE A PRO

Paint Like a Pro

3 Remove the sanding dust. A vacuum with a brush attachment removes most of the dust. Wipe off the rest with a damp rag.

4 Sand after priming. Sand out any imperfections in the prime coat. Shine a light across the surface at a low angle to accentuate imperfections. If you find any spots that need an extra dab of filler, mark them with tabs of masking tape.

Prep tips

Pros often paint doors in place. But from prep to painting, you'll get better results if you remove the door. Working in your garage, shop or basement, you can control lighting and drying conditions better. And laying the door flat minimizes runs in the paint job. Here's what to do after you remove the door:

- Clean the door with a household cleaner. Almost any cleaner will do, as long as it cuts grease. Areas around doorknobs are especially prone to greasy buildup.
- Remove all the door hardware to get a neater paint job and save time. If you're dealing with more than one door, avoid hardware mix-ups by labeling plastic bags that will hold the hardware for each door.
- Fill dents and holes with a sandable filler such as MH Ready Patch. You'll probably have to fill deep dents twice to compensate for shrinkage.
- Remove old paint from the hardware. Start with a product intended to remove paint splatter such as Goof Off Pro Strength Remover or Goo Gone Painter's Pal. You can use paint strippers, but they may also remove clear coatings from the hardware or damage some types of finishes.

Sanding tips

If your door is in good shape, all it needs is a light sanding with sandpaper or a sanding sponge (180 or 220 grit). That will roughen the surface a little and allow the primer to adhere better. But most likely, you'll also need to smooth out chipped paint and imperfections from previous paint jobs. This is usually the most time-consuming, tedious part of the project. Here are some tips for faster, better results:

- Paint often sticks to sandpaper, clogging the grit and making it useless. So be sure to check the label and buy sandpaper intended for paint. You may still get some clogging, but you'll get less. This goes for sponges and other abrasives too.
- Start with 120 or 150 grit. You can switch to coarser paper (such as 80 grit) on problem areas, but be sure to follow up with finer grit to smooth out the sanding scratches.

CAUTION: If your home was built before 1979, check the paint for lead before you sand. For more information, go to hud.gov/offices/lead.

- On flat areas, a hard sanding block will smooth the surface much better than sponges or other soft-backed abrasives (Photo 2).
- Try a finishing or random-orbit sander on flat areas. It might save you tons of time. Then again, the sandpaper may clog immediately from heat buildup. It depends on the type and age of the paint.
- Buy a collection of sanding sponges and pads for the shaped areas. Through trial and error, you'll find that some work better than others on your profiles.
- Inspect your work with low-angle lighting (see Photo 4).

Tips for a perfect workspace

After the messy job of sanding is done, set the door aside and prep your workspace. For priming and painting, you want a work zone that's well lit and clean. Sawdust on your workbench will end up on brushes; airborne dust will create whiskers on the paint. The conditions in your work area should allow paint to dry slowly. Slower drying means more time for you to smooth the paint before it becomes

5 Paint the edges and wipe off the slop. Brush or roll paint onto all four edges. Immediately wipe any paint that slops onto the face of the door with a rag or foam brush. You don't have to completely remove the paint, but you do have to flatten it to prevent ridges (see photo below right).

6 Brush around the panels. Work the paint into the corners and grooves, then drag the brush over the paint to smooth it. Wipe away any slop around the panel as shown in Photo 5.

gummy and more time for the paint to level itself. Here's how to prep your space:

- Clean everything. Vacuum work surfaces and sweep the floor.
- Minimize air movement for less airborne dust and slower drying. Close doors and windows. Turn off forced-air heating or cooling.
- Don't rely on overhead lighting; you may even want to turn it off. Instead, position a work light 4 to 5 ft. above the floor. This low-angle light will accentuate any drips or ridges.
- Have all your tools and supplies ready, including a pail of water to dunk your paint tools in as soon as you're done.
- If you're working in the garage, unplug the garage door opener so it can't be opened while you work. An opening door raises dust.

Priming tips

You can "spot-prime" a door, coating only patched dents or areas you sanded through to bare wood. But priming the whole door is best; the new paint will stick better and you'll get a more uniform finish. Here are some tips for this critical step:

- Your choice of primer is just as important as your choice of paint. At the paint store, ask for a primer that's compatible with your paint, levels out well and sands smoothly.
- Have the primer tinted, based on the color of your paint.
- Apply the primer with just as much care as the paint and following the same steps (see Photos 5 – 9). Also check out the painting tips in the next section.

Water-based alkyd is best

If you want a smooth finish, choose a paint designed for that. Some paints, even good-quality paints, just aren't formulated for smoothness. Smooth paints are usually labeled "enamel" or "door and trim." But the label alone doesn't tell you enough; some brands of "enamel" are much better than others. Advice from the store staff, and the price, are the best indicators. Super-smooth paints often cost $25 to $30 per quart! But I'm happy to spend an extra 10 bucks per door for first-class results.

Among the paints I've used, one category stands out for smoothness: water-based alkyds. These paints dry slowly for extra working time and level out almost as well as traditional oil-based alkyds. After applying them with a high-quality roller, I was able to skip the brush-out step shown in Photos 7 and 9 and still got perfect results. Cleanup is as easy as with any other water-based paint. The disadvantages of water-based alkyds are a very long wait before recoating (16 to 24 hours) and a high price tag. I've used Benjamin Moore Advance Waterborne Interior Alkyd and Sherwin-Williams ProClassic Interior Waterbased Acrylic-Alkyd Enamel. To find a dealer, go to benjaminmoore.com or sherwin-williams.com.

The wrong paint Some paints show brush marks, ridges and roller stipple no matter how skillful or careful you are. Others go on smoothly and then level out beautifully, even if you're not a master painter.

7 Roll, then brush the panels. Coat the panels quickly with a roller. Then smooth the paint with a brush. Be careful not to touch the profiles surrounding the panel.

8 Roll the rails and stiles. Roll the door in sections, coating no more than one-quarter of the door at a time. Then brush out the paint. Be careful not to slop paint over the edges around the panels.

■ For an ultra-smooth paint job, apply two coats of primer. With a thick build of primer, you can sand the prime coat glassy-smooth, without sanding through to the old paint.

■ Lightly sand the primer with 220-grit, inspecting as you go (Photo 4). A couple of quick passes is all it takes. If you're not in a rush to get the door back in service, let the primer dry overnight before sanding. The longer it dries, the better it will sand.

Make the door flippable

Drive one screw into one end and two into the other. That lets you coat both sides of the door without waiting for the first side to dry. Drill pilot holes and drive 5/16 x 5-in. lag screws about halfway in. Smaller screws can bend and let the door drop just as you're finishing the final coat. (I learned this the hard way.)

Painting tips

Painting a door is a race against time. You have to lay down the paint and smooth it out before it becomes too sticky to work with, or so stiff that brush marks won't level out and disappear. Keep moving. Don't stop to answer the phone or get coffee. Minutes count. In warm, dry conditions, even seconds matter.

■ Consider a paint additive to slow down drying and improve leveling. Your paint dealer can recommend one that's compatible with your paint.

■ Start with a dust-free door; wipe it down with a damp rag just before painting.

■ Wet the floor. Two benefits for the price of one: A wet floor prevents you from kicking up dust that will create dust nubs in your finish. Better yet, it raises the humidity, which extends the time you have to smooth out the paint and gives the paint more time to level out. In my informal experiments, raising the humidity doubled the working time of the paint. (I also discovered that slick floors get even slicker when wet, which can lead to Three Stooges–style paint accidents. Be careful.)

■ Spend at least $10 to get a quality brush for a smoother finish. Pro painters disagree about the size and type to use. I prefer a 2-in. sash brush.

■ Don't use cheap roller sleeves or you'll get fibers in the finish. I use a mini roller and get good results with microfiber, mohair and FlockFoam sleeves. Foam sleeves also leave a smooth finish, but they hold very little paint, which slows you down.

■ Paint all four edges of the door first (Photo 5). Here's why: when painting edges, some paint inevitably slops onto the faces of the door. It's better to have that happen before the faces are painted.

9 Brush with the grain. Brush across the joints where door parts meet. Then drag your brush in a straight line along the intersection. That way, any visible brush marks will look more like a wood grain pattern and less like sloppy brushwork.

- Brush on a light coat. A heavy coat of paint covers better and sometimes levels out better, but runs are more likely and brush marks are deeper. So start out lightly, then lay it on a little thicker as your brush skills improve.
- Roll on the paint where you can. Rollers lay on paint much faster than a brush, giving you a few more precious minutes to work the paint before it begins to stiffen.
- Brush out rolled paint. Brushed paint usually levels out better than rolled paint, and any brush marks are less noticeable than roller stipple. *But you might be able to skip the brush-out step altogether.* With top-quality enamel and roller sleeves, roller results can be super smooth. This depends in part on drying conditions, so try it on a closet door or a primed scrap of wood first.
- Keep a pair of tweezers handy. Pluck out paintbrush bristles or rescue stuck insects without messing up the paint. This works great with other finishes too. For marital harmony, don't return the tweezers to the medicine cabinet. Buy a new pair (another lesson learned the hard way).
- Plan to apply at least two coats and lightly sand between coats with 220-grit to remove any dust nubs.

The ultimate smooth finish

Even the most skilled painter can't match the perfection of a sprayed-on finish. There are two types of sprayers: "airless" and "HVLP" (high-volume, low-pressure). Both can apply a flawless coat in minutes, but HVLP is more forgiving; it produces a finer spray, which reduces your chances of blasting on too much paint and creating runs. Many HVLP sprayers won't spray acrylic/latex paint. For a model that will, expect to spend $100 to $150, well worth it if you have a house full of doors to paint. Aside from finish quality, a sprayer will also save you hours of brushwork if you have several doors to paint. For more on both airless and HVLP sprayers, go to familyhandyman.com and search for "paint sprayers."

GreatGoofs®

Shoe renew

While painting my garage recently, I needed to stir the primer. I removed the lid on the primer can and started to stir with an attachment chucked into my drill. Everything was going smoothly until I switched the drill to "high." In an instant, I saw a third of the can of paint rise to the brim and then fly over the top of the can onto the grass and soak my tennis shoes. The only silver lining here was that my shoes were nearing the end of their useful life and the paint was water based, so cleanup was mostly successful!

—Joshua T. Timm

Paint Like a Pro

7 TIPS FOR CUTTING IN

Get a clean edge with these easy techniques

by **Jeff Gorton, Associate Editor**

Painters call it cutting-in or cutting, and it's the process of painting the perimeter of walls or ceilings with a brush before rolling the walls. Cutting in corners where the two adjoining walls are the same color is straightforward. But where beginners run into trouble is along ceilings, moldings and other areas that require a perfectly straight line of paint. In this article we'll give you some tips and pointers to help you increase the speed and improve the accuracy of your cutting-in technique.

1 Buy a good-quality, angled sash brush

I've seen many pro painters cut in perfectly with a big square-edge brush, but for most people, angled sash brushes like the ones shown here are easier to control. You can fan the angled tips out to get a fine line of paint, and the angle makes it easier to get into corners. A 2-1/2-in.-wide brush is about right for most interior room painting. But if you're painting windows or other small woodwork, buy a smaller brush too. It's easier to paint accurately with a smaller brush.

2 Work from a small pail and pat, don't wipe, to load the brush

Transfer about 1 in. of paint to a small container rather than dipping into the can the paint comes in. A small amount of paint prevents dipping your brush too deep. Look at a paint store or home center for small plastic or metal paint pails with handles built in, like the one shown here (about $5).

Dipping the paintbrush and then wiping off the paint on the edge of a bucket is a common practice, but it's not very efficient for cutting in. It's better to leave more paint on the brush by dipping the bristles about an inch into the paint and then just patting the brush against opposite sides of the pail. With that amount of paint on the brush, you'll be able to cover more surface before you need to reload.

3 Wiggle into corners

Wiggling the brush a little bit helps the paint release into tight corners. Wiggling the brush is also a good technique for filling in missed areas as you make a second pass. Don't wiggle too hard. Just a little vibration is all that's needed to get great results.

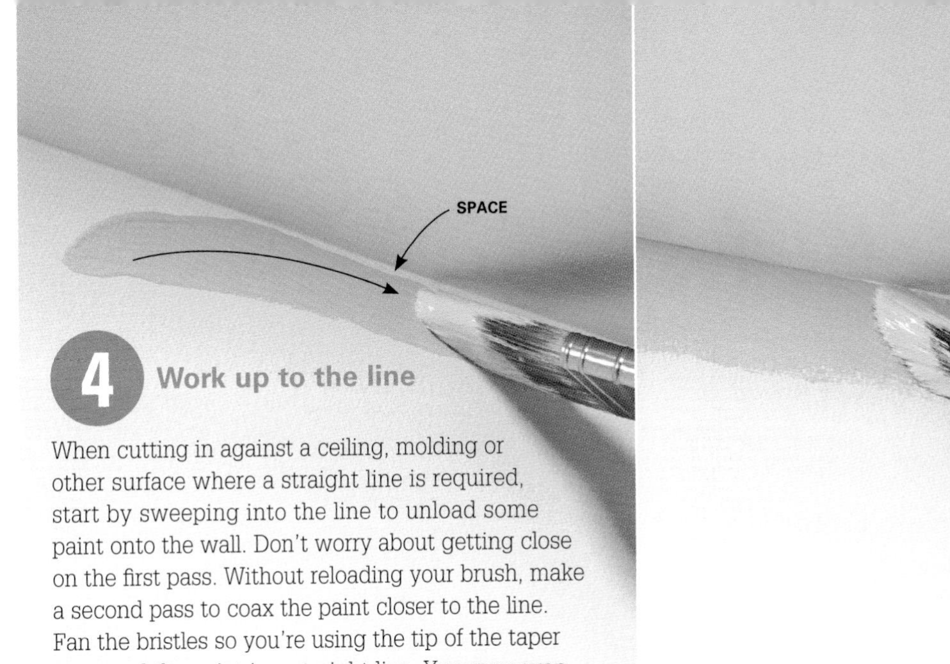

4 Work up to the line

When cutting in against a ceiling, molding or other surface where a straight line is required, start by sweeping into the line to unload some paint onto the wall. Don't worry about getting close on the first pass. Without reloading your brush, make a second pass to coax the paint closer to the line. Fan the bristles so you're using the tip of the taper to spread the paint in a straight line. You may even have to make a third pass to get a perfectly straight cut-in line. Afterwards, feather the edge (below).

5 Feather the edge

When you're happy with the cut-in line (above), finish up by feathering or thinning the edge. Without reloading the brush, drag the tips of the bristles lightly over the outside edge to spread the paint in a thin layer and get rid of any ridges or paint buildup. This feathering step ensures that your cut-in paint won't show as a stripe after you roll paint onto the walls.

6 Mask only the tops

When you master cutting in, you need to apply masking tape to only the tops of windows, doors and the base-board. And the only reason you do this is to avoid spattering the woodwork when you roll paint onto the walls. Masking less saves you time and money, and you don't have to worry about paint creeping under the tape or the paint job getting messed up when you pull off the tape.

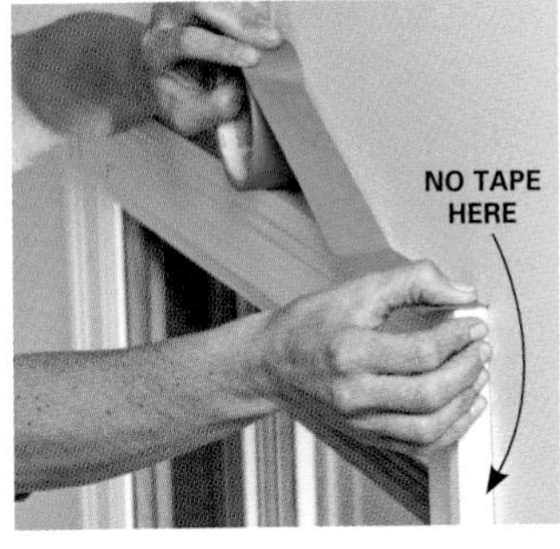

7 Get in a good position with bright light

To paint an accurate cut-in line, you have to get your body into a position where you can see the line clearly, and you need bright light. One of our Field Editors sent us this tip—to use a headlamp—and it really helps. For cutting-in along the ceiling, get your head close to the ceiling for the best view of the cut-in line.

MASKING A ROOM FOR PAINT

How to choose—and use—today's masking tape

by **Jeff Gorton, Associate Editor**

With all the new types of masking tape available today, it's easier than ever to prepare a room for painting. You can buy low-adhesion tape to protect delicate surfaces; edge-sealing tape to create crisp, bleed-free lines; and tape kits to mask textured walls.

But there's more to successful masking than having the best tape for the task at hand, and there are ways you can speed up the job. Here are some tips to help you make the most of whatever modern tape you choose.

Clean moldings before you apply tape

Even the stickiest masking tape won't stay put if you apply it to a dusty, dirty surface. You'll save yourself a lot of time and frustration if you start every masking job by cleaning the moldings or the wall you're applying the tape to. Usually a thorough dusting with a damp rag is all that's required. But if the surface is greasy, you'll have to wash it with a detergent solution. TSP-PF (phosphate free), available at home centers and paint stores, is the go-to detergent for most painters. Wait for the surface to dry completely before masking.

Speed up masking with a tape applicator

If you really want to speed up and simplify your masking job, buy a tape applicator. Shown is the ScotchBlue Painter's Tape Applicator from 3M. It's available at home centers and paint stores for about $9 with a roll of tape, and it's designed to help you precisely mask using the adjacent surface as a guide. You simply roll it along the molding, wall or ceiling to apply the tape. Then use the built-in cutter to slice the tape at the end of the run. With this tool, even a novice can get great results with only a few minutes' practice.

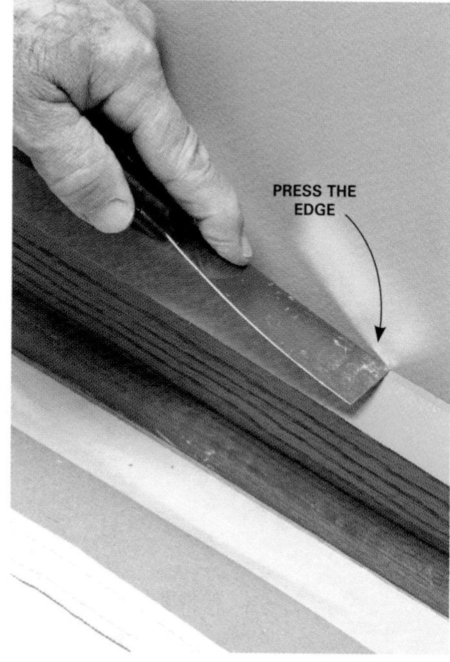

Press the tape to ensure a good bond

This may be old news to you seasoned painters. But if you're just starting out, it's probably the most important masking tip you can learn. After you apply the tape, make sure to press down the edge to seal it. Otherwise paint is sure to seep under the edge of the tape. A flexible putty knife works great. Start at one end of your tape run and pull the blade along the tape while applying downward pressure. Tilt the putty knife blade slightly so you're applying pressure right along the edge of the tape.

1 Cut off the excess tape. Make a crease with a putty knife. Then cut off the extra tape with a utility knife for a perfect corner.

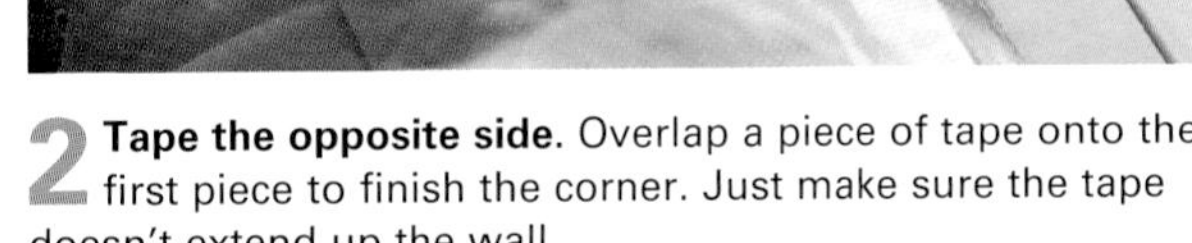

2 Tape the opposite side. Overlap a piece of tape onto the first piece to finish the corner. Just make sure the tape doesn't extend up the wall.

Simple corner masking

It's easy to get a perfect fit on inside corners with this simple technique. Start by running the first piece of tape up the wall, making it a little long. Press the tape down into the corner with a putty knife. Then cut along the crease with a sharp utility knife (**Photo 1**) and remove the cutoff piece. Now you don't have to be so careful with the next piece (**Photo 2**).

Quick and easy wall protection

If you're spray texturing or painting a ceiling, draping lightweight plastic sheeting is the best way to cover your walls. The photos below show a quick and easy way to hang the plastic. Use 1-1/2-in.-wide tape with medium to high holding strength. But test first in an inconspicuous area to make sure the tape doesn't pull paint from the wall. Super-thin "painter's plastic" is a good choice for this type of masking because it's inexpensive and lightweight, and it produces less waste. Overlap the plastic at doorways to create an opening.

1 Apply tape along the ceiling. Press the top edge down, but leave the bottom loose. It should curl up slightly to expose the sticky underside.

2 Hang the thin plastic. Stick the edge of the lightweight plastic sheeting to the tape and let it hang to the floor. You don't need to tuck the plastic underneath the tape. Just curl the tape back onto itself and stick the plastic to the exposed adhesive.

Inside corner painting tips

When you're changing wall colors at an inside corner, it can be tricky to get a nice straight line, especially if the corner is rounded or has built-up layers of paint. The tip is to paint around the corner with the first color. Then when the paint dries, mask off the painted side using a top-quality edge-sealing tape (FrogTape Multi-Surface is one example).

But don't try to tape right down the corner. Instead, move the tape about 1/8 in. from the corner where it'll be easier to get a perfectly straight line. Nobody will ever notice that one paint color extends slightly past the corner, and you'll end up with a straight, crisp color change.

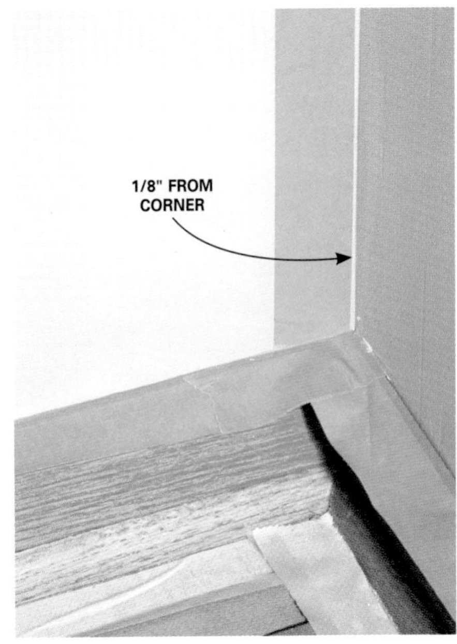

Paint Like a Pro

Foolproof window masking

Unless you have a super-steady hand for painting windows, it's faster and easier to simply mask off window glass—especially if you use this super-quick method we learned from a pro painter. The photos below show how. If you're spray painting instead of brushing, start by cutting a piece of paper about an inch smaller than the glass and putting it under the first piece of tape you apply.

1 Mask the sides. Apply strips of tape to the sides, leaving the ends long. Then press the ends of the tape into the corner with a flexible putty knife.

2 Cut the tape. Use a razor knife to cut off the excess tape. A sharp utility knife would work well too.

3 Fill in the top and bottom. Now it's easy to fill in between the side pieces. You don't have to worry about getting the tape the perfect length.

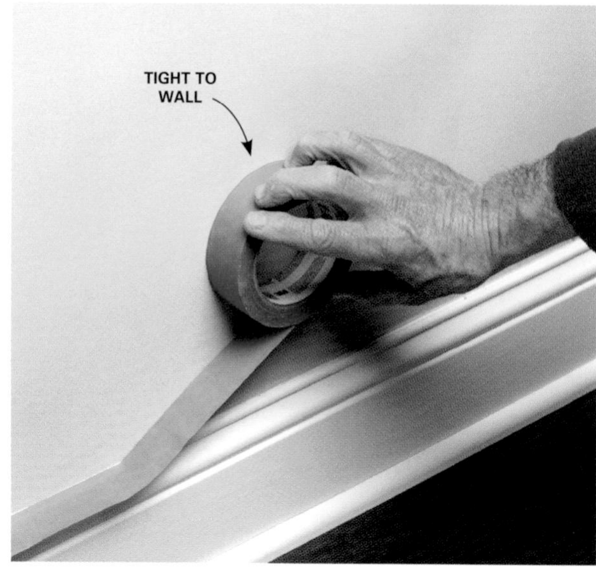

Speedy taping *without* a special tool

Here's a technique to help you apply tape quickly and precisely, without any special tools. Stick a few inches of tape to the molding and unroll about 6 more inches of tape. Then while you hold the roll of tape tight against the wall, rotate it down to stick this section of tape and repeat the process. It takes a bit of practice, but mastering this technique will dramatically increase your masking speed and accuracy.

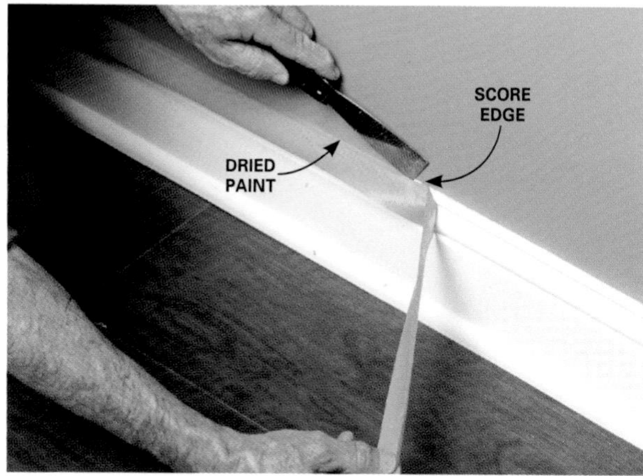

Score tape before pulling it off

Ideally you would remove masking tape right away, while the paint is still wet. But in reality this isn't very practical. In the first place, modern water-based paint dries pretty fast. By the time you're through painting a room, the paint where you started is already starting to dry. And if you have to apply a second coat of paint, you certainly don't want to remove the tape and then have to reapply it.

The solution is to let the paint dry completely. Then score the edge of the tape with a putty knife before you pull it off. This will break any bond that has formed with the paint and ensure that the masking tape will come off cleanly without damaging your paint job.

2 Electrical & High-Tech

IN THIS CHAPTER

Home Care & Repair....................................64
Repair a buried cable, fix crooked switches and outlets, save money on electronics recycling and more

Great Goofs....................................67
Missing the signals

Fishing Wire....................................68

Working with PVC Conduit....................................72

Get Faster and Better Wi-Fi in Your Home....................................76

Handy Hints....................................78
Energy-saving outlet strip, lithium for long life, better electrical circuit ID and more

Great Goofs....................................79
Flash of brilliance

REPAIR A BURIED CABLE

If you're planning to dig holes in your backyard, you should always call 811 a few days beforehand to get all the underground utilities marked. Unfortunately, privately owned wiring will not be marked, so it's still possible to strike an electrical cable. It's especially likely if you're digging between the house and a freestanding garage, shed or yard light. If you do cut a power line, though, it's easy to fix. Here's how.

Assess the damage

Turn off the circuit breaker to the cut cable and double-check at the damaged area with a voltage sniffer to be sure it's really off. Then enlarge the hole to a 2-ft. diameter. If the cable is cut cleanly, you can just splice it back together with a single underground splice kit. But if it's cut or nicked in several places, you'll have to remove the damaged section and splice in a "jumper" piece of UF (underground feeder) cable using two splice kits.

Two types of splice kits

Underground AC splice kits come in two varieties: heat-shrinkable tubing and gel-filled shield. Both use a brass splicing block to connect the wires. But they differ in how they protect the splice.

The most common type of kit protects the splice with an 8-in. length of heat-shrinkable tubing filled with watertight hot-melt adhesive. (The Gardner Bender HST-1300, about $14, is shown on the left in the photo below.) Slide the tubing over the cable before you connect the wires to the splice block. Then slide the tubing over the connector and shrink it with a heat gun (best) or a torch (gently!). The other type is a corrugated plastic shield filled with an encapsulating gel. (Shown at far right and in **Photos 1 – 5** is the Tyco Electronics PowerGel Wraparound UF Splice Kit; about $30). It's twice the price as the heat-shrinkable model, but it installs much more quickly, is goof-proof and is very long lasting.

Make the splice

Start by cutting out the damaged sections. Then cut, separate and strip the ends of the buried cable (**Photo 1**). Do the same for the additional section of cable (if needed). Next, secure the wires in the brass holder (**Photo 2**). Locate the splice block in the protective shield (**Photo 3**). Wrap the shield around the splice and secure it (**Photo 4**). Then repower the circuit to make sure the splice works.

To make it easier to locate the splice in the future, mark it with bright-colored surveyor's tape (**Photo 5**). Then refill the hole.

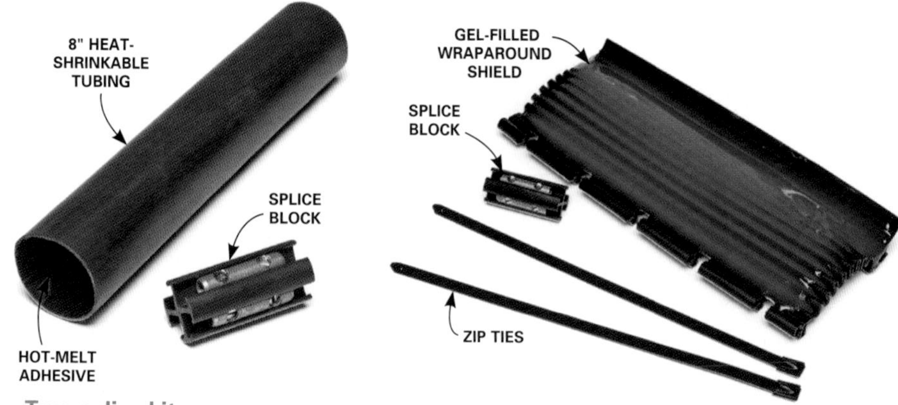

Two splice kits
On the left, one with heat-shrinkable tubing. On the right, one with gel. For both, the wires are connected in a splice block.

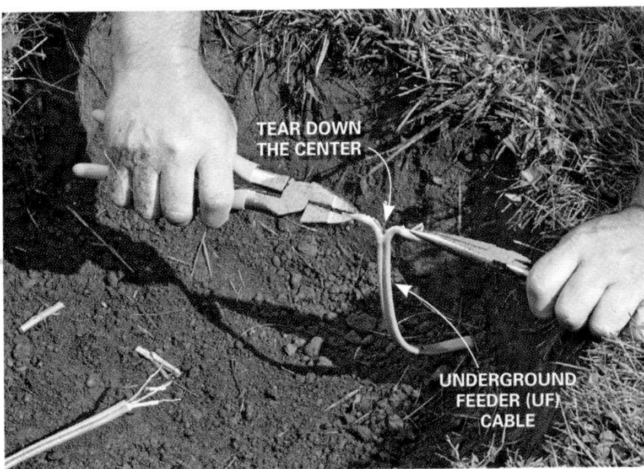

1 Twist and pull to separate. Grab each of the side conductors with pliers. Then twist your hands in opposite directions to start the tear. Pull the conductors 180 degrees away from each other to separate and expose a length of 1-1/2 in. Strip 3/4 in. of insulation off the black and white wires.

2 Match the colors and splice. Slide the black wires into opposite ends of the brass barrel and tighten the screws. Then do the same for the white and bare copper wires.

3 Position the splice on the shield. Place the splice block dead-center over the gel-filled shield. Clean off any debris that may have fallen into the gel. Then press the splice into the gel.

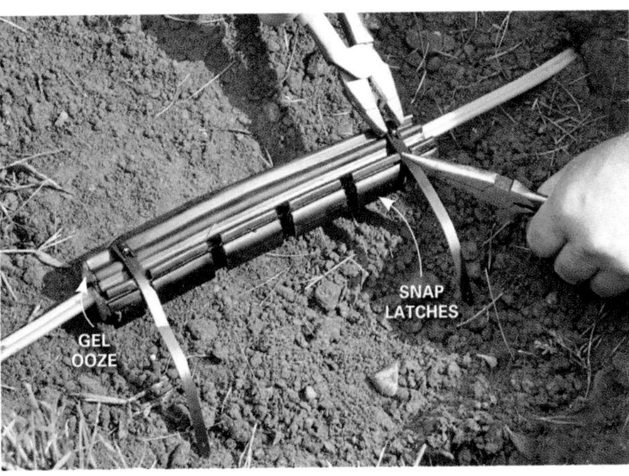

4 Roll and snap. Roll the shield around the splice and align the plastic latches. Snap the latches, starting at the center and working toward the edges. Then install the zip ties and tighten with pliers.

5 Mark the location. Tie bright-colored surveyor's tape around the splice and fill the hole with soil. Replace the grass and trim the tape at soil level so you can find it again.

Splicing low-voltage cable

Besides underground power cable, it's also possible to slice through low-voltage lighting, irrigation and telephone cable and coaxial cable. Since they're low voltage, you may be tempted to just twist the wires and wrap the splice with electrical tape. It won't work. Instead, head to a home center and get a couple of low-voltage connectors for direct burial. They rely on gel to encapsulate the splice to prevent water intrusion and corrosion.

For low-voltage stranded cable, like you might find on lighting, use the wire nut/gel-filled tube style. Twist on the wire nut, plunge the connector into the tube until the gel oozes out the top, then snap the lid. For solid irrigation and telephone wire, shove the wires in an insulation piercing gel-filled connector and snap it closed.

LANDSCAPE WIRING CONNECTORS

INSULATION-PIERCING GEL-FILLED SPLICE CONNECTOR

WIRE NUT

GEL-FILLED CAPSULE

FIX CROOKED SWITCHES AND OUTLETS

Here's a handy tip from one of our electrical consultants. The screws that attach an outlet or a switch to the box go in a slot that allows the device to be adjusted. But you don't always have to remove the cover plate to fix crooked switches or outlets. Instead, try pushing a flat-blade screwdriver against the cover plate. Use a screwdriver with a sharp blade. A rounded-over blade will just slip off. You may have to push from more than one corner to fix really crooked devices.

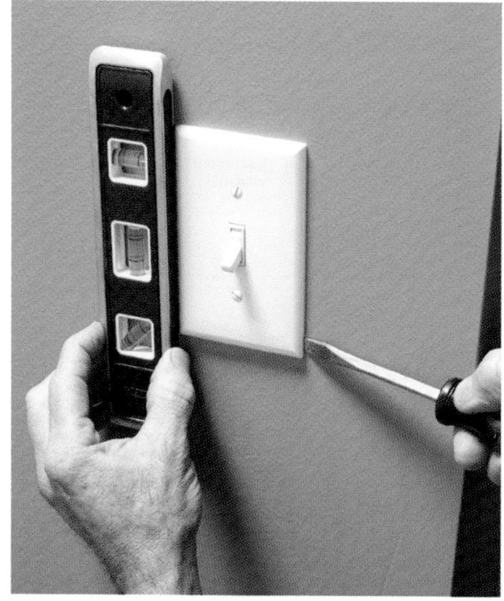

USE THE RIGHT BATTERY IN YOUR SMOKE DETECTOR

You may have heard that lithium batteries are the best choice to use in smoke detectors because they last longer than alkaline batteries. However, even though lithium batteries may last longer, once they start to run out of juice, they die quickly. That shortens the length of time the detector broadcasts a low-battery chirp signal. So it's possible to miss the warning chirp and be left with a dead smoke alarm. Not good!

However, the user's manual for some smoke detectors state that lithium batteries can be used. To clear up the confusion, we contacted a major smoke detector manufacturer. It turns out that the low-battery detection software in smoke detectors is designed to work only with the types of batteries listed in the owner's manual. If your manual says lithium batteries are approved, you're good to go. If it doesn't, then don't use them—further proof that it really *is* a good idea to read the user's manual.

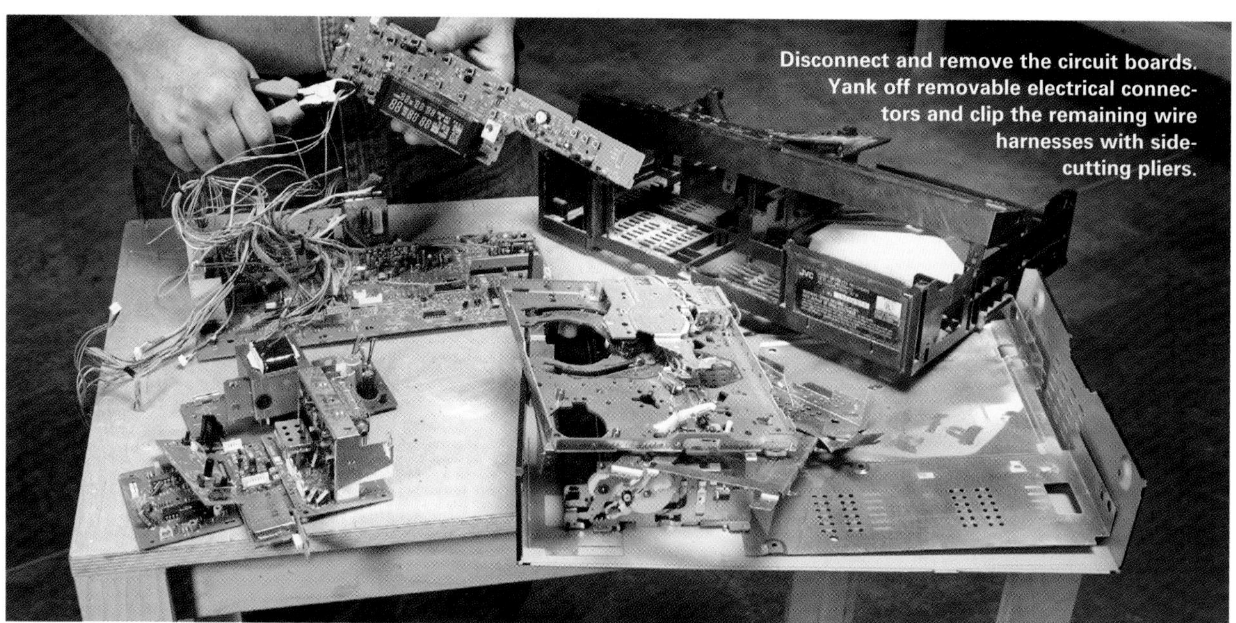

Disconnect and remove the circuit boards. Yank off removable electrical connectors and clip the remaining wire harnesses with side-cutting pliers.

SAVE MONEY ON ELECTRONICS RECYCLING

Many communities offer free electronics recycling. But others charge a flat fee per piece, depending on the type of device and its weight. An old VCR, for example, can cost $10. If you have to pay to get rid of electronics, here's how to save some money. Find an electronics recycler that'll accept removed circuit boards and charge only by the pound. Then disassemble the devices by removing the cover and front panel. Remove the circuit boards as shown and take them to the electronics recycling center. Recycle the metal and plastic parts with your household recycling.

FIX COMPUTERIZED APPLIANCES YOURSELF

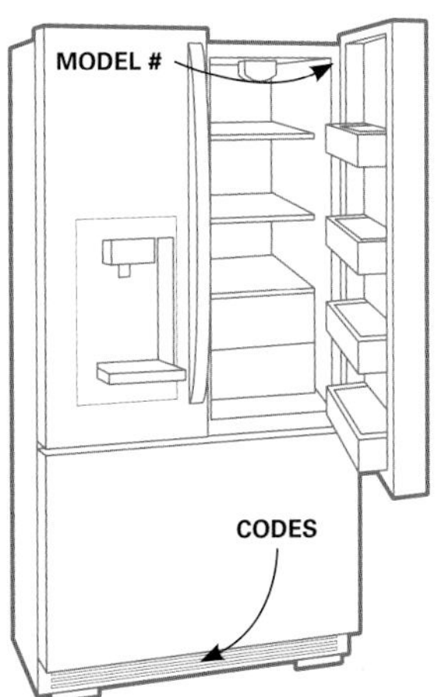

Many newer appliances include computerized touch pads and control boards. You may think they're too complicated to repair yourself. Wrong. They're actually easier to work on because the computer does all the diagnostic work for you. Once the computer detects a problem, it stores a fault code in memory. All you have to do is put the computer into readout mode and consult the fault code chart to discover which part failed. Fortunately, most manufacturers pack the code retrieval procedure and code translation information right inside the machine.

The trick is to find them. The diagrams here show typical locations. Remove the cover panel and look for the fault code instructions in a plastic bag. Follow the instructions to put the computer into code retrieval mode, then count the blinks or read the fault code from the display. Once you learn which part failed, copy the model and serial number off the tag and buy a replacement part.

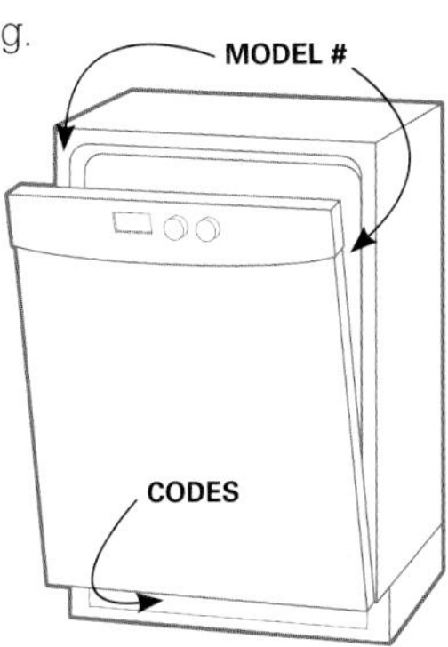

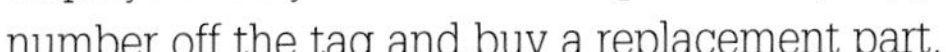

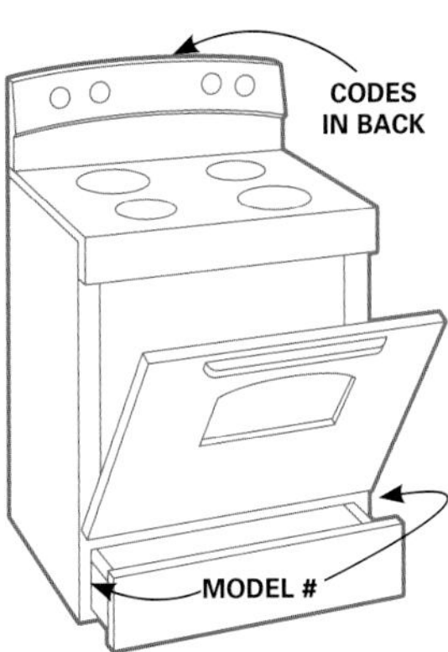

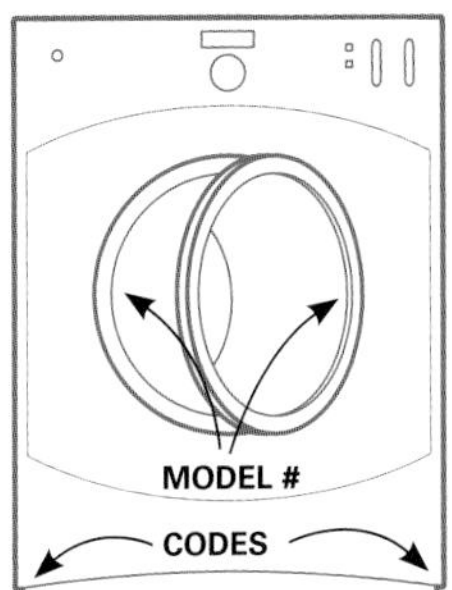

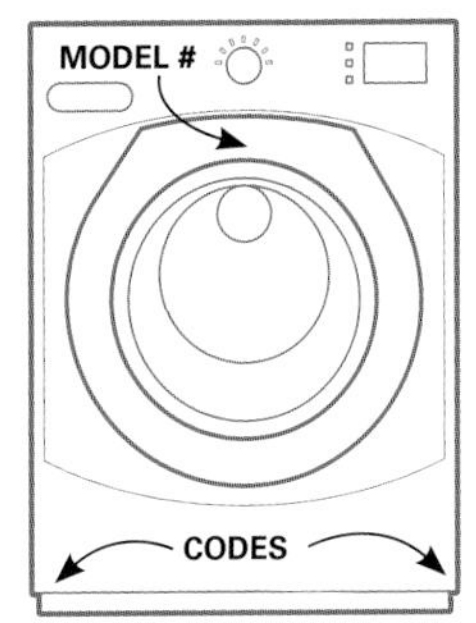

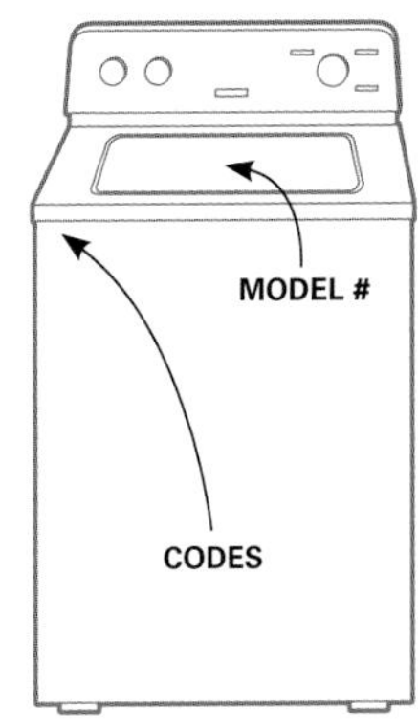

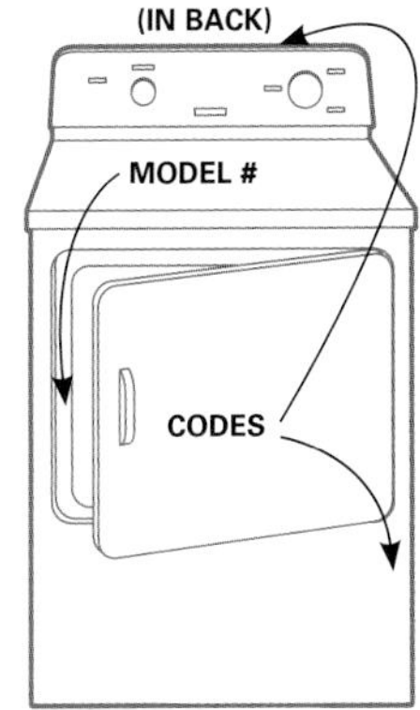

Find the model number and the fault code sheet
Here are the typical locations on various appliances. (You may need to remove a cover panel to find them.) With the fault codes, the appliance diagnoses itself!

GreatGoofs®

Missing the signals

It was chilly in the house, so my wife decided to turn up the thermostat. We waited several hours, but it still felt like an icebox, so I announced that I would fix the problem while she ran a few errands. I jacked up the temperature, but there was still no heat.

I ventured into the attic to check our gas heater. Not seeing any obvious problem, I called for a furnace repair. The technician quickly noticed that the attic unit wasn't receiving a signal from the thermostat. Then came the painful question: "When was the last time you replaced the batteries in your programmable thermostat?" To add insult to injury, my wife called right then to suggest that I try changing the thermostat batteries! Completely red-faced, I wrote the "repair" check. On the upside, I'm enjoying toasty warm mornings. I just wish there were a quick fix for humiliation!

—John P. Williams

FISHING **WIRE**

A pro shares secrets for running wire

by **Mark Petersen, Contributing Editor**

Fishing wires and cables through finished walls can be a perplexing and intimidating assignment. It's tempting to cut in access holes all over the place, but you don't have to do that if you play it smart. With a few simple tools and these tips from our expert, Tim Johnson, you'll avoid a whole bunch of drywall patching, and have more time for real fishing!

MEET AN EXPERT

Tim Johnson works for Norske Electric in Savage, MN. He became an electrician 15 years ago after finishing a stint with the U.S. Navy. He works on both commercial and residential projects, and even spent a couple of years wiring up wind turbines 265 ft. in the air!

Buy extra wire

Have plenty of extra wire or cable on hand, because it's not likely that you'll be able to fish a wire in a straight line from Point A to Point B. There's also the possibility that your wire might get hung up on something, and you'd have to abandon it and start over.

The tools you need

Flex bits and glow rods are the go-to tools Tim uses to fish wires. Flex bits are great for drilling holes in hard-to-reach spaces (see "Invest in a Bumper Ball," p. 70). The two most common lengths are 5 ft. and 6 ft., but extensions are also available. A 3/4-in. x 54-in. flex bit costs about $50 at home centers. Buy a bit that has a hole on the end of it so you can use the bit itself to pull wires (more on that later).

Once your hole is drilled, you can shove a glow rod through the hole, attach your wire to the eyelet at the end and pull it back through. Glow rods can also be used to hook wires to pull them out. As their name suggests, glow rods glow in the dark. This makes them easier to spot when you're working in dark areas (which is most of the time).

Glow rods come in various lengths and thicknesses, and you can combine as many sections as the job requires. Thinner rods flex more and work better when you have to make sharp turns. A thicker rod can span longer distances and is better for hooking wires that are more than a few feet away. A 9-ft. glow rod kit costs about $37 at home centers. Expect to pay about $60 for a 24-ft. kit.

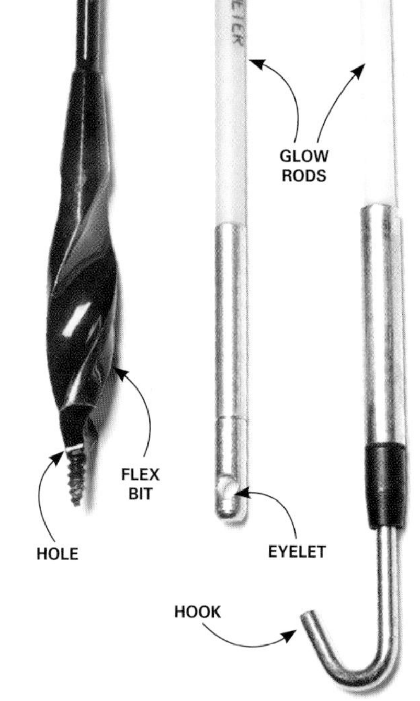

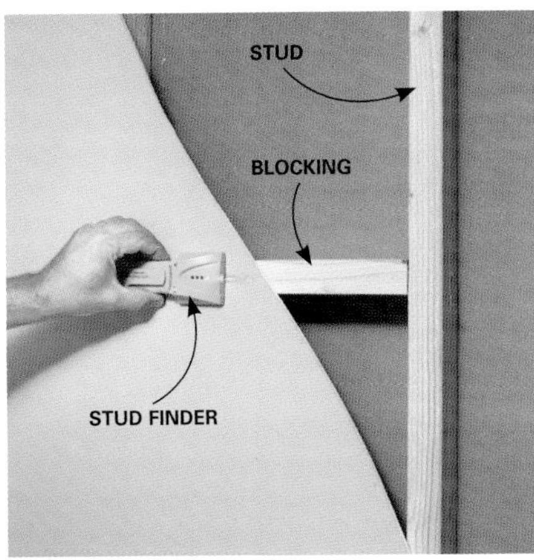

Check the whole wall cavity with a stud finder

A decent stud finder is a must-have for every wire-fishing job, but don't throw it back in your pouch after you've located the studs. Use your stud finder to check the whole wall cavity for obstacles like blocking and abandoned headers. You don't want to find out the hard way that you should have fished your wire one stud cavity to the left or right.

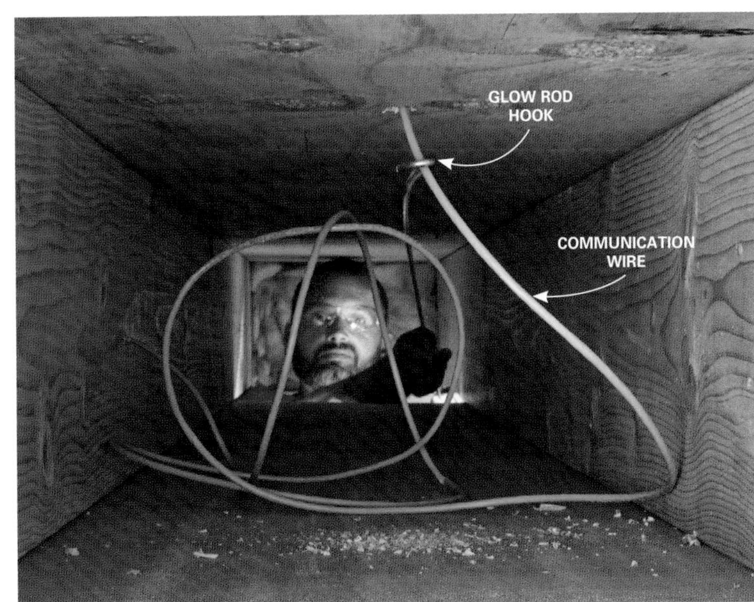

Push through more than you need

When hooking a wire to pull it toward you, make sure there's more than enough wire to hook on to. Sometimes it's a real challenge to grab hold of a wire, and once you have it hooked, you don't want to lose it. Tim always makes sure that he has at least 5 or 6 ft. of extra wire to keep up the tension on the hook the whole time he's pulling on it.

Get a better view with an inspection mirror

You know your wire is in there somewhere, but you just can't seem to find it. It's probably hung up on another wire or pipe, but guessing isn't going to solve the problem. Tim shines a flashlight onto an inspection mirror to find out exactly what's going on. This is a simple, inexpensive tip that can save you a lot of time and frustration. Pick up an inspection mirror at an auto parts store for less than $10. Or bump it up a notch and pay a few more bucks for a mirror with small built-in lights, so you can see exactly what's going on.

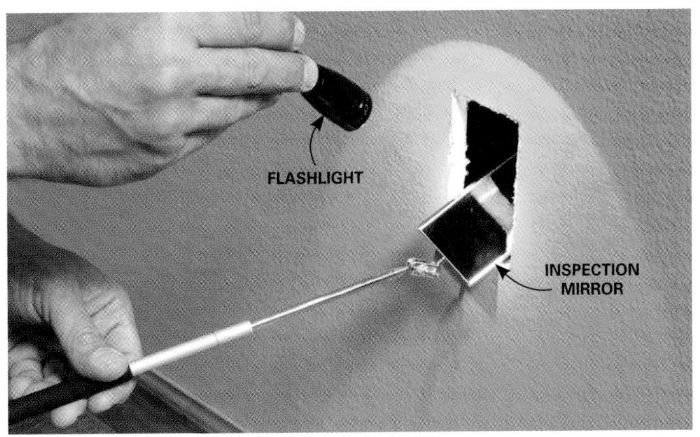

Seal the holes

If you're drilling holes through top and bottom plates or running wires through a fire wall in the garage, you must seal those holes with a fire-resistant caulk or foam sealant to comply with fire and energy codes. Most building officials won't make you bust out large holes in ceilings and walls in order to access hard-to-reach holes, but check with your local official before you begin your project. A can of fire-blocking insulated foam sealant costs about $7 at home centers and hardware stores.

Don't spin the bit in insulation

The best advice for fishing wires through insulation is "Avoid it if you can." The potential is always there to damage the vapor barrier or bunch up insulation, leaving cold spots in the wall. If you must fish wires through exterior walls, the best tip is to avoid spinning the flex bit until you make solid contact with the wood you plan to drill through. If you drill too early, you'll end up creating a large insulation cotton candy cone, which will make retrieving your bit difficult, if not impossible.

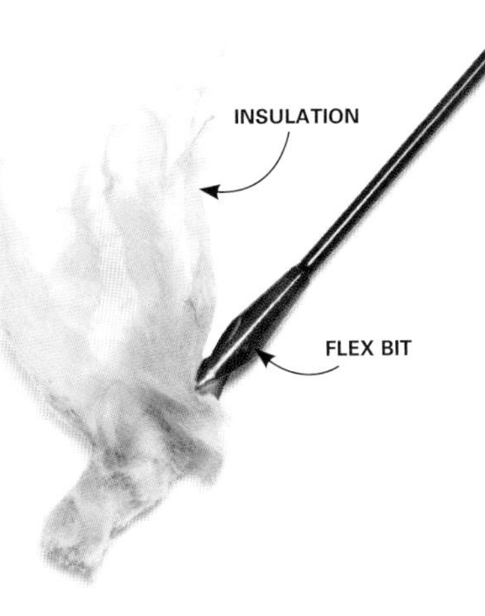

Hook on to a flex bit

Sometimes you don't need to use glow rods at all. Most flex bits have holes in the ends of them. If you have access to where the flex bit pops out, attach your wire directly to the bit and fish the wire through that way. Tim twists the wire and tapes it up to make sure it doesn't come off when he's pulling it back through (see "Get a good hook-up," p. 71). Remove your bit from your drill before pulling so you don't accidentally spin the bit and twist up your wire.

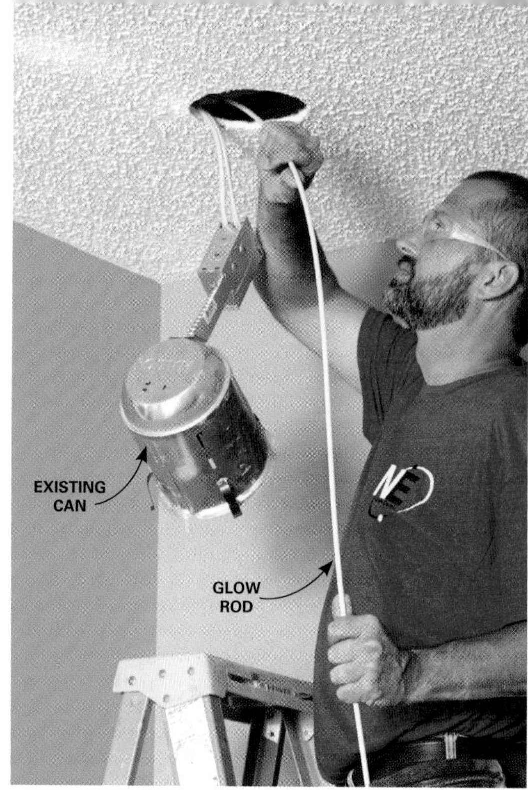

Fish wires through the holes for recessed lights

When you're installing new recessed can lighting, fishing wires from one light to another is easy because you have a great big hole to pull the wires through. But even if you're not installing new lighting, you can use the existing openings. Many cans can be easily popped out of the opening by removing a few screws.

Invest in a Bumper Ball

Wires aren't supposed to be installed any closer than 1-1/4 in. from a penetrable surface (the outside of the drywall). That means you shouldn't be drilling holes right next to the drywall. But it's not always easy to control where a flex bit goes. A Bumper Ball flexible drill bit guide installed on the end of your flex bit will help maintain the proper space between the bit and the outside of the wall cavity. You can buy a set of two at electrical suppliers or at licensedelectrician.com for about $13.

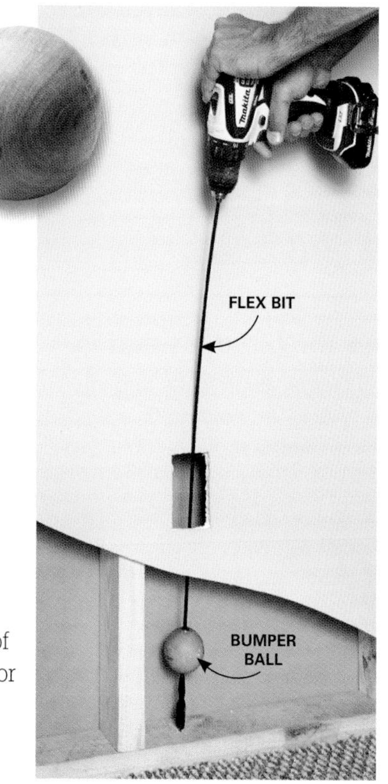

Protect drywall with a mud ring

Mud rings, also called drywall brackets or low-voltage "old-work" brackets, are great for protecting the drywall when you're drilling with a flex bit or cranking on a glow rod. They're easy to install (just tighten two screws) and cost less than $2 at home centers. Once the wires are connected, you can screw the wall plate to the mud ring.

Mud rings are approved only for low-voltage wires like communication and coaxial cables. If you need to install a regular gang box for an electrical outlet or wall switch, install the mud ring temporarily to protect the drywall while you fish the wire, then remove it.

Install conduit inside cabinets

Additional outlets above the counter space—that's one of the most popular electrical retrofits. Tim loves these jobs because he just fishes his wire through a flexible conduit installed right through the base cabinets. If you drill the holes for the conduit as far back and as high as you can, no one will ever notice.

Get a good hook-up

When Tim hooks cable to the eyelet of a glow rod, he strips the plastic sheathing back about 6 in., then cuts off the hot and neutral wires. He then wraps the remaining ground wire through the rod's eyelet and wraps it back around the wire's sheathing several times. Finally, he wraps the whole area with electrical tape.

When hooking coaxial cable, Tim just tapes the whole wire to the glow rod. He's never lost a wire using just tape.

Tim uses the same technique when working with communication cable like phone wire. If you try to hook one of the small communication wires, you could stretch and damage that individual wire several feet down inside the sheathing.

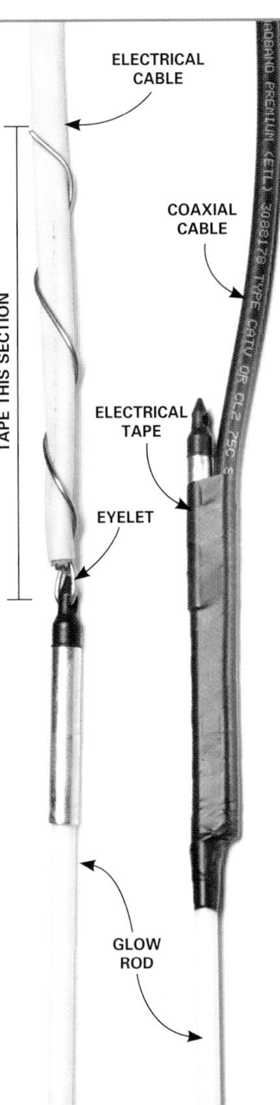

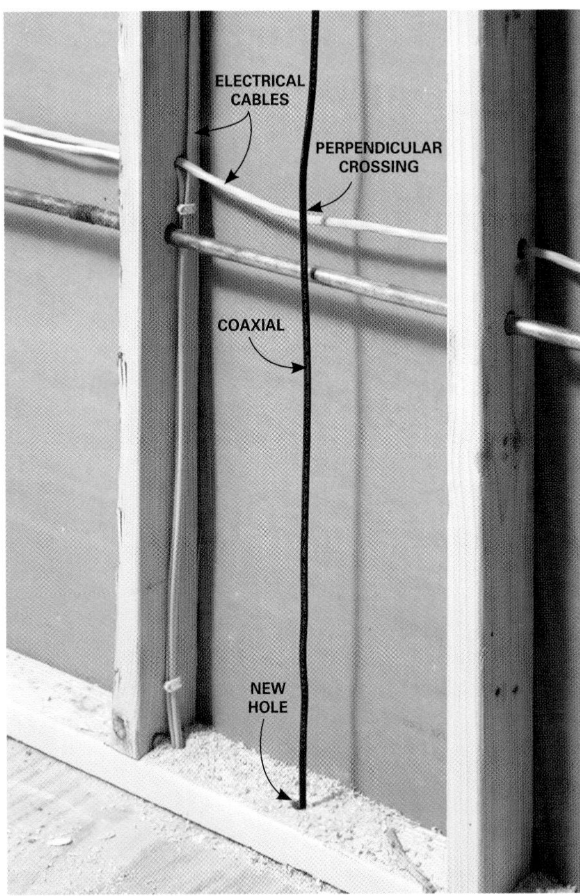

Keep low-voltage wires away from electrical cables

It's really tempting to fish low-voltage wires (like coax and Cat-5e) through existing holes occupied by electrical cables, but don't do it! Even though cables are insulated, the high-voltage current can interfere with the signal in the low-voltage wires. This could result in bad TV reception or unreliable phone and Internet service. Drill a new hole, and keep the new low-voltage wire several inches away from electrical cables. It's OK to run low-voltage wires perpendicular to cables, and it's also OK to run low-voltage wires next to electrical wires that are encased in conduit or metal sheathing.

Don't spin apart the glow rods

Sometimes you need to twist and spin glow rods in order to snake them past ductwork, pipes and other obstructions. A great way to lose a rod or attachment in a wall or joist space is to twist it so many times in the same direction that it unthreads and comes apart. Some pros wrap a little electrical tape around the connections to keep them secure.

WORKING WITH **PVC CONDUIT**

PVC conduit is easy to work with—if you know the tricks of the trade

by **Mark Petersen, Contributing Editor**

For outdoor wiring—hooking up a hot tub, adding outlets to a deck, powering a shed—installing conduit makes a lot of sense, and many times it's required. Conduit even has its uses inside, wherever wires would otherwise be exposed and could be damaged. And if you have a circuit you may want to extend someday, conduit will enable you to pull additional wires.

We're going to show you how to install plastic (PVC) rigid conduit rather than metal conduit. Plastic conduit is less expensive, lighter and much easier to work with. Here are great tips from commercial electrician Jason Bouchard to help you make wiring runs with conduit.

Larger conduit and bigger boxes

Install 3/4-in. conduit instead of 1/2-in. if (1) you need to pull more than three wires through one section of conduit; (2) there's any chance you'll add wires in the future; or (3) if you have a long and winding run. The 3/4-in. conduit doesn't cost that much more, and it's a heck of a lot easier to pull wire through. Whatever size conduit you use, don't fill it more than 40 percent with wires.

Single-gang electrical boxes will work, but if you have two or more conduit sections connecting to one box, buy double-gang. The male connectors on the ends of the conduit take up quite a bit of room inside the box, leaving little room for devices. GFCI outlets and other large devices, like dimmers, fit better in deeper boxes (2-1/8 in.).

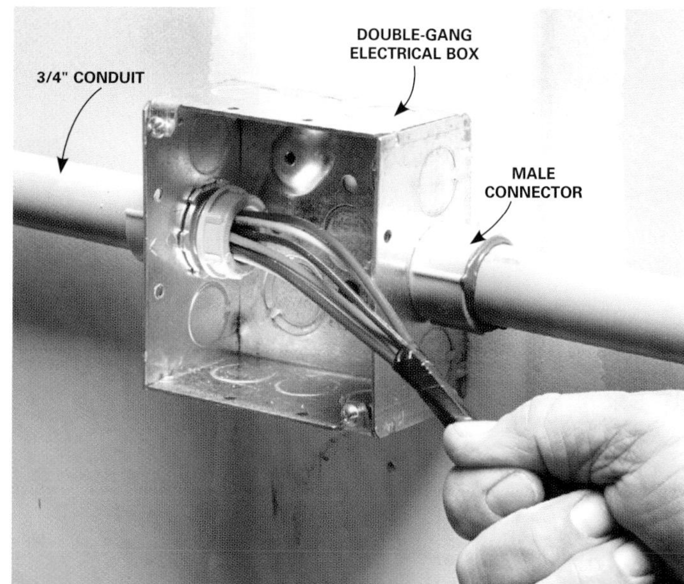

Buy THHN wire

THHN (thermoplastic high heat-resistant nylon-coated) is the best wire for pulling through conduit. Other types of wire have a sticky rubber sheathing that makes them almost impossible to pull. Stranded THHN is used on most commercial jobs—it's more flexible than solid wire, which makes it easier to pull, and it doesn't spring back when you push it into the box.

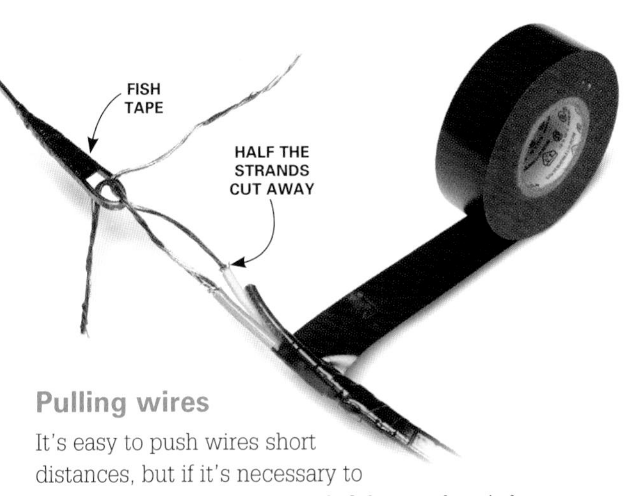

Pulling wires

It's easy to push wires short distances, but if it's necessary to pull them a long distance with fish tape, here's how our expert ties them on: First he strips 4 in. of sheathing off two wires. Then he cuts half the strands off the two exposed wires (less bulk to pull through). Next he loops the remaining exposed wires through the eyelet of the fish tape. Finally, he wraps all three wires in electrical tape all the way up to the eyelet of the fish tape.

Drill a hole to let water out

There's still a strong possibility that water will get inside your weatherproof box. Jason drills a 1/4-in. hole in the bottom of the box, so if water gets in, it can get out. You can drill the hole before or after you install the box.

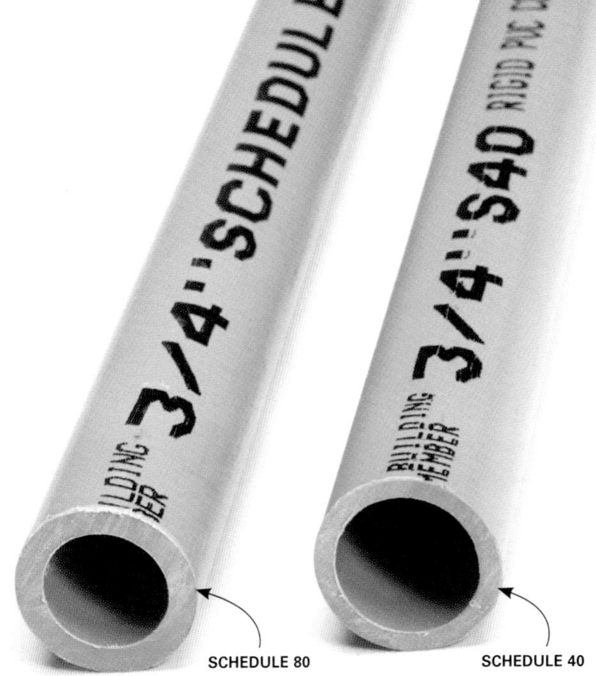

Schedule 40 vs. 80

Schedule 40 conduit is cheaper and has a larger inside diameter, so it's easier to pull wires through it. The plastic on Schedule 80 is thicker, but the conduit has the same outside diameter as 40, so the inside diameter is smaller. Always install Schedule 80 conduit in high-traffic areas or any other areas where it could get damaged, like behind your woodpile. By the way, the fittings (such as adapters and turns) are the same for each type.

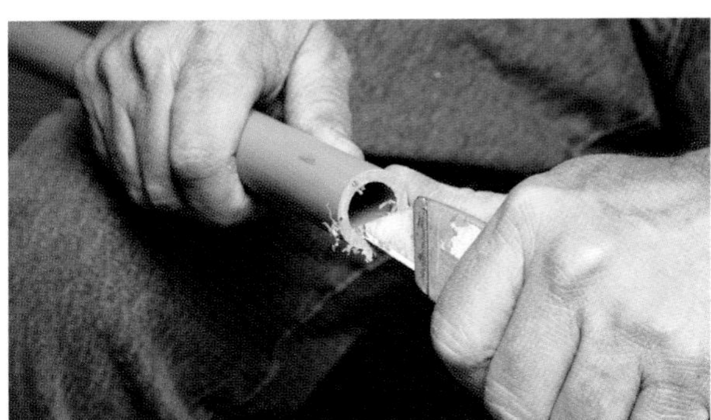

Deburr with a utility knife

If you do end up with a rough cut, don't forget to deburr the inside of the conduit. Burrs can damage the insulation on the wires. There are a lot of fancy deburring tools available, but Jason just spins a utility knife on the inside of the conduit to smooth it out.

MEET AN EXPERT

Jason Bouchard has been a journeyman commercial electrician for more than 19 years. He's worked on everything from traffic lights to waste incinerators. He even wired and lit the huge torch featured in the 1996 Summer Olympics in Atlanta.

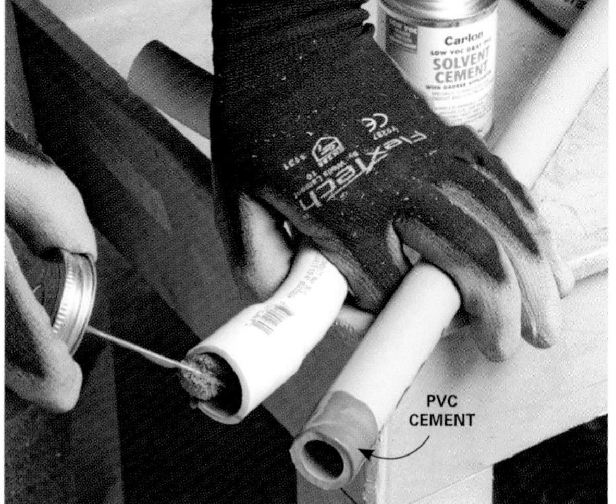

Conduit doesn't need primer

Some PVC pipes require primer, but you don't need to use primer when gluing conduit and fittings. Home centers usually sell the appropriate cement near the conduit and fittings.

Measure as carefully as you can so you can avoid dry-fitting your connections. Unlike PVC plumbing pipes, PVC conduit and fittings can be difficult to pull apart once you shove them together. And always wear gloves, unless you want to spend half the evening picking glue off your hands.

Cut it with a circular saw

There are lots of ways to cut PVC conduit, but a circular saw fitted with a metal blade gives you a smooth, fast, burr-free cut. If you don't have a metal blade, a regular construction blade will do the job, but you may have to deburr the end of the conduit after you cut.

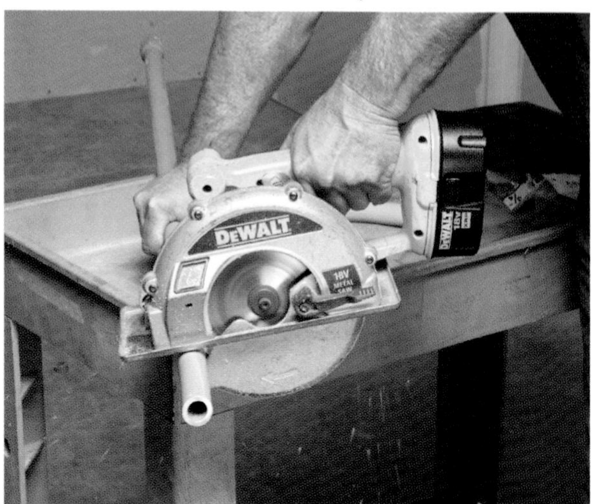

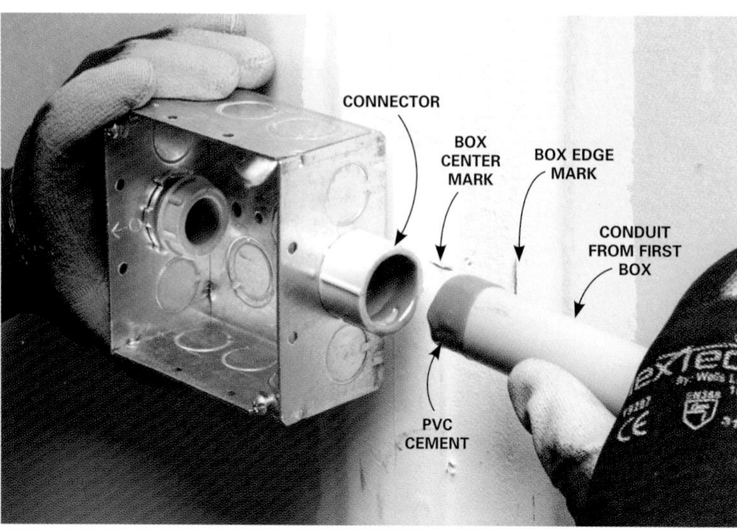

Mount the first box, then the conduit, then the next box

It's tempting to start by attaching all the boxes to the walls and ceiling first and then run the conduit, but don't do it. It's easier to secure one box and then run the conduit from that box to the next one. Fasten the second box to the wall or ceiling after you fasten it to the conduit. Then you won't have to fight the conduit trying to bend it into position. This is especially important if you have two boxes in close proximity because it's difficult to bend short sections of conduit. This process makes it easier to fasten the connectors, nuts and bushings (see p. 75) to the box first and then glue the conduit to the connector.

Metal hangers work best

Use metal hangers even with PVC conduit; they hold up better than plastic. Choose the single-hole type. One screw is more than enough support, and compared with the two-hole strap, installation will go twice as fast.

Your job will look better if you install the kind of hanger that offsets the conduit the same distance from the wall as the knockout on your boxes. For 1/2-in. through 1-in. conduit, the maximum spacing between supports is 3 ft.

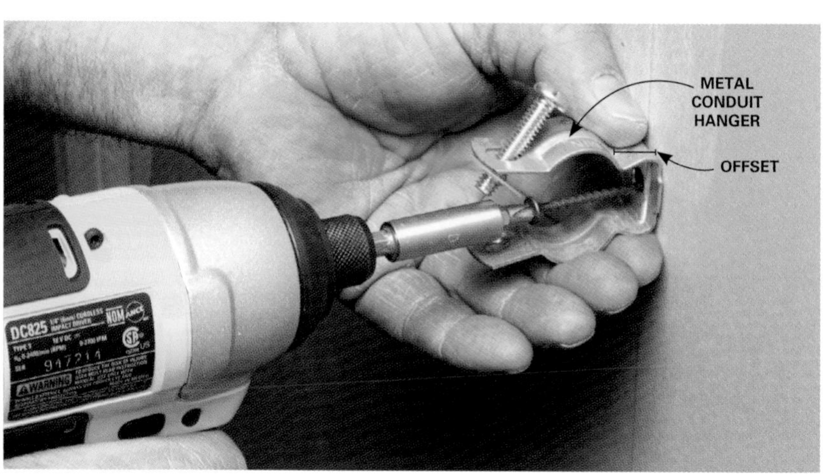

Install metal locknuts

It's OK to use plastic conduit locknuts, but just as with conduit hangers, Jason prefers the metal ones. He says plastic locknuts can strip out and break.

Hook on old wires to pull new ones

If you're adding wires to existing conduit and have to pull them a long distance, hook the new wires to an existing one—including a replacement wire for the one you're using—and pull them through that way. You'll have to buy extra wire, but you'll save a lot of time and frustration.

Use weatherproof boxes outdoors

Install weatherproof boxes (sometimes called bell boxes) outside. Unlike regular boxes, weatherproof boxes usually have threaded knockout holes to create a water-resistant connection. Many come with caps to plug the hole you don't use. Make sure the box you buy has holes where you need them.

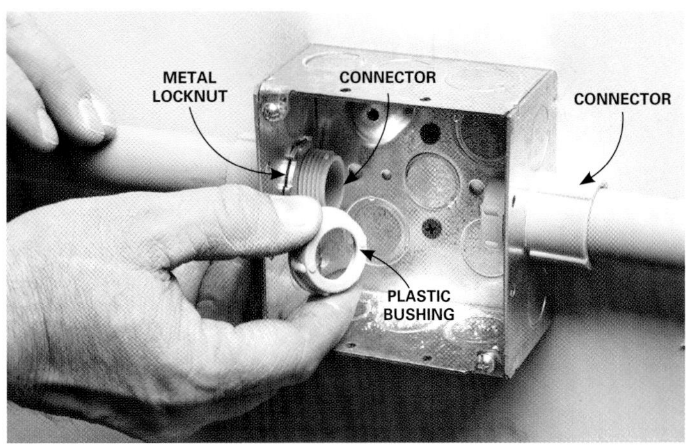

Bushings protect wires

Even if you deburr the end of your pipe, you can still damage wires when pulling them past conduit edges. A bushing provides a nice rounded, smooth surface for the wires to slide by. It's cheap insurance, and your electrical inspector will be impressed.

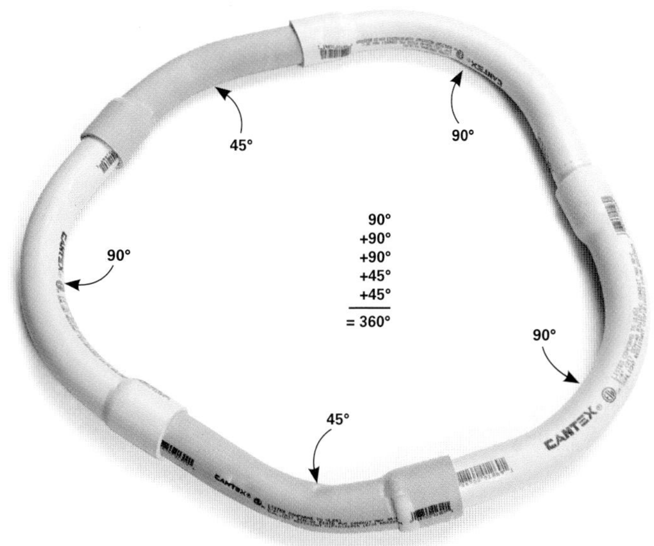

Keep elbow totals no more than 360 degrees

If you have a long run with a whole bunch of twists and turns, consider splitting up the span with junction boxes. Every elbow you install makes pulling wire more difficult. And installing turns totaling more than 360 degrees (four 90-degree elbows) is not allowed on one run. Jason rarely goes beyond 180 degrees because it's easier to install an additional box and pull the wire a shorter distance.

Conduit in a trench

If you're running rigid PVC conduit, most trenches need to be 18 in. deep, but ask your electrical inspector how deep to dig the trench for your specific project. You can run Schedule 40 in a trench, but use Schedule 80 wherever the conduit comes up out of the ground (see "Schedule 40 vs. 80," p. 73). Assemble all the conduit first and plop the whole thing into the trench when you're done. Much easier and cleaner than working in a trench!

GET **FASTER AND BETTER** WI-FI IN YOUR HOME

Take care of your family's need for speed—throughout your home

by **Rick Muscoplat, Contributing Editor**

If you have a wireless (Wi-Fi) router in your home, chances are you have areas with a strong signal and fast speeds—but also areas where you can't connect to the Internet at all. That's especially true of large or sprawling homes.

You can fix some Wi-Fi coverage and speed problems by tweaking router settings, relocating the router or adding an expander device. However, if you're using a router with outdated Wi-Fi technology, you may be fighting a losing battle. In that case, you're better off buying a new router that has the latest Wi-Fi technology. We'll show you how to check your existing router to see whether it's worth tweaking it, or time to bite the bullet and buy a new one. You don't need any special tools, but you'll need the owner's manual for your router. If you don't have it, we'll show you how to get it.

Is your Wi-Fi system up to date?

All Wi-Fi router manufacturers follow industry standards developed by the Institute of Electrical and Electronics Engineers (IEEE). The original standard was IEEE 802.11, and each successive standard includes a letter suffix. The oldest and slowest residential router standard is 802.11b, followed by 802.11g and 802.11n. The newest, the 802.11ac standard, represents a monumental leap in terms of speed and reliability. We won't go into all the techno mumbo jumbo, but trust us, if your router isn't at least an 802.11n vintage, there's no way you're going to improve your Internet speeds.

So your first job is to find out the generation of your current router. Locate the specifications for your router in the owner's manual. If you don't have it, download it from the Internet (**Photo 1**). Then find the specifications page and look for the IEEE standard (**Photo 2**).

If your router is older than 802.11n, buy a new 802.11ac router. If you lease a combination modem/router from your cable or DSL provider, contact the company and ask if it has newer equipment available. If it doesn't, you'll save money in the long run by returning the leased equipment and buying your own modem and an 802.11ac router.

If you already have an 802.11n router

First, update the router's "firmware" (the software that operates your router). Find the latest firmware on the manufacturer's website. You can often solve connection and speed problems by simply installing the most recent firmware version. To discover the current firmware version in your router and learn how to obtain and install firmware updates, see the instructions in your owner's manual.

Next, try changing the channel

Wi-Fi routers and wireless devices work like walkie-talkies in that two people can't talk at the same time on the same channel. If your neighbors' routers are using the same

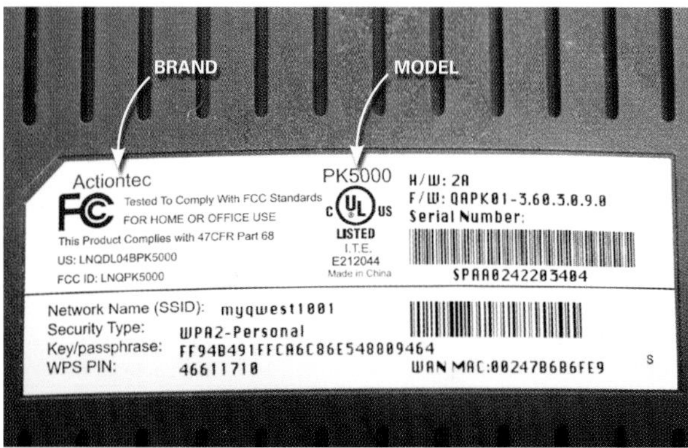

1 **Find the make and model.** Locate the FCC label on your router. Note the make and model. Then go to the "support tab" on the manufacturer's website and download the owner's manual.

Wireless	IEEE 802.11g ← 802.11g STANDARD IEEE 802.11b IEEE 802.1x WPA/WPA2 WEP 64/128/256 bit encryption SSID Broadcast enable/disable	Multi SSID WMM WPS Auto Chann MAC Addre Authentic
Ethernet	ISO/IEC 8802-3; ANSI/IEEE standard 8(	

2 **Find the router's Wi-Fi standard.** Look for the Wi-Fi standard on the specifications page of your owner's manual. It may be listed as a single standard like IEEE 802.11b, 802.11g or 802.11n. Or the manual may list something like 802.11ngb to denote a router that meets the 802.11n standard, but is also backwards-compatible with "g" and "b" laptops and older devices.

3 Temporarily relocate the router. Disconnect the modem/router from its present location and run a longer cable to a central location in your home. Then connect the modem and router to the temporary cable and recheck signal strength in all rooms.

4 Check signal strength. Turn on the Wi-Fi in your smartphone, tablet or laptop and move it from room to room, noting the number of Wi-Fi bars (not cell phone bars).

5 If needed, add a range extender. Install either a desktop or a wall plug-in range extender halfway between the Wi-Fi router and the weak/dead area. Access the extender with your laptop and program it with your router password.

6 Install an adapter on your old laptop. Slide an 802.11ac adapter into a USB port on your old laptop. Enter the password for your new 802.11ac router and reap the benefits of high-speed Wi-Fi.

channel as yours, both routers can slow to a crawl. In that case, changing the channel may help.

If you're leasing the modem/router from your Internet provider, call its tech support line and ask how to change the channel. If you own your router, follow the log-in and channel changing instructions in the manual. If the new channel gives you faster Internet speeds, you're done. If not, move on to the next step.

Relocate the router

If your router is located in a corner room, you may be able improve speeds and coverage by simply moving it to a central location. The signal may be degraded by having to traverse layers of drywall, bricks or other materials. Since rewiring is a lot of work, first try hooking it up in a central location with temporary wiring to see if it helps the signal strength. Here's how:

If you have cable Internet service, buy a 50-ft. coaxial cable and a male/male connector. Disconnect the coax cable from your modem/router and install the connector and then the extension cable. Then move the modem/router to a central location and connect the extension (**Photo 3**). If you have DSL service, plug the modem/router into the phone jack closest to the center of your house (or buy a longer phone cable to reach the center).

Next, use a smartphone, tablet or laptop to check the Wi-Fi signal strength in each room (**Photo 4**). If relocating the router provides a noticeable improvement, you've found the answer—move the router. If you still have a signal strength problem, try adding a range extender.

Rebroadcast the signal to remote rooms

Range extenders receive the signal from the router and rebroadcast it so you get coverage over a wider area. They're available in different speeds and power ratings (two examples are the Netgear EX6200 High Power Wi-Fi Range Extender, about $120, and the Netgear EX6100 plug-in Wi-Fi Range Extender, about $90; available online). Plug the extender into a standard outlet and follow the programming instructions to make it work with your existing router (**Photo 5**).

Buy a new 802.11ac router and USB adapter

The newest 802.11ac routers provide the fastest speeds and the most features. For example, some models manage data traffic to all devices in your home so no single device can hog all the bandwidth. That's an important feature if someone wants to use the Internet while another family member is streaming video or gaming. Plus, some 802.11ac routers provide a whole-house backup feature so you can keep data from every device in one place. And you can install a USB adapter to let your old laptop receive the 802.11ac signal (**Photo 6**).

Note: When adding a range extender or updating your laptop with a USB adapter, we recommend buying the same brand as your router to ensure compatibility and receive the best technical support from the manufacturer. The Netgear devices shown here are just one brand. But many other companies, such as Asus, D-Link, Linksys, Apple and ZyXEL, also make 802.11ac components.

HandyHints®

FROM OUR READERS

AUTOMATIC ON AND OFF!

I bought an energy-saving outlet strip for my TV and its components. One outlet controls several other outlets on the strip, so when I turn off my TV, the adjacent controlled outlets (VCR, DVD player and receiver) sense that no current is going to the TV anymore, and those outlets shut off.

Then I decided to try it out in the shop. I use it with my router table, disc sander and orbital sanders, so when I flip one of them on, my shop vacuum also starts up to take care of dust collection. It also has two outlets that are independent for other accessories you'd like on all the time. Energy-saving outlet strips range from about $25 to about $90 for a higher-end model like the one shown.

—D. Linley

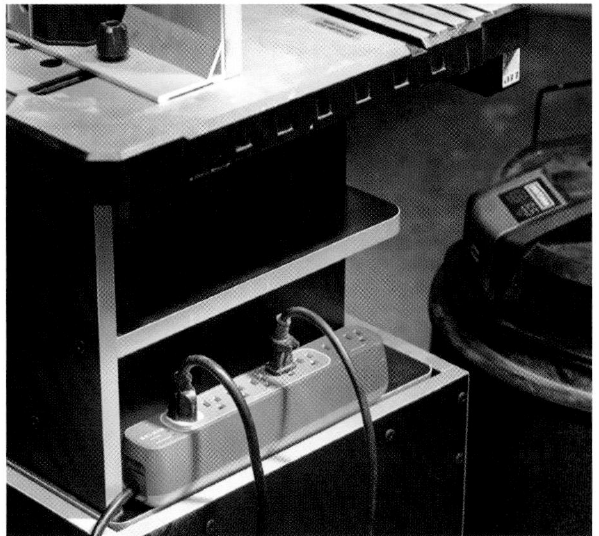

GREASED LIGHTING

We've all been there: A lightbulb breaks away from its base when you try to remove it, and then you're stuck with broken glass and a tough-to-get-out bulb base. You can solve this problem easily (especially in damp areas like porches and bathrooms) with Bulb & Socket Lube. I just smear a dab on the threads of the base and tighten the bulb as usual. Look for Bulb & Socket Lube at your home center or hardware store.

—H. Ed Chapman Sr.

PREVENT PORT DAMAGE TO YOUR SMARTPHONE OR LAPTOP

My 3-year-old granddaughter thought the USB ports on my son's laptop would be a great place to hide her hairclips. It was powered up at the time, and the clips shorted out the $800 main board (he had to remind himself how precious she is).

The service guy said port damage is common, and not just from little gremlins jamming hairpins in them. Dust, dirt and metal fragments can accumulate in the ports and cause damage when you jam the plug in. So my son sealed his smartphone and laptop ports with silicone anti-dust stoppers (one choice is the Cosmos stopper/plug set; $6 at amazon.com). It's really cheap insurance against costly repairs.

—Rick Muscoplat, Contributing Editor

LITHIUM FOR LONG LIFE

Lithium batteries offer long shelf life and long run-time, but cost more than alkaline batteries. So when does it make sense to use them? One use is emergency lights. Stick them in a flashlight and it can sit on a shelf for 10 years and still work when you need it. Another is smoke alarms. It's a pain to replace alkaline batteries every year. Lithium lasts five years or more. Check to be sure your smoke alarm will work properly with lithium batteries (see "Use the Right Battery in Your Smoke Detector," p. 66).

Many cameras require lithium batteries because the devices need a lot of juice. And since I'm a camper, I love lithium batteries for use in my headlamp; they're lighter, last longer and do better in the cold. The cost is the only downside: about $1.65 for a "double A" when you buy a handful at a time. For many of us, just reducing the hassle of changing batteries is worth the extra bucks.

—Ken Collier, Editor in Chief

ELECTRICAL & HIGH-TECH

CLEVER CORD CONTROL

I've got a small kitchen and tangled cords drive me crazy! After the toaster and bread maker tumbled onto the floor while I was putting away the rice cooker, I finally had to take action. My solution was to buy Command Clear Medium Cord Clips (available at home centers and amazon.com). I attached one to each appliance so I could wrap the cord around the appliance and through the clip, effectively eliminating any cord disasters. The clips are inexpensive (about $2 for six) and you can remove them without harming the paint or finish.

—Kyle May

BETTER ELECTRICAL CIRCUIT ID

Doing electrical work at home got a lot safer when I began using this nifty labeling technique. I took the time to identify which electrical circuit breaker controlled the current to each outlet and switch, then I removed each cover plate. On the back of the cover plates, I wrote the number of the corresponding circuit breaker. Now, when I change a fixture or do other electrical work, I unscrew the plate and see which breaker I need to shut off before I start.

—Matt Kelly

GreatGoofs®

Flash of brilliance

Recently, I helped my brother install a new motion sensor light in his mother-in-law's bedroom bathroom. We adjusted the setting so the light would stay on for five minutes when it was activated and then shut off. In her adjacent bedroom, the bed was positioned so she could easily get up to use the bathroom at night. About a week went by before she started complaining that the light stayed on most of the night.

I stopped by that evening and observed that the light came on even without any apparent motion in the room. I then shut the pocket doors on the bathroom and discovered it worked properly. Shortly, however, I found the culprit. She had placed a small digital picture frame on her dresser. Every time a new photo flashed on, it activated the sensor of the light. I moved the frame to another location, and the problem was solved.

—Mark Moran

Adding Outlets

THE BASICS

Whether you're adding an outlet inside or out, here are some basics you need to know.

AFCI protection

Arc-fault circuit interrupters (AFCIs) are designed to detect dangerous, abnormal arcing in branch circuits and cut off the power before a fire can start. Newer electrical codes require AFCI protection for all branch circuits supplying outlets, switches, light fixtures and other devices in essentially all locations in the dwelling except bathrooms, unfinished basements and attics. Garages and outdoor locations may be exempt from this requirement. Contact your local electrical inspector before you begin your project to learn the requirements for your area.

An AFCI circuit breaker provides the most protection, but they are not available for all brands of electrical panels, and can't be used if the branch circuit is sharing its neutral with another branch circuit. If you can't use AFCI circuit breakers, you may be able to use AFCI outlets (below) rather than replacing the panel; your electrical inspector will help you determine how to proceed.

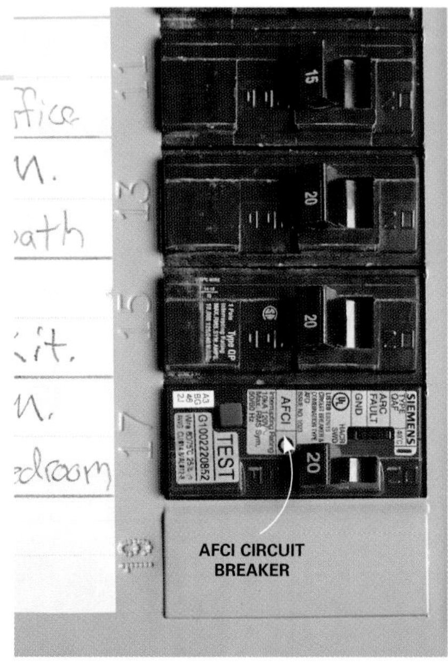

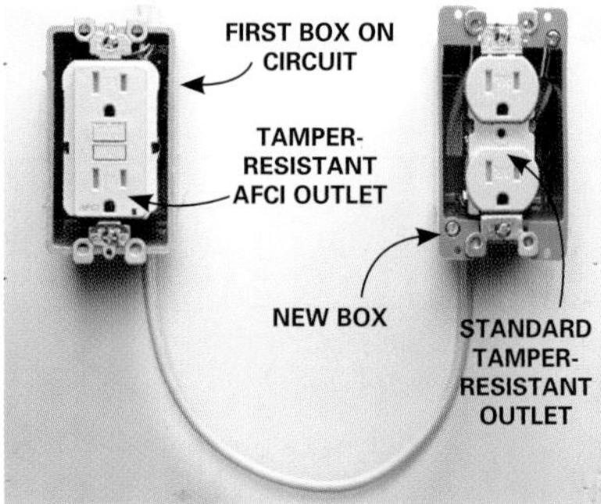

Install an AFCI outlet at the source

When you pull power from an existing outlet for a new outlet, the electrical code requires AFCI protection for both the existing wiring and the new wiring. The easiest way to do this is to install an AFCI outlet at the first outlet of the existing circuit. The AFCI outlet will provide downstream protection for the new extended wiring. Your electrical inspector can provide you with details that apply to your situation.

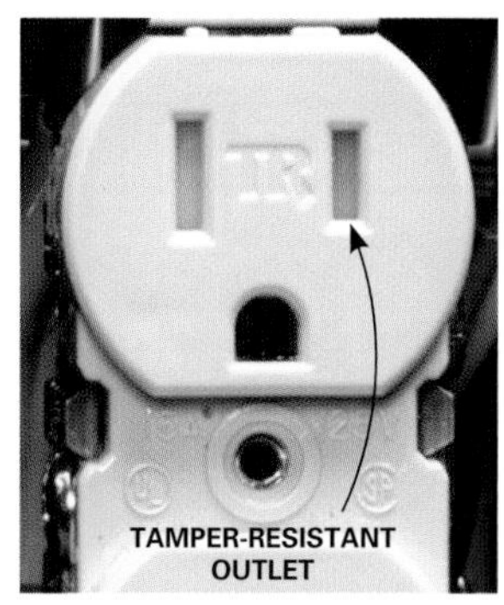

Install tamper-resistant outlets

Tamper-resistant outlets feature shutter-like coverings over the prong openings. They are designed to help prevent children from shoving a metal object into an outlet. Tamper-resistant outlets are now required at all indoor and outdoor locations for dwelling units.

How to calculate box size

Count the wires currently coming into the box:*		Add cable for the new outlet:	
1 red wire	1	1 new black wire	1
2 black wires	2	1 new white wire	1
2 white wires	2	1 new ground wire (combined with other ground wires)	0
All ground wires (count as 1)	1		
1 switch (counts as 2)	2		
TOTAL IN BOX	**8**	**TOTAL BEING ADDED**	**2**

**Your box will probably have a different wire configuration*

For 14-gauge wires, add both totals and multiply by 2 cu. in. (For 12-gauge wires, multiply by 2.25.)

The minimum box size needed for the configuration at left is 20 cu. in. (10 x 2) for 14-gauge wires.

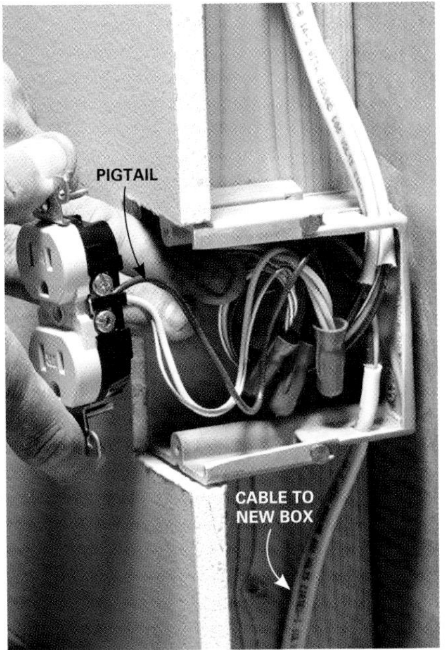

Fold—don't cram—wires into the box

Connect all the wires together and then run short individual wires (pigtails) to the outlet, as shown above. Pigtails also ensure that the rest of the circuit remains energized downstream even if this outlet fails. Try to fold all the wires as neatly as you can and push them into the back of the box. Cramming outlets into a crowded box can result in loose connections and damaged wire insulation, which can cause a fire.

Use the same gauge wire

If you're pulling wire from a circuit that has 12-gauge wire, don't install 14-gauge wire to the new outlet or vice versa. The new outlet should be wired with the same gauge wire as the source.

Don't overload an existing circuit

If you're planning to add your new outlet to an existing circuit, calculate the current load on the circuit, then determine if there's enough capacity to add another outlet to it without overloading the circuit. To learn more, search for "electrical overloads" at familyhandyman.com. You also may have to add a larger electrical box to accommodate all the wires; see "How to Calculate Box Size" on p. 80.

POWERING YOUR NEW OUTLET

Where to get power for indoor outlets

When you're choosing which circuit to add on to, the ease of pulling the wire to the new outlet will likely be the most important factor. Here are some acceptable options:

- General-purpose outlet circuits in living areas, attics and unfinished basements
- Light switch and light fixture locations where unswitched 120-volt power is available
- Smoke detector locations

Where to get power for outdoor outlets

Consider a new circuit. It may seem like overkill to run a whole new circuit to power just one outlet, but a new circuit has several advantages. First, you can be sure that the entire capacity of the circuit is available at the outlet. If you're planning to operate power tools or lawn equipment, this is a big advantage. In fact, for the additional cost of 12-gauge wire, you can run a 20-amp circuit with plenty of power for practically any tool you want to use. With a new circuit, you don't need to calculate the load on the circuit or worry about overcrowding an existing box.

Of course, a new circuit requires running a new cable all the way from your outdoor outlet to the electrical panel, which may be difficult in some situations. And when you get to the main electrical panel, you'll have to connect the wires for the new circuit to a new circuit breaker in the box, a job best left to a licensed electrician unless you're an experienced DIYer. If you choose this option, go to familyhandyman.com and search for "add a new circuit" for more information on breaker box safety and how to add a circuit.

Add a circuit
Running a cable from your new outlet to the circuit breaker box and connecting it to a new circuit breaker is a good alternative to connecting to an existing circuit.

Where *not* to get power for new outlets

You can't add on to just any circuit in your house. Here are some circuits you definitely want to avoid:

- Dedicated kitchen, bathroom and laundry circuits.
- Individual circuits for motor-operated appliances like garbage disposers, refrigerators, furnaces, dishwashers and trash compactors.
- Circuits for specialty appliances like microwave ovens.
- A box with too many wires (see chart on p. 80).

Adding Outlets

5 TIPS FOR **ADDING** AN **INDOOR OUTLET**

Make a starter hole with a screwdriver

Drywall keyhole saws are often called "jab saws" because they can be used to jab through the drywall to start a hole. But you'll probably damage less drywall if you make a couple of starter holes in opposite corners with a skinny, flat-head screwdriver.

When you're cutting, let the saw do the work. Overaggressive sawing can tear the paper on the back side, which will weaken the drywall significantly. It's important to stay inside the lines; a hole that's too big will be unusable. If a hole ends up too small, you can carve away at the edges with a utility knife.

Find the wall cavity with a clothes hanger

When you're pulling power up from an unfinished basement, here's a simple way to figure out where to drill the hole for the new cable. First, drill a small "finder" hole near the base of the wall. Then use a wire cutter to make a 45-degree cut on a long, straight piece of wire clothes hanger. Chuck the coat hanger into your drill with the angled end down, and use it as a drill bit. The hanger will bore through carpeting, hardwood floors, subfloor and even drywall. Leave the hanger in the hole, and then go downstairs and measure over about 3-1/2 in. (3/4-in. quarter round, 1/2-in. base trim, 1/2-in. drywall and half the width of a 2x4 = 3-1/2 in.). That's where to drill your new hole. Patching the finder hole is a piece of cake.

The same trick works when pulling power from the attic. Drill up into the attic where the wall intersects the ceiling, using a piece of coat hanger that's long enough to extend above the attic insulation. Because there's no trim, measure over only 2-1/4 in. from the hanger instead of 3-1/2 in. Find wire hangers at a dry cleaner; most stores sell only plastic ones these days.

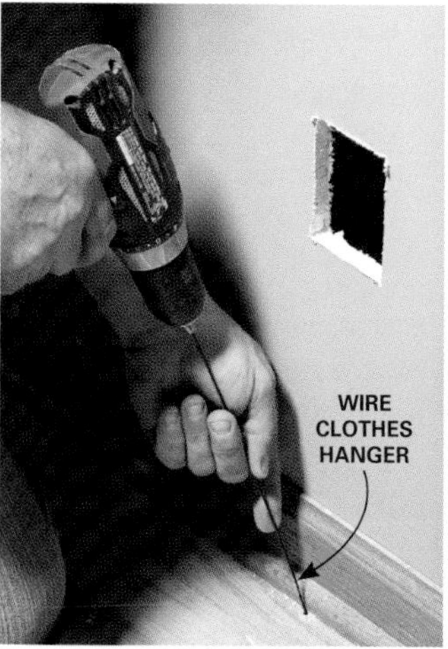

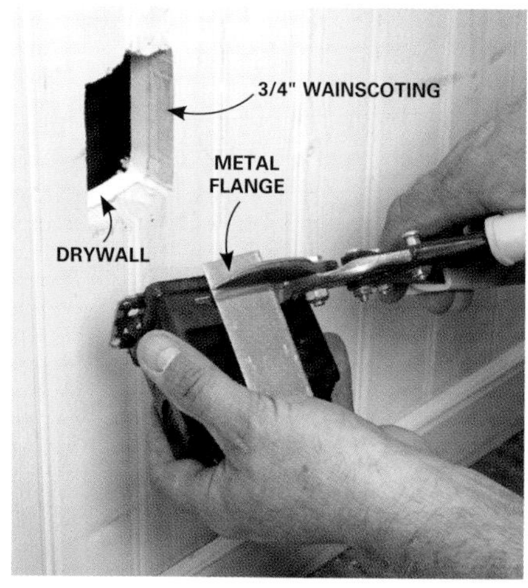

3 Trim the metal supports for thicker walls

Some experienced electricians prefer working with the "old work" boxes that have metal flanges. These boxes provide more support than the boxes with flip-out wings. One drawback of old-work boxes is that they aren't made for thicker walls. So when you need to add an outlet to a wall with drywall and thick wain-scoting, you'll have to cut about 3/4 in. off both metal flanges with an aviator snips before installing it. Make straight cuts or the box will end up crooked in the hole.

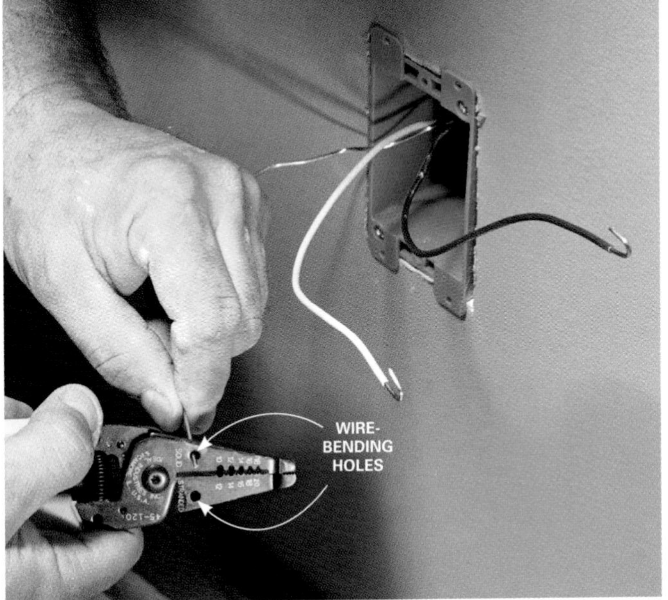

4 Strip cables before pulling them into the box

It's a lot easier to remove the sheathing from the cables before you install the box. Make sure there's at least 1/4 in. of the sheathing pulled inside the box beyond the cable clamp. And at least 6 in. of wire should be left in the box, measured from the front edge of the box opening. After the box is installed, bend the end of the wires using the hole on your wire stripper.

GLASS-AND-TILE DRILL BIT

TILE-CUTTING BIT

5 Cut holes in tile with a rotary tool

A rotary tool is a great, safe way to cut through tile. Set the depth of the tile-cutting bit shallow to avoid hitting plumbing or wires in the wall cavity. Whenever possible, use grout lines for two sides of the hole because they're much easier to cut through. Drill starter holes in two opposite corners with a glass-and-tile drill bit.

"Old work" boxes

There are several kinds of "old work" boxes, sometimes called "remodel" boxes. Some are easier to find than others (but all are available online), and some are easier to install and more durable (details below). Instead of being nailed to a stud, "old work" boxes are clamped onto the drywall. Here are a few of the most common styles.

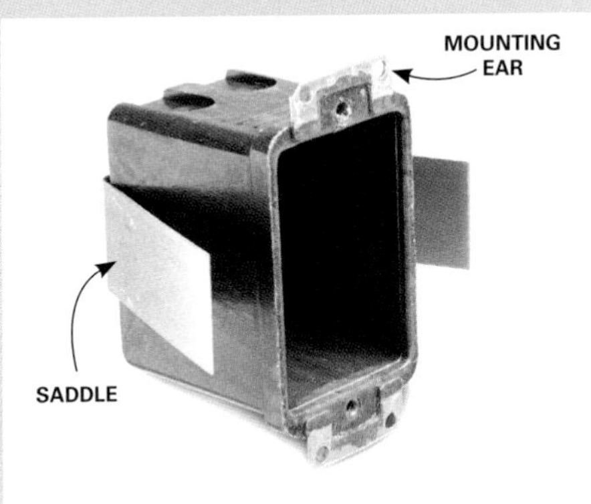

This tough fiberglass box is a favorite of many contractors although it's a bit more expensive ($3). They like it because the rugged clamping system is much more secure than that of cheaper styles. These boxes aren't always available at home centers, but you can find them at electrical supply stores. Or search online for "Carlon 70108." Choose this style if the outlet gets a lot of use.

This PVC box is the least expensive (98¢ for a 14-cu.-in.) and most readily available, but it's also the flimsiest. Some pros complain that the clamping tabs aren't strong enough and the screws strip out the plastic.

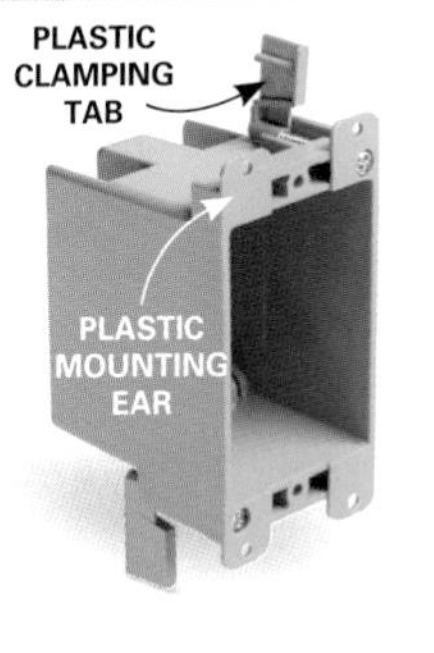

This fiberglass box is a good choice. It's reasonably priced ($1.70), available at many home centers and stronger than the PVC version.

Adding Outlets

5 STRATEGIES FOR **GETTING POWER TO AN OUTDOOR OUTLET**

Wiring a new outdoor outlet isn't complicated. But getting wire to the right spot—without tearing into walls—can be a huge challenge. In this article, we'll help you choose the best strategies for locating and powering your new outlet. We won't go into depth about how to mount the outlet box or connect the wiring. For this information, go to familyhandyman.com and search for "outdoor outlet." There you'll find instructions for adding an outdoor outlet to your wall or a post in your yard as well as detailed wiring diagrams.

We'll show you some of the different wiring techniques you can use to provide power to your new outlet and tell you the pros and cons of each. As with any electrical project, before starting, make sure to talk to your local electrical inspector to find out what permits and inspections are required.

1 Run cable from the basement or crawl space

The rim joist is the wide board that rests on the foundation and supports the exterior walls. If your basement ceiling is unfinished, installing an outlet on the rim joist is a simple project. But there are a few things to watch out for.

If you want to put the outlet on the rim joist that runs parallel to the floor joists, make sure you can reach into the space from the basement. Sometimes the joists are too close together to allow easy access. If you want to add the outlet to the rim joist that runs perpendicular to the floor joists, make sure the outlet is near the center of a joist space so you aren't drilling into the end of a floor joist. Use a long 1/8-in. drill bit or a section of stiff clothes hanger to drill a locator hole in your desired spot. Then you can see from inside whether the spot you've chosen is easily accessible. You'll probably have to remove insulation, and in older houses even pry out concrete or rubble, to get good access to the rim joist near the new outlet.

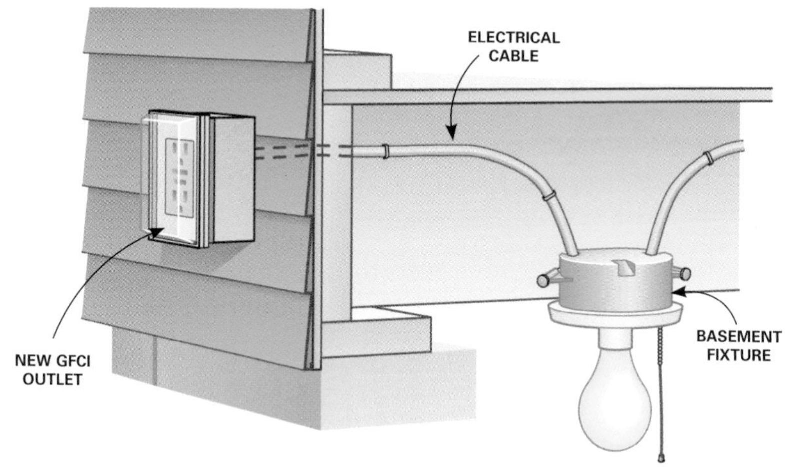

Through the rim joist
If you have a crawl space or an unfinished basement, this is the best way to go. It's easy and your choice of power source and outlet location is unlimited.

From the rim joist, it's usually easy to run the new cable to the circuit breaker panel or to an existing basement lighting circuit. If the circuit is in a crawl space or an unfinished basement (with no laundry area), you probably don't have to add AFCI protection; ask your electrical inspector about the requirements in your area.

2 Connect to an interior outlet

This option is one of the easiest, especially if you don't have an unfinished basement or crawl space. You simply find a spot on the outside of your house that lines up with an outlet on the inside. Then you can fish new wires from the interior outlet to the one outside. But keep in mind that you may have to add AFCI protection if it doesn't exist. Ask your electrical inspector to be sure. There's an article at familyhandyman.com that provides detailed how-to information for adding an outdoor outlet using this technique. Search for "outdoor outlet."

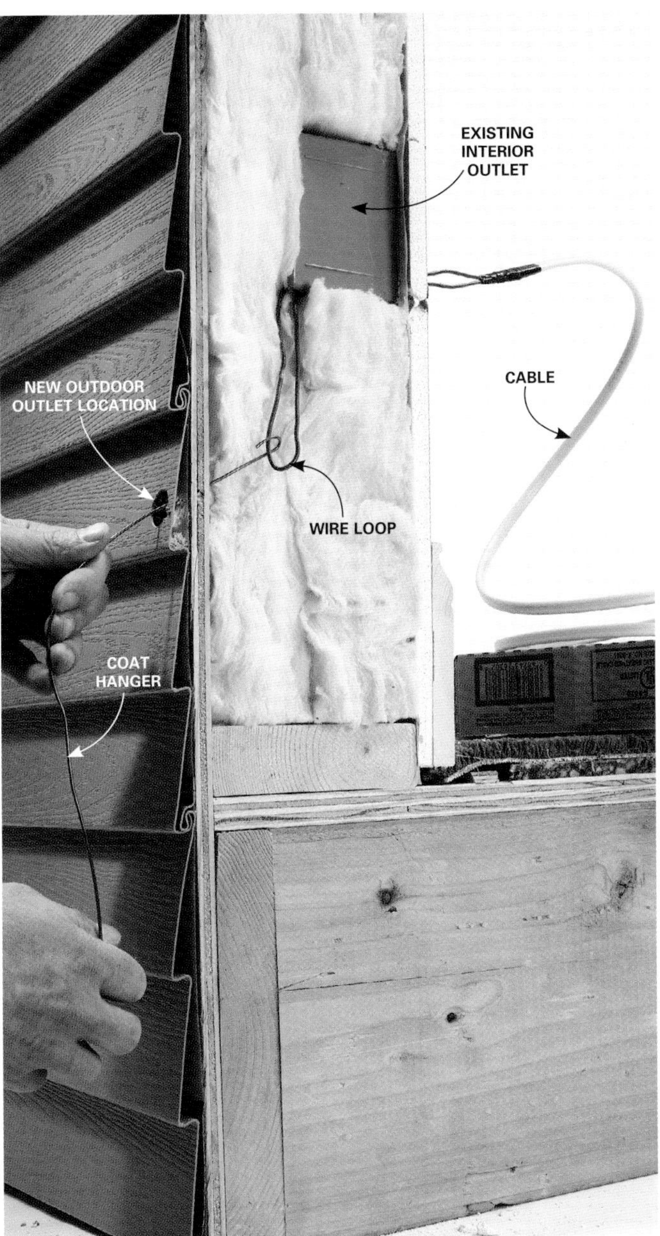

Through the wall
You can run wiring from an interior outlet without tearing up walls. But your options are limited with this approach: Your exterior outlet has to be within a few inches of an existing interior outlet.

Outlets and boxes

Exterior wiring requires outlets and boxes that provide protection against moisture and shocks. The outlet looks similar to those used in kitchens and bathrooms, but it offers additional protection against weather.

You'll also find several different types of boxes. All feature weatherproof covers, but have different mounting strategies. Below are details on three good choices.

Buy the right outlet
When you shop for an exterior outlet, first make sure it's a GFCI protected outlet like the one shown here. Then look for the labels WR (weather resistant) and TR (tamper resistant).

Standard outlet boxes
A standard plastic or metal box cut into the wall is a good option if you want to avoid a surface-mounted box. Finish the job by installing an in-use cover to protect outlets from water while cords are plugged in.

Boxes with built-in covers
For a sleeker look, install a box with the in-use cover built in, like this InBox by Arlington Industries. There are many variations of this box to fit different situations. If your home center doesn't have them, you can buy one online.

Weatherproof surface-mount boxes
One advantage of a surface-mount box like this is that you only need to drill a hole for the cable or conduit to enter through the back. Plus, this type of box easily accommodates surface-mount conduit.

Adding Outlets

3 Run conduit from an existing outlet

If you have an existing exterior outlet and don't mind the look of surface-mounted conduit, this is a good option for adding an outlet. If your existing outlet is surface mounted, you can simply remove one of the knockouts in the weatherproof box and connect your conduit with a weatherproof fitting. But if your outlet is recessed, you'll have to add a weatherproof box extension to allow for a conduit connection. Use an LB fitting to turn a corner with conduit. For more information on working with metal or plastic conduit, go to familyhandyman.com and search for "conduit."

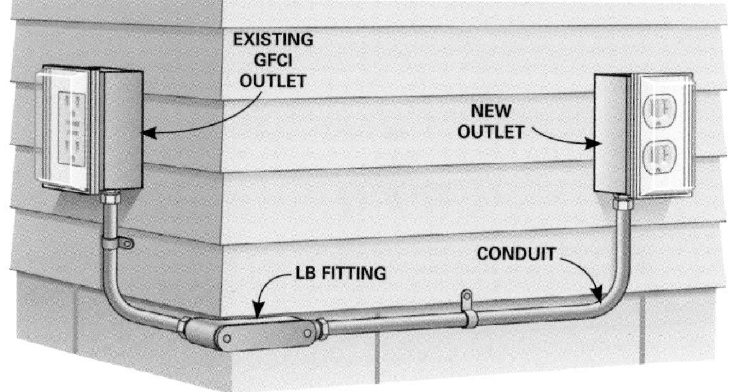

Tap into another outlet
Extending conduit from an existing outlet is a great way to add another outlet without running new cable through walls, basements or attics. You can run the conduit under a course of siding or near the ground to make it less conspicuous.

5 Run underground cable from an existing outlet

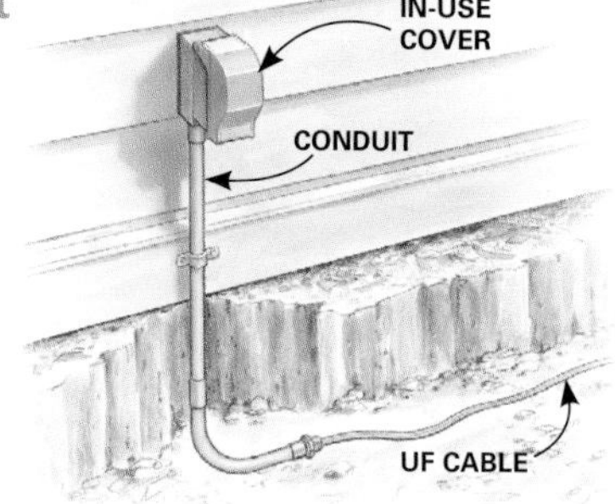

Run power underground
If you don't want to run exposed conduit, you can run power underground instead. A 12-in.-deep trench is all you need for UF cable.

This option is similar to No. 3 above, but rather than run the conduit on the surface of your house, you can run it underground to the new outlet. You also have options for handling the underground wiring, depending on how deep you want to dig. The easiest method doesn't require running conduit underground. Instead it uses UF cable buried 12 in. deep.

There are a few caveats, though. The cable must be protected by a GFCI. If the existing outlet isn't GFCI protected, simply replace it with a GFCI outlet. Also, you must protect the cable with a plastic or metal conduit sleeve from the outlet boxes to a depth of 12 in. below the surface of the ground. You can use this same method to run wiring to a post in your yard (go to familyhandyman.com and search for "outdoor outlet").

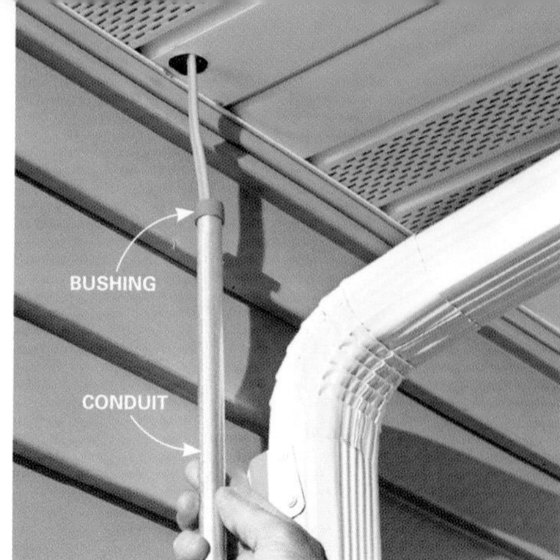

4 Run a cable from the attic

If you don't have a basement or crawl space, this is a good option for getting power to an exterior outlet without fishing wires through the wall. Basically, you run UF cable through a hole in the soffit and through the attic to your power source, leaving enough cable to reach the new outdoor outlet plus an extra foot. Then you slide the conduit, with bushing, over the cable until the conduit extends a few inches into the soffit. To finish, connect the box to the conduit, add straps and wire the new outlet. Insulation and the cramped space can make getting wire through the attic a nasty job. Consider this option as a last resort.

Here are a few tips for running the cable:

- Choose a spot for the new outlet that's alongside a downspout or exterior trim where the vertical conduit will be less conspicuous.
- Use UF (underground feeder) cable, not regular NM (nonmetallic).
- Connect the conduit to the Bell box with a weatherproof compression fitting, not a setscrew-type conduit connector.
- Install a bushing on the top of the conduit sleeve to protect the cable from the sharp edge of the conduit.

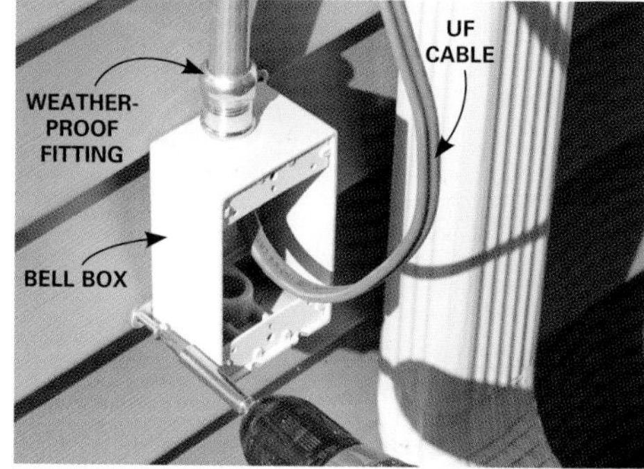

Down from the attic
Run UF cable through the attic and down through a sleeve on the wall to the new outlet.

3 Plumbing, Heating & Appliances

IN THIS CHAPTER

Home Care & Repair....................................88
Fix a refrigerator leak, easy appliance leveling, refresh the fridge and more

Working with PEX.......................................90

Can You Count on Your Sump Pump?.......94

Great Goofs...97
Taking the heat

Air Conditioner Repairs...............................98

Choose a Faucet You'll Love......................102

Great Goofs..105
Drill baby drill, an open-and-shut case, a knockout tub surround

Installing Faucets.......................................106

FIX A BOTTOM-FREEZER REFRIGERATOR LEAK

If you discover water on your kitchen floor near the refrigerator, first check for leaks in the water line to the ice-maker. If the water line and valve are dry, chances are you have a clogged evaporator drain line. The water is from frost and ice buildup on the evaporator coil that melts off during the defrost cycle. Normally this water just drains into a pan in the bottom of the refrigerator. Then, the condenser fan motor blows warm air across the pan and the water simply evaporates.

But if the drain line clogs, the water overflows and seeps down the interior walls of the freezer and onto the floor. You can fix the problem yourself in just a few hours and save an expensive service call. All you need is a pair of tweezers and a short piece of flexible 1/4-in. O.D. tubing from any hardware store. Here's how to remove the clog.

To reach the drain, you'll first have to remove the access panel from the back of your bottom freezer. The refrigerator in the photos below has been cut so you can see where all the components are. But every refrigerator is different, so do an Internet search for instructions on how to remove the access panel on your particular refrigerator.

Start by removing all the frozen food from the freezer. Put it in a cooler. Then remove the freezer drawer and slides (Photo 1). Next remove the access panel (Photo 2). Clean debris from the evaporator gutter and drain (Photo 3). Then pour hot water into the gutter to melt the ice and snake the drain with the tubing (Photo 4). Then flush water through it again. If it flows, you're done and can reassemble everything. If it still doesn't flow, call a pro.

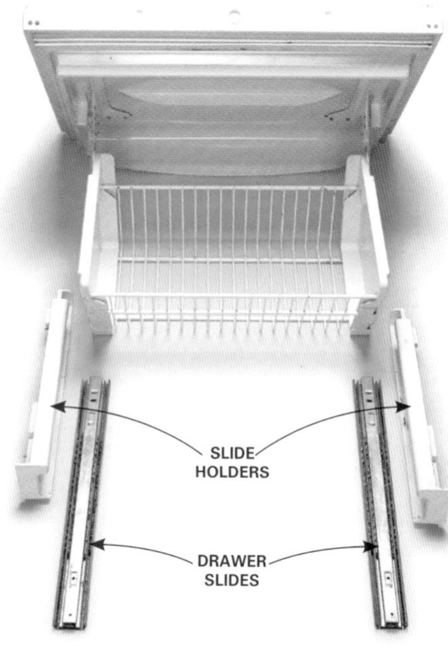

1 Remove these components first. Pull the freezer door all the way out and lift if off the slides. If the slides prevent you from removing the access panel, unscrew or unsnap them and remove them. If the drawer slide retainers block access to the access panel, remove the screws and lift off the retainers.

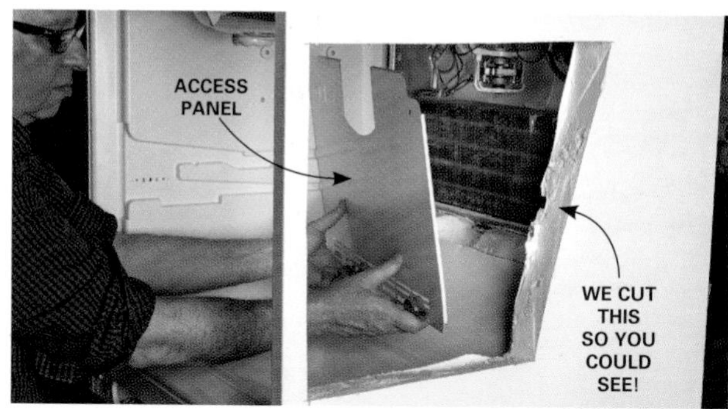

2 Remove the access panel. Use a nut driver to remove the access-panel retaining screws and pull the panel forward. Disconnect any lights or sensors attached to the panel. Then set the panel aside.

3 Remove drain debris. Pluck the clog out of the drain with a pair of tweezers.

4 Snake the drain. Thread flexible 1/4-in. tubing down the drain and rotate it as you push it to break the clog. Stop pushing when you hear it hit the drain pan under the refrigerator. Flush the drain with hot water and make sure it all goes into the drain pan (remove the bottom front grille and shine a flashlight through the opening to see the drain pan).

CONSULTANT: COSTAS STAVROU, NICOLLET APPLIANCE SERVICE

FIX BROKEN AGITATOR DOGS ON A WHIRLPOOL WASHER

Whirlpool washing machines use a ratcheting-style agitator. The ratcheting pawls (called "dogs") can wear out with age, or break if you overload the machine. When that happens, the agitator won't rotate. The parts are cheap (less than $5 at appliance repair stores) and the repair is easy. Whirlpool used two ratchet designs, depending on whether the washer has a plain agitator or one equipped with a fabric softener dispenser. Replacing the dogs in a plain agitator is more complicated and that's the one we show here.

Remove the agitator cap by prying up around the outer edge with a small flat-blade screwdriver. Then unscrew the center hold-down (Photo 1). Reach in and remove the ratchet assembly. Turn it upside down and remove the snap-in retaining plate (Photo 2). Then install the new dogs and retaining plate (Photo 3). Then reinstall the ratcheting assembly, tighten and pop on the lid.

If your washer has a fabric softener dispenser, remove it and unscrew the ratchet assembly retaining bolt. Then lift the agitator out and tip it upside down. The ratchet assembly will fall out—there's no retaining plate. Replace the dogs as shown here. Then load the ratchet assembly into the upside-down agitator, flip it over and tighten the bolt. Snap on the fabric softener dispenser.

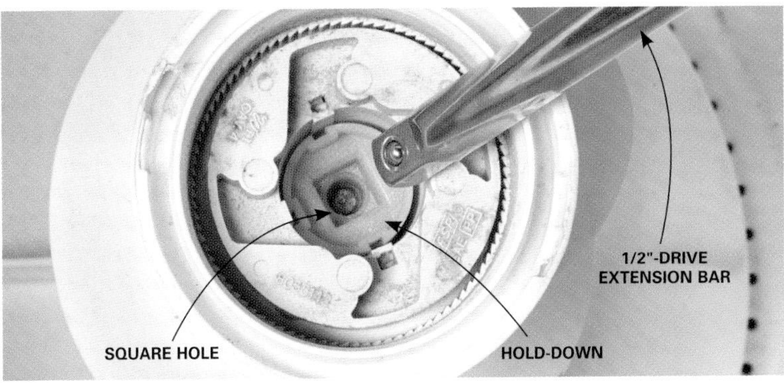

1 Unscrew the hold-down. Slide a 1/2-in.-drive, 6-in.-long socket extension bar into the square hole in the hold-down and unscrew. Then remove the hold-down.

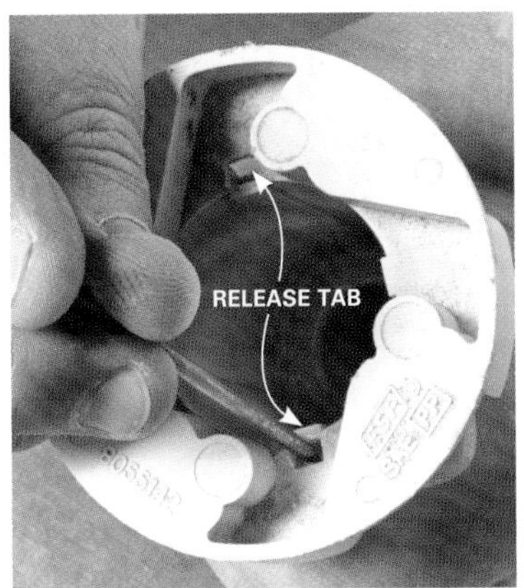

2 Remove the plastic plate. Poke a nail or small flat-blade screwdriver into the recess on each side of the ratchet assembly to unlock the retaining plate. Then pull it off to expose the dogs.

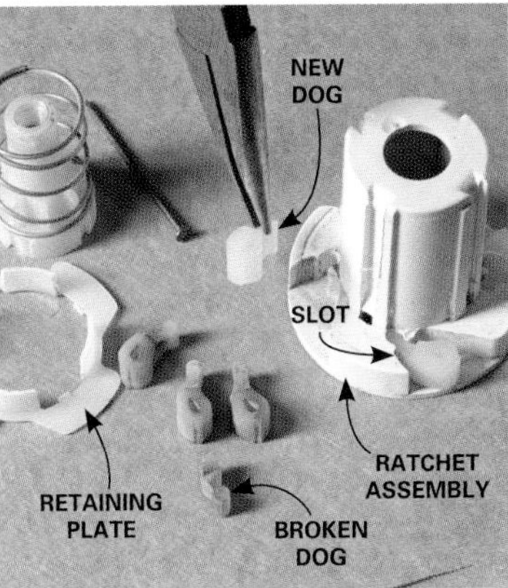

3 Replace the dogs. Drop four new dogs into the round slots. Then snap on the retaining plate.

EASY APPLIANCE LEVELING

Here's a two-part tip for leveling appliances. First, use a magnetic level to free up both hands. Most torpedo levels have a built-in magnet and work great for appliance leveling. The second part of the tip is to lift the front of the appliance with a pry bar to take pressure off the leveling feet. It's much easier to turn the feet when they're off the ground.

REFRESH THE FRIDGE

If you've ever dealt with a fully stocked refrigerator that has lost power for several days, you truly understand the definition of "putrid." Even after a thorough cleaning/disinfecting, the stench can linger for an eternity. Try stuffing your fridge with crumpled newspapers and charcoal. The odor will be gone within several days.

WORKING WITH **PEX**

PEX offers many advantages over copper

by **Mark Petersen, Contributing Editor**

There are a lot of reasons why PEX (cross-linked polyethylene) plumbing pipe is so popular. PEX is less expensive than copper. It can be run in long lengths without any fittings, which reduces the chance of leaks. It's less likely to burst in low temperatures. And the biggest advantage of PEX is that it's super easy to work with. But just because it's easy doesn't mean you can't screw it up. We asked Les Zell, our resident expert, to share some tips, preferences and techniques to help your PEX install go as smoothly as possible.

MEET AN EXPERT

Les Zell has been a plumber for almost 30 years. He is the owner/operator of Zell Plumbing & Heating in Hudson, Wisconsin.

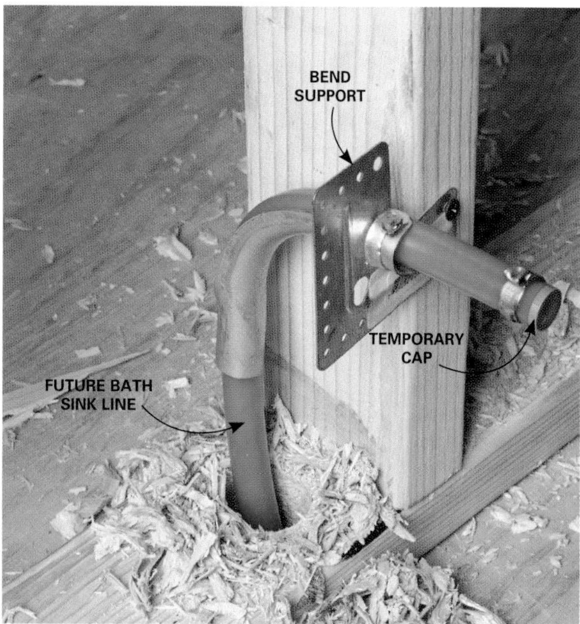

Install PEX directly to the fixtures

Les prefers to run PEX directly to the fixtures so he won't have to bury fittings behind the walls. It's hard to keep PEX perfectly straight when PEX exits the wall, so another option is to use a 90-degree copper stub-out when you run a line to a toilet or other fixture where your shutoff valve will be visible.

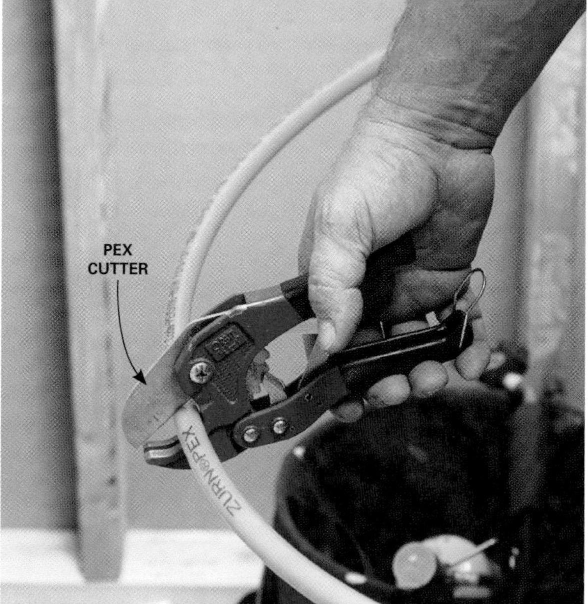

CUT IT STRAIGHT

There's no reason to spend a bunch of money on a fancy PEX cutting tool. The one our expert is using costs less than $15. Whether you use a $100 cutter or just a utility knife, the most important thing is to cut straight. A pipe that is cut at an angle won't fit properly against fittings, and that increases the risk of leaks.

Protect your PEX

PEX expands and contracts with changes in temperature, which causes the pipes to move back and forth. Several years of even the slightest movement can wear a hole in PEX pipes, especially if they're rubbing against something abrasive.

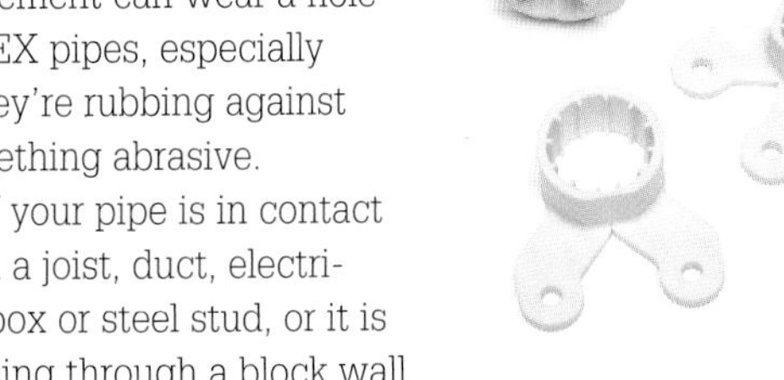

If your pipe is in contact with a joist, duct, electrical box or steel stud, or it is passing through a block wall or concrete slab, it needs to be protected. You can protect your pipe with abrasion clips, cover the pipe with inexpensive pipe insulation, or enclose it with a larger pipe. Pipes that are encased in concrete (for in-floor heating, for example) are OK because the concrete holds them in place. And pipes running straight through wood studs and joists are fine too—just protect the pipe in areas where it bends as it passes through.

Home runs are best

You can install PEX with main lines and branches to each fixture, but "home runs" are better. A home run is one line that runs directly to a fixture, starting at a manifold (below). Home runs require more piping but deliver a stronger and more consistent water flow. Also, installing home runs is fast and requires only two connections (one at the manifold and another at the fixture end), which reduces leaks.

You can also use a hybrid system where you run 3/4-in. hot and cold lines to a set of fixtures—for example, in a bathroom—and install a smaller manifold behind an access panel. Then make short runs of 1/2-in. lines to each fixture. Another cool thing about home runs is that each fitting has its own shutoff at the manifold. That means you can shut off just that fitting to do some work—you don't have to shut off the water to the whole house.

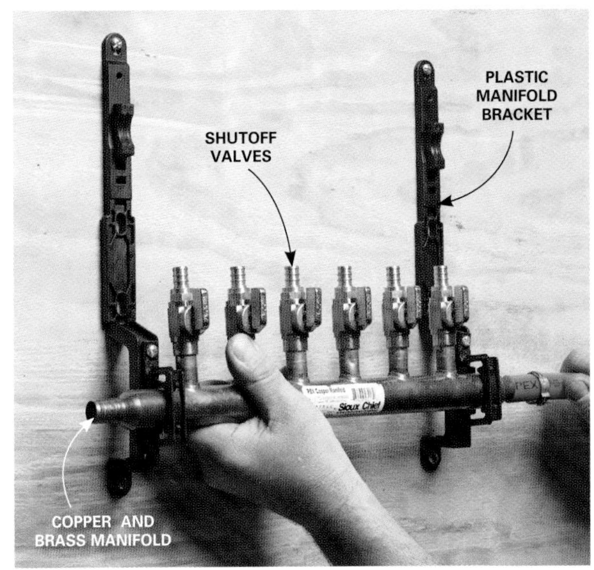

Cinch clamps are easy

There are many different ways to connect PEX to fittings, but Les prefers cinch clamps. They're readily available and relatively inexpensive, and you know when they're installed properly because the tab of the clamp will be visibly pinched.

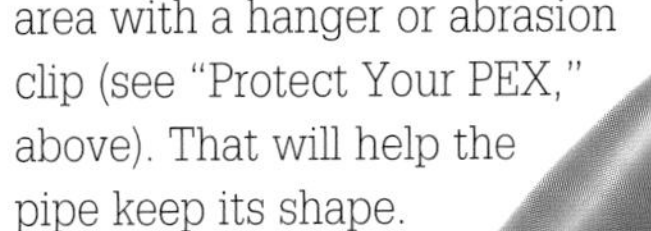

Repair or replace kinks

Kinks happen. You can repair kinks with a heat gun, but PEX tends to rekink in the previously kinked spot, especially if the pipe needs to make a bend at the kinked location. It's best to cut kinks out and use the shorter sections of pipe elsewhere. If you get a minor kink in the middle of a long, straight run and you don't want to cut it out, heat the pipe with a heat gun and then cover the damaged area with a hanger or abrasion clip (see "Protect Your PEX," above). That will help the pipe keep its shape.

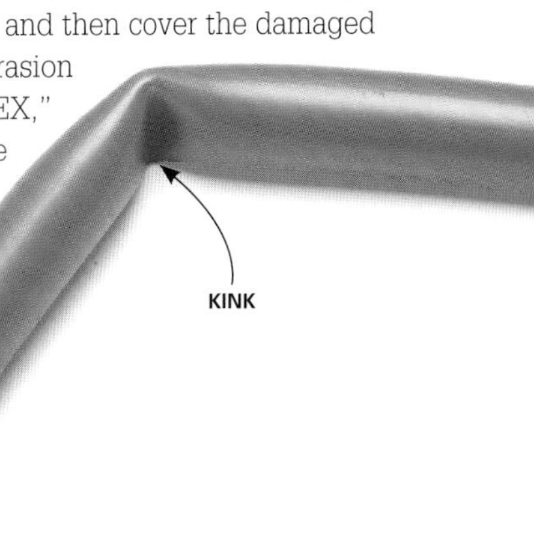

Control your coil with an elastic cord

One complaint about working with PEX is that the coils have a mind of their own. As soon as the banding is removed from the coils, they tend to explode out in every direction. Les's tip is to use bungee cords to help keep your coils in check. He leaves the cords on and unrolls just the amount he needs. If your coil comes wrapped in plastic, don't remove it. Sometimes you can just feed out pipe from the innermost section of the coil. If you have just a few smaller runs or short lengths to install, buy sections of straight pipe—it's a lot easier to work with.

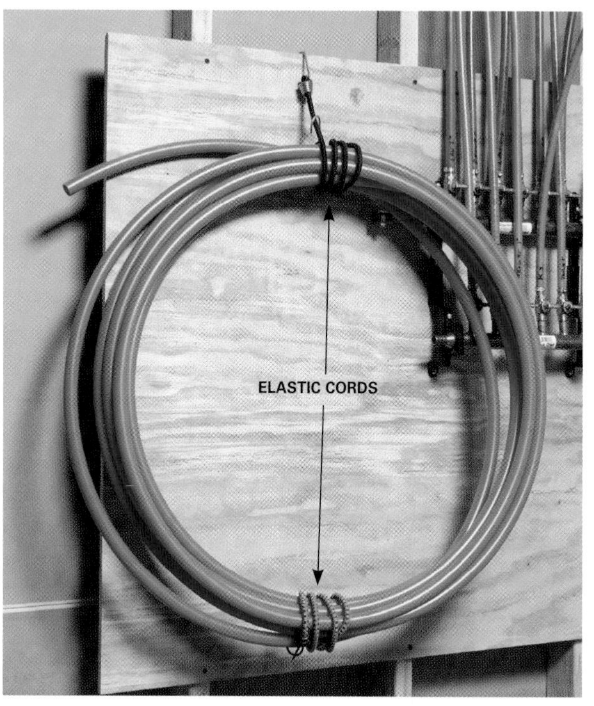

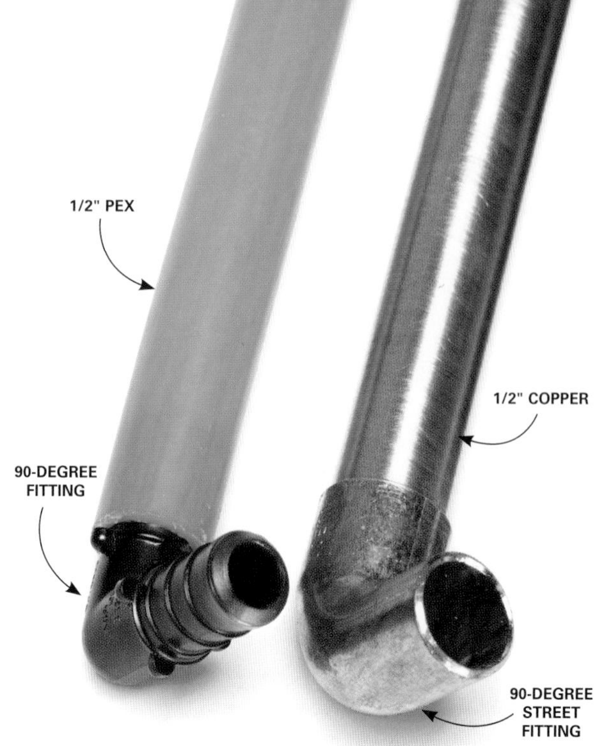

Upsize to avoid poor pressure

The inside diameter of 1/2-in. PEX is smaller than that of 1/2-in. copper (and even smaller with fittings). If you're tearing out copper and replacing it with the same size PEX pipe, the water flow to the fixtures may be noticeably lower when you're done. If you're working on a house that has less than 45 lbs. of pressure or a flow rate of less than 4 gallons per minute, make sure you install home runs (see p. 91), and consider going up in size to 3/4-in. pipe. A simple way to test water pressure is to hook up a hose bib pressure gauge (about $16 at home centers) to your spigot. To check your flow rate, just see how many gallons of water flow into a 5-gallon bucket in one minute.

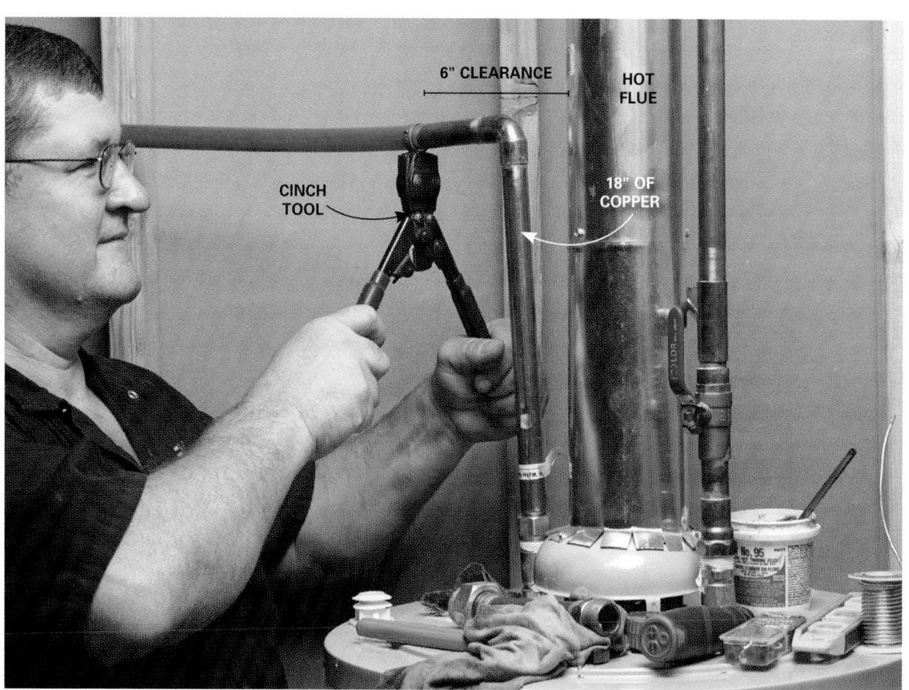

Keep PEX away from hot stuff

PEX is plastic, and plastic melts. So keep your PEX pipes away from hot stuff. Codes commonly require PEX to be at least 18 in. away from the water heater and 6 in. away from single-wall flues on gas water heaters. And stay well clear of furnace flues, wood-burning stove pipes and any other item that gets hot.

Warm up cold pipes

Our expert, Les, knows a plumber who did a job in northern Wisconsin in the middle of winter. The building had no heat, and all the pipes and fittings were freezing cold. When the furnace was fired up and the water turned on, they sprang dozens of leaks. Most PEX manufacturers recommend you work with pipe at temperatures above freezing. The whole length of the pipe doesn't need to be warm, just wherever you make a connection. You can heat those cold pipes and fittings with a heat gun or hair dryer, leave them in a warm vehicle for a while or keep fittings in your pocket. Heck, you can even warm a pipe in a thermos of hot water.

Use the same stuff

There are several different manufacturers of PEX. It is very important that you know which brand of pipes you're working with and install only that manufacturer's connectors and fittings. If you mix and match materials, you will void your warranty and may fail your inspection. Worst-case scenario: You'll end up with leaky pipes, water damage and a job that may need re-doing. Not all products have recognizable markings on them, so leave a few of the packaging labels on-site so the inspector can see what you're using—and keep them for future reference.

Avoid kinks

PEX's flexibility makes it easy to work with. It can be bent around pretty sharp corners without the need for an elbow fitting. But if you try to bend it too much, you'll end up kinking it. Installing a bend support will prevent this, and it will also protect the pipe from abrasion.

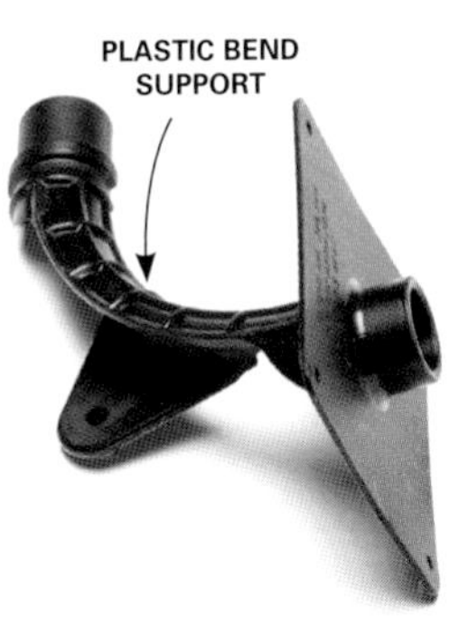

PLUMBING, HEATING & APPLIANCES

CAN YOU COUNT ON YOUR **SUMP PUMP?**

A dead pump can lead to disaster. Here's how to avoid trouble

by **Rick Muscoplat, Contributing Editor**

A sump pump is one of the most important (and most ignored) disaster prevention devices in a home. When this simple system fails, the results can be catastrophic, leading to thousands of dollars in damage, daily disruptions caused by major repair work and higher insurance premiums for years to come. So spending some time and money on avoiding failure makes a lot of sense. This article will show you how.

How to buy a primary sump pump

Home centers sell a confusing array of sump pumps that range from $50 to $300. But don't despair. We've reviewed all the specs, talked to the engineers and boiled it down to five simple buying tips:

1. Horsepower means nothing. It's the pumping volume in gallons per hour (GPH) that counts. Check the capacity of your current pump. If your current pump keeps up with the flow during the heaviest rainstorms, buy that capacity again. If not, buy a pump with a higher GPH rating. To find your current pump's rating, locate its make and model number on the label and find the specs on the manufacturer's Web site.
2. Check the "head" on the manufacturer's GPH rating. Head is the height that water has to be lifted from the pump to the horizontal discharge pipe. More height means harder work for the pump. The GPH rating on most good-quality pumps includes the head (typically 10 ft.). But some manufacturers rate pump capacity without head ("3200 GPH at 0 head," for example). That gives an unrealistic—and misleading—estimate of pump capacity.
3. Spend at least $125 to get a quality sump pump. Look for a caged or vertical float switch, a motor with a UL and a CSA rating, and a pump made with a stainless steel, cast aluminum or cast iron impeller and pump body. Avoid pumps made from epoxy-coated parts.
4. Buy an energy-efficient pump. Once you find a pump with the correct GPH rating, look for a model that consumes the fewest amps. This isn't about saving electricity; high-amp pumps run hotter and burn out the float switch faster.
5. If your sump accumulates gravel or sand, buy a "top suction" pump that's "solid passing" to prevent a stall/burnout caused by trapped gravel. Or raise a "bottom suction"-style pump on a few bricks to keep it off the bottom of the sump.

While you're at the home center, buy a new male fitting to fit the pump outlet; pipe primer and cement; a new check valve and rubber couplers.

Sizing a pump

Whether you're buying a replacement pump or a backup system, you'll have to determine the pump capacity. Here's how: Disconnect your existing pump, pull it out of the basket, and check the GPH rating on the label or check the pump's specifications on the manufacturer's Web site. Buy a new pump with at least that much capacity. If your existing pump sometimes can't keep up with the incoming water, select a model with a higher GPH rating.

What causes primary pumps to fail?

The most common reason for pump failure is a power outage, not some problem with the pump itself. Common events besides power outages can also cut off the supply of electricity. For example, lightning can trip GFCI outlets, or someone can unplug the pump and forget to plug it back in.

Assuming the power stays on, sometimes the pump itself fails. Many inexpensive sump pumps are simply too small to handle the flow from a major downpour or rapid snowmelt. And because inexpensive pumps are built with less durable materials, they lose pumping efficiency. So the pump runs more often and burns out early. Or the motor runs but the pump doesn't eject water.

Float switches are also a frequent cause of pump failure. "Wide angle" tethered float switches, the kind that free-float around the sump basket, are the biggest trouble-makers. They swirl around the sump basket, making them far more likely to get trapped against the pump, discharge pipe or power cord. Once trapped, they can't switch on the pump. Inexpensive switches can also simply wear out or cause motor burnout.

Know when your pump is dead

Homeowners often don't discover a sump pump failure until they see the damage. But there are ways to avoid that:

If you buy a new AC sump pump run by a controller, it'll have some type of alarm to let you know if the pump fails or the power goes out. The same holds true for most new battery-powered systems.

■ **Local alarm.** Detects water at the top of the sump basket using either a probe or a float and sounds an audible alarm (such as the BWD-HWA Basement Watchdog Water Sensor and Alarm; about $10 at home centers). Local alarms are great if someone is home at the time of the failure.

■ **Verbal message via landline.** Detects water at the sump and dials a preprogrammed phone number and plays a recorded message (one choice is the Control Products WA-700 Water Alarm; about $55 at homesecuritystore.com). Also sounds an audible alarm. Must have a landline.

■ **Text messaging.** Detects water at the sump and sends a text to three different cell phones (one choice is the Blue Angel BCPA1; $189). Requires an adequate Verizon signal at the sump pump and a $4 monthly fee. Find a dealer at blueangelpumps.com.

Backup systems

Some homeowners keep a replacement pump on hand in case their pump dies. That's a good idea (home centers often sell out of pumps during storms or floods). But having a replacement handy won't help you if you're on vacation during a power outage or if your pump dies while you're slumbering through a stormy night. That's the beauty of backup systems: No matter what the reason for the pump failure, a backup system will save the day. Here are your options:

BATTERY BACKUP SYSTEMS: $175 TO $700

Manufacturers of battery backup systems usually sell three models: good, better and best. The "best" units come with a larger battery and a more sophisticated battery charger. The larger battery gives you a longer run-time, and the better charger prolongs the life of the battery.

So how long will a battery backup system keep your basement dry? That depends on how much water is entering your sump basket (which determines how often the pump will run). Here's an example: one manufacturer's system comes with a 40-amp/hour battery that's projected to last up to 53 hours (pumping at the rate of 2,300 GPH once every five minutes). But, if you have serious water problems such that the pump runs once a minute, that same battery will last only 12 hours. That's hardly enough battery capacity to get you through an extended power outage. In that case, buy a system with a larger battery, or a system with a charger large enough to keep two batteries fully charged.

If you have minor seepage and rarely experience power outages, you're probably safe buying a less expensive battery backup system. Then again, that $400 savings could cost you big-time if just one 100-year storm knocks out your power and turns a sump trickle into a flood.

Advantages of battery backup systems

- Simple installation—connect to existing discharge pipe or run a separate pipe
- Unlike water-powered systems, battery backup systems work when there's no water supply

Disadvantages

- Battery may run down before power comes back on
- Battery water levels must be checked every few months
- Battery terminals must be cleaned twice a year
- Battery must be replaced every five years (prices start at $100 and go up from there).

Figure A: Battery backup pump

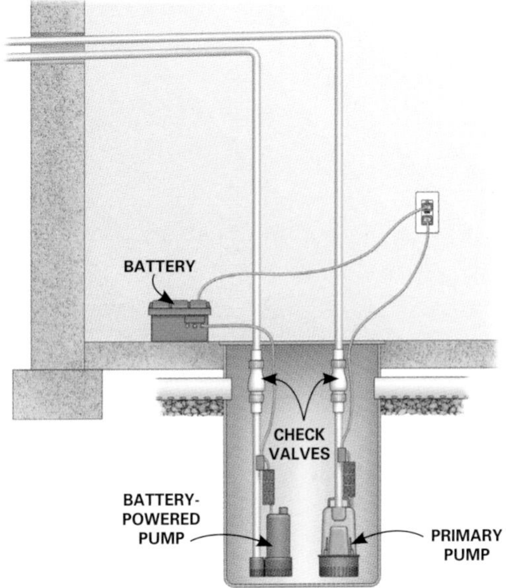

If the primary pump fails, the battery-powered pump takes over and ejects water. A maintainer keeps the battery at full charge.

WATER-POWERED BACKUP: $150 TO $400

A water-powered backup pump uses water pressure to siphon water out of your sump. Most use 1 gallon of city water for every 2 gallons of sump water they remove. So a pump that's capable of removing 1,500 GPH will use 750 GPH of city water. And that's created a lot of controversy. In fact, a few municipalities prohibit their use due to already severe water shortages. So check with local ordinances before buying a water-powered sump pump. In an area with high water costs, the water bill can run as high as $170 a day. But keep that in perspective. If your power goes out for a couple of days, you'd happily pay a $300 water bill to avoid a flood.

Water-powered pumps require at least 40 psi and a 3/4-in. feed line to achieve maximum pumping rates. And they require a separate drain line and some type of backflow prevention to prevent cross-contamination with potable water.

Water-powered pumps come in two styles: **in-sump** and **above-sump**. An in-sump pump (such as the Liberty No. SJ10 SumpJet pump; $175 to $200 at home centers and online) is always immersed in drain water, which raises the risk that drain water could contaminate the drinking water supply. To prevent that, most local codes require the installation of an expensive reduced pressure zone (RPZ) backflow prevention valve (starting at about $165). RPZ valves must be professionally installed and tested annually by a licensed plumber. That adds an annual cost to the system. So check with your local building inspection department before you buy an in-sump system.

An above-sump unit (like the Basepump RB750-EZ; $300 at basepump.com) mounts well above the sump, which reduces the risk of drinking water contamination. Therefore, many plumbing inspectors require only a less expensive atmospheric vacuum breaker (AVB), which costs about $40.

Advantages of water-powered backup systems

- No limit to run-time; works as long as you have water pressure
- No battery replacement costs
- No routine maintenance

Disadvantages

- If you have a well, this setup won't work during a power outage
- More difficult installation because it requires a new water line, backflow preventer and new drain line
- Annual fee for RPZ valve testing (if required by local code)
- May be expensive to run in areas with high water costs

Figure B
Above-sump water-powered pump

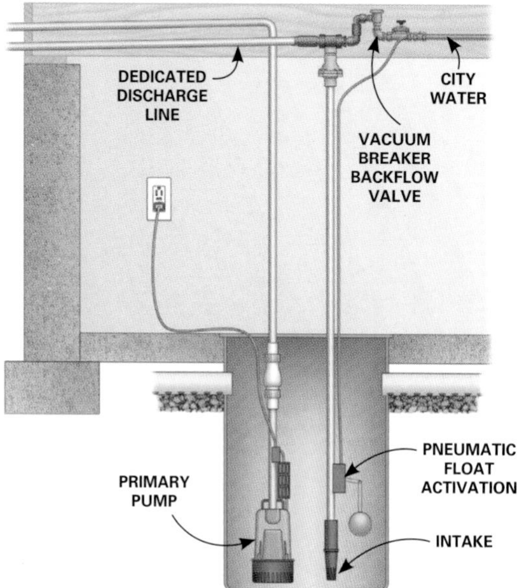

This pump operates like an in-sump unit, using city water to pump sump water. Both kinds of water-powered systems require a separate discharge line.

Figure C
In-sump water-powered pump

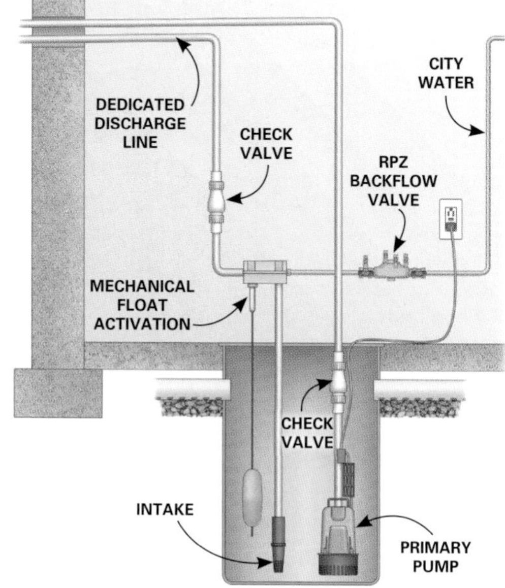

When the primary pump fails, a water-powered pump uses city water pressure to siphon water out of the sump. With an in-sump version, your local inspector may require an RPZ valve to prevent contamination of drinking water.

GENERATOR-POWERED SUMP PUMP

During a power outage, a generator can pay for itself in a dozen ways. One of those ways is powering a sump pump. A typical sump pump draws about 9 amps, so it won't add much load to the generator. But a generator isn't a perfect substitute for a backup system. A battery- or water-powered system kicks in automatically, whether you're home or not and no matter what the failure. A portable generator works only if you're around to connect it. And a generator (standby or portable) won't help if your primary sump pump is kaput.

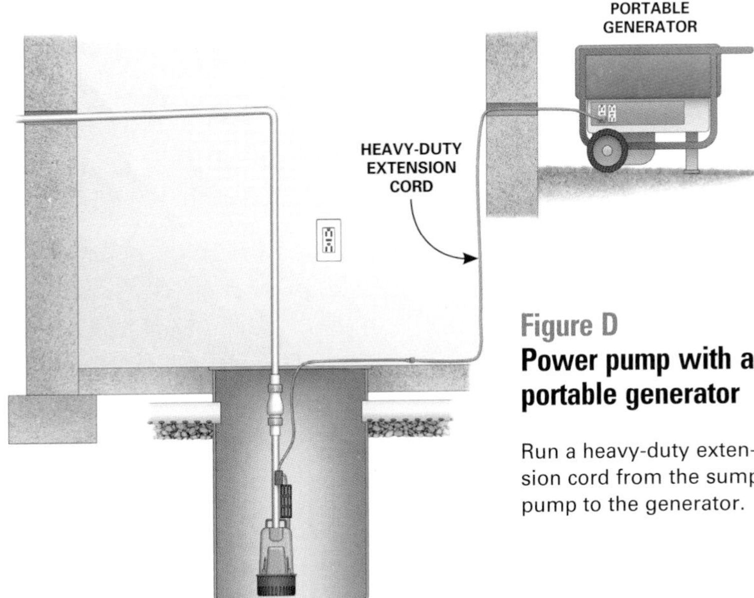

Figure D
Power pump with a portable generator

Run a heavy-duty extension cord from the sump pump to the generator.

GreatGoofs®

Taking the heat

Last winter, my very "handy" husband spent an entire day laying a wood floor in our attic and was very pleased with himself and the extra storage space he had created. That night the house got very cold. First thing in the morning, we placed an urgent call to our heating company to have a technician come out. It didn't take long for the technician and my husband to discover the problem, and when they came downstairs, my husband's face was quite red. It turns out that the previous day, he had "snipped" our thermostat wire in the attic, mistaking it for an old TV antenna wire. Needless to say, he took a lot of heat for that mistake.

—Diana L. Hamill

Diana's husband, Scott

AIR CONDITIONER REPAIRS

Learn what you can do yourself—and when it's time to call a pro

by **Rick Muscoplat, Contributing Editor**

When a central A/C unit fails during a heat spell, you may have to wait days for a technician to show up. If you're lucky, you'll only have to pay about $300 for the repair. But if you're comfortable working around electricity and are willing to spend about $50 on parts, you can probably fix your A/C yourself in about two hours and save about $225 on parts markup and labor.

We talked to Ross Johnson, an HVAC technician at Superior Heating, Air Conditioning & Electric in Anoka, MN, to get his best do-it-yourself A/C repair and maintenance tips. They'll help you with the most common "low cooling" and "no cooling" problems. You'll need an inexpensive multimeter, a voltage sniffer, an assortment of screwdrivers and a socket set. Here's how to start.

Buy parts

The contactor (relay) and start/run capacitor(s) (see illustration below) fail most often and are inexpensive. So it's a safe bet to buy and install those parts right away, especially if your A/C unit is older than five years. The condenser fan motor can also fail, but it runs about $150—hold off buying that unless you're sure that's the culprit.

To buy replacement parts, find the nameplate on the

Anatomy of a central air conditioner

Central A/C systems consist of two major components: a condensing unit that sits outside your house, and the evaporator coil (often referred to as an A-coil) that sits in the plenum of your furnace or air handler. The refrigerant in the A-coil picks up the heat from your home and moves it to the outdoor condensing unit. The condensing unit fan blows outside air through the condensing coil to remove the heat. The condensing unit houses the three parts replaceable by a DIYer: the contactor, the start/run capacitor(s) and the condenser fan motor. The condensing unit also houses the compressor, but only a pro can replace that. The A-coil has no parts that can be serviced by a DIYer.

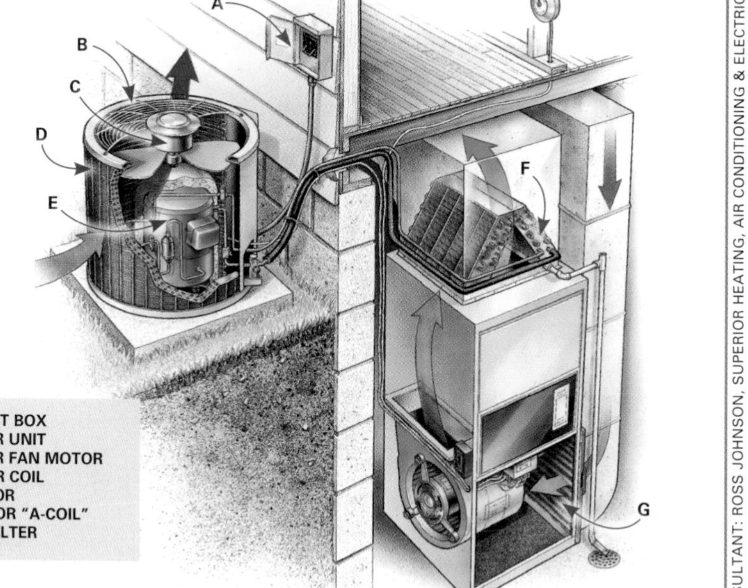

A. DISCONNECT BOX
B. CONDENSER UNIT
C. CONDENSER FAN MOTOR
D. CONDENSER COIL
E. COMPRESSOR
F. EVAPORATOR "A-COIL"
G. FURNACE FILTER

CONSULTANT: ROSS JOHNSON, SUPERIOR HEATING, AIR CONDITIONING & ELECTRIC

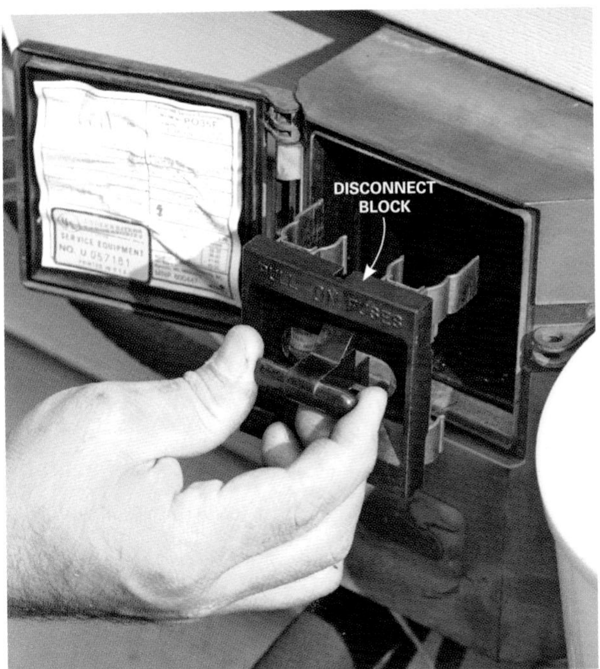

1 Shut off the power. Open the electrical box next to the condensing unit and pull the disconnect block straight out. Check inside the box with a voltage sniffer to make sure the power is really off.

2 Clean the condenser coils. Aim your garden nozzle upward into the top of the condenser coil to remove the crud build-up under the lid. Work all the way around the coil. Then aim the nozzle down and flush the debris down the coil fins. Adjust the nozzle to a gentler stream and shoot water directly into the coils to flush out any remaining debris.

condensing unit (not your furnace). Jot down the make, model and serial number (or take a photo). Get the parts at an appliance store, furnace dealer or online (arnoldservice.com is one source).

Start with the easy fixes

If you're getting little or no cold air, check these three things first. Make sure all the registers in the house are wide open. Then be sure the furnace filter is clean. Then go outside and clean off the condenser coils (Photo 2). If several registers were closed or the filter was clogged, the reduced airflow could have caused the evaporator coil to ice up and stop cooling your home. If you've changed the filter and opened all the registers and you're still not getting airflow at the registers, deice the A-coil. Move the thermostat mode switch from "Cooling" to "Off" and move the fan switch from "Auto" to "On." Let the blower run for at least 30 minutes or until there's good airflow at the registers. Then turn the A/C back on to test it. If it works for the next 12 hours, you've solved the problem.

If the condenser coils are clogged, the compressor can overheat and shut down. You'll experience intermittent periods of minimal cooling, followed by no cooling. Even if you're "sure" the condenser coils are clean, clean them again. Turn off the power. Flip the A/C and furnace circuit breakers in your main electrical panel to the "Off" position. Next, turn off the power switch right at the furnace or air handler. Then yank the disconnect block (Photo 1) and clean the condenser coils (Photo 2).

If the A/C still doesn't work properly after you've cleaned the condenser coils, installed a new filter and opened all the supply vents, proceed with the following repairs.

Test the fuses

Many disconnect blocks contain two cartridge fuses. Check them before you proceed with repairs (Photo 3). A blown fuse is a sign of a failing part inside the condensing unit. So don't just replace it and think you've solved the problem. Instead, replace the parts we show here. Then install new fuses and fire up the unit. If it blows again, call a pro—you've got more serious issues.

Inspect the inside of the access panel

Follow the electrical conduit from the house—that's where you'll find the access panel. With the power off, remove and store the access-panel retaining screws and remove the panel. Before you replace any parts, check for rodents' nests or evidence of chewing on wires and electrical connectors.

If you find broken wires or chewed insulation and can safely handle electrical repairs, discharge the capacitor first (Photo 4). Then repair the wires and clean out the nest. Otherwise, call a pro.

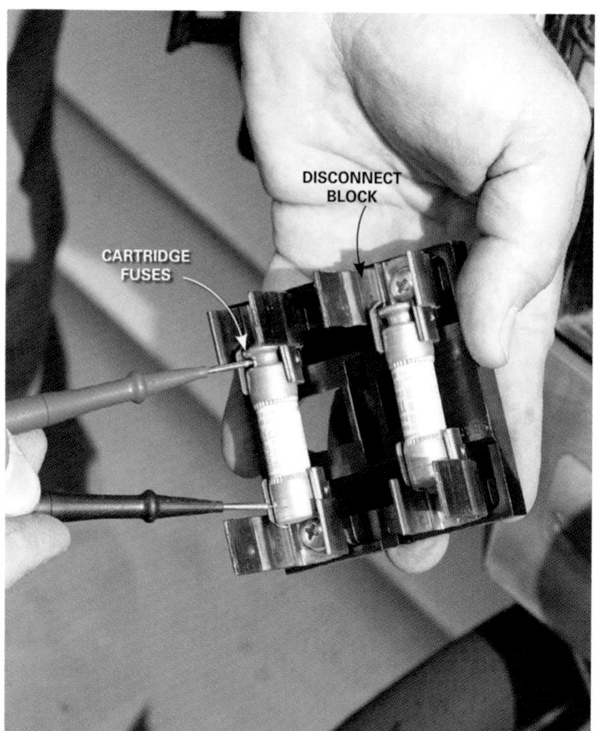

3 Check the fuses in the disconnect block. Set your multimeter to the Ohms scale and touch the red and black leads to opposite ends of each fuse. If you get a numerical reading, the fuse is good. But a zero, a minus symbol or an infinity symbol (∞) indicates a blown fuse.

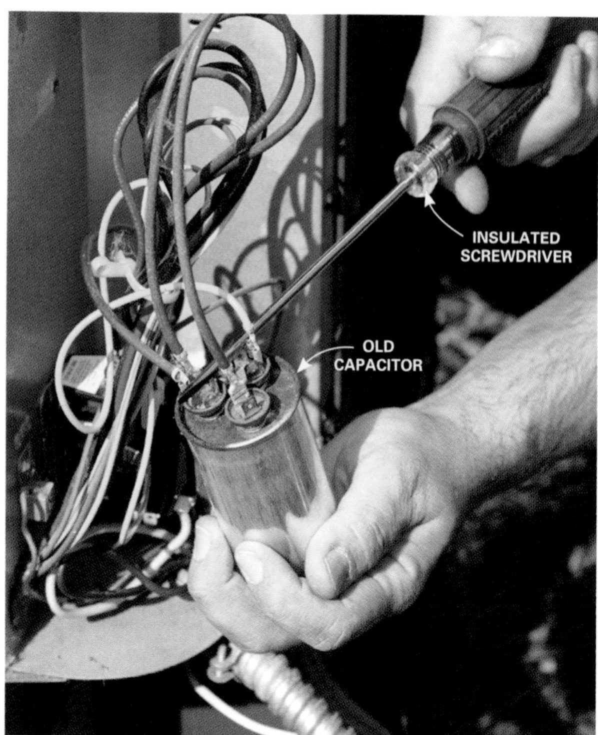

4 Discharging a dual start/run capacitor. Remove the capacitor from the retaining bracket. Then touch an insulated screwdriver between the HERM (or "H") terminal and the COMMON (or "C") terminal. Do the same between the FAN (or "F") terminal and the "C" terminal. On single-mode capacitors, just make a short between the two terminals.

Replace the start/run capacitor(s)

All A/C units have at least one capacitor. The capacitor stores electricity and releases it during compressor and condenser fan startup to give both motors an extra jolt of power. And it smooths out voltage fluctuations to protect the compressor and condenser fan motor from damage.

Capacitors can degrade slowly, providing less startup power over time. Or they can fail in an instant. Gradual capacitor failure can go unnoticed for a long time, stressing the compressor and condenser fan motor windings, resulting in their early failure. Since capacitors are cheap (less than $25 each), it pays to proactively replace yours about every five years.

Be patient at startup

A/C units and thermostats have built-in delay features when they're shut down and then repowered. The delay can be as long as 10 minutes. And, if you've subscribed to an energy-saving device from your local power utility, the unit can take even longer to reset. If you've installed the parts shown and reinstalled the disconnect block, repowered the circuit breaker, turned on the switch at the furnace, moved the thermostat to A/C mode and lowered the temperature below the indoor temperature, and the unit doesn't fire up after 30 minutes, it's time to call a pro.

Replacing a capacitor is easy. Just take a photo of the wires before disconnecting anything (you may need a reference later on). Then discharge the stored energy in the old capacitor (Photo 4). Use needle-nose pliers to pluck one wire at a time from the old capacitor and snap it onto the corresponding tab of the new capacitor. The female crimp connectors should snap tightly onto the capacitor tabs. Wiggle each connector to see if it's tight. If it's not, remove the connector and bend the rounded edges of it so it makes a tighter fit on the tab. When you've swapped all the wires, secure the new capacitor (Photo 5).

Replace the contactor

A contactor is a $25 mechanical relay that uses low-voltage power from the thermostat to switch 220-volt high-amperage current to the compressor and condenser fan. A/C contactors can wear out and are at the top of the list of common A/C failures. Even if your contactor is working, it pays to replace it every five years or so. Unscrew the old contactor before removing the wires. Then move the wires to the new unit (Photo 6).

Test your repairs

Reinstall the access panel and disconnect block. Turn on the circuit breaker and furnace switch. Then set the thermostat to a lower temperature and wait for the A/C to

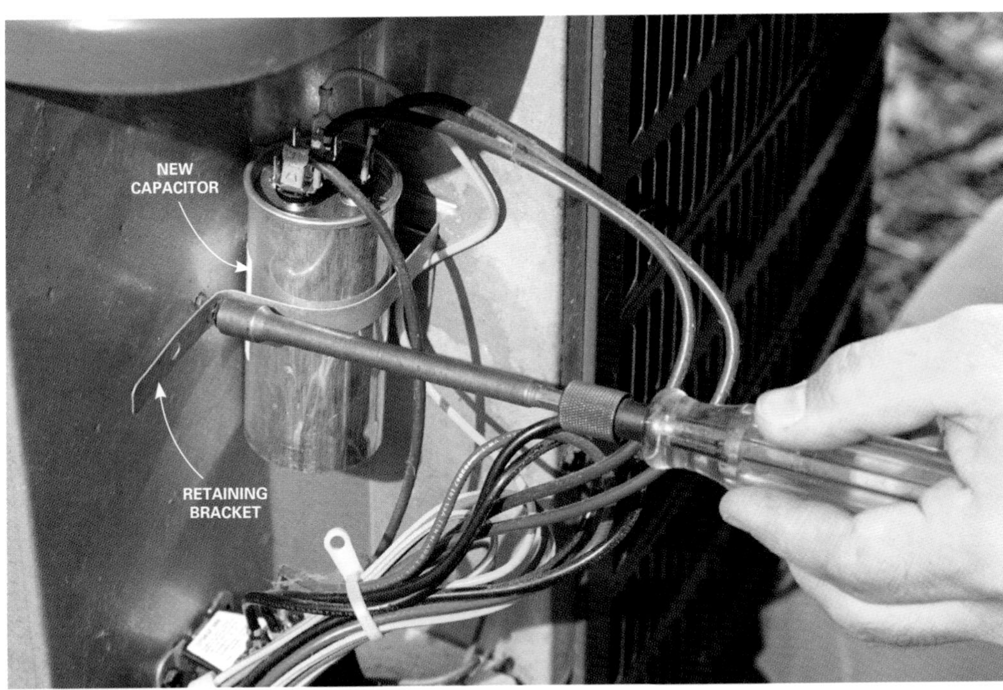

5 Install the new capacitor. Slide the new capacitor into the retaining bracket and tighten the bracket screw. Secure the wires with a zip tie.

6 Swap out the contactor. Yank a connector off the old contactor and move it to the same location on the new part. Tighten the connectors where needed. Then secure the new contactor in the condensing unit.

7 Replace the fan motor. Mark the blade to show which side is up. Loosen the fan blade setscrew and carefully pull it off the motor shaft. Then swap in the new motor. Route the motor wires through the old conduit and secure with zip ties where necessary. Don't skip the zip ties or the blade could cut the wires.

start (see "Be Patient at Startup,," p. 100). The compressor should run and the condenser fan should spin. If the compressor starts but the fan doesn't, the fan motor is most likely shot. Shut off the power and remove the screws around the condenser cover. Lift the cover and remove the fan blade and motor (Photo 7). Reinstall the blade and secure the cover. Then repower the unit and see if the fan starts. If it doesn't, you've given it your best shot— it's time to call a pro.

CHOOSE A **FAUCET** YOU'LL LOVE

Style is critical, but don't forget the practical factors

by **Gary Wentz, Senior Editor**

Most people choose a faucet based on looks alone. And that's a mistake. Looks are important, but you can usually get the look you want without compromising on convenience and long-term dependability. For advice on those practical considerations, we talked with faucet designers, manufacturers, retailers and plumbers. Here's what we learned.

Spend enough but not too much

Plan to spend at least $65 for a bath faucet and at least $100 for a kitchen faucet. You might get a great faucet for less, but it's more likely that you'd get a low-quality faucet. If you spend much more, you're paying for extra features or style rather than basic reliability or durability.

Watch the spout height and reach

Faucet spouts vary a lot in height and reach, and most of the time you can just choose the look you like best. But if you have a shelf above the sink, a tall spout may not fit. With a three-bowl kitchen sink, a spout with a short reach may not extend to all the bowls. A bath faucet with a short reach might cause you to slop water behind the spout when you wash your hands.

Pull-down sprayers are better

If you've ever had a "side" sprayer (a spray handle mounted in the sink), you've probably had dribbles or leaks. And you might assume you'd have similar (and more expensive) trouble with a faucet-mounted sprayer like the one shown here. Probably not. All of our experts told us that "pull-down" sprayers have proven much more reliable than the old side sprayers.

Choose ceramic valves

If you want to avoid having a faucet that drips, get one with ceramic valves. Other types of valves are usually drip-free for years, but they can't match the long-term reliability of ceramic. Faucets with ceramic valves cost about the same as other faucets.

Some finishes are tougher than others

Here's Rule No. 1 of faucet finishes: Choose a finish that matches nearby cabinet hardware, towel bars, etc. Mismatches look bad. If you plan to replace existing hardware, your choice of faucet finishes is wide open. The vast majority of faucets have polished chrome, satin nickel or bronze finishes. All of these finishes are durable and keep their good looks for years. But some are more durable than others.

Chrome is the most durable finish and the easiest to keep clean—that's why it's always been the favorite for commercial kitchens and public bathrooms. If your faucet gets heavy use, it's your best bet for long-term toughness.

Nickel finishes are usually labeled "brushed," "satin" or "stainless steel" and have a dull shine. They're durable but prone to fingerprints and water spots, so they're harder to keep clean. Some have a coating that reduces stains and smudges, but that coating isn't as durable as metal and may chip or wear.

Bronze faucets have a brownish tone and are often called "oiled" or "rubbed" bronze. But the surface is a coating (such as epoxy) rather than metal. This coating is tough stuff, but can be chipped or scratched more easily than metal.

Count the holes in your sink

If you want to switch from two handles to one, you have to think about the number of holes in the sink. Most sinks have three holes: one for the hot handle, one for the cold and one under the spout. Some single-handle faucets include a cover plate to hide the extra holes. But some don't, so check the label. If you currently have a "wide spread" bathroom faucet with two handles far from the spout, you can't switch to a single-handle model.

If you want a kitchen faucet with a "pull-down" sprayer mounted in the spout, there will be an empty sprayer hole. But the solution is simple: install a soap dispenser ($20 and up). Your new faucet may even include one.

A single handle is more convenient

Two-handle faucets have a stylish symmetry that suits many bathrooms, especially traditional ones. But in practical terms, single-handle faucets have all the advantages. They're just plain more convenient; water temperature adjustment is easier and there's one less handle to clean.

CONSULTANTS: BRAD CROZIER, MOEN; GRAY UHL, AMERICAN STANDARD; SEAN MURPHY, BUILD.COM

EASIER INSTALLATION

Installing a new faucet often earns a "PG" rating for the foul language involved. But faucet makers have been striving for a "G" rating with ingenious engineering that takes some of the frustration out of installation. Here are some innovations:

Instant-change faucets

Moen's M-PACT system consists of a valve kit that contains below-the-sink components, and a kit containing the handles and spout. With the valves installed, adding the handles and spout takes less than five minutes. When styles change, you can buy new components and install them instantly. Faucets for the M-PACT system may or may not include the valve kit—check before you buy. There's also a version for showers.

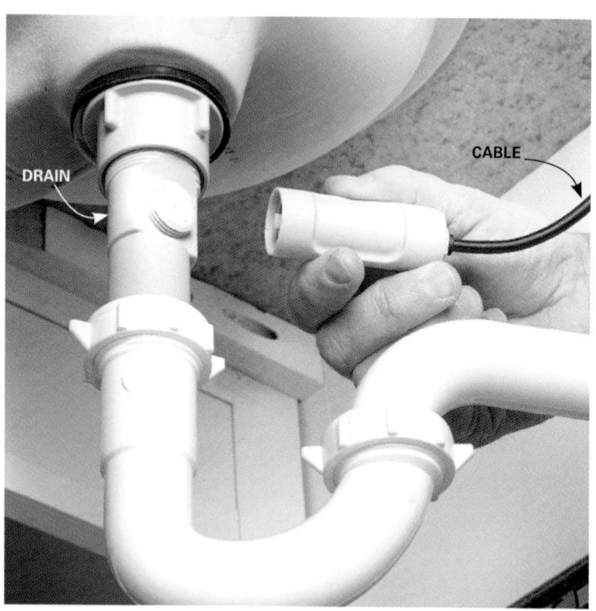

No-adjust stopper

Pop-up sink stoppers are frustrating. You make fussy adjustments when you install it and readjustments later. American Standard's SpeedConnect system eliminates all that. Just connect the cable—no adjustments, no readjustments. From above the sink, the system looks and operates just like the traditional system. Most American Standard bath faucets include the SpeedConnect drain.

Faster, easier faucet mounting

Delta's EZ Anchor system lets you mount the faucet without crawling under the sink. First, you install the anchor; all it takes is turning a couple of screws. Then set the faucet body onto the anchor. As you turn the hub, barbed fingers lock the faucet solidly onto the anchor. You still have to reach under the sink to connect the preattached supply lines, but you'll avoid lying on your back and reaching up, cramming your hand behind the sink and dropping tools on your face. Only a few Delta kitchen faucets feature EZ Anchor (we hope that changes soon).

Super-simple stopper

Pfister's Push & Seal pop-up assembly is the ultimate in stopper simplicity. There's no linkage between the stopper and the faucet, nothing to connect or adjust. The spring-loaded locking mechanism under the stopper provides a tight seal. The Push & Seal drain is included with most Pfister bath faucets.

Save money with WaterSense

If you're buying a bathroom faucet, look for the WaterSense label. To get this EPA label, a faucet has to have a low flow rate (1.5 gallons per minute) but feel like a high-flow faucet. As one of our experts put it, "You're saving water, but you can't tell." In areas with high water costs, a WaterSense faucet can pay for itself in one year. WaterSense labels don't apply to kitchen faucets.

GreatGoofs®

Drill baby drill

While installing tubing for our automatic ice cube maker, I had to climb into the crawl space below the house to drill holes. I proceeded to cut through some insulation, and came to some 2x4 framing that had to be drilled through in order to feed the tubing up through the floor and into the kitchen above. I started drilling but somehow couldn't get through the wood.

After several minutes, a blister on my thumb, and a very sore shoulder from lying on my back on the gravel, I decided I had better consult my husband. He came to my rescue only to find that I had accidentally knocked the drill lever into reverse before drilling. After I swallowed my pride, the job went smoothly. Believe me, I earned that first glass of ice water!

Beth Dreher

PLUMBING, HEATING & APPLIANCES

An open-and-shut case

Our gas dryer wasn't getting the clothes dry, so I checked the vent to see if it was clogged. There was plenty of dryer lint—I spent an hour cleaning the vent with my shop vacuum. Then I tried the dryer, but it still didn't get warm. I reopened the dryer, checked all the electrical connections and the igniter position, but I just couldn't find the problem. I gave up and called an appliance repair shop.

When the technician arrived, he knelt down, looked in with a flashlight, then reached inside. He got up with a grin and said, "All fixed." I said, "You're kidding—what was wrong?" He said the gas valve was shut off. "You probably pushed it closed with the vacuum cleaner." He was there all of 10 minutes, apologized for his company's minimum billing and went off with a check, still smiling.

—Dave Gurrie

A knockout tub surround

As a young homeowner, I attacked my first-ever bathroom remodeling project with great enthusiasm. I purchased a new vanity, sink, medicine cabinet and light bar, and special-ordered a new tub and a separate one-piece tub surround. I installed the tub according to the instructions, even setting it in wet concrete to give it a nice firm base. The next day, I went to swing the tub surround into place against the back wall of the bathroom. At that moment I painfully realized why two-piece tub surrounds are manufactured. My one-piece unit just wasn't going to fit in the opening around the tub no matter what I tried.

It could be argued that as a mechanical engineer, I should have predicted this outcome! I ended up knocking out 4 ft. of the wall between the bathroom and the adjacent bedroom to get the tub surround to fit.I was just lucky I was still single at the time.

—Russell Zell, PE

INSTALLING FAUCETS

Tips and tricks for modern faucets

by **Jeff Gorton, Associate Editor**

Today's faucets are easier than ever to install. In fact, you can even buy faucets that install entirely from the top of the sink so you don't have to crawl underneath. But there are still things you should know for a quick, easy and leak-free installation. Here are our best tips for helping you with your next faucet installation.

Stuck shutoff valves

If your shutoff valve is stuck open, you can often free it by loosening the packing nut slightly. This relieves pressure on the valve stem and allows you to turn the valve more easily. Retighten the valve stem nut just enough to prevent leaks around the valve stem.

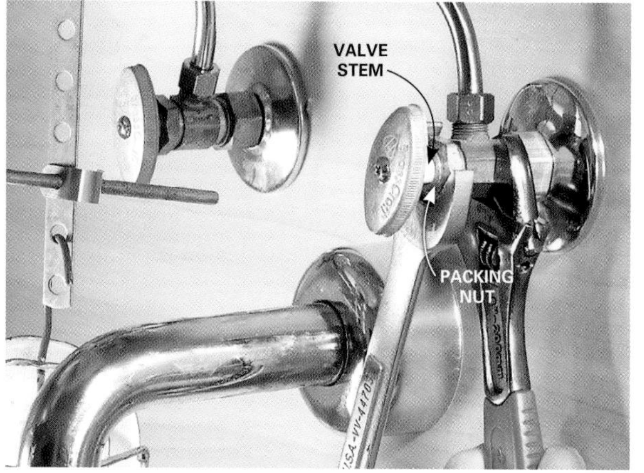

You may need a basin wrench

A basin wrench is a standard plumbing tool that is indispensable for removing and installing most faucets. The wrench allows you to reach into the cramped area behind the sink to loosen or tighten the nuts that hold the faucet to the sink, and the nuts that connect the supply lines. You may not need a basin wrench if you can get the old faucet out by cutting the nuts (see "Cut out the old faucet," p. 107) and if the new faucet includes a wrench or some other means of installing the faucet without a basin wrench. Check inside the package when you buy the faucet to see what's required. If you do need a basin wrench, plan to spend about $20 to get a good one.

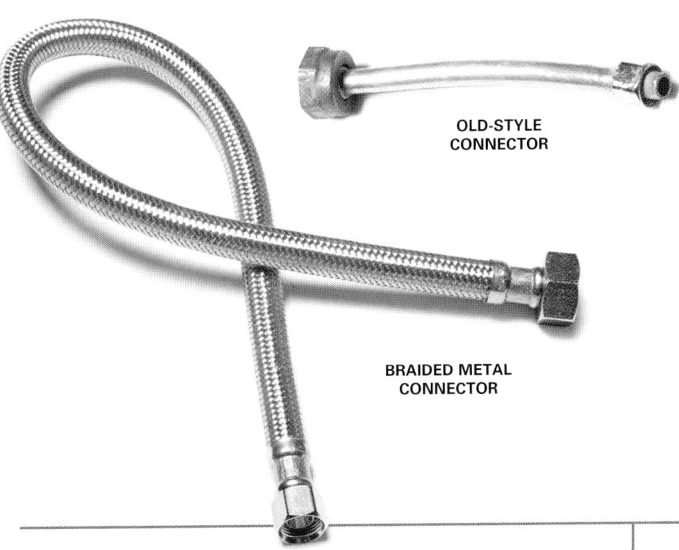

Upgrade your supply lines

One of the most difficult parts of installing a new faucet used to be connecting the supply lines so they didn't leak. But the new-style connectors with braided jackets have gaskets built into each end that make connections virtually foolproof. They cost more—about $5 each—but are worth every penny. You don't need to crank the nut very tight for an effective seal. Just thread it finger-tight and then add about a half-turn with a wrench. So save yourself headaches and replace those old supply lines with braided stainless steel connectors.

Cut out the old faucet

Even with a basin wrench, it can be nearly impossible to break loose corroded nuts holding older faucets to the sink. If you don't care about wrecking the faucet, cut off the nuts instead. You can use either a rotary tool (Dremel is one brand) with a grinding disc or oscillating tool with a metal-cutting blade. Cut through one side of the nut. Then use a screwdriver to pry the nut away from the faucet body. You can also cut off other stubborn parts, like the pop-up drain assembly on a bathroom sink.

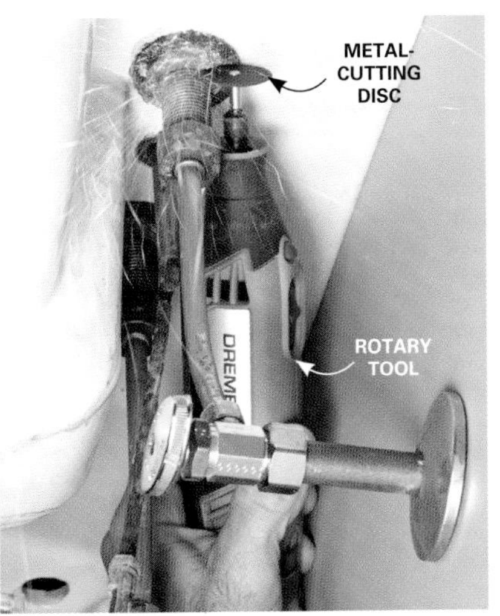

Measure for the supply lines

Many new faucets include supply lines, but they may not be long enough, or they may not have the right threads to connect to your shutoff valves. To determine the length of the supply lines you'll need, measure from the underside of the sink near where the faucet connects to the shutoff valve and add a few inches. If the supply lines included with your new faucet aren't long enough, buy extensions. To make sure the threads on your new supply lines match those on your shutoff valves, take one of your old supply lines with you to the store and match it with the new supply lines.

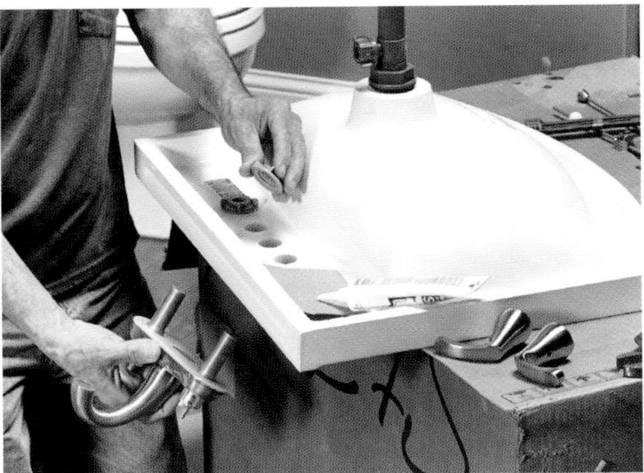

Premount the faucet on new sink installations

If you're installing a new sink along with your faucet, mount the faucet to the sink before you install the sink. It's much simpler than lying on your back inside the sink cabinet to install the faucet. Even if you're not installing a new sink, you may find it easier to remove the old sink to get better access for removing the old faucet and installing the new one. Plus, removing and reinstalling the old sink will allow you to clean off old caulk and gunk that's accumulated around the edge and renew the seal between the counter and the sink with fresh caulk.

Remove the aerator before you turn on the water

Messing around with plumbing often dislodges minerals or other debris that has built up inside the pipes and valves. To prevent that stuff from clogging the aerator in your new faucet, remove the aerator before turning the water back on. The aerator is the device on the end of your faucet that has a screen or perforated plastic covering the end. Most aerators simply unscrew counterclockwise. Some new faucets include a special tool for removing the aerator.

If you're installing a pullout faucet, the aerator can be tricky to remove. If this is the case, simply unscrew the entire spray head from the supply tube and point the tube into the sink while you turn on the water. Let the water run a few seconds. Then replace the aerator or spray head. If your faucet ever starts to run slowly, remove the aerator and clean it. This will usually fix the problem.

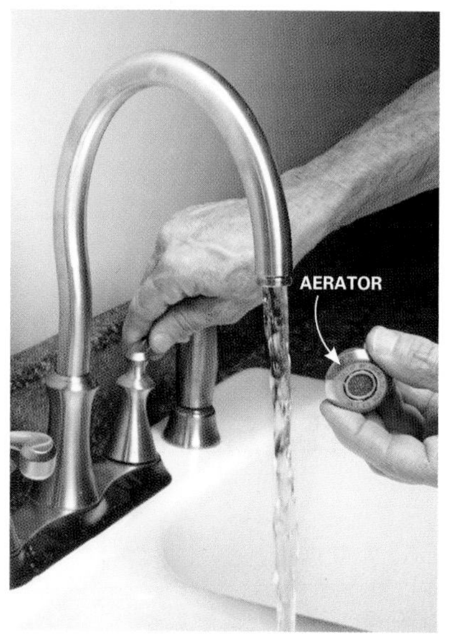

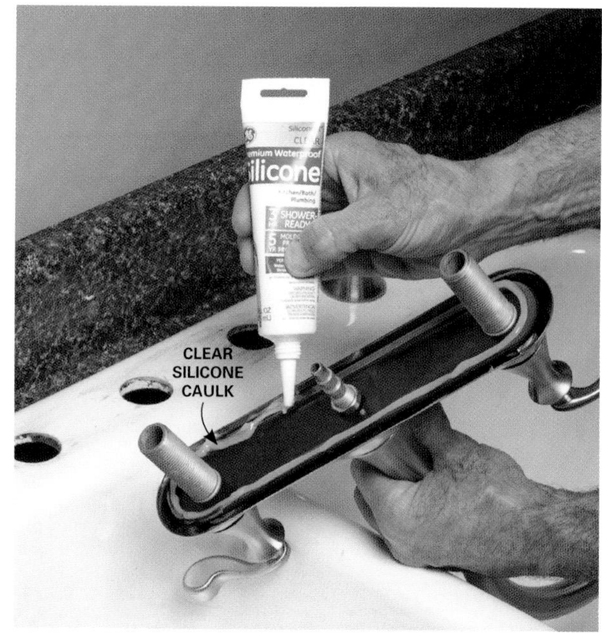

Mount the faucet with silicone

If water gets under your faucet, it can corrode the faucet or worse, damage your countertop or cabinet. Most new faucets include a gasket of some type to create a seal between the faucet and the sink, but it's still a good idea to apply a bead of clear silicone caulk to the bottom of the faucet and the bottom of the gasket to ensure a good seal. Also, the silicone acts as an adhesive to prevent the faucet from moving around if the connection nuts loosen. Clean up any silicone that oozes out, first using just a paper towel, then mineral spirits.

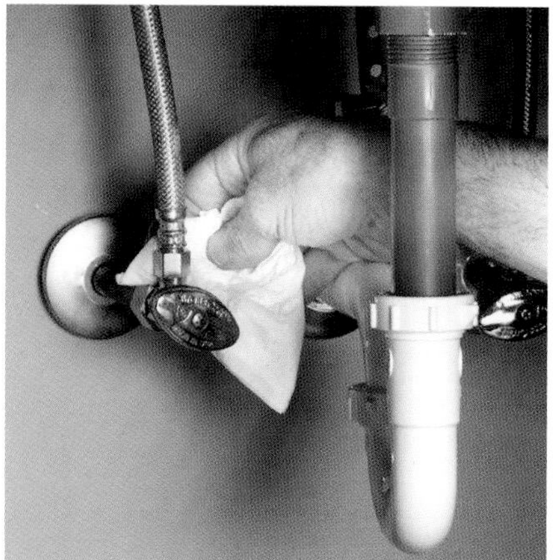

Check for leaks

When you're done with the faucet installation, check for leaks. Turn on the water and let it run for two or three minutes. Then crawl under the sink with some tissue and wipe around the joints with it. Even a tiny leak will show up as a wet spot on the tissue. Tighten the connection near any leak you find.

Save the instructions and parts in a freezer bag

Many new faucets include wrenches, aerator removal tools, and other parts or tools that you should keep. An easy way to keep track of this stuff, along with the instruction sheet, is to put it all in a big freezer bag and hang it inside the sink cabinet, where you'll always be able to find it.

4 Woodworking & Workshop Projects & Tips

IN THIS CHAPTER

Hide-the-Mess Lockers 110

Advanced Trim Tips 114

Top 10 Tips for Gluing Wood 120

Tips for Tighter Miters 124

Table Saw Helpers 128

Ken's Favorite Shop Tips 131

Sharpening Knives and Tools 136

Driving Screws 140

A Classic Workbench 143

Building Face Frame Cabinets 148

Master the Reciprocating Saw 152

Finish a Tabletop 156

Handy Hints 160
Spray-foam super tube, protect your tools, easy-to-read tool markings and more

Hardware Organizer 164

10 Simple Woodworking Jigs 167

Get Creative with Tools 172

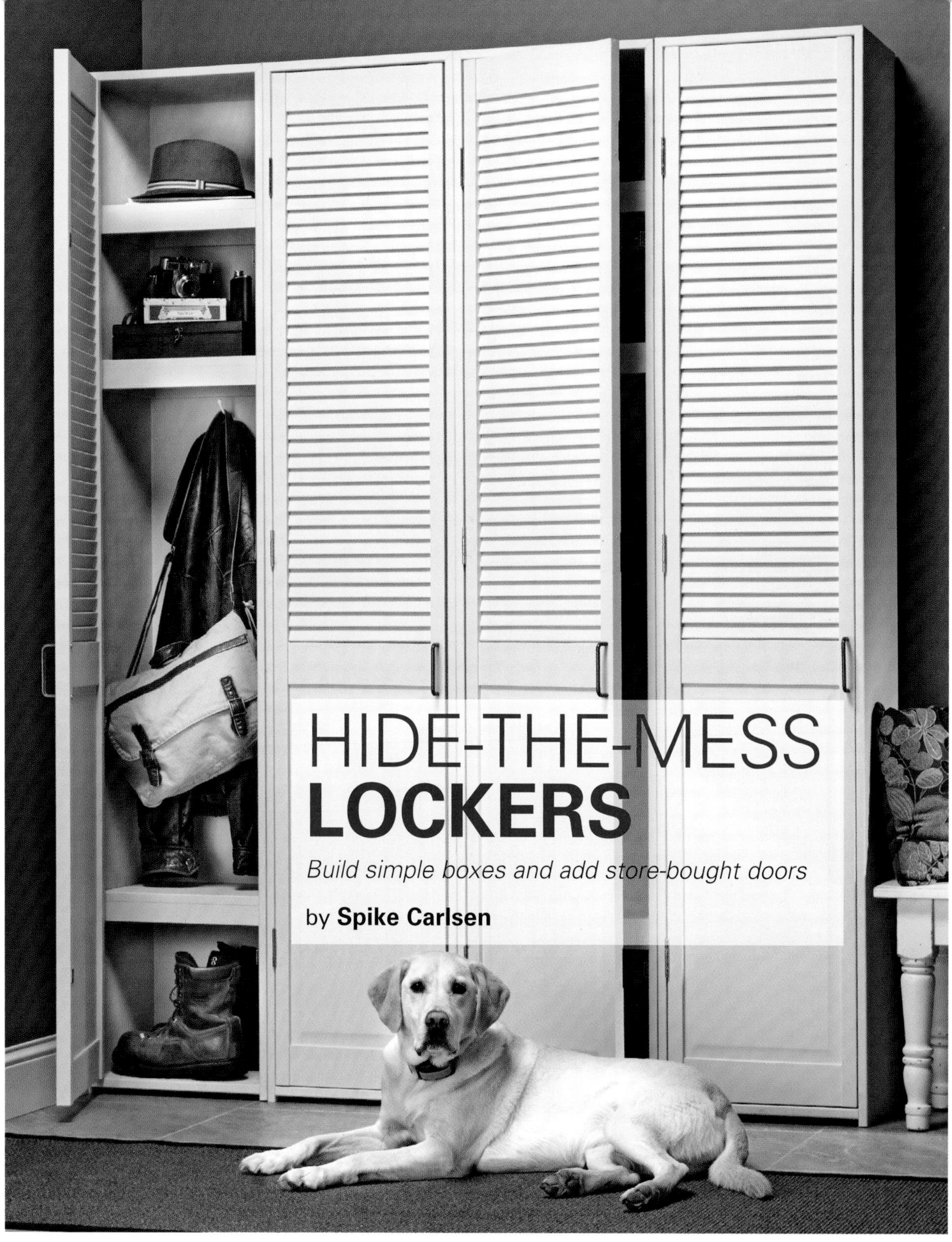

HIDE-THE-MESS **LOCKERS**

Build simple boxes and add store-bought doors

by **Spike Carlsen**

My daughter, Kellie, recently bought a nice little house with a nice big coat closet by the front door. The problem is, since the garage is in the back, everyone, including the dog, uses the back door.

I designed and built these hide-the-mess lockers with people like Kellie in mind. Each locker is big enough to stash a coat, backpack, boots, hats, and odds and ends that normally wind up on the floor. Since they're modular and space efficient, you can build one for each member of the family—including the dog (leashes, toys, food, you name it). Now everyone has a personal place for stashing stuff—and the responsibility for keeping it organized.

The louvered door is made from one of a pair of closet bifold doors, which you can buy at almost any home center. Since the doors come in pairs and you can get two locker "boxes" from each sheet of plywood, you'll make the best use of materials by building them in twos. Here's how to do it.

Money, materials and tools

My total materials cost was just under $100 per locker. Since I was planning to paint the lockers, I used inexpensive "AC" plywood. If you plan to stain your lockers, and use hardwood plywood such as oak or birch and hardwood doors, you'll spend about $150 per locker. On a row of lockers, only the outer sides of the end lockers show, so you can use inexpensive plywood for the inner parts and more expensive material for the outer parts. Expect to spend at least a day buying materials, rounding up tools and building a pair of lockers. Set aside another day for finishing.

A table saw is handy for cutting up plywood, but a circular saw with a guide will provide the same results. To see how to build a guide, search for "cutting guides" at familyhandyman.com. You'll also need a miter saw to cut the screen molding. A finish nailer will help you work faster, but hand-nailing will work too as long as you drill holes to prevent splitting.

Buy the doors first

There are a variety of bifold doors available. If you need more ventilation, use full louvered doors; if ventilation isn't an issue, use solid doors. The doors you buy may not be exactly the same size as mine, so you may have to alter the dimensions of the boxes you build. Here are two key points to keep in mind as you plan your project:

- You want a 1/8-in. gap surrounding the door. So to determine the size of the box opening, add 1/4 in. to the height and width of the door. Since my bifold doors measured 14-3/4 x 78-3/4 in., I made the opening 15 x 79 in.
- To determine the depth of the shelves, subtract the door thickness from the width of the sides (including the 1/4-in. screen molding). My doors were 1-1/8 in. thick, so I made the shelves 10-7/8 in. deep (12 minus 1-1/8 equals 10-7/8 in.). When the doors are closed, they'll rest against the shelves inside and flush with the screen molding outside.

Get building!

Use a table saw or straight-cutting guide to cut the plywood sides (A) and top and bottom (B). The Cutting List on p. 113 gives the parts dimensions for my lockers. If you plan to paint or stain the lockers, it's a good idea to prefinish the insides of parts. Once the lockers are assembled, brushing a finish onto the insides is slow and difficult.

Assemble the boxes with 2-in. trim-head screws (Photo 1). Trim-head screws have smaller heads than standard screws and are easier to hide with filler. Cut the

MEET AN EXPERT

Spike Carlsen is a carpenter, author and former editor at *The Family Handyman*. You can find his books in stores and at online booksellers. Find out more at spikecarlsen.com.

1 Build a simple box. Cut the plywood parts and assemble them with trim-head screws. Make sure the box opening is 1/4 in. taller and wider than the door itself.

2 Square it up. Take diagonal corner-to-corner measurements, then adjust the box until the measurements are equal and the box is square. Install the back, using one edge of the back to straighten the box side as you fasten it. Check once again for squareness, then secure the other edges of the back.

3 Cover the plywood edges. Install screen molding over the front edges of the box. Apply wood glue lightly and use just enough nails to "clamp" the molding in place while the glue dries.

4 Build slatted shelves. Plywood shelves would work fine, but slatted shelves allow better ventilation so wet clothes and shoes can dry. Space the slats with a pair of wood scraps.

5 Install the shelves. Stand your locker up and position the shelves to suit the stuff that will go in it. Mark the shelf locations, lay the locker on its back and screw the shelves into place. Make sure the shelves are inset far enough to allow for the door.

6 Mount the hinges. Remove the hinges from the doors (they'll be pointed the wrong way) and reinstall them on the door based on the direction you want it to swing. Prop up the door alongside the box and align the door so there will be a 1/8-in. gap at the top and bottom of the box. Then screw the hinges to the box.

1/4-in. plywood back (C) to size. Make certain the box is square by taking diagonal measurements (they should be equal; see **Photo 2**), and then secure the back using 1-in. nails. Use the edges of the back as a guide to straighten the edges of the box as you nail the back into place.

Cut 1/4 x 3/4-in. screen molding and use glue and 1-in. finish nails or brads to secure it to the exposed front edges of the plywood (**Photo 3**). Cut the shelf front and back (D), sides (E) and slats (F) to length, then assemble the three slatted shelf units (**Photo 4**). With the locker box standing upright, position the shelves and hold them temporarily in place with clamps or a couple of screws. Adjust the shelf spacing based on the height of the locker's user and the stuff that will go inside. Once you have a suitable arrangement, lay the locker on its back and screw the shelves into place (**Photo 5**). The shelves are easy to reposition in the future as needs change.

Add the hardware and finish, and then install

Remove the hinges that hold the bifold doors to each other. Determine which way you want the door to swing, then mount the hinges onto the door accordingly. (Note: You'll need to buy another set of hinges if you're building two lockers.) Remember, you want the louvers to point downward on the outside! With the locker on its back, position the door and secure the hinges to the plywood side (**Photo 6**). Install door handles and magnetic catches to hold them closed.

Remove the doors (but don't finish them yet!) and install the locker boxes. Your lockers can stand against baseboard, leaving a small gap between the backs of the lockers and the wall. Or—if you remove the baseboard—they can stand tight against the wall. Either way, installing them is a lot like installing cabinets: Fasten all the boxes together by driving 1-1/4-in. screws through the side of one locker into the next. Then screw the entire assembly to wall studs.

Install the unfinished doors to make sure they all fit properly, then remove them again. This may seem like a waste of time, but there's a good reason for it: Your locker boxes may have shifted a little during installation, and the doors may not fit properly. If a door or two need some edge sanding, you want to do that before finishing.

When you've checked the fit of all the doors, remove them one last time for finishing. Whether you're using paint or a natural finish, louvered doors are a real pain. If your plans include a clear coat, consider polyurethane or lacquer in spray cans: You'll get better results in far less time, though you'll spend an extra $5 to $10 per door. After finishing, install the doors and load up those lockers!

Figure A
Locker construction

Overall Dimensions:
16-1/2" wide x 81" tall x 12-1/4" deep

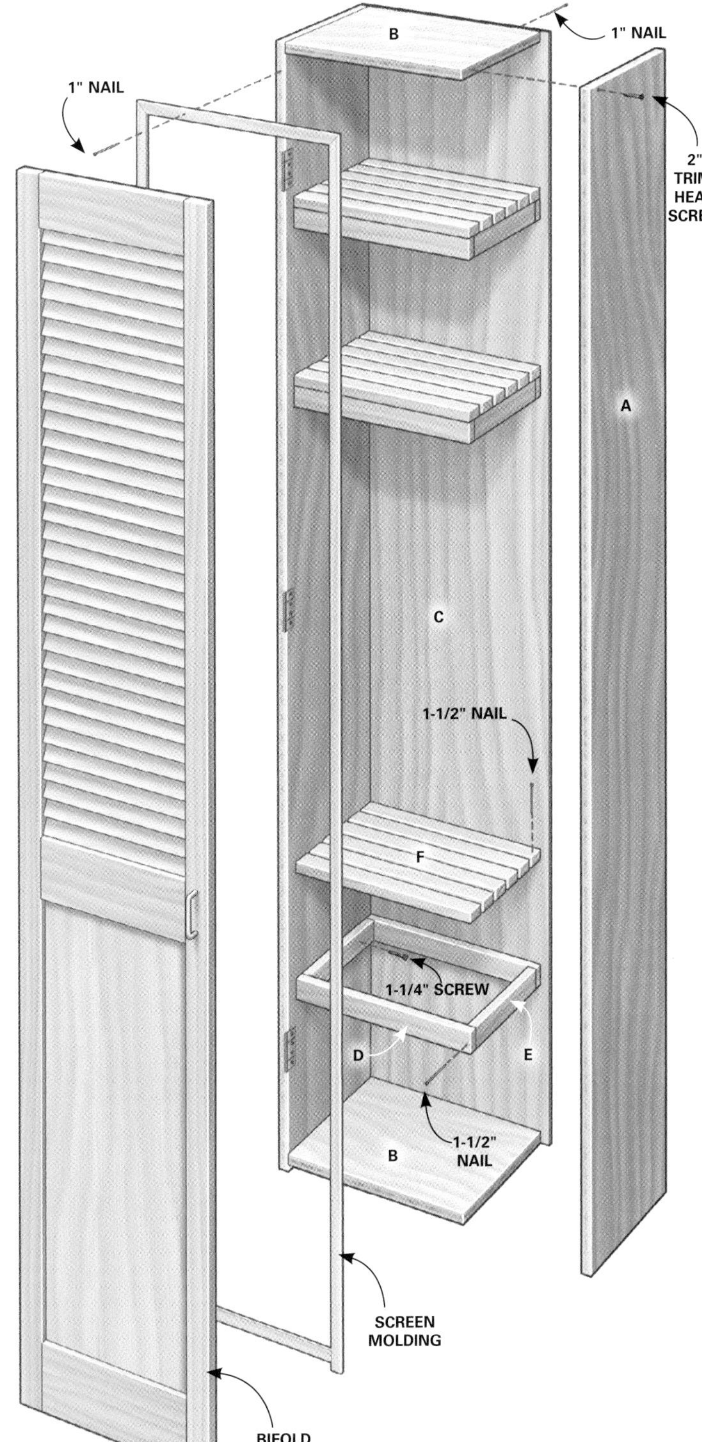

MATERIALS LIST

(for two lockers)

Because bifold doors are sold in pairs, and one sheet of 3/4-in. plywood yields two lockers, you can make the best use of materials by building an even number of lockers.

ITEM	QTY.
30" bifold door pack (2 doors)	1
3/4" x 4' x 8' plywood	1
1/4" x 4' x 8' plywood	1
1/4" x 3/4" x 8' screen molding	5
3/4" x 1-1/2" x 8' solid wood	9

2" trim-head screws, 1-1/4" screws, 1" nails, 1-1/2" nails, wood glue, no-mortise hinges, door handles and magnetic catches.

CUTTING LIST

(for one locker)

These locker parts suit a door measuring 14-3/4 x 78-3/4 in. Verify the exact size of your doors before building.

KEY	QTY.	SIZE & DESCRIPTION
A	2	11-3/4" x 80-7/8" sides (3/4" plywood)
B	2	11-3/4" x 15" top/bottom (3/4" plywood)
C	1	16-1/2" x 80-1/2" back (1/4" plywood)
D	2	3/4" x 1-1/2" x 15" shelf front/back (solid wood)
E	2	3/4" x 1-1/2" x 9-3/8" shelf sides (solid wood)
F	6	3/4" x 1-1/2" x 15" shelf slats (solid wood)

Figure B
Cutting diagrams

3/4" PLYWOOD

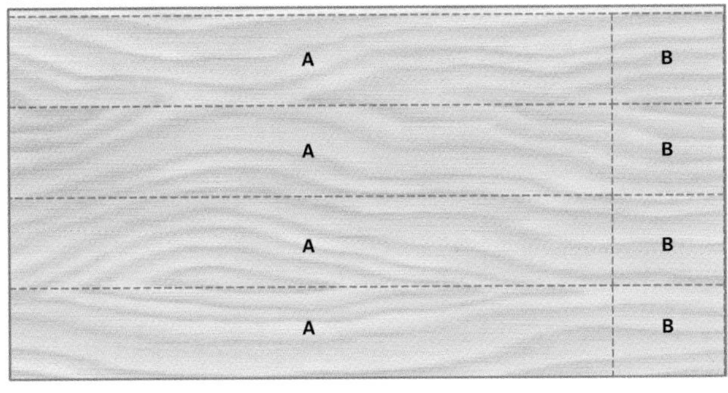

1/4" PLYWOOD

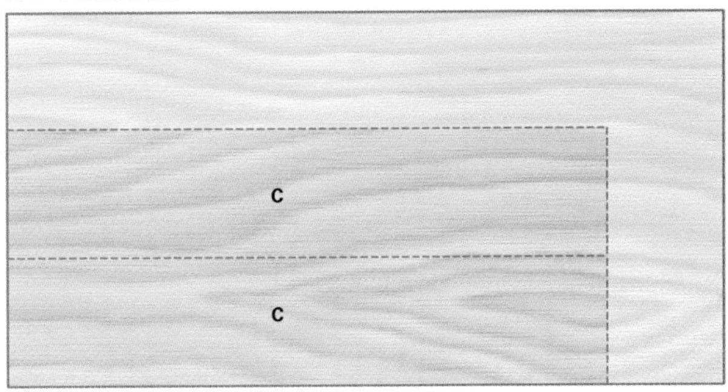

WOODWORKING & WORKSHOP PROJECTS & TIPS

ADVANCED **TRIM TIPS**

Great results, even in bad situations

by **Jeff Gorton, Associate Editor**

Wavy walls, crooked studs, uneven floors and out-of-square corners are the norm in most houses, and they all add to the challenge of getting your moldings to fit just right. To help you out, we've collected problem-solving tips from three veteran carpenters with a wide range of trim carpentry experience.

Tighten up open miters

Uneven walls or misaligned jambs make it hard to get tight-fitting miters. If your miter has a consistent gap at the front, there's a good chance that putting a slight back bevel on both moldings will fix the problem. If you own a compound miter saw, you could tilt the saw about a half-degree, but that requires fussy adjustments.

The quickest and easiest way to cut a slight back bevel is to shim the molding so it's resting at an angle to the saw blade. A pencil makes a handy shim and is just about the right thickness. You can adjust the position or thickness of the shim to compensate for all kinds of wall variations. You can even shim just the back or the front to mimic how the trim rests on uneven drywall.

Problem: An open miter
This doorjamb protrudes a bit beyond the wall, and the result is that the trim can't lie flat and the front of the miter joint can't close.

**Solution:
Cut a "back bevel"**
You could tilt the saw blade to back-bevel the miters, but tilting the trim is faster and easier. Slip a pencil or shim under the molding, just behind where the cut will be. Cut both sides of the miter with shims in the same position. Then test the fit and make adjustments as needed.

Cut steep angles on your miter saw

It's not common, but occasionally you'll run into a situation that requires miters greater than the 45- or 50-degree angle available on miter saws. The photo at right shows one solution.

Problem: Miter saws don't cut steep angles
This miter saw won't cut the 60-degree angle we need.

Solution: Clamp to an angled block
Cut a block of wood at a 45-degree angle and cut a flat spot for the clamp. Clamp the molding to the block and line up the miter saw with the mark to make the cut.

Scribe trim to fit uneven walls

Learning how to scribe moldings to fit tightly to uneven surfaces is a vital trim carpentry skill. And once you get the hang of scribing, you'll find all kinds of situations where it'll come in handy. Here we're showing how to fit a casing against an out-of-plumb wall. You can also scribe door bottoms, inside corners of wainscoting, and even shelving or cabinets that abut crooked walls.

There are several types of scribing tools, but the simple compass with a wing-nut lock shown is a favorite with many trim carpenters. The photo at right shows how to use the compass to scribe a line. Then finish up by cutting and trimming to the line for a perfectly fitting piece (photo below).

Problem: The trim won't fit
This casing is wider than the space between the door and the wall, so the casing needs to be cut. That cut will need to fit tightly against an uneven wall.

Solution: Step 1
Scribe a line on the casing
Set the scribing tool to the distance between the wall and the mark on the casing. Scribe a line by running the point of the tool against the wall, being careful to keep the tool perpendicular to the wall.

Solution: Step 2
Cut along the line
Next, remove the molding and tack it to a board. Carefully saw along the line with your circular saw. Stay a little outside the line. Then finish up by belt-sanding or planing up to the line.

Angle a nail to close baseboard gaps

Sometimes you can't force baseboard tight against the wall because there's no stud behind the gap. This is especially common at outside corners if there's a buildup of joint compound. But there is a bottom plate that you can reach with a well-placed nail. For the best control and maximum hold, set aside your nail gun for a minute and reach for a hammer and an 8d finish nail. The cutaway photo below shows how the angled nail catches the plate.

Problem: Ugly gap, no stud
This gap seems impossible to close because there's no stud to nail into. This is common near outside corners where there's a buildup of joint compound.

Solution: Nail into the plate
If there's no stud where you need to pull in the molding, drive an 8d finish nail at an angle into the plate. In hardwood trim, drill a pilot hole. Use a hammer and a nail set to set the nail head slightly below the surface.

Make blocks for tough transitions

Used tastefully, transition blocks can be a real problem solver. Rather than struggling to align moldings or fudging to match profiles, you can make a nice transition with a decorative block. You can buy ready-made blocks, but it's easy to make your own. Cut the block to the height and width you think look good. Then cut or rout the top or add a small molding to complement your trim style. Use transition blocks where stair skirts intersect baseboards, where floor levels change, or at the bottom of door casings where the baseboard is thicker than the casing.

Problem: Moldings don't line up
A change in floor heights creates an ugly jog in the baseboard.

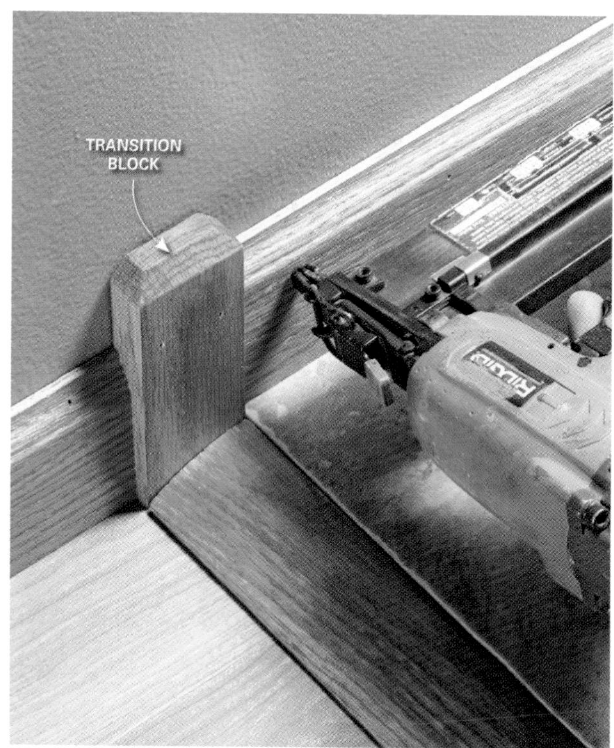

Solution: Cut a decorative block
Cut a block of wood that's a little thicker than the baseboard. Then finish the top with a bevel or a routed profile.

Big humps require surgery

Careful framing is the key to easy trim installation. But in the rush to get the walls put up, framing carpenters sometimes get a little sloppy. A stud that's not lined up with the plate causes a big hump in the wall, making it difficult to get the baseboard tight. But if you're courageous enough to cut into your wall, the fix is simple. Start by cutting out a little chunk of drywall right at the hump to see what the problem is. There could just be a chunk of drywall or other debris trapped between the drywall and the bottom plate. Or the stud could be misaligned. If this is the case, see the photo below for the solution.

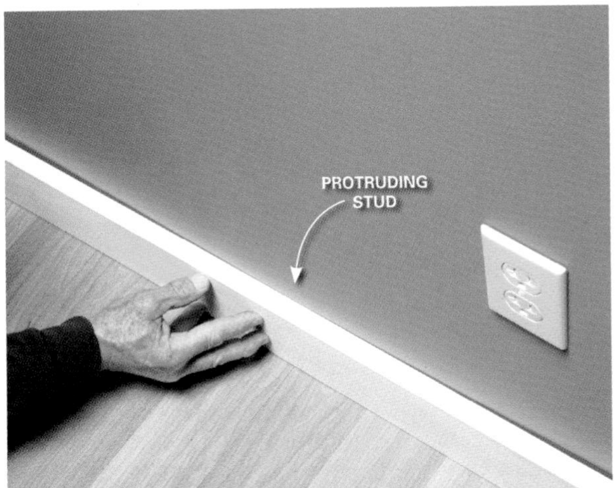

Problem: A hump causes baseboard gaps
Even if we could draw the baseboard tight to the wall on both sides of this hump, the baseboard would still look wavy. It's better to get rid of the hump.

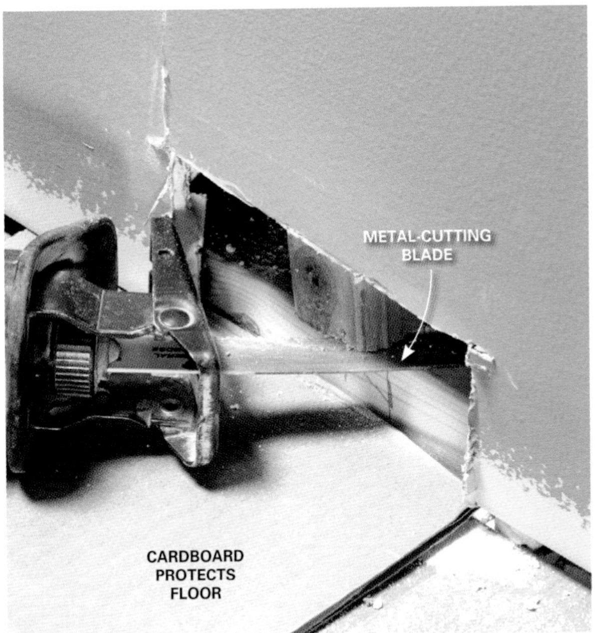

Solution: Move a protruding stud
Cut the nails that hold the stud to the plate. Then push the stud back until it's lined up with the plate and reattach it with an angled screw.

Clean out corners before you start

Even careful drywall tapers can end up with an accumulation of joint compound near the bottom of inside corners. The problem is that all that extra mud prevents the baseboard from fitting well. The trick is to scrape off the buildup before you start installing the base. You can use a small pry bar with a sharp edge, a dull chisel or a stiff putty knife scraper. Before you start scraping, mark the top of the baseboard on the wall. Then scrape below the line where it won't show.

Problem: Sloppy mud in corners
Lumps and ridges will lead to gapped or tilted baseboard and open joints.

Solution: Scrape out the corners
Mark the top of the baseboard on the wall. Then scrape away any excess mud below the line.

Keep an oscillating multi-tool handy

On every trim job, there's at least one situation where an oscillating multi-tool can save the day. Whether it's trimming the bottom of an installed casing or notching a transition piece, an oscillating tool with a woodcutting blade is the perfect choice. And now that you can buy one for as little as $40, it's a tool every trim carpenter can afford.

Problem: Transitions get in the way
You could notch the base to fit over this transition piece. But it would be easier and look better if you cut the transition instead.

Solution: Notch with an oscillating tool
Mount a fine-tooth blade in the oscillating tool. Then use a scrap of baseboard as a guide to cut the wood transition.

Keep baseboard from tipping

Most drywall is installed with the tapered edge parallel to the floor and with at least 1/2 in. between the drywall and the floor. The combination of the space along the floor and the drywall taper can allow the baseboard to tip in at the bottom. This isn't a big problem along the length of walls, but at inside corners, the tilt can make fitting coped corners difficult. The photo at right shows a simple fix.

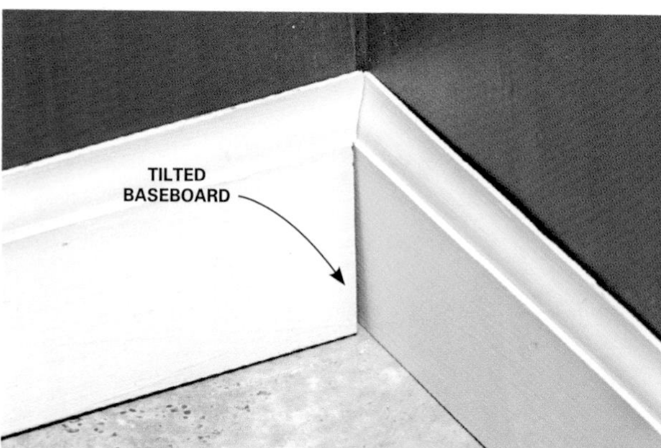

Problem: Tilting base creates a gap
The tapered drywall edge allows the baseboard to tilt—and that means a gap in the corner.

Solution: Spacer blocks prevent tilting
Cut strips of wood to the thickness of the drywall and cut off small pieces to use as spacers at inside corners or wherever they're needed. The spacers prevent the trim from tipping and make fitting inside corner joints much simpler.

Join moldings with biscuits

Strengthening trim joints with biscuits may seem like overkill, but it's a great way to keep miters tight and prevent misalignment when you nail moldings to the wall. This tip is especially useful for larger casings, which are harder to hold in alignment. But you can add biscuits to just about any joint that's wide enough to accommodate them. The photos below show how.

You'll need a biscuit joiner ($80 to $200) and some biscuits. If you're not familiar with this tool, go to familyhandyman.com and search for "biscuit joiner" for tips and operating instructions.

Cut and fit the miters first, then cut the biscuit slots. The photo below right shows how to cut biscuits on a profiled molding. On new doors and windows that are perfectly square, some carpenters cut and assemble the casings with biscuits and nail the assembly to the wall after the glue dries. Or you can use the technique we show here and add the biscuits as you go.

Problem: Joints open when nailed
Perfect-fitting miters can become misaligned as you nail them to the wall.

Solution: Step 1
Cut biscuit slots
Clamp the molding (face down if it has a profile) and cut a slot with the biscuit joiner. Cut a biscuit slot in the same location on the other molding.

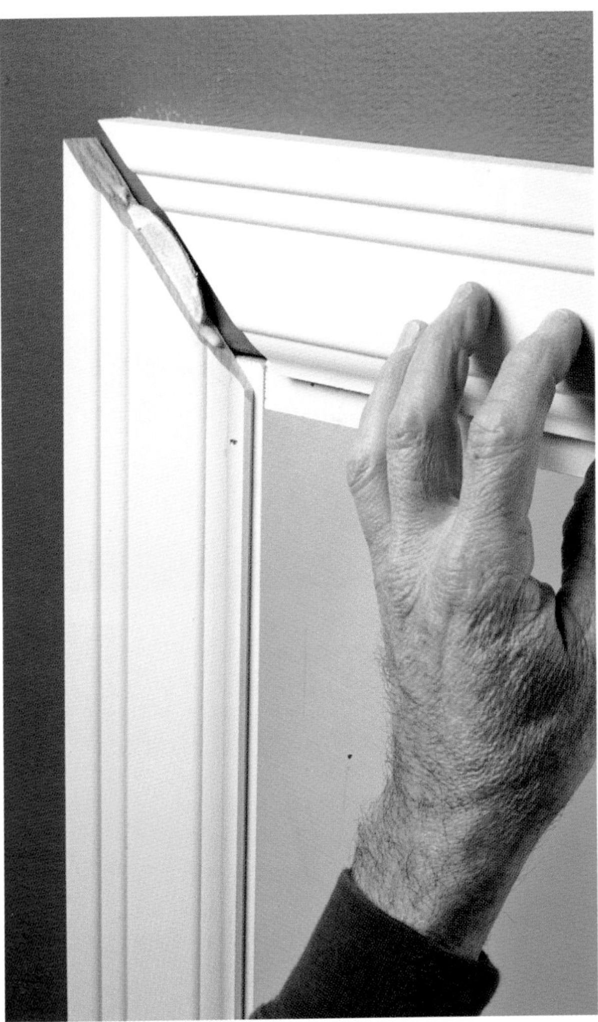

Solution: Step 2
Join moldings with a biscuit
Nail one casing to the jamb and wall. Spread glue on the miter and the biscuit and assemble the miter.

TOP 10 TIPS FOR GLUING WOOD

Get a top-quality glue-up with these easy tips

by **Jeff Gorton, Associate Editor**

Modern wood glue formulas make it easier than ever to create strong, long-lasting and even waterproof joints in wood. But despite the improvements in wood glue, there are still plenty of tips and techniques you can use to speed up the job and improve the quality of the glue connection. Here are 10 of our favorites.

1 Mask glue joints before prefinishing

Finishing the parts of your project before you assemble them can be a great time-saver and allow you to get a better-quality finish. But for a strong glue joint, you have to keep the joints free of finish (glue doesn't stick to varnish or stains very well). The solution is to apply masking tape to the surfaces that will be glued. Then remove it to expose raw wood when you glue up the project. Any good-quality masking tape will work. If you'll be using a water-based finish, you'll get the best results with a "no-bleed" tape such as green Frog Tape and ScotchBlue painter's tape.

2 Apply wood glue with a flux brush

Flux brushes, available in the plumbing department of hardware stores and home centers, are just right for applying and spreading glue. They work especially well for gluing intricate joints like the ones in the coped door rail shown here. You can store a wet brush for a few days in water and then wash and use it over and over again.

3 Cover bar clamps with wax paper

When you use steel bar clamps or pipe clamps, and wood glue comes in contact with the clamp, the moisture in the glue can cause the steel to leave a dark mark on your wood. Lay a sheet of wax paper over the clamps to prevent this "dark spot" problem. It will also catch glue drips that would otherwise get all over your clamps and workbench.

4 Add one board at a time

When you're gluing several boards together, it can be difficult to get all the top surfaces perfectly aligned. Here's a tip that solves the problem. Rather than glue and clamp all the boards at once, add one board at a time. Let the glue joint set up for about 20 to 30 minutes, then release the clamps and add another board. This method will take a little longer. But it makes it a lot easier to keep all of the boards' top surfaces flush, which makes for much easier flattening and sanding of the surface.

5 Attach small pieces with superglue

Of course you reach for a superglue (cyanocacrylate glue, or CA) to fix a broken teacup handle. But did you know that it works on wood, too? In fact, CA glue is really handy for attaching small trim pieces that would be hard to clamp. Just put three or four drops onto the parts and stick them together. We like the gel version of CA glue because it doesn't run off and make a mess.

The right amount of glue

With a little experience, you'll develop a feel for how much glue is just enough. Too little glue creates a "starved joint," which will be weak. Too much glue makes a mess and wastes glue. With practice, you'll know just how much to apply. You should see a continuous line of small glue beads. When this perfect glue joint sets up a little, you'll find it easy to scrape off the jelled excess, and you'll have very little cleanup to do.

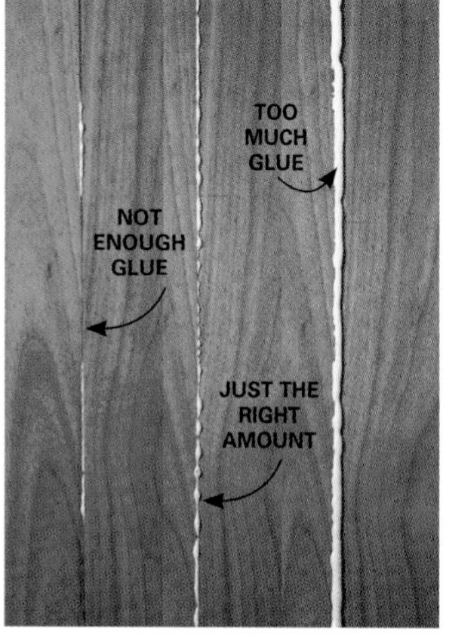

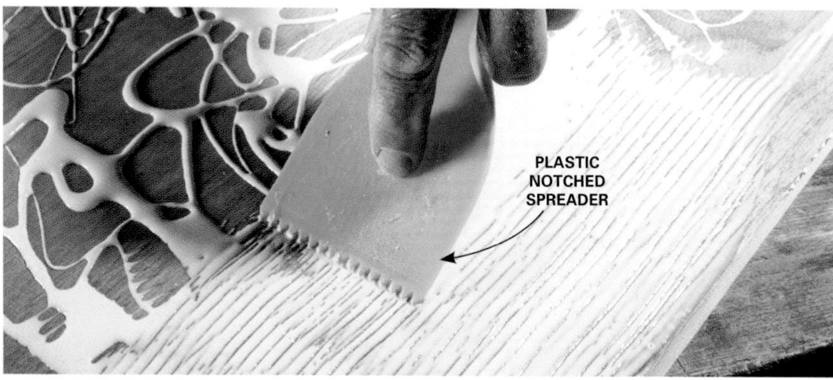

6 Spread glue with a notched trowel

When you're gluing large surfaces, an inexpensive notched plastic trowel works great for spreading the glue. To find one, look in the flooring or tile section of the hardware store or home center. If you have a "pinking" shears in the family sewing basket, you can make our own spreader from an expired credit card.

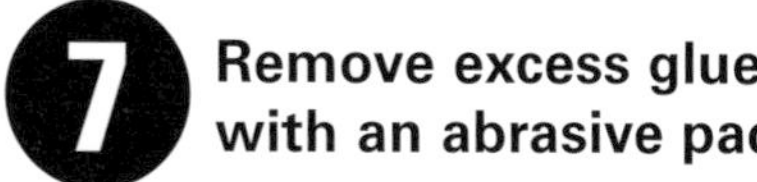

7 Remove excess glue with an abrasive pad

It can be difficult to remove excess glue with a rag. And if you don't get it all off the surface when it's wet, the dried glue can show up as light spots when you finish your project. But a synthetic abrasive pad, dampened with water, works perfectly to remove the glue. Dip the pad in a container of water. Unlike a rag, which is hard to rinse glue from, the pad has a loose synthetic weave that releases glue easily. After rinsing out the pad, shake it to remove most of the water. Then use it to scrub off excess glue. When you're done, dry the surface with a clean rag. Green abrasive pads are found with the cleaning supplies at grocery stores, hardware stores and home centers.

8 Let it jell, then shave it off

Look at any woodworkers' forum and you'll likely find a debate about the best way to remove glue squeeze-out. Some woodworkers insist that you should clean it up immediately with a damp rag. Others let it dry completely, then scrape it off. We think that in most cases the best method is to wait about 30 to 60 minutes—just until the glue turns a darker color and changes to a gel—and then shave it off with a sharp chisel. This will remove almost all of the glue without making a mess. You may still have a little cleanup to do (see Tip 7), but it's a lot less work than cleaning up wet glue or removing hard glue (see Tip 9).

9 Remove hardened glue with a paint scraper

We've all been there. You glue up your project and then quit for the night. The next day you discover the rock-hard glue and realize that you forgot to scrape off the glue squeeze-out. Don't despair. A sharp paint scraper makes fast work of hardened glue. Either a sharp steel scraper or, better yet, a carbide paint scraper will pop off all those glue beads in a heartbeat.

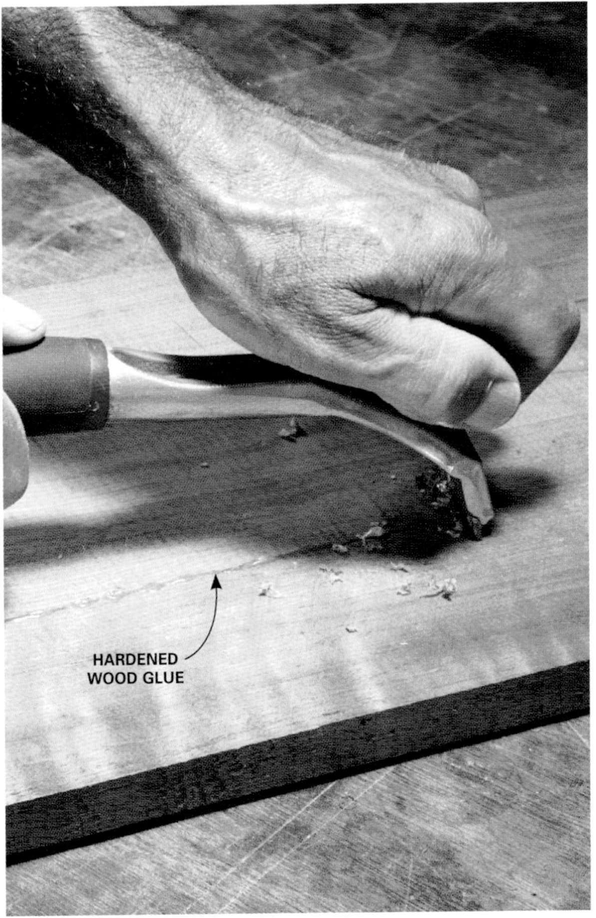

10 Tack—then clamp

Wood glue makes boards slippery, so it can be hard to keep them lined up correctly while you apply clamps. An easy solution is to hold the parts in alignment with a few strategically placed brads before you apply the clamps. For leg glue-ups like we show here, cut your parts extra long and place the brads where they'll get cut off during the finishing process. Otherwise, just place brads where the filled holes won't be too visible.

TIPS FOR **TIGHTER MITERS**

Miter joints don't have to look sloppy!

by **Barry Shoultz, Field Editor**

When they're done well, mitered joints look good. They hide end grain and match face grains nicely. But they're also a pain in the neck, requiring precise cuts and fussy fastening. In pursuit of the perfect miter joint? These tips for tighter miters cover common situations you'll undoubtedly encounter in your workshop.

Use scrap wood guides for a perfect fit

It's dang near impossible to get the length and position of a mitered part right unless you can butt it up against the adjoining miters. To provide a guide, tape or clamp mitered scraps in place. Remove the scraps as soon as you glue the part in place—otherwise, stray glue might make those temporary guides permanent.

Align with biscuits

It's not easy to align and clamp miters, especially when they're lubricated with a coat of slippery glue. That's why woodworkers often use biscuits on miter joints even where extra strength isn't needed. Cutting biscuit slots is a minor job that provides major help at glue-up time.

Match wood grain

Whether you're banding a tabletop or making a picture frame, make sure the wood color and the grain pattern match at the miters. Selecting matching wood at the lumberyard takes only a few extra seconds and gives you much better-looking miters.

Miter, assemble then rout

Shaped moldings can be tough to miter, align and clamp. So make life easier by starting with plain square stock. Then, after assembly, grab your router and shape the edges. The risk with this method is that you'll gouge or splinter parts that are already in place. The best way to avoid disaster is to make a series of shallow passes instead of one full-depth cut.

Square up with corner clamps

With some miter-clamping methods, you need to grab a square and make sure the corner is exactly 90 degrees. Not so with corner clamps; they automatically hold parts perfectly square. They're available at home centers or online for $10 to $50 apiece.

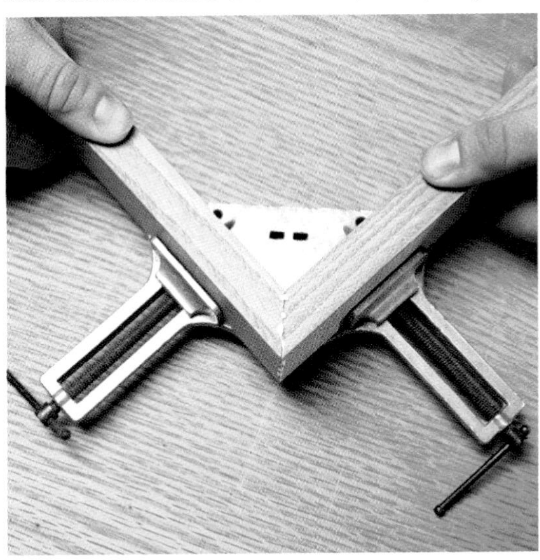

Slow down your glue

It's hard enough to align and clamp miters without rushing to get it done before the glue begins to set (in five to 10 minutes, and even faster in warm, dry conditions). That's why there are slow-setting wood glues, which give you an extra 10 minutes or so.

If you can't find a slow version at your favorite home center, make your own. If you add one part water to 20 parts wood glue, you'll gain about five minutes of working time. The water will also weaken the bond very slightly. So if strength is critical, order slow-setting glue online. Titebond Extend is one common brand.

Rehearse before you glue

A dry run—complete assembly with clamps but without glue—is the best way to ensure a smooth, successful glue-up, whether you're assembling miters or anything else.

Clamp with your hands

When you're dealing with small or other hard-to-clamp parts, your hands make the best clamps. Simply rub the glued surfaces together and hold them tightly on a flat surface for about a minute. Let go and allow the joint to set for 30 minutes before handling it.

Micro-adjust with paper shims

If you've ever tried to adjust the angle of your miter saw by one-tenth of a degree, you already know how hard micro-adjustments are. Here's an easier way: Slap a few sticky notes on the fence, make test cuts and add or remove sheets until you get exactly the angle you want.

Feel the difference

When you're building a box or frame, the opposite sides have to be exactly the same length. To make sure they are, do the touch test: Set the parts side by side and run your finger over the mitered ends. You may not be able to see a slight length difference, but you'll feel it.

Close ugly gaps

You can close a miter gap by rubbing it with a screwdriver shank or any hard, smooth tool. We used the end of a utility knife. That crushes the wood fibers inward to make the gap disappear. Even professional woodworkers sometimes resort to this crude trick.

Make your own corner clamps

This is an old favorite among woodworkers: Clamp on notched blocks, then add a bar clamp or two to squeeze the joint. This allows you to put a lot of pressure on the joint without buying any special clamps. If you're assembling a four-sided project such as a picture frame, join two corners first. Then, after the glue has set, join the two halves of the frame.

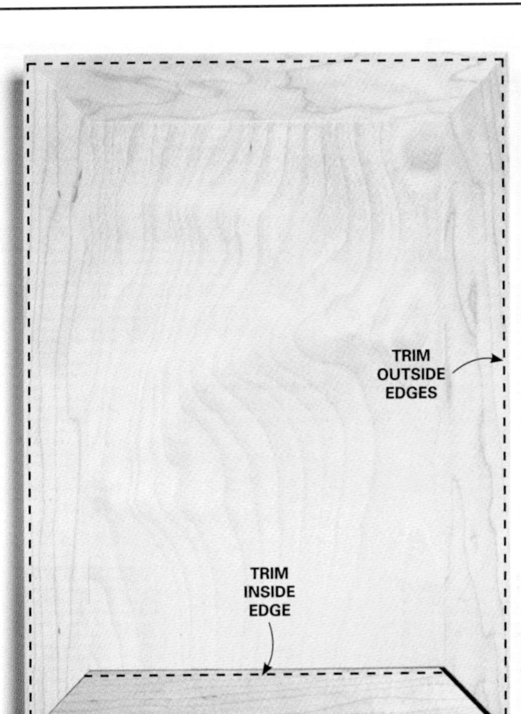

'Lengthen' a board

Ever cut that last part just a bit too short? There's a solution for that: First, trim off the inside edge of the too-short part. By cutting off the short edge, you effectively make the mitered part longer. Then trim the same amount off the outer edges of the other three sides. Your edging will be a little thinner than you had planned, but nobody will notice.

Bond joints instantly

Trim carpenters have used this system for years: Apply a few dabs of cyanoacrylate adhesive (aka "superglue") to one surface and apply activator (or "accelerator") to the other. Immediately press the parts together and they'll bond in seconds. No waiting, no complicated clamping setup. Activator is sometimes sold separately ($5 and up), sometimes with the glue. Look for it at home centers or shop online; rockler.com carries a good selection of glues and activators.

Upcycled miter saw stand

This year we got a new gas grill. I hated the idea of throwing away our old one. One day while I was using my miter saw on the ground, it occurred to me that my old grill could provide the perfect saw base. I removed the grill housing from the frame and built center framework that allowed the saw to sit flush with the wings of the grill. I can remove my saw and store it below, giving me a mobile workbench as well.

Troy Heller

READER PHOTOS

WOODWORKING & WORKSHOP PROJECTS & TIPS

TABLE SAW HELPERS

Make your saw do more—and do it better

by ***The Family Handyman* Editors**

The Family Handyman has been dishing out table saw wisdom for more than 50 years. The saws themselves have improved dramatically over that time, but even the best modern saw can benefit from some old-fashioned ingenuity. So we selected some of our favorite tips from the past few decades to help you get more from your saw, whether it's an antique or the latest model.

Cut skinny strips safely

Cutting thin strips can be dangerous. There's no space between the blade and the fence for a push stick, and on some table saws you have to remove the blade guard. Five minutes and a 6-in.-wide scrap of plywood or particleboard are all you need to cut safely and quickly. Just screw a wooden "heel" to the scrap and you've got a sliding guide that lets you leave the guard in place and keeps your fingers safe. Add a handle to make it easier to pull the guide backward after each cut.

Use your blade guard!

To show some of these tricks more clearly, we removed the blade guard. For others, the guard must be removed. Use your guard whenever you can—and keep your fingers attached to your hands.

Upstanding support

Upright cuts—for lap joints, tenons or rabbets—aren't a good job for a table saw. That is, unless you build a simple box to guide and support the workpiece. Precise cuts depend on a precise box, so take the time to build it square and sturdy. And as always, make your adjustments and mistakes using scraps before cutting precious wood.

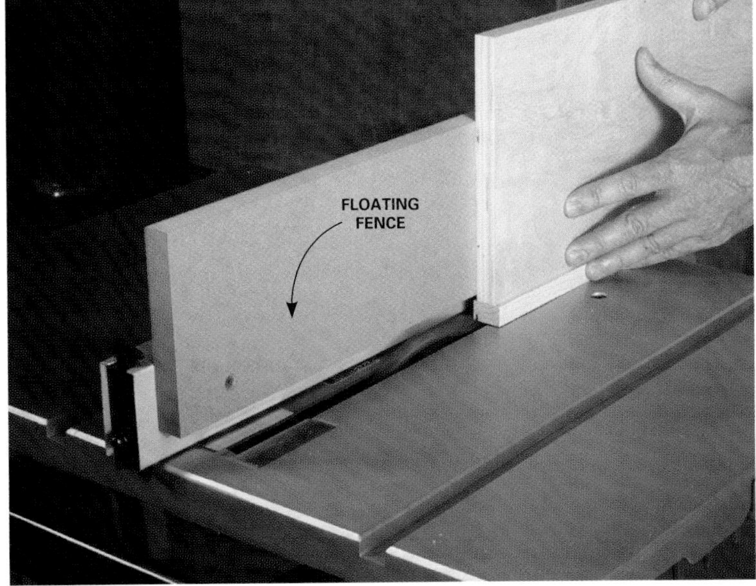

Fast, flawless plywood edging

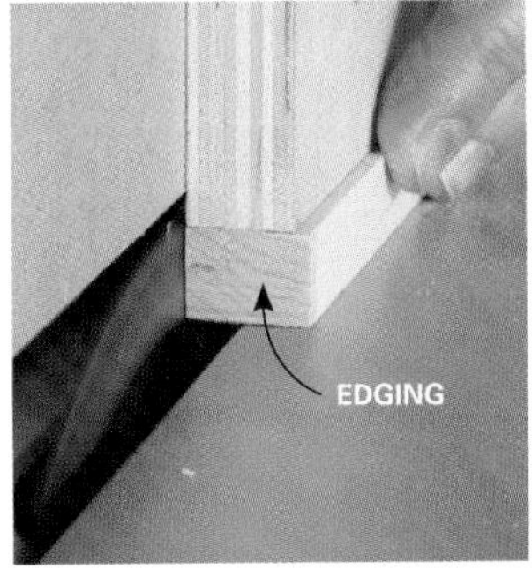

If you've ever covered plywood edges with solid wood, you know how hard it is to position the edging flush with the plywood surface. Next time, try this: Start with edging that's about 1/8 in. wider than the thickness of the plywood. That way, you can attach the edging fast, without worrying about a flush fit. To trim off the excess edging, clamp or screw a tall "floating fence" to your table saw fence. Then position the floating fence so it's flush with the outer edge of the blade. Finding the perfect position requires a couple of test runs. But when you get it right, you'll be able to trim the edging in seconds. And if you use a good-quality smooth-cutting blade, you can remove the saw marks with only light sanding.

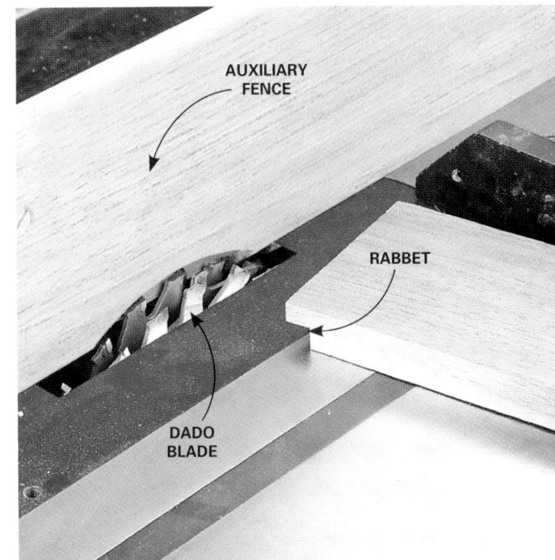

Cut rabbets with a dado blade

A dado blade in a table saw is the fastest way to cut notches, or "rabbets," along the edge of a board. And here's a way to make the process even faster: Set the blade to cut slightly wider than the rabbet width. Then clamp or screw an auxiliary fence to the saw's fence. Now—instead of fussing with dado adjustments—you can precisely adjust the width of the rabbet by moving the fence and allowing the dado blade to cut into the auxiliary fence.

Instant stand and outfeed

With a few minutes, a couple of 2x4s, a slab of plywood and a pair of sawhorses, you can build a stand for a benchtop saw, plus a long outfeed table. On the version shown here, the 2x4s are notched so that the saw table is flush with the plywood. Screw the plywood to the 2x4s and the 2x4s to the horses. Also screw or clamp the saw to the 2x4s.

Straighten a crooked board

To cut a straight edge on any board, all you have to do is mount the crooked board to a larger carriage board and run the whole assembly across your table saw. You can fasten the crooked board with screws or—if you don't want to put screw holes in the board—hold it firmly in place with 4-in.-long screwed-down cleats at both ends. Set your saw's fence to match the width of the carriage board. That way, you can tell exactly where the blade will cut the crooked board.

Avoid laminate disaster

An auxiliary fence mounted tightly against the table is essential when cutting plastic laminate (or any other thin material) on a table saw. Without it, skinny stuff can slip under the fence and cause a crooked cut, major chipping, kickback and injury, and ruin an expensive sheet of laminate.

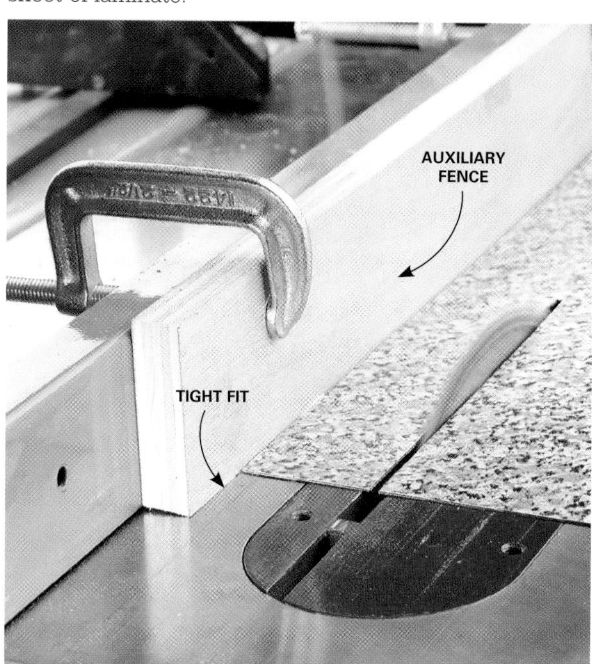

Precision crosscuts

For easy and accurate crosscuts, mount a tall backer board to your miter gauge. Run the board across the blade and you've got a kerf that shows you exactly where the blade will cut. No more guesswork and no more squinting to align the cutting line with the blade.

Inexpensive accuracy

Think of the markings on your miter gauge as approximate, not exact. For real accuracy, drop by a woodworking store or an art supply store. For a few bucks, you can get a setup tool that's as accurate as the most expensive square. Use it to set your miter gauge to 45 or 90 degrees. This works with your miter saw and other tools too.

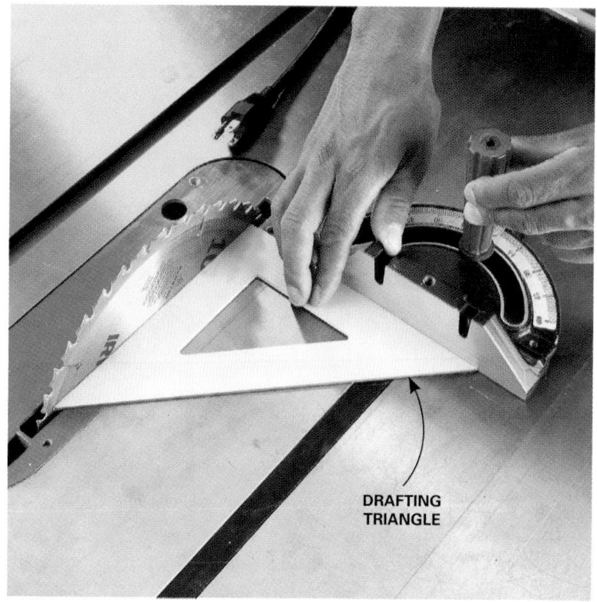

KEN'S FAVORITE **SHOP TIPS**

by **Ken Collier, Editor in Chief**

I was a cabinetmaker when I started working for *The Family Handyman*. That was almost 30 years ago, so I've seen a lot of shop tips come and go. Some of them I've used once or twice and then forgotten. Others I've used so often that they've become essential parts of the way I work in the shop. Here are a few of my favorites.

MEET AN EXPERT

Ken Collier is Editor in Chief of *The Family Handyman* and a longtime woodworker.

Finishing stand-offs

These simple little contraptions are immensely useful for staining and finishing. Make them from scrap, but be careful to countersink all the screws to the same depth so their points all protrude the same length. For many projects, you can stain or finish both sides at once. The little mark left by the screw tip won't be detectable.

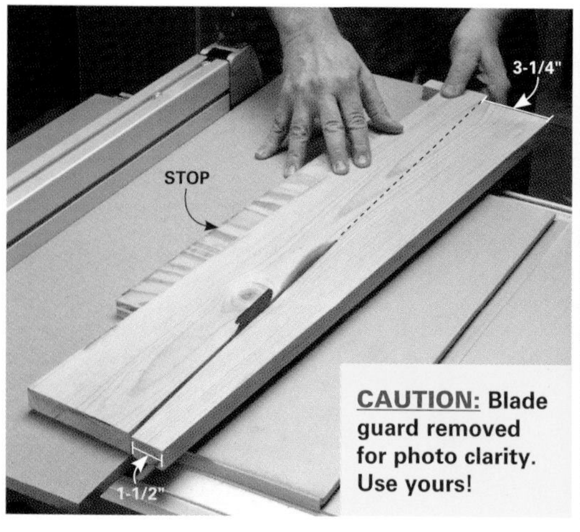

Quick table legs

If you need to build a quick table, here's a great way to make the legs. I've used this design to make tables for our cabin, and utility tables for the shop and yard. Each leg is made from a 1x6, ripped to make two tapered pieces. Glue and nail (or screw) the two pieces together, sand as much as you feel is necessary, and you're done. The taper jig is quick to make, but it works only for this particular taper.

Fail-safe drill stop

I used to use a metal drill stop (you know the kind—a little ring that goes over the bit and tightens with a setscrew). Then one time while I was drilling dozens of shelf support holes, the setscrew slipped and I drilled a hole right through the side of an expensive cabinet! Now I use a wooden stop instead. It just takes a minute to make out of scrap, and you can fine-tune the depth of the hole by readjusting the bit in the chuck of the drill. Your bit will never, ever drill too deep.

Clamp holders

Anything that gives you more control when gluing is a good thing. These simple-to-build clamp bars, made of 2x4s, will keep clamps from tipping, and can be set up on a couple of sawhorses to free up space on your bench. Screw the two 2x4s together so you can cut the notches on both at the same time.

Overhead rag storage

My shop is in my basement, so I end up storing all sorts of things in the ceiling. One of the handiest is a box of paper shop towels. A box of 200 towels from Scott costs about $10 and fits neatly between the floor joists above my workbench. Just reach up and pull one down to wipe up errant glue or stain.

Plastic laminate labels

I use scraps of plastic laminate for drawer labels. Round the corners, smooth the edges and attach them with hot-melt glue. You can write on the labels with pencil or marker, and erase them with a little solvent.

Shop-made parts boxes

Have you priced those plastic parts bins? Too expensive for me! So years ago I started making my own out of scrap. The trick is to keep them modular. I make the front, back and bottom from 3/4- or 1/2-in. material, and the sides from 1/4-in. plywood. Nailed and glued together, they're plenty tough. Mine are 12 in. front to back (to fit in old kitchen upper cabinets), 3 in. tall, and either 3-1/2 in. or 7 in. wide. Save up some scrap and you can make a couple dozen in an hour or so.

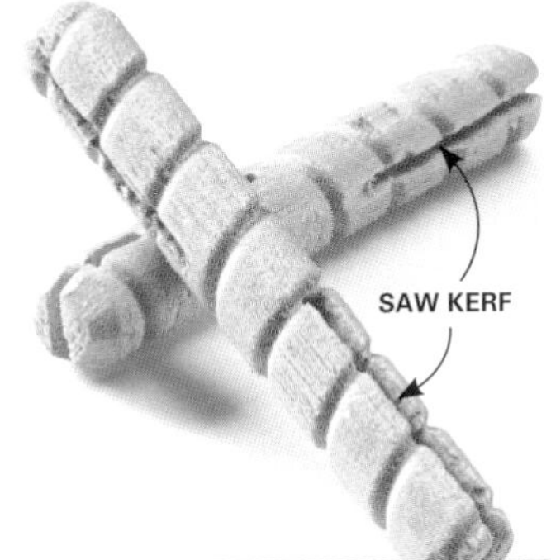

Test-fitting dowel joints

When you make dowel joints , it can be difficult to test the fit of the joint, because the dowels often fit so tight the joint is hard to disassemble. Here's what to do: Simply cut a couple of saw kerfs in the test dowels, and they'll be easy to remove.

The slop can

I use polyurethane varnish a lot, so cleaning out brushes in mineral spirits is a regular chore. I use tin cans to rinse the brushes, and pour the used solvent into a "slop" can. The varnish solids settle to the bottom and congeal, leaving pretty clean solvent at the top. That recycled mineral spirits gets used for the first couple rinses of a brush, followed by one final rinse of fresh solvent. Eventually the slop can fills up with congealed goop, at which point I use a can opener to remove the entire top. When the goop hardens, into the trash it goes.

Bright lights for final inspection

I learned the hard way that the room where cabinets end up is usually much brighter than a workshop, making flaws much easier to see. So when I'm ready for finishing, I go over the whole piece with a trouble light flat against the surface, looking for flaws. A light coat of mineral spirits helps reveal any glue stains.

Cabinetmaker's triangle

This marking system is the quickest way to avoid mixing up parts during assembly. It's easy, once you get the hang of it, and goes back to the old days of hand woodworking. I use it all the time. It's particularly useful for indicating the layout of door parts or the order of boards that are being edge-glued. The photos tell it all.

1 Fold in half

2 Fold in half again

3 Tear halfway along crease

4 Fold one half inside the other

5 Sand

Fold sandpaper into a pad

For sanding edges and curves by hand, this sandpaper trick can't be beat. Take a quarter sheet of sandpaper and fold it as shown above. It makes a firm but flexible pad, and the inner surfaces don't wear against each other. When the two outer surfaces are used up, simply refold to expose the two inner surfaces. Slick, huh?

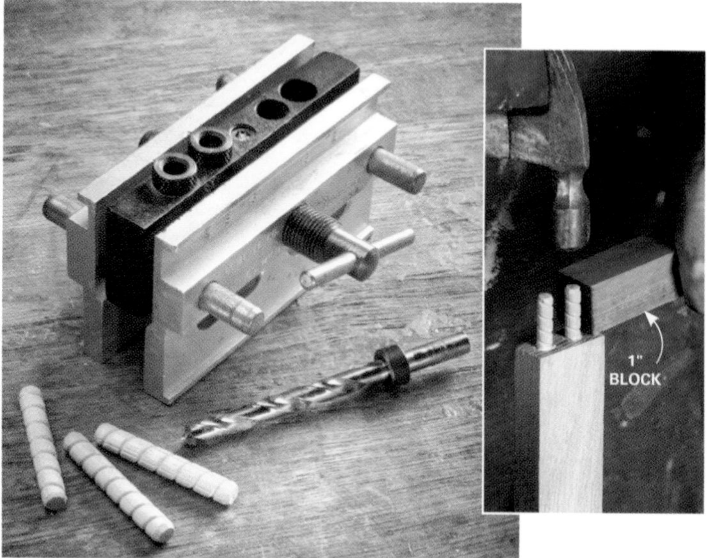

Dowel joints are DIY-friendly

I'm a fan of old-fashioned dowel joints, especially if you use a self-centering dowel jig like this classic model from Dowl-it (typically $65 to $75), which does two holes at a time. Dowel joints are especially handy for making a quick pair of doors, windows, and mirror frames and many other little projects. Use dowels made for joints, a stop on your drill bit to control depth, and a 1-in.-thick block to help you pound in the dowels to a consistent depth. I spread glue inside the hole, not on the dowel itself.

Multipurpose T-bars

These are wonderfully simple versatile shop aids. Most of the time I use them to raise a project off the bench for clamping, but sometimes I'll clamp or even screw parts to them to keep things flat. I made mine from 5-in.-wide strips, with a double thickness on the upright. A little masking tape on the top edge makes them easy on finished surfaces and keeps glue from sticking.

Marking gauge with pencil

This is one of my favorite and most-used tools: a marking gauge (starting at about $15) with a hole drilled in it to accept a pencil. I use it when I want to align screws, drawer pulls or other hardware that doesn't require a high level of precision. It's an exceptionally useful tool.

Right-angle clamping jig

Here's a little helper that you can make in about two minutes. It's like a third hand for holding cabinet parts together for assembly, or for clamping miter joints.

Hand countersink

One of my handiest tools is this countersink with a handle. It's made from a bit designed for an old-fashioned hand drill, but you could make a similar one from a power-drill countersink. Besides making a quick countersink, this tool will quickly remove splinters from the edges of a hole. And when I make dowel joints, I use it to chamfer the edges of the dowel holes so excess glue doesn't squirt out.

T-SQUARE

ALIGN SLOT WITH YOUR CUTTING LINE

T-square router fence

If you need to cut dadoes or grooves across the sides of a cabinet, this tool is the way to go. Build the T-square for one particular router and one particular bit, and test it on a scrap. Once the "head" of the T-square has been cut, you can use that cut to perfectly position the rest of the cuts.

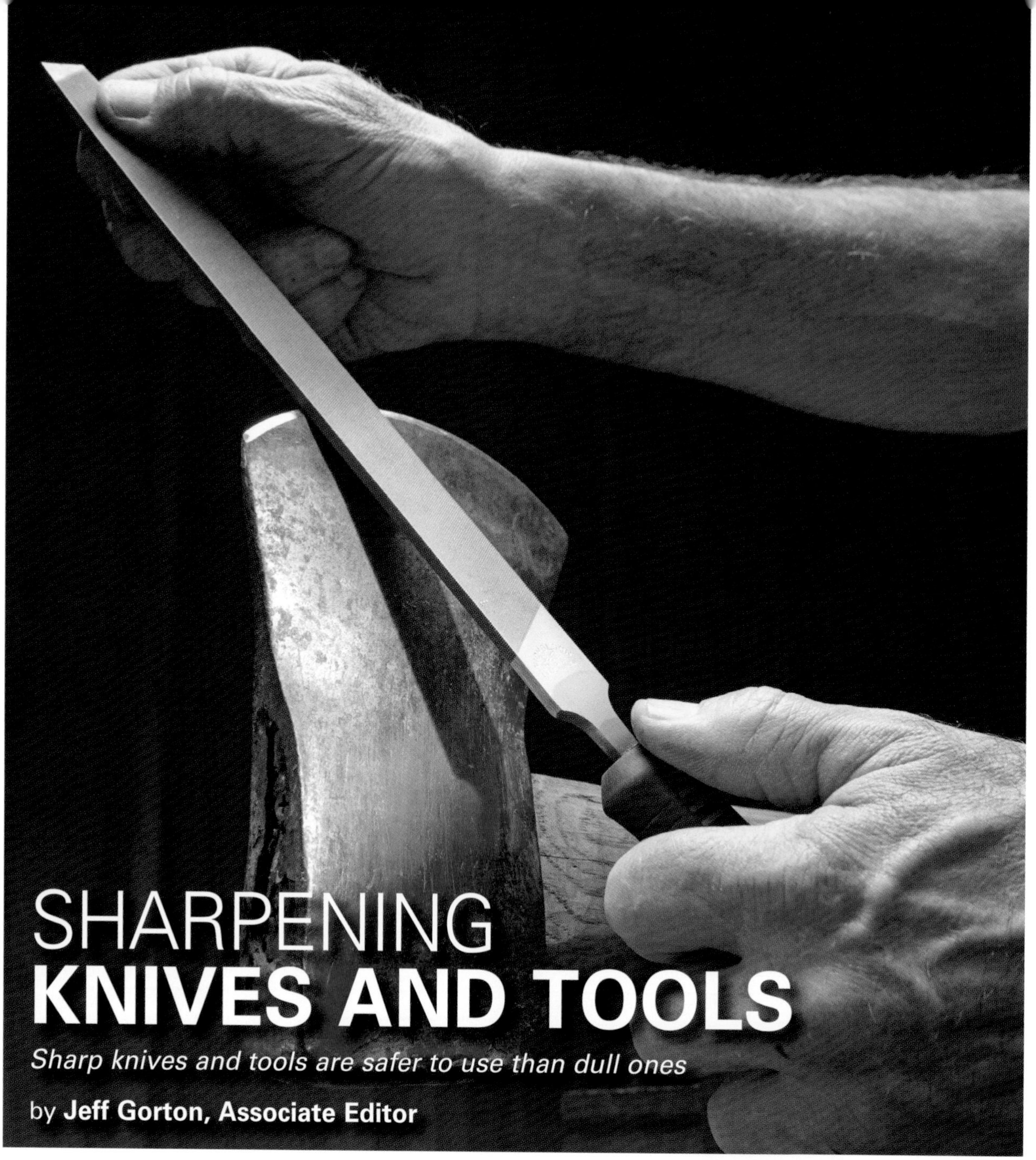

SHARPENING KNIVES AND TOOLS

Sharp knives and tools are safer to use than dull ones

by **Jeff Gorton, Associate Editor**

If sharpening your dull kitchen knives or blunt chisels sounds like drudgery, we can help. We'll show you some cool sharpening tips and tools that'll motivate you to tune up the edges on all the dull tools and knives in your shop and kitchen.

We don't have space here to teach every sharpening step, but we've collected tips to help you get started on the most common sharpening tasks. For more detailed sharpening information, go to familyhandyman.com and search for the topic you're interested in.

It's easy to keep your spade bits sharp

Most of us grab a spade bit instead of our expensive Forstner bits when it's rough material that needs drilling. But this abuse takes a toll. Luckily, a spade bit doesn't have to be sharpened with precision to work better. A few strokes along the bottom with a file and you're back in business.

Clamp the bit in a vise and file the cutting edges, making sure to maintain the existing angle. A tapered triangular file works well for many sizes of spade bit.

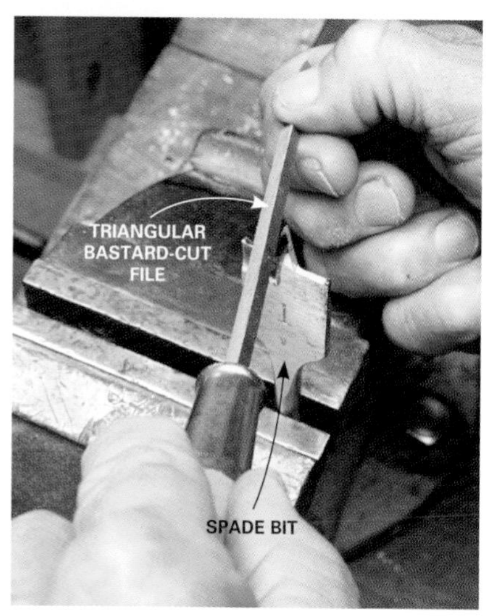

Flatten the back of chisels and plane blades

It's impossible to get a sharp edge on a chisel or a plane if the back of the blade isn't flat. If you're using the glass and sandpaper method of sharpening ("Foolproof chisel and plane sharpening," p. 138), press the back side of the blade against the sandpaper and move the blade back and forth, being careful to hold it perfectly flat. Sand the back of each blade until it's uniformly shiny along the cutting edge. Do this with each grit as you move through the progression from coarse to fine. Use the same technique with natural or diamond sharpening stones.

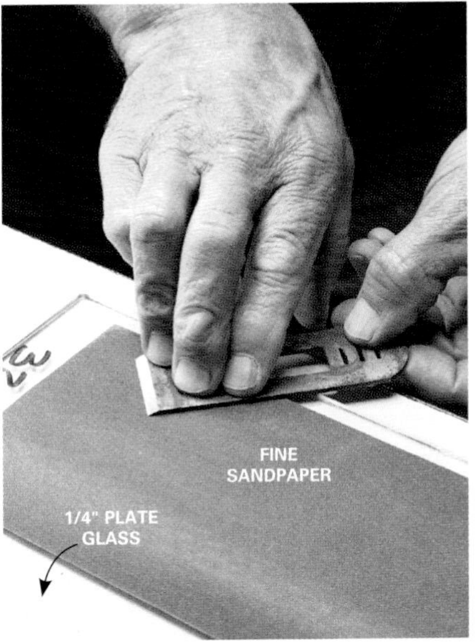

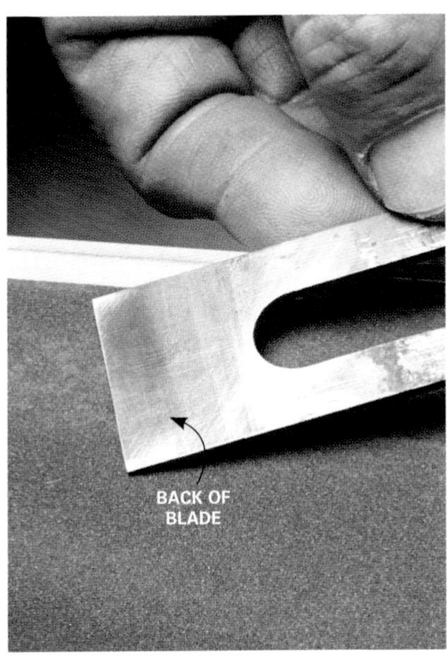

Keep a handheld sharpener in your kitchen drawer

Most of the time you don't need a power tool or an expensive knife-sharpening system to keep a workable edge on your kitchen knives. Regular use of a handheld sharpener will be fine. The Wusthof sharpener we're using costs about $35 and works great. Other brands may work equally well, but we haven't tried them. The sharpener has carbide steel rods to shape the blade, and diamond rods to finish the edge. Follow the instructions to quickly sharpen kitchen knives that have standard beveled edges. You'll have to use another sharpening tool if your knives have unusual or asymmetrical angles.

Sharpen serrated bread knives with a diamond sharpening steel

The only hard part of this tip is finding the right size diamond steel. The curve of the steel has to fit the scallops on your serrated knife. Take your knife to a cookware store and find a diamond-coated steel (from $30) that matches the scallop size on your knife. If you're shopping online, you can find the diameter you need by holding drill bits against the scallops. Then use this dimension to order the right diameter sharpener. Another option is to buy a tapered, pocket-size diamond steel (the one shown is $15) that accommodates a variety of different scallop sizes.

You'll notice that one side of the blade is flat and the other tapered. Sharpen only the tapered side. Starting at one end, sharpen each scallop with two or three strokes, matching the original angle. When you're done, run the knife through corrugated cardboard to remove metal filings.

Sharpen hatchets and axes with a file

You don't need a power tool to sharpen hatchets or axes, just a sharp mill bastard file with a handle (starting at about $8). Buy a good-quality American-made file brand like Nicholson. And pick up a file brush while you're at it. You use the file brush to clean the metal filings from the file's teeth to keep it cutting well.

Clamp your hatchet to your bench or in a vise. Then file the edges, following the original angle. The file cuts only on the push stroke, so don't go back and forth with a sawing motion. Start your stroke on one end of the blade and push the file up and across, applying a little pressure. Make three or four passes on one side, then do the same on the other side. Keep the number of passes equal for both sides. File until the edge is uniformly sharp. Look directly at the sharp edge with a strong overhead light. Dull spots will show up as bright reflections.

File hatchets or axes used for cutting or felling wood at about a 25- to 30-degree angle on each side. Splitting axes work better with a blunter angle, so for them you should increase the angle to about 35 to 40 degrees. Filing will get your hatchet or ax blade back in shape, but if you want it really sharp, you'll have to follow up with a stone or diamond hone.

Don't throw away those old drill bits

If you've ever tried to sharpen a drill bit on a grinder, you know what a hit-and-miss proposition it is. It's hard to maintain the correct angle, keep the chisel point centered and avoid burning the bit.

Drill Doctor offers several versions of a special tool that makes drill-bit sharpening almost foolproof. The least expensive tool (about $50) is perfect for the home shop. You simply follow the instructions for chucking the drill bit into the tool and rotate it on the grinding wheel to sharpen. Go to drilldoctor.com to compare features of the different models and to get tons of great information on sharpening drill bits.

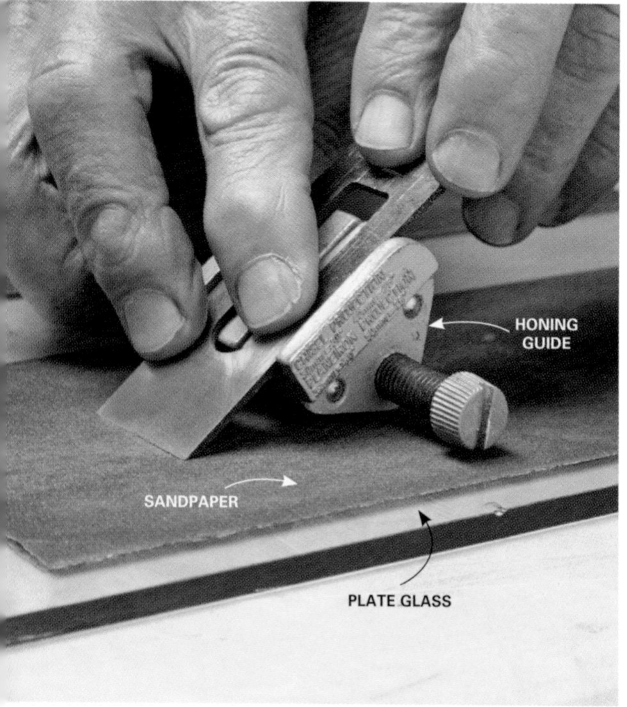

Foolproof chisel and plane sharpening

There's nothing like working with a razor-sharp plane or chisel, and nothing more frustrating than trying to use dull ones. Arkansas or Japanese stones are the traditional tool, but they're expensive to buy and take practice and skill to use. But there's an easy and inexpensive way to get great results without stones or much practice. The key to success is the honing guide, which ensures a consistent bevel. The guide we're using (about $15 at woodworking stores) works for both chisel and plane blades. You'll also need a 12-in. square of 1/4-in. plate glass to provide a perfectly flat honing surface. You can order one at any hardware store, but be sure to have the sharp edges sanded smooth. You'll glue sandpaper to the glass and use it like a sharpening stone.

Use spray adhesive to attach half sheets of silicone carbide sandpaper to the glass. Cover one side with 220- and 320-grit paper and the other with 400- and 600-grit. The sharpening angle is determined by how far you extend the blade before clamping it to the guide. Dimensions on the side of the guide show where to set chisels and planes to maintain 25- and 30-degree angles.

Clamp the blade in the guide and roll it back and forth on the coarsest paper until the edge is uniformly shiny. It should take only 15 or 20 seconds. Repeat this process for each progressively finer grit.

A 1-in. belt sander is a versatile sharpening tool

Most carpenters know that a belt sander is a good ad hoc tool for getting a reasonably acceptable edge on a dull chisel. And knife-makers and professional sharpeners often use special belt grinders to shape and sharpen blades. You can get many of the benefits of a professional belt grinder for a fraction of the cost with a 1 x 30-in. benchtop belt sander. The one we're using is from Grizzly Industrial (about $95). Buy 180- and 240-grit belts and you'll be set for serious knife sharpening. Plus, you can use the belt sander to grind other tools like axes and chisels, and to sand small woodworking projects.

For really dull knives, start with a 180-grit belt and finish with a 240-grit belt. Practice on an inexpensive knife until you get the feel of holding the knife at the correct angle as you move it across the belt. Try to maintain the angle that's on your knife. This is usually about 20 degrees. For a razor-sharp edge, buy a leather belt ($18 to $20) along with honing compound and mount it on your sander for the final sharpening step.

Touch up a knife with a honing steel

You've probably seen chefs on cooking shows brandishing a knife and a steel like a samurai swordsman and thought it was just for pros. But a honing steel isn't hard to use and is perfect for restoring a sharp cutting edge to your knives. You can't fully restore a dull blade with a steel, but you'll be surprised how quickly you can take a slightly dulled edge to almost razor-sharpness with just a few strokes.

The safest method for using a steel is to rest the tip on a surface that's not too slippery, like a wooden cutting board. Then pull the knife down and across, alternating sides. Keep the knife at about a 25-degree angle so you're just tuning up the edge. The steel doesn't actually sharpen. It simply straightens out the wavy edge so the knife slices through material better. Eventually you'll have to resharpen the knife. But for between-sharpening tune-ups, you can't beat a steel. You can buy a steel for $8 to $40 wherever good knives are sold.

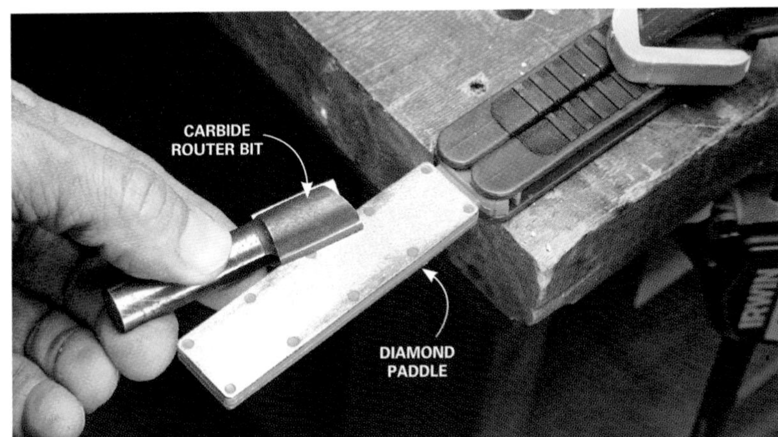

Tune up carbide router bits with a diamond paddle

Chipped or severely dulled carbide router bits require professional sharpening, but you can restore a slightly dulled edge with a diamond paddle. The one we're using is available online and at sporting goods and woodworking stores for about $20.

To avoid changing the cutting profile of the bit, sharpen the back of the cutters only. A handy method is to clamp the diamond paddle to your workbench and move the bit back and forth over the diamond-impregnated surface. Start with the coarser-grit side of the paddle. Then switch to the fine side. The sharpened carbide should have a consistent shiny band along the cutting edge.

DRIVING SCREWS

10 tips to help you avoid the most common pitfalls

by **Jeff Gorton, Associate Editor**

For such a simple task, it's surprising how many things can go wrong when you drive screws. Stripped screw heads, split board ends and broken screws are just a few common problems. We'll show you how you can avoid all the frustration just by using the right screws and a few special tools.

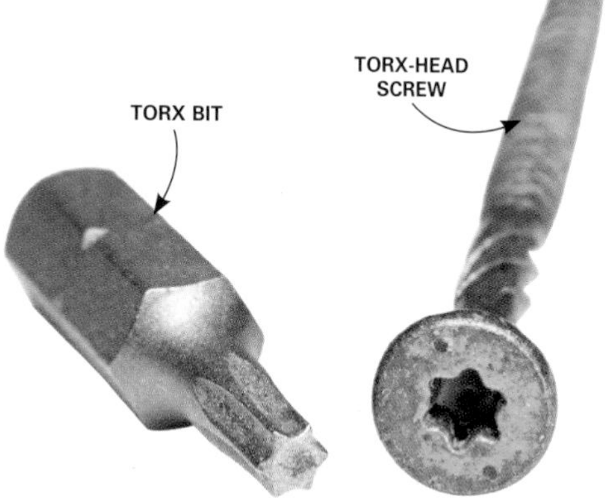

Look for Torx-head screws

Torx-head screws have been common on automobiles for a long time, but now they're available for general construction use too. Star-shaped Torx bits fit tightly into the star-shaped recess in the head of the screw, providing a firm grip that rarely slips out or strips the screw head. It's easier to drive these screws because you don't have to press down as hard to maintain good bit contact. Plus, most Torx-head screws are premium-quality fasteners available with other features like self-drilling points, self-setting heads and corrosion-resistant coatings.

Torx-head screws require star-shaped bits that are labeled with a "T" followed by a number. Some screw packages include a driver bit, but if yours doesn't, check the package to see what size is required. If there's a downside to Torx-head screws, it's the price. You wouldn't want to use them to hang drywall.

Trim-head screws aren't just for trim

Trim-head screws are slender screws with very small heads. Originally they were designed to attach wood trim to walls built with steel studs. But now you can go to the fasteners department in any home center or full-service hardware store and find trim-head screws in several colors, long lengths, corrosion-resistant finishes or stainless steel, which make them perfect replacements for nails in many situations. When sunk slightly below the surface, the heads on these screws are small enough to be covered easily with wood filler or color putty.

Here we're using trim-head screws to connect a fence rail to a post. But you can also use them in place of galvanized casing nails to install exterior doors and windows, or to attach exterior trim. Trim-head screws have several advantages over nails. They hold better and are easier to install in tight areas. Plus, if you're not an experienced carpenter, they allow you to install trim without worrying about denting it with an errant hammer blow. Keep a supply of trim-head screws of various lengths on hand and you'll be surprised how often you reach for them rather than nails.

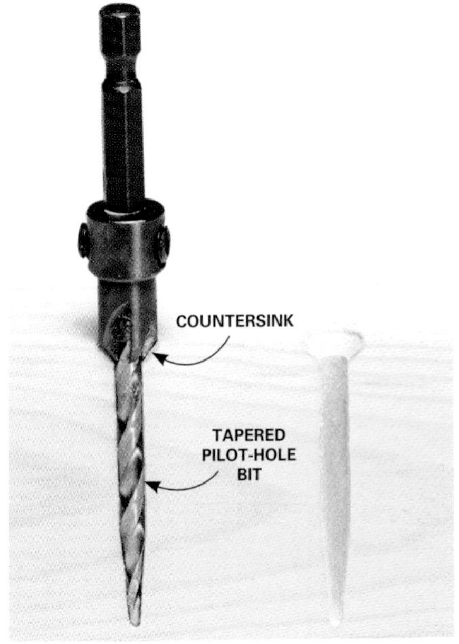

Buy a set of countersink bits

Drilling a pilot hole for the screw and then creating a recess, or countersink, for the screw head is standard practice on cabinets and furniture projects. The pilot hole bit creates a hole that reduces friction to make screw driving easier, and the countersink allows you to set the screw head flush with or below the surface. With a set of countersink bits like these, you can complete both operations in one step. Even though they cost a little more, we prefer the combination pilot/countersink bits with the tapered drill bit. Tapered countersink bits cost start at about $10 each, or you can buy a set of the three most common sizes for under $25.

Get a cordless impact driver

Nothing beats impact drivers for driving screws easily. Impact drivers ($60 to $150 for the cordless version) combine hammer-like blows with rotation to apply plenty of torque to the screw head. The hammer action means you don't have to press down hard to keep the bit in contact with the screw. This allows you to drive screws one-handed in spots that would be hard to reach otherwise. But beyond this advantage, the extra torque makes it simpler to drive any screw, especially long ones.

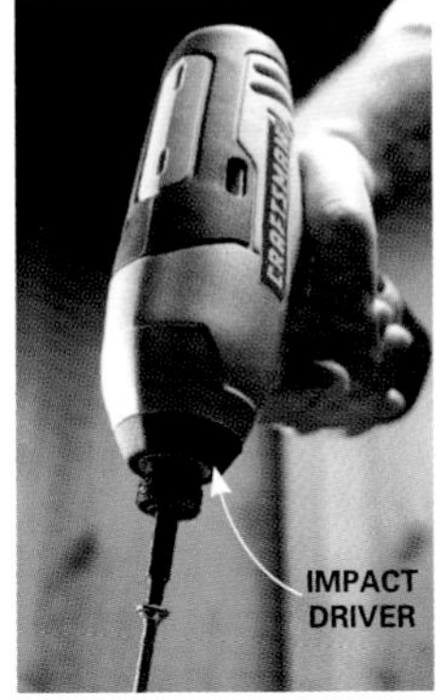

Tack first, then drive screws

It can be frustrating and time consuming to try to hold parts in place while you drill pilot holes and drive screws. Here's a trick that solves the problem and speeds up assembly too. Tack the parts together first with a brad or finish nail gun. That enables you to align the parts with one hand while you tack with the other. Once everything is held in the right position, it's simple to drill the pilot/countersink holes and drive the screws.

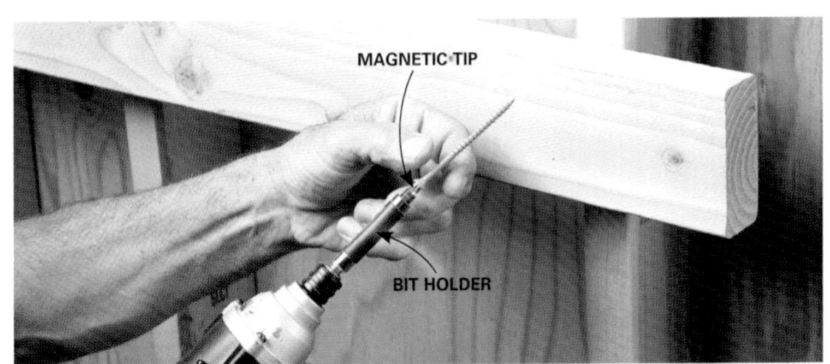

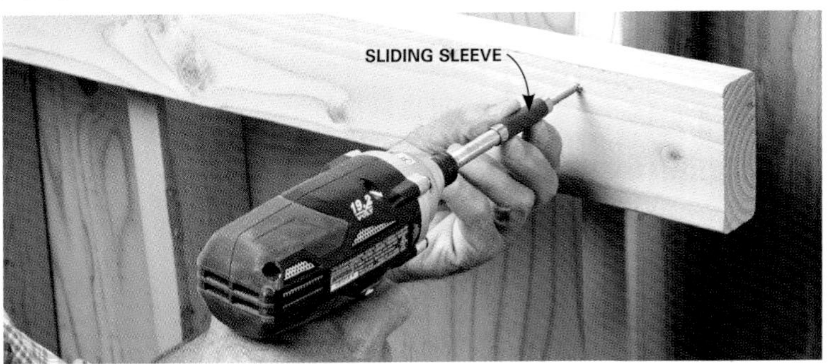

Use a magnetic bit-tip holder

If you're new to driving screws with a drill, you may not know the many benefits of using a magnetic bit holder. First, and most obvious, is that it holds any driver bit with a standard 1/4-in. hex-shape base, making it super quick and easy to change bits. But there are other advantages too. The bit holder extends the length of the bit, making it much easier to get into tight spots. The magnet in the bit holder magnetizes the tip, allowing you to hold ferrous-metal screws in place on the end of the bit for easier driving (top photo). And if you buy a bit holder with a sleeve, like the one shown here, you can use it to hold long screws upright as you drive them in (bottom photo). Look for a magnetic bit holder that's at least 3 in. long and includes the sleeve (about $6 for a top-quality bit holder).

Ditch the lag screws

STRUCTURAL SCREW

The next time you build a deck, gazebo or fence that requires lag screws, consider using a modern version instead. These new structural screws are just as strong but skinnier, and they have specially designed tips and threads to make it easier to drive them in. You don't even have to drill pilot holes. And you can drive them with a standard drill, impact driver or strong cordless drill. They cost a little more than conventional lag screws. But if you've got better things to do than waste time with lag screws, they're worth every cent.

Install drywall with special tools

DRYWALL SCREW GUN

If you're considering driving drywall screws with a cordless drill and a regular Phillips-bit driver, don't. Drywall screws have to be driven to exactly the right depth. Too shallow, and you won't be able to cover them with joint compound; too deep, and you'll break through the paper face of the drywall, which will give you ugly drywall screw pops later. It's nearly impossible to drive screws quickly and accurately without special tools.

Here are your choices. If you only have a few sheets of drywall to hang, you can buy a special tip for your cordless drill that limits the depth you can drive the screw. These drywall screw tips (bottom photo) cost just a few dollars and work well if you're careful. A better option is a driver drill that's built to drive drywall screws. You can buy a time-saving auto-feed version ($100 to $300; photo at left) that uses special collated screws, or a dedicated drywall screw gun ($70 to $200; photo above left) that drives regular drywall screws. Both versions have adjustable nosepieces for precise depth control. If you only need the tool for one drywall job, consider renting one for a day or two.

CORDLESS AUTO-FEED DRYWALL SCREW GUN

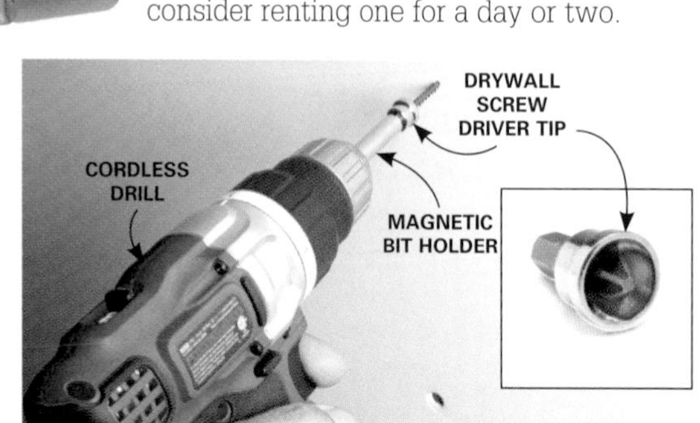

Center starter holes with a self-centering bit

When you drill pilot holes for hardware mounting screws, it's tough to keep the hole centered. That's where self-centering pilot bits come in handy. Just choose the right size self-centering bit, press the nose into the hole in the hardware, and the cone-shape guide keeps the bit centered while you drill the hole. A set of bits that work for screw sizes No. 6, 8 and 10 costs about $24.

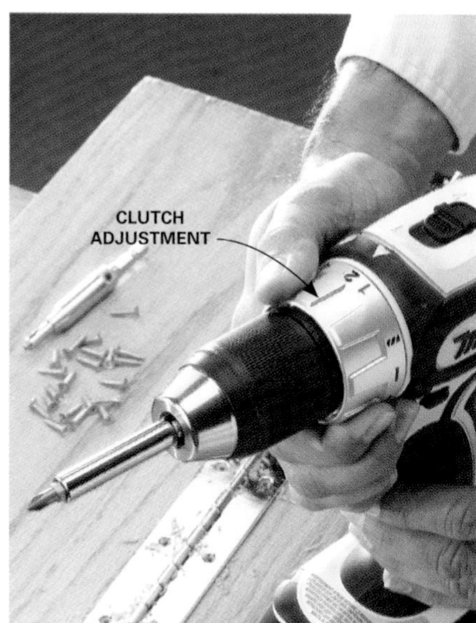

Adjust the clutch to avoid stripped screw heads

Most cordless drills come equipped with a clutch. If your drill has a clutch, try it out the next time you use the drill to drive small brass or aluminum screws that are easily damaged. Start with the lightest clutch setting and increase it until the proper driving depth is reached. The clutch will prevent you from accidentally stripping the screw heads.

A CLASSIC WORKBENCH

A timeless design that's simple and strong

by **Jeff Gorton, Associate Editor**

What it takes

TIME: One day

COST: $85

SKILL LEVEL: Beginner

TOOLS: Circular saw, Speed square, drill, No. 6 countersink bit

If this workbench looks familiar, it's probably because you've seen one a lot like it in your father's or grandfather's shop. Variations of this design have been around for decades, and for good reason: The bench is strong, practical and super easy to build. You can run to the lumberyard in the morning, grab a few boards, and by noon you'll have a perfectly functional workbench.

The workbench isn't fancy—it's built from standard construction lumber. But you can easily customize it with drawers or other features now or later. To see some of the improvements you can make, go to familyhandyman.com and search for "workbench upgrade."

If you can cut a board, you can build this bench. And you don't need any fancy tools either. In addition to a small square and a tape measure, you'll need a circular saw to cut the parts and a drill to drive the screws.

Getting started

You'll find all the materials at a lumberyard or home center (see Materials List on p. 144). Choose lumber that's straight and flat, and that doesn't have too many

Figure A
Exploded View

Overall dimensions:

60" wide x 28-1/4" deep x 36" tall plus a 7-3/4" backboard

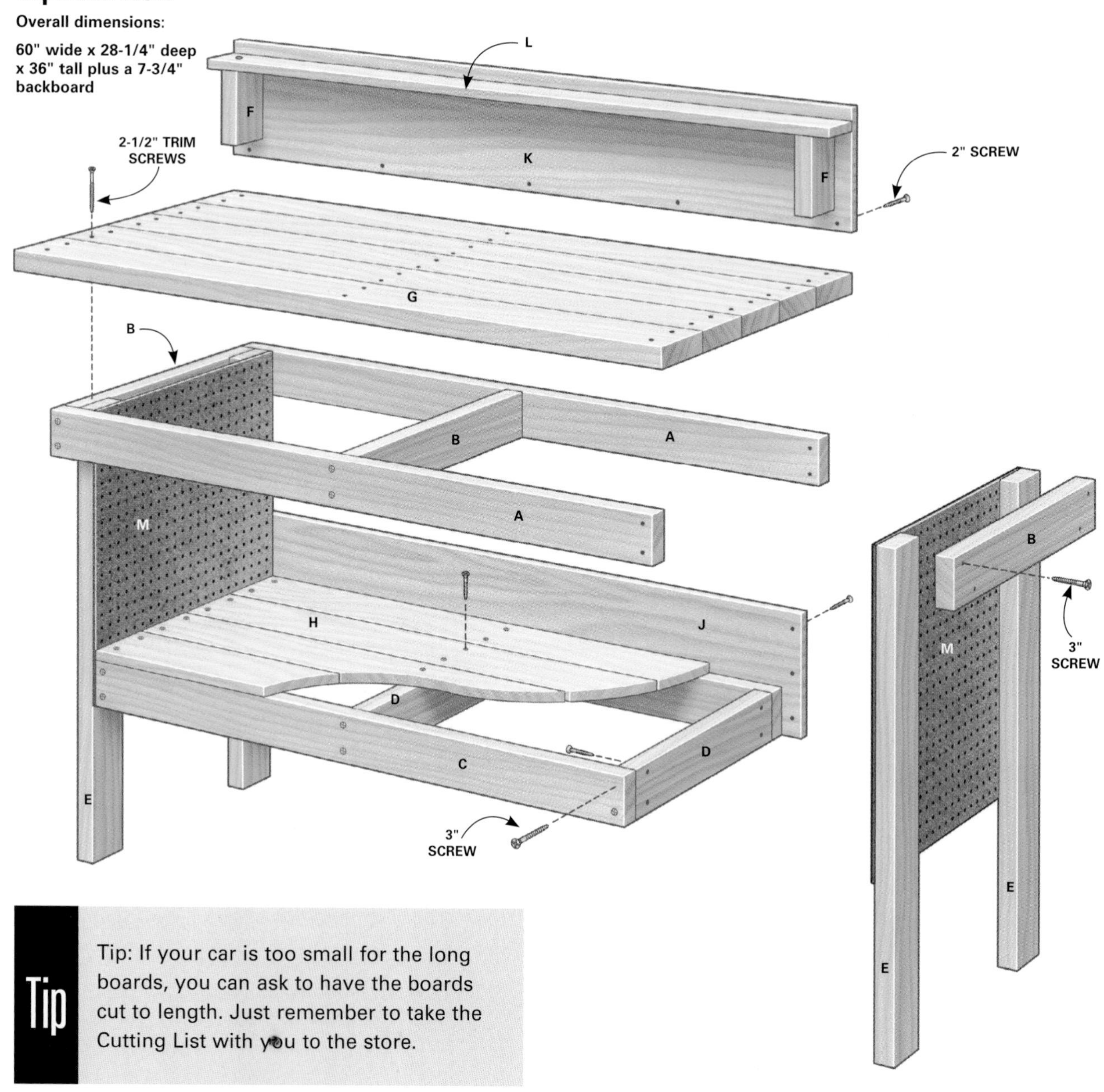

Tip

Tip: If your car is too small for the long boards, you can ask to have the boards cut to length. Just remember to take the Cutting List with you to the store.

MATERIALS LIST

ITEM	QTY.
2x4 x 8' pine	6
2x6 x 10' pine	2
2x6 x 8' pine	1
1x10 x 10' pine	1
1x6 x 10' pine	2
1x4 x 6' pine	1
2' x 4' x 1/4" pegboard	1
3" self-drilling screws	42
2" self-drilling screws	50
1-1/4" self-drilling screws	20
2-1/2" trim screws	30
Tube of construction adhesive	1

CUTTING LIST

KEY	QTY.	SIZE & DESCRIPTION
A	2	1-1/2" x 3-1/2" x 56" top frame front and back
B	3	1-1/2" x 3-1/2" x 22-1/2" top frame crosspieces
C	2	1-1/2" x 3-1/2" x 49-1/2" shelf frame front and back
D	3	1-1/2" x 3-1/2" x 19-1/2" shelf crosspieces
E	4	1-1/2" x 3-1/2" x 34-1/2" legs
F	2	1-1/2" x 3-1/2" x 6" back shelf supports
G	5	1-1/2" x 5-1/2" x 60" top boards
H	4	3/4" x 5-1/2" x 49-1/2" shelf boards
J	1	3/4" x 9-1/4" x 53" back brace
K	1	3/4" x 9-1/4" x 60" backboard
L	1	3/4" x 3-1/2" x 60" backboard shelf
M	2	22-3/8" x 22-3/8" x 1/4" pegboard leg braces

gouges, slivers or cracks. We used Torx-head screws with self-drilling tips. But you can substitute any construction screw. If you're not using screws with self-drilling tips, drill pilot holes to avoid splitting the wood.

Cut the parts according to the Cutting List on p. 144. We used a miter saw, but a circular saw will work fine. Mark the 2x4s with a Speed square or combination square. Then carefully cut the boards to length. If you plan to stain or paint the bench, now is the time to sand the parts. And to really simplify your job, you could also stain or paint the parts before you assemble the bench.

Start by building the top and shelf frames

We used an old door propped up on sawhorses as a work surface, but the floor will work too. Lay the 2x4s for the front and back of the top and shelf on the work surface and mark the centers. Remember, if you're not using self-drilling screws, drill pilot holes for the screws. Photo 1 shows how to assemble the frames. Set the top frame aside and screw the shelf boards to the shelf frame (Photo 2).

Build and attach the leg assemblies

Photo 3 shows how to build the leg assemblies. You'll notice that the leg assemblies are 1/8 in. narrower than the inside dimension of the top. That's so you can install the legs without binding, which would cause the pegboard to bow. Also, if the only pegboard you can find is thinner than the 1/4-in. pegboard specified, add the difference to the front and back of the shelf frame (C). For example, if you buy 1/8-in. pegboard, add 1/4 in. to parts C.

The pegboard is useful for hanging tools, but its real function is to stabilize the workbench as a brace. We added the construction adhesive to make sure the assemblies stayed strong and rigid. Be aware, though, that some of the adhesive will be visible through the holes.

The pegboard holes are a little too big to use as screw holes, so use a No. 6 countersink bit to drill pilot holes and make countersinks for the screws. Secure five evenly spaced 1-1/4-in. screws into each leg.

1 Build the frames. Use 3-in. screws to assemble the frames that support the top and the shelf. To avoid splitting the 2x4s, either drill pilot holes or use self-drilling screws. Build both frames and set the top frame aside.

2 Attach the shelf boards. Attach the outside boards first. Then position the two remaining boards to create equal spaces between them and screw them to the frame. Before driving screws, drill pilot holes with a countersink bit.

3 Assemble the legs. Drill five holes about 2 in. from the edge of the pegboard with the countersinking bit. Spread a bead of construction adhesive on the legs and attach the pegboard with 1-1/4-in. screws. If glue oozes through the holes, wait for it to dry. Then shave it off with a sharp chisel.

4 Screw the legs to the top frame. Apply construction adhesive where the legs contact the top frame. Then attach the legs with screws.

5 Add the shelf. Rest the bench on one end. Slide the shelf between the legs and line it up with the bottom of the pegboard. Screw through the shelf into the legs.

6 Mount the top boards. Starting at the back, align the first 2x6 flush to the back and measure for the 2-in. overhang on the side. Attach the 2x6 with trim screws. Attach the rest of the boards the same way. The front 2x6 will overhang the frame about 2 in.

7 Install the backboard. Attach the 1x4 shelf to the 1x10 backboard. Then add a 2x4 block at each end. Rest the backboard assembly on the workbench and drive screws through the back to hold it in place.

The next step is to attach the legs to the top frame. Apply construction adhesive to the top 3 in. of the legs. Then attach the leg assemblies with 3-in. screws (**Photo 4**).

Add the shelf and top

Stand the workbench on one end. Then it's simple to slide the shelf into place and line it up with the pegboard (**Photo 5**). Drive 3-in. screws through the shelf frame into the legs to support the shelf.

The top of this bench is 2x6s, placed tight together. The boards overhang the frame 2 in. on the sides and front. The overhang makes it easier to use clamps on the edges of the workbench. **Photo 6** shows how to get started. We attached the 2x6s with trim screws, but you could substitute 16d casing nails.

Attach the back brace and backboard

The 1x10 back brace keeps things from falling off the back of the shelf, but it also stiffens the bench to prevent side-to-side rocking. Apply construction adhesive before attaching the brace with 2-in. screws.

The backboard is a 1x10 with a 1x4 shelf attached. On the side of the 1x10 you want facing out, draw a line the length of the board, 1-3/4 in. down from the top. This is where you'll align the bottom of the 1x4. Draw a second line 1-3/8 in. from the top. Drill pilot holes with the countersink bit every 8 in. along this line. Now ask a helper to hold the 1x4 on the line while you drive 2-in. screws into the shelf through the pilot holes. After the shelf and 2x4 blocks at each end are attached, screw the backboard to the workbench (**Photo 7**).

You can modify your bench to fit your space and work style. We mounted an inexpensive woodworking vise on the front of the workbench and drilled holes in the 1x4 shelf to hold screwdrivers. If you've got a pint-size carpenter in the family, check out the mini version of the bench on p. 147. It would make a great project to build with your kids or grandkids.

MINI-CLASSIC FOR MINI DIYERS

Here's a plan for a downsized version of the workbench. All of the construction steps are the same; it's just smaller to fit the young carpenter in your family. The height is about right for a 42- to 48-in.-tall DIYer, but you can easily increase the height just by making the legs longer.

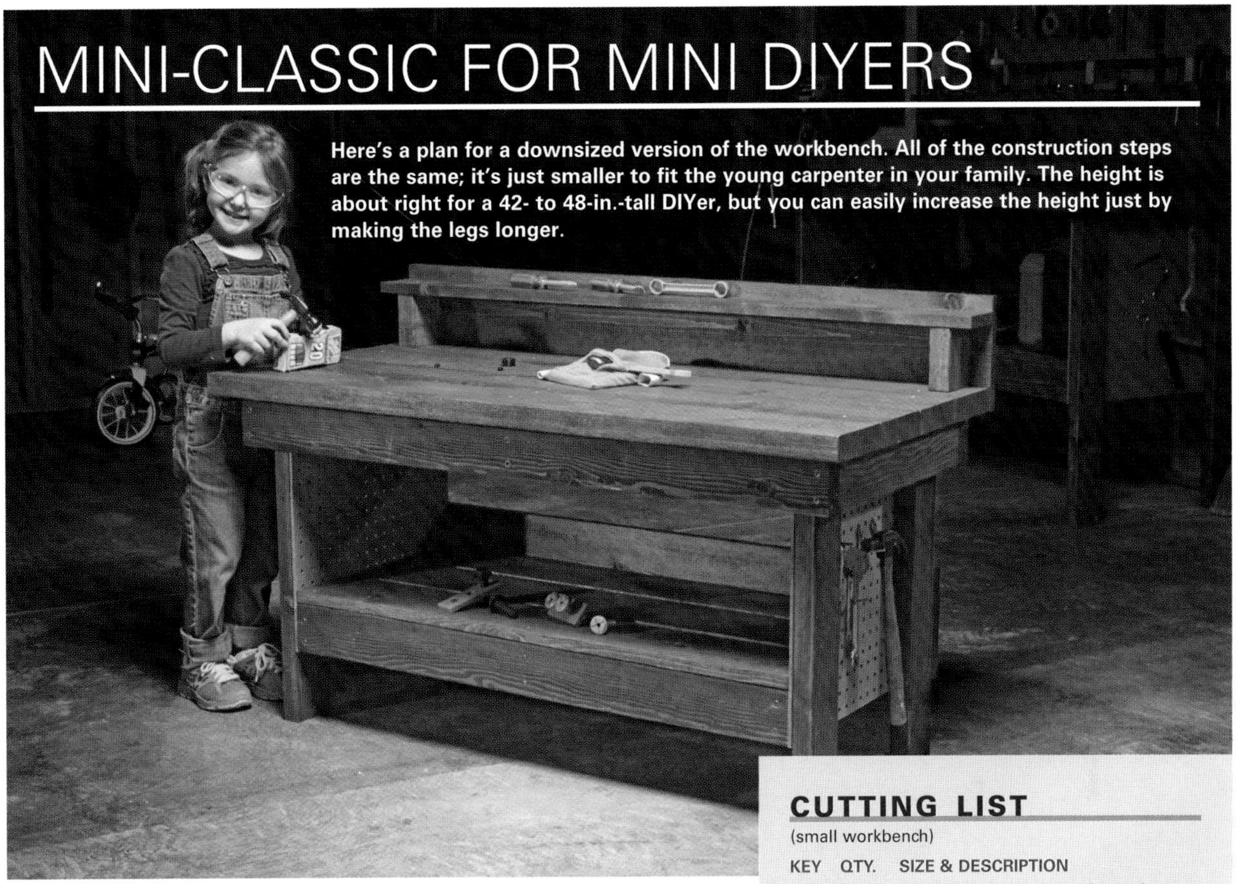

CUTTING LIST

(small workbench)

KEY	QTY.	SIZE & DESCRIPTION
A	2	1-1/2" x 3-1/2" x 45" top frame front and back
B	3	1-1/2" x 3-1/2" x 17-1/2" top frame crosspieces
C	2	1-1/2" x 3-1/2" x 38-1/2" shelf frame front and back
D	3	1-1/2" x 3-1/2" x 14-1/2" shelf cross-pieces
E	4	1-1/2" x 3-1/2" x 22-1/2" legs
F	2	1-1/2" x 3-1/2" x 4" back shelf supports
G	4	1-1/2" x 5-1/2" x 48" top boards
H	3	3/4" x 5-1/2" x 38-1/2" shelf boards
J	1	3/4" x 7-1/4" x 42" back brace
K	1	3/4" x 7-1/4" x 48" backboard
L	1	3/4" x 3-1/2" x 48" backboard shelf
M	2	17-3/8" x 17-3/8" x 1/4" pegboard leg braces

Figure B: Small bench

Overall dimensions: 48" wide x 22-3/4" deep x 24" tall plus a 5-3/4" backboard

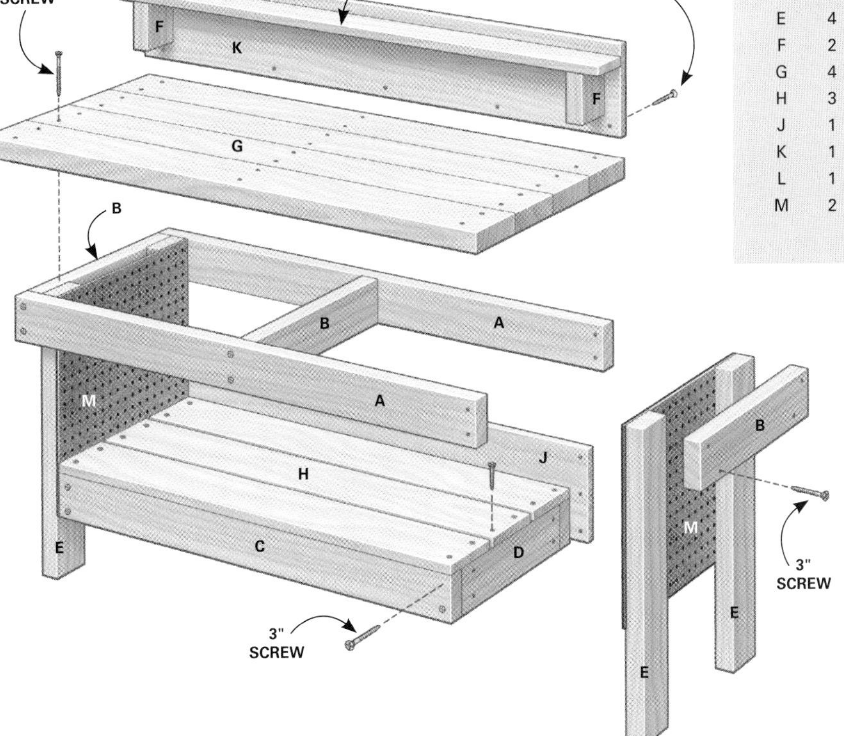

MATERIALS LIST

(small workbench)

ITEM	QTY.
2x4 x 8' pine	4
2x6 x 8' pine	2
1x8 x 8' pine	1
1x6 x 10' pine	1
1x4 x 4' pine	1
2' x 4' x 1/4" pegboard	1
3" self-drilling screws	42
2" self-drilling screws	40
1-1/4" self-drilling screws	16
2-1/2" trim screws	24
Tube of construction adhesive	1

BUILDING FACE FRAME CABINETS

Tips and tricks for pro-quality cabinet face frames

by **Mark Petersen, Contributing Editor**

A classic way to make cabinets is to build plywood boxes (aka carcasses) and cover the front with a hardwood face frame. Cabinets like this are strong and handsome and relatively easy to build. And the editors at *The Family Handyman* have the experience to prove it. Some have built dozens of face frame cabinets; a couple of us have built hundreds. For this story, we've compiled a list of tips that we felt could help experienced cabinetmakers as well as those just starting out.

While these cabinets provide a sturdy support for door hinges, we won't cover door building here. See "Build the cabinets, buy the doors" on p. 149 for some ideas.

Label your face frame parts first

Dry-fit face frame parts so the best side of all the boards will be seen, avoiding stark grain color variations at joints. Label all the pieces with a pencil so the frame goes back together the same way you laid it out. The pencil marks also come in handy when you're ready to sand the assembled frame. You'll know you have flat joints when the pencil marks disappear.

Leave off the back until you apply finish

If you plan to finish your project before you install it, leave the back off until after you've applied the finish. It makes getting into all those nooks and crannies a lot easier, especially in deeper cabinets. Wood glue won't stick to finished wood, so if you want to glue on the back, you'll have to use polyurethane glue.

Build the cabinets, buy the doors

Building cabinet doors is doable but can be tricky. It sometimes requires powerful and expensive wood-shaping equipment. And if you have a bunch to build, you'll need a lot of clamps and even more space. Unless you have unlimited free time, consider building your cabinets but buying your doors. You'll find many door makers online (search for "buy cabinet doors"). Cabinet doors can be ordered in a variety of styles and in increments as small as 1/16 in. It's always nice to be able to see and touch, so check out your local cabinet shop as well.

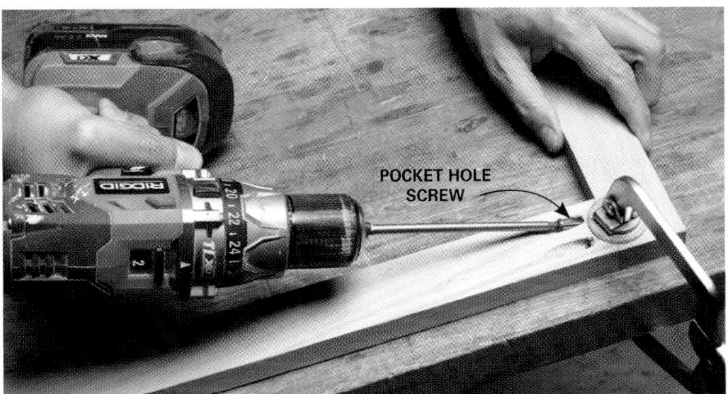

Assemble the face frame with pocket hole screws

Pocket hole screws are a fast and easy way to join a face frame. You don't need a lot of clamps or wood glue, and it's way easier than making mortise-and-tenon joints. An entry-level pocket screw jig will cost you less than $50, but if you plan to build several face frame projects, spend about $140 to get a top-of-the-line jig. For more on pocket screw joinery, go to familyhandyman.com and search for "pocket screws."

Trim some face frames flush

Face frames on furniture look best when they're flush with the cabinet sides. But it's still better to build the face frame a little bigger (about 1/16 in.), and trim it off with a flush trim router bit. Adjust the bit depth so the cutting edges are only slightly deeper than the face frame. (Also see "Build face frames larger" on p. 150.)

FLUSH TRIM BIT

WOODWORKING & WORKSHOP PROJECTS & TIPS

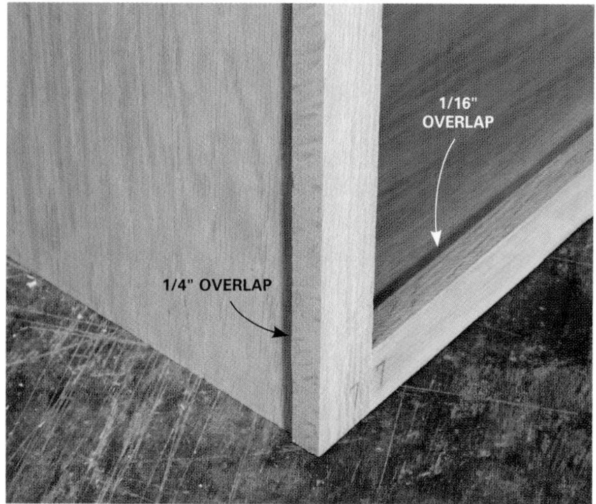

Build face frames larger

A main function of a face frame is to hide the exposed plywood laminations. A face frame does a better job of this if it overlaps the box edges a bit. Making the face frame run past all the plywood edges provides a little wiggle room and hides not-so-perfect saw cuts on the plywood. Face frames on sides of kitchen cabinets should overlap 1/4 in. on the outside edge. This makes room for adjustments when installing them next to one another. Build the face frame so that the bottom rail ("rails" are horizontal boards and "stiles" are vertical boards) projects 1/16 in. above the bottom shelf of the cabinet.

Gang up on your components

Even with a high-end table saw, it's difficult to reset the fence to exactly replicate previous cuts, so plan ahead and cut all your face frame parts at the same time. Gang-planing your stiles and rails will save time and ensure all the parts are exactly the same width and thickness. Gang-sand board edges by clamping them together. That not only speeds up sanding but also keeps you from rounding over edges. And always make more parts than you need. It's better to have a couple of pieces left over than to have to cut, plane and sand one replacement board if you make a miscut. Also, having extra allows you to choose the best boards of the lot.

Nail the face frame to boxes

One of the easiest ways to attach face frames to carcasses is with a thin bead of wood glue and an 18-gauge brad nailer with 2-in. brads. Be sparing with brads; their main duty is to hold the frame in place while the glue dries. A couple per side and wherever there's a void should do the trick. A little putty will make the brad holes almost invisible.

Leave the end stile off to scribe

Leave one end stile off when you install cabinets that butt against walls at both ends. With a complete face frame, you won't be able to push the cabinet into place or scribe and adjust the stile to fit. Cut that last stile a bit oversize to leave room for scribing, and rip a 45-degree back bevel for easier planing to your scribed line. The bevel also makes it easier to twist the stile into place.

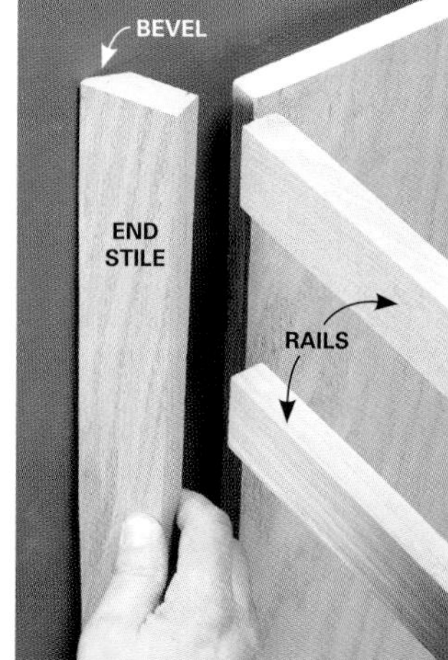

Assemble the whole face frame on your workbench with pocket screws, then remove the last stile. That way you'll be guaranteed a perfect fit when you reattach it after planing. Or attach it with a bit of glue and a few brads.

Don't settle for what's in the home center

Home centers and lumberyards typically have only a few cabinet-grade plywood options in stock, but almost all of them can order what you need. You can order sheets with more plies for stability; pick the orientation of the wood grain; buy sheets with hardwood on one side and melamine on the other; choose marine-grade plywood for outdoor projects ... the options go on and on.

It takes a little planning ahead, and ask about minimum orders, but don't limit yourself to oak if you really want cherry.

Don't cut rabbets if they're not needed

It's common practice to cut a rabbet (a notch to receive the 1/4-in. back panel) on the back edge of cabinet carcasses so the back panel will be recessed. But that's not necessary if the cabinet sides won't be visible—the back panel edges won't be either. Save some time and just tack on the back panel with a brad nailer. Make sure to take into account the overall depth of your cabinets—they'll be 1/4 in. deeper if you go this route.

Build individual boxes

Moving and installing long one-piece cabinets can be a tough job, and it may not even be possible to get the assembly into the room. Instead of creating such a monster, build individual cabinet carcasses. Add the face frame after they're all in place.

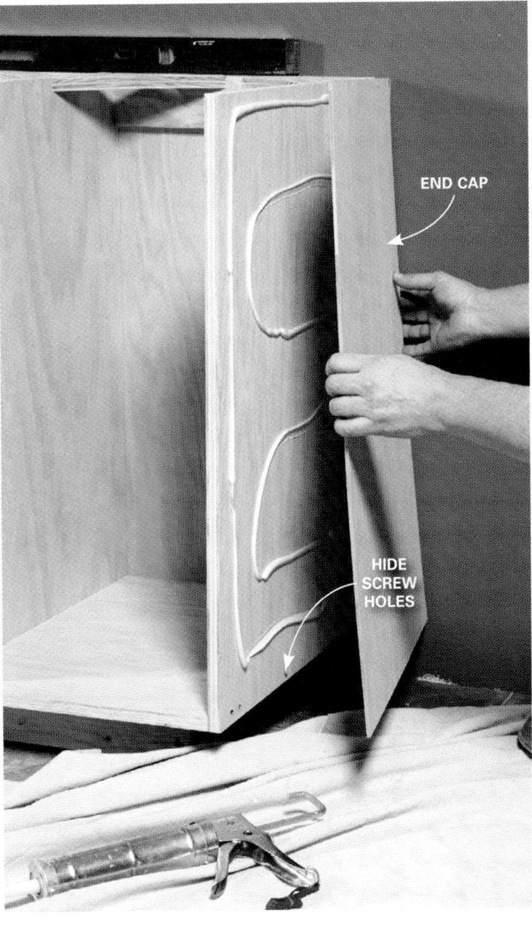

Cap end cabinets

If you cap the end cabinet with 1/4-in. plywood, you don't have to hide the fasteners you used to build your boxes. That means you can use large, sturdy screws without worrying about ugly putty-filled holes. You'll also need an end cap if you choose to build a separate base. Use construction adhesive and a few small brads to fasten the panel in place, and make sure you extend the outside face frame stile an additional 1/4 in. to account for the thickness of the plywood.

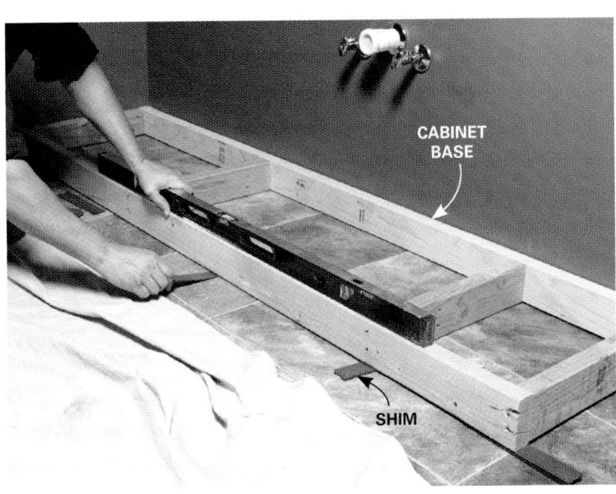

Build a separate base

Most factory-built cabinets have a recessed "toe-kick" that's typically about 4 in. high and deep. But you can also make a separate base that's the total length of the cabinet assembly and build shorter cabinets to make up the difference. With this method, you won't have to mess around with figuring out and cutting toe-kick profiles on your cabinets.

This is also a handy technique when you have an uneven floor because you need to level and shim only one base instead of several individual cabinets. It's important to use dead-straight wood for bases so it'll be flat for setting the cabinets. Once your cabinets are installed, finish off the base front with a strip of 1/4-in. plywood that matches the cabinets.

MASTER THE **RECIPROCATING SAW**

Get the most out of this multi-use tool

by **Mark Petersen, Contributing Editor**

A reciprocating saw is a powerful, versatile tool that can cut a huge variety of materials and get into tight spots other saws can't. It's a must-have for any demolition job, but there's not a framer, plumber, electrician or roofer worth their salt who doesn't have one in their truck at all times. I learned a thing or two during the hundreds of dusty hours behind my recip saws. In this story, I'll show you a few tricks to help you get more out of your saw, avoid the dreaded kickback and extend the life of your blades.

Bend longer blades to cut flush

Longer blades aren't just for cutting wider stuff—they also work great for flush-cutting. Bend the blade so a good portion of it rides flat along the floor or whatever surface you're working on, and use the end portion of the blade to do the cutting.

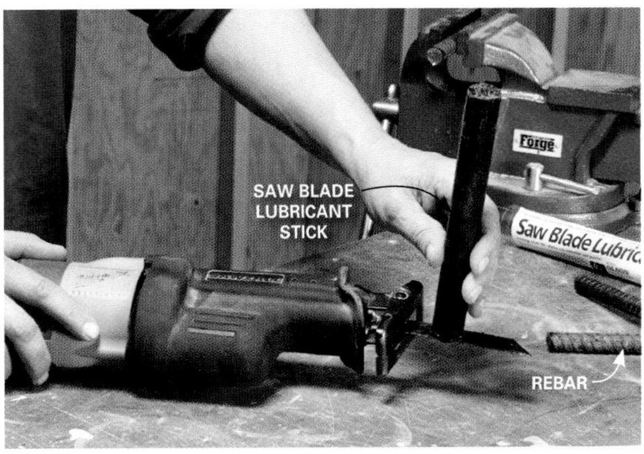

Extend blade life with lubrication

Blades heat up as you cut, especially when you're cutting metal, and a hot blade dulls quickly. If you have a lot of metal to slice, rub on blade lubricant between cuts. Blade lubricant helps keep the blades cooler and the teeth free of clogs from metal chips. You can get the Olson Saw Blade Lubricant stick shown here for about $10 online.

Cover the shoe to protect the surface

There's nothing subtle about a reciprocating saw. It's a downright brute and usually unsuitable for delicate jobs. The saw's violent vibrations can mar surfaces, and unlike on jigsaws, covering the shoe with tape is not enough to protect the surface. When I have to cut a hole through a finished floor, I slice a small section of cheap pipe insulation in half and tape it to the shoe. It's a cheap and easy way to avoid costly floor repairs.

Use framing as a blade guide

Cut the plywood out of window openings with a longer blade and bow it a bit so it rides along the framing. I end up with a nice, clean cut every time. And don't forget to warn the guys outside so they don't get conked on the noggin with a chunk of plywood.

Pound out a bent blade

Kickbacks are inevitable when working with a recip saw, and a kickback often results in a bent blade. Blades are relatively inexpensive these days, but if you're down to your last one or want to avoid a trip back to the truck, you can bend them back into shape. Grab a block of wood and pound down the raised section. Try to avoid pounding directly on the teeth so you don't damage them.

Change angles for cutting faster

When cutting through thick material, periodically change the angle of the blade. It reduces the surface area being cut, which reduces the friction and makes for a faster cut. And whenever possible, keep the shoe tight up against the cutting surface to avoid kickbacks and to keep the material from rattling around.

Flip the blade to get down close

Blades can be inserted into most recip saws with the teeth facing up or down (some new saws accept blades in four directions). When cutting something that's lying flat on the ground, like the bottom plate of a newly framed door opening, insert the blade with the teeth pointing up and flip the saw upside down. That way the handle won't get in the way and you'll be able to cut more parallel to the ground, which will reduce the chance of kickback.

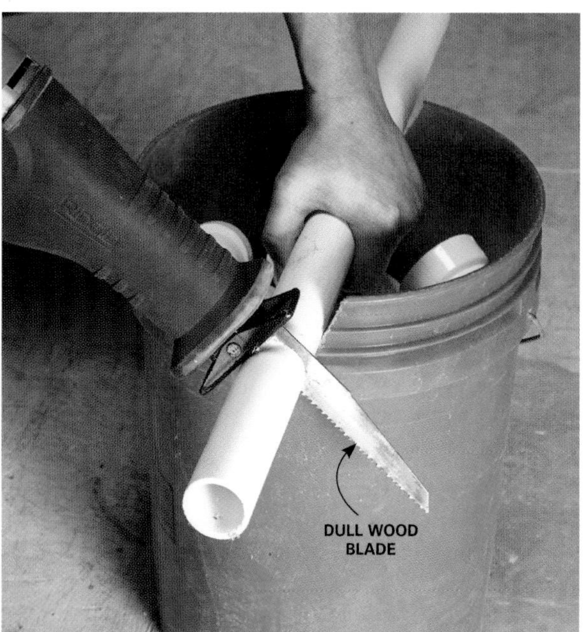

Cut plastic with dull blades

In some cases a dull blade is preferable: Cutting plastic pipe with a sharp, aggressive blade can cause the teeth to grab the pipe and jerk it back and forth instead of cutting it. A dull wood blade cuts through plastic almost as well as a blade specifically designed for the task.

Save a couple old blades

Some jobs can dull a reciprocating saw blade in just a few seconds. Don't sacrifice your good, sharp blades on jobs like these. Instead, keep a few well-used blades for rough work like cutting through shingles.

Adjust the shoe to extend blade life

Pushing the shoe up against the work surface is a good way to avoid kickbacks and reduce vibration. The problem is that the teeth right next to the shoe always wear out before the teeth on the rest of the blade. Recip saws with adjustable shoes are nice because you can adjust the shoe so the cutting action occurs at different spots on the blade.

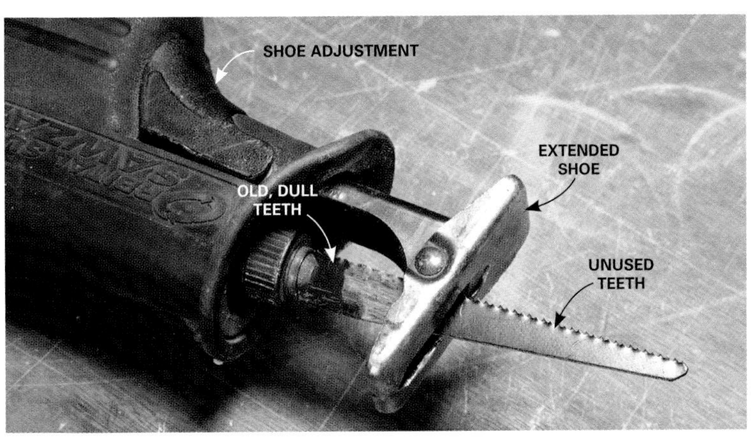

There's a blade for that

There's a reciprocating saw blade for cutting just about anything you can think of. There are also other attachments, which makes this versatile tool even handier. Here are some examples of the more popular blades and attachments available in home centers:

- Bimetal demolition blade for nail-embedded wood
- Diamond-grit blade for cast iron
- Carbide grit for tile and clay
- Fine-tooth metal-cutting blade
- Carbide-tip blade for cutting bricks and masonry. Is that cool or what?
- Blade for ripping through plaster
- Scraper; handy for pulling up old vinyl tiles
- Double-edged bore blade for multidirectional cuts, with rounded end for easy plunge cutting
- Bidirectional-tooth pruning blade
- Wire brush attachment; handy for scraping rusty metal or flaking paint

Avoid waggle — use smaller blades

Blades for reciprocating saws come in different lengths for a reason. Cutting smaller material with longer blades can cause the end of the blade to violently waggle back and forth. This can result in a slower cut, a whole lot of vibration and possibly a bent blade. So choose a blade only a couple inches longer than whatever you're cutting.

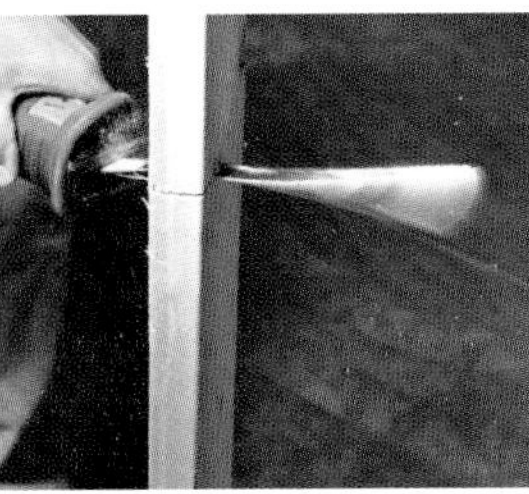

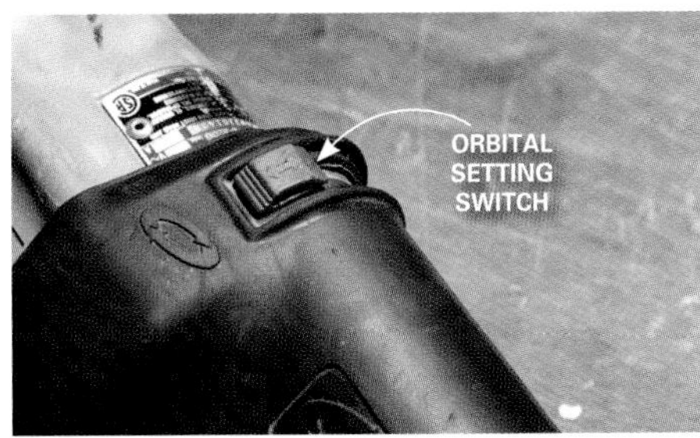

Set your saw to orbital for faster cuts in wood

Some recip saws have an orbital cutting feature. This causes the blade to cut in a slight orbital pattern instead of back and forth in a straight line. Set the saw to full orbital when cutting through wood. If your saw has an adjustable orbital feature like this one, set it halfway when cutting through nail-embedded wood. Turn the feature completely off when cutting through metal. If you don't, the blade will bounce off the work surface, slowing down the cut and rattling your fillings loose.

FINISH A TABLETOP

21 tips for glass-smooth perfection

by **Gary Wentz, Senior Editor**

Finishing a tabletop is tricky. On a big table especially, coating the entire surface before the finish becomes too sticky is the ultimate test of speed and skill. And your work has to be perfect. More than any other furniture surface, a tabletop reflects light and shows off every little flaw.

But that doesn't mean you can't do it. These tips will make the tough parts easier and help you achieve a perfect finish.

1 Declare war on dust

Airborne dust is the wood finisher's nemesis. It settles on wet coatings and creates ugly pimples in the dried finish. You can sand them out, but it's better to minimize that labor by minimizing dust. Clean up the work area and change out of the dusty clothes you wore while sanding.

Wetting the floor also helps prevent you from kicking up dust. Don't use so much water that the floor is slippery. A spray bottle or damp mop should do the trick. (A side benefit is that a damp floor raises the humidity, so polyurethane dries more slowly and remains workable longer.)

If you're using water-based finishes, control airborne dust by turning off forced-air heating or cooling, and by closing windows and doors. This doesn't apply to oil-based finishes; with those, adequate ventilation is required to remove harmful fumes.

2 Work fast

Depending on the conditions, oil-based polyurethane may become too sticky to work with after just five to ten minutes. Water-based poly dries even faster. So have all your supplies lined up and ready to go before you start. And once you've started, there's no time for coffee or bathroom breaks.

3 Tent the work area

Open rafters and trusses are an endless source of falling dust. So if you're working under an open ceiling, hang plastic sheeting above. Keep the plastic at least 12 in. from light fixtures or remove the bulbs. Sometimes, adding plastic "walls" is a lot easier than cleaning up the entire area. If you're using oil-based finishes, hang the sheets about a foot from the floor to allow for ventilation.

4 Prevent regrets

The very best way to avoid wood finishers' remorse is to test your finishes on wood scraps of the same species as your masterpiece. Sand the scraps in exactly the same way you sand the table: Sanding lighter or harder or using different grits will change the look of any finish you apply.

5 Sanding tips

■ **Sand every square inch the same.** Any variation in sanding steps can show up in the final finish. If, for example, you run out of 80-grit sanding discs halfway through the initial sanding, you might be tempted to switch to 100-grit. But don't. Even after sanding with higher grits, stain may look different in differently treated areas.

■ **Don't oversand.** Most professionals stop at 150-grit on coarse-grain woods like oak or walnut and 180-grit on fine-grain woods like cherry or maple. But that doesn't apply to end grain, which shows sanding scratches more than face grain; you may have to sand to 220- or even 320-grit.

■ **Skip grits when sanding.** You don't have to use every available grit as you progress from coarse to fine. Instead, you can jump from 80-grit to 120- to 180-grit, skipping 100- and 150-grit.

■ **Sand between coats.** A quick hand-sanding between coats flattens out flaws before the next coat. Polyurethane tends to gum up sandpaper, so use paper or pads that resist clogging (320-grit). On shaped edges, use synthetic steel wool, such as Scotch-Brite pads, labeled "very fine."

■ **Do a final sanding by hand.** A random orbital sander is perfect for most of the sanding. But do a five-minute final sanding by hand using the same grit. Hand-sanding with the grain removes swirls and torn wood fibers left by the orbital action of the sander.

6 Prop up the tabletop

Set the top on screws so you can easily finish the edges.

7 Avoid blotches

Most common wood species—pine, birch, maple and cherry—absorb stain unevenly. For a more consistent finish, apply a prestain conditioner.

8 Remove the legs

A disassembled table is much easier to move and the legs are easier to finish. On a typical table, removing each leg is as simple as unscrewing a nut.

9 Seal end grain

The end grain of wood soaks up finishes and often turns much darker than the face grain. Check for this on your test scrap (see Tip 4). If you get an ugly result, pretreat the end grain with a dose of finish that will limit absorption (wood conditioner, sanding sealer, shellac or polyurethane thinned 50 percent). Apply the treatment with an artist's brush and be careful not to slop onto the face grain.

10 Vac and tack

A vacuum with a brush attachment will remove 99 percent of the sanding dust. But that's not enough. This photo shows how much dust is left over. After vacuuming, wipe with a tack cloth (available at home centers) if you plan to use oil-based stain or coatings. If you're using water-based finishes, use a lint-free rag dampened with mineral spirits.

11 Customize your lighting

Overhead lighting is great for most shop work, but it's bad for finishing. Try this instead: Turn off the overhead lights and position a bright light 4 to 5 ft. off the floor. The low-angle glare will highlight every flaw.

12 Inspect your sanding work

Stain will highlight any flaws in your sanding job (swirls or cross-grain scratches). Then you'll have to resand—and sanding stained wood is a real pain. To find flaws before you stain, use low-angle light (see Tip 11, above). Wiping on mineral spirits also helps to reveal problems.

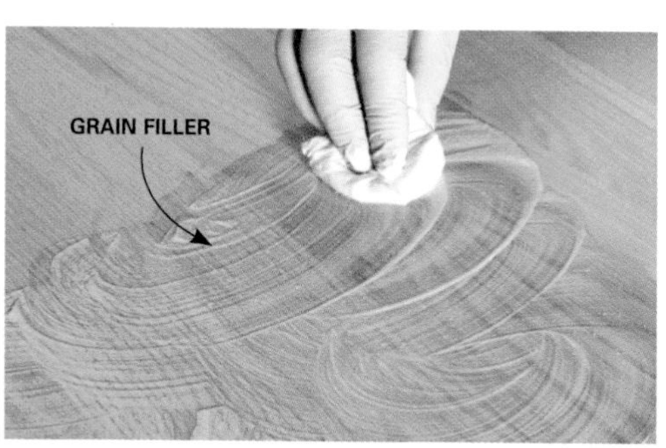

13 Fill the grain

The deep grain lines in woods like oak or walnut will telegraph through the clear finish, no matter how many coats you apply. And that's fine; it's part of the character of coarse-grain woods. But if a perfectly smooth surface is the look you want, use a grain filler. You'll find several products online or at woodworking stores. With most, you wipe on the filler, squeegee off the excess with a plastic putty knife and then sand after it's dry for a smooth-as-glass surface.

14 Go with polyurethane – and apply it properly

There are lots of clear finishes. But for a combination of usability and durability, you can't beat polyurethane. Oil-based poly, which dries slower than water-based, is best for beginners because it allows more working time. The other important difference is clarity: Water-based poly is absolutely colorless, while oil-based has an amber tone, which can be good or bad depending on the look you want.

■ **Start with high-gloss poly.** A few coats of semigloss or satin polyurethane looks like a sheet of dull plastic over the wood. So build up coats of gloss poly first. Then, if you want less sheen, dull the finish by wet sanding or wiping on a couple coats of satin or semigloss.

■ **Roll on oil-based poly.** Coating a big surface with a brush—before the poly becomes gooey—requires speed and skill. Rolling, on the other hand, is faster, easier and almost goof-proof.

Rolled-on poly looks terrible at first, but the bubbles disappear in minutes, leaving a smoother surface than most of us can achieve with a brush. Beware of ridges formed by the edges of the roller and humps where you start and stop. You can minimize both of those flaws by applying lighter coats. We experimented with several kinds of rollers and got the best results with microfiber mini rollers. We also tried rolling on water-based poly; don't do it.

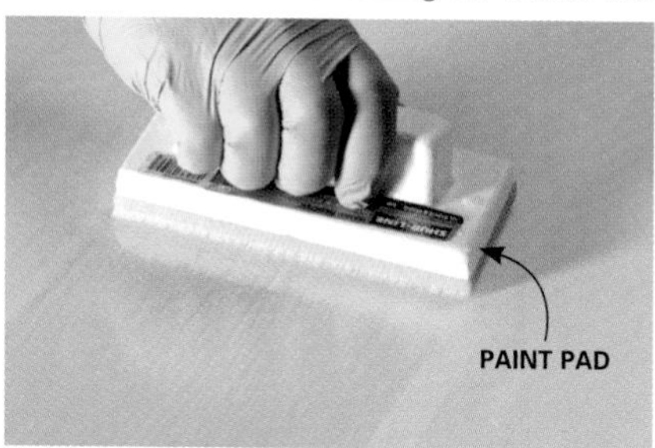

■ **Apply water-based poly with a pad.** Water-based poly dries faster than oil, so it's even harder to brush over a big surface. The solution is a paint pad, which applies poly quickly and smoothly. Just dip the pad into a pan of poly and drag the pad across the surface. Be sure to smooth out any ridges pushed up by the edges of the pad.

■ **Spray the legs.** Table legs—especially shaped legs—are almost impossible to coat smoothly with a brush. So instead, hang them from the ceiling with wire and use a can of spray poly to coat them.

15 Pluck out problems

Tweezers are an essential emergency tool. If a fly, brush bristle or lint ends up in the finish, you can surgically remove it.

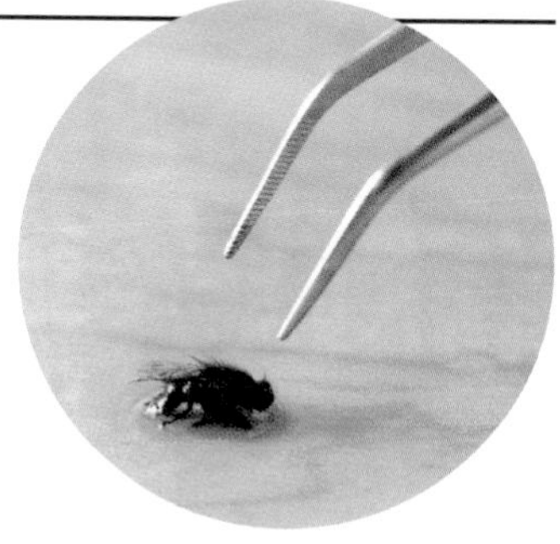

Apply at least three coats

With a thicker layer of protection, damage to the underlying wood is less likely—so your tabletop will look better longer, and reviving the finish will be easier. Some finishers apply four or even five coats.

17 Underside and edge details

■ **Coat the underside.** Wood absorbs moisture from the air, shrinking and swelling with changes in humidity. Finishes slow that absorption. So if you coat only the topside, the unfinished underside will shrink or swell at a different rate. That means a warped table. But one coat on the underside will stabilize the tabletop.

■ **Keep an eye on edges.** Regardless of how you apply poly, you'll likely end up with some runs on the edges. So constantly check the edges as you work and be ready to smooth out runs with a brush.

■ **Wipe away drips.** After the table is completely coated, wrap a rag around your finger and wipe off any drips along the underside.

Don't sand through

If you sand through the poly and remove some stain, you can touch up with more stain. But the repair won't be perfect, so take pains to avoid that mistake. Sand very lightly after the first coat, just enough to remove the dust whiskers. After the second coat, you can sand a little harder to flatten larger flaws. Be careful around the table edges; that's where it's easiest to sand through.

19 Wet-sand before final coats

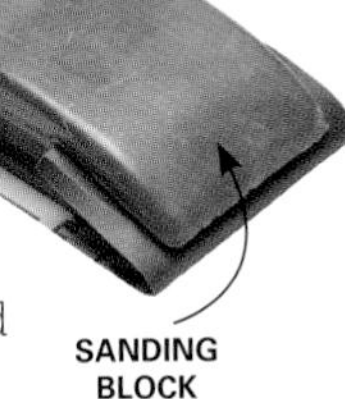

Load a sanding block with 600-grit wet/dry paper, dribble on some soapy water and rub the finish smooth. Then wipe the table dry, look for flaws and rub some more. Don't stop until you achieve perfection. Smooth shaped edges with synthetic steel wool.

Clean off the white stuff

As the table dries after wet-sanding, a white residue will appear. Be sure to clean it off completely. Residue left in the grain lines of coarse-grain wood will be trapped under the final coat and haunt you forever.

21 Wipe on the final coats

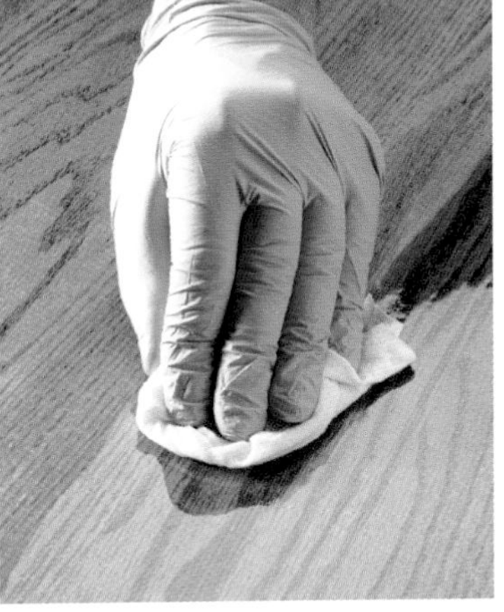

Wet-sanding leaves the surface perfectly smooth but dull. To restore the shine, apply two coats of wipe-on polyurethane (available in gloss, semigloss and satin). Wiping results in a very thin, fast-drying coat, so flaws like dust nubs or sags are less likely.

Never use wax or polish

All you need for routine cleaning and care of your table is a damp cloth. When normal wear eventually dulls the finish, you can renew it in just a few minutes with another coat of wipe-on poly. But if you've ever used furniture wax or polish, a fresh coat of poly may not stick.

HandyHints®

FROM OUR READERS

MAGNET IN A BAG

Cleaning up metal shavings around my drill press almost always got me a metal sliver or two. Using a magnet works fine, but it's no fun to get all those shavings off the magnet. Then I decided to put the magnet inside a plastic bag that was turned inside out. Now I can attract the shavings to the bag, seal it and pull it free, and throw them away without touching a single shaving.

—Robert Black Sr.

SCREW HOLDER

While doing some remodeling, I wanted to spray-paint the switch plate covers and screws to match the new colors. I didn't have any Styrofoam to hold the screws, so I found an old advertising sign that had corrugated edges (old political signs work great too). I cut a strip and the screws fit perfectly.

Kari Schuster

EASY LABEL REMOVAL

I've always loved to reuse plastic containers for storing parts and fasteners. But I've never loved getting the old label off. Recently, I discovered that if I fill the container with hot water, the label will peel right off after a few minutes. If the water is hot enough from your tap, just fill the container; wait for the adhesive to soften and then peel the label. If you heat the water on the stove, don't boil it! Keep the water at about 160 degrees F—if it gets too much higher, your container can sag and lose its shape!

—Shirley Fringer

A TRIM FOR FLUX BRUSHES

I use flux brushes for all sorts of tasks, from glue spreading to touch-up painting. I find that the bristles are too long, making them too soft to push glue or paint. They work a lot better if you cut off about 1/4 in. of the bristles. If you trim the bristles at an angle, you can also make a nice cut-in brush for small parts.

Dan Doshan

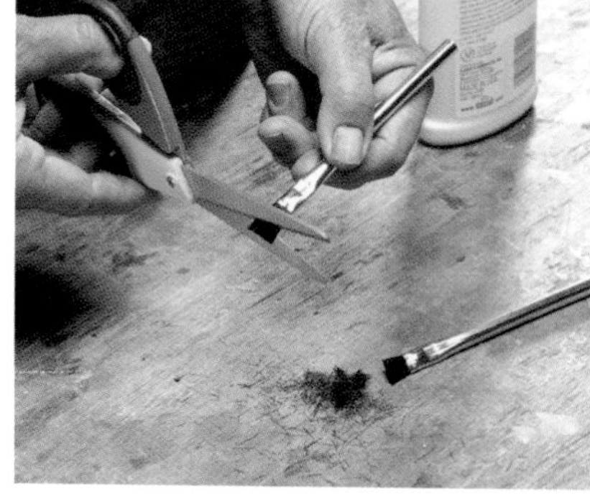

PLASTIC-CARD PUTTY KNIVES

Don't throw away your old credit cards or membership cards. You can use them as flexible putty knives to spackle or fix holes in drywall. If you round the edges, you can use them to smooth caulk. They're easy to clean and keep on hand for the next project.

Phyllis Bryant

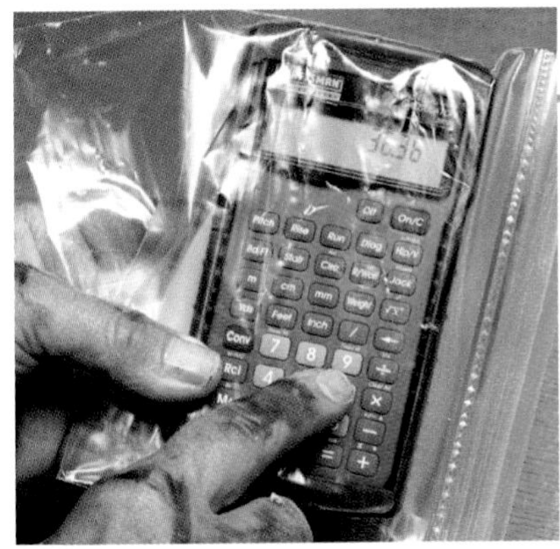

DUST-FREE SHOP CALCULATOR

I had to throw out my last calculator because the keys started sticking from all the gunk that had built up on the keyboard while it was in the shop. To protect my new one, I keep it in a plastic bag. When the bag gets grimy, I just toss it instead of the calculator!

—David Hassler

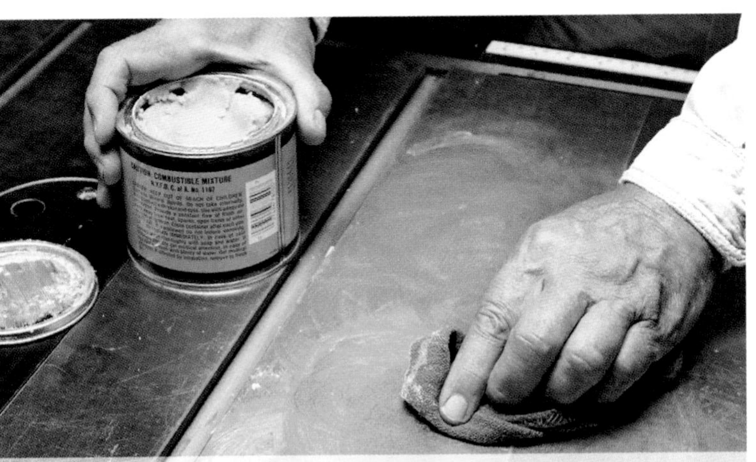

SLICK TABLE SAW

I find the best way to protect my cast-iron table saw top is to occasionally rub on a coat of paste wax. This gives me a nice, slick top for easier material feeding, and if I drip glue on the surface, it won't stick. It also helps prevent surface rust when the air is humid.

—Jack Linden

SPRAY-FOAM SUPER TUBE

While sealing tiny openings along my home's foundation, I was having a bugger of a time positioning my inverted spray foam can just right. That's when I decided to look around the shop for a solution. I found some 1/4-in. clear flexible tubing that I'd picked up at the hardware store. It fit on the end of the nozzle nice and tight after I ran it under hot water to soften and expand it slightly. Once it was outfitted, I could hold the can in a comfortable spot and then move the end of the tubing to fill the cracks with foam.

—Glenn Copeland

NO SAWDUST IN THE HOUSE!

We have this policy at home that I can't come into the house from the garage with even a speck of sawdust on my clothes (somehow my vote didn't count!). To keep the dust off my clothes, I picked up a pair of nylon athletic pants and a nylon rain jacket at a thrift store. I just slip them over my street clothes when I'm kicking up dust in the shop — nothing sticks to them. My clothes seem to be lasting longer too!

—David Radtke

HandyHints®

PROTECT YOUR TOOLS

Tarps do a decent job of protecting tools from the elements, but it's hard to keep them in place, especially when you're traveling down the road. The wind always seems to catch underneath, which can send them sailing.

The next time you have to take your tools on a road trip, try wrapping them in a grill cover. The size and shape of a grill cover make it much easier to secure with a strap or bungee. The cover also protects your tools from rain or morning dew if you plan to leave them out overnight in your backyard. Home centers and discount stores carry grill covers in various sizes costing from $15 to $50.

Kirk Pennings,
Field Editor

ONE HANDY DRILL BIT

STEP BITS

There's nothing better than a step bit for drilling through thinner metal. It's designed to drill incrementally larger holes the deeper you drive the bit, so you can drill several size holes with one bit. It creates a nice clean hole and doesn't catch and kick back like a twist bit.

Electricians use step bits all the time to drill electrical boxes and circuit panels. I've used mine to prep storm door hardware and drill large starter holes in gutters so I could cut out a downspout hole with a tin snips. A good-quality 1/8-in. to 1/2-in. 13-hole step drill bit costs about $20. One that creates a 1-in. hole will cost around $30. You can save money by buying them in a set.

—Matthew Kelly, Field Editor

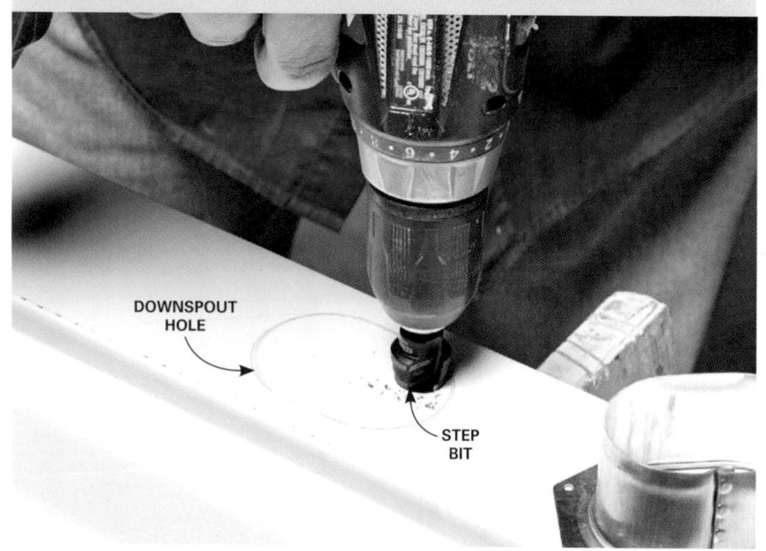

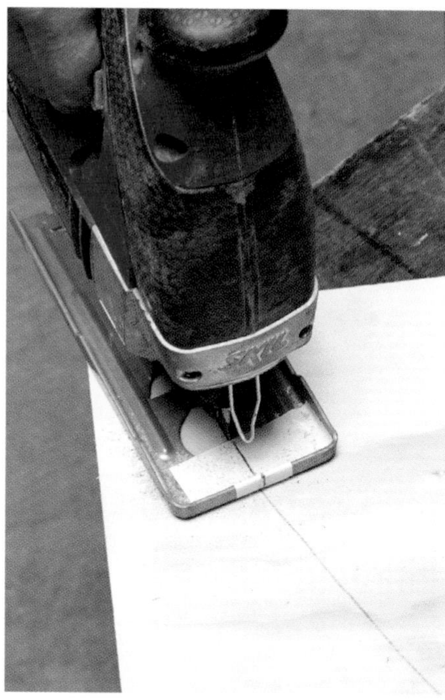

SIMPLE JIGSAW GUIDE

I have a small workshop for DIY projects, so I use a jigsaw for most of my cutting. Sometimes the lighting or sawdust makes the blade hard to see. To solve this, I put a piece of tape on the front edge of the saw boot and marked a line coinciding with the path of the blade. Now I can easily follow my layout and cut clean, accurate lines.

Ramanand Rao

CAULK TUBE ORGANIZER

Tired of having your caulk tubes lying all over the workbench or your shelves? Make this organizer from a scrap of 2x8 and a piece of 1/4-in. plywood. Just lay out a pattern for your 2-in. hole saw to follow and drill holes through the 2x8. Then glue the plywood to the bottom. Now you can set it on a shelf and easily identify the tube you're looking for.

—Burnie Lorenz

EASY-TO-READ TOOL MARKINGS

Stamped-in tool markings can be tough to read. To solve this, I bought some white fingernail polish, brushed it on the tool and quickly wiped it with a clean cloth. The white polish stays in the grooves, and the numbers are easy to read at a glance. You can use lacquer thinner to wipe it if the polish dries too quickly.

—Graig Grequire

FRESHEN UP YOUR WORK BOOTS

At the end of the day, before I retire my work boots to the hall closet, I fill them with cedar chips. (Actually I slide in an old sock that's filled with cedar chips.) I've tried several store-bought products, but cedar chips seem to work the best at absorbing moisture and eliminating odors. I bought a bag of chips sold as animal bedding at my local pet store for $10, and it will last me for years. I change out the chips every month or so.

—Byron Derringer, Field Editor

REPLACEMENT SANDER PAD

The rubber cushion on my old palm sander was wearing thin around the edges. Because of its age, I couldn't find a replacement pad. As I was drinking my beverage with a foam can cover around it, I realized I could cut the foam to fit the sander and glue it on. I peeled off the old pad, cleaned the metal base and attached the foam with contact cement. Works for clamp-on as well as stick-on sanding squares! You can find can covers at discount and convenience stores.

—Allen J. Muldoon

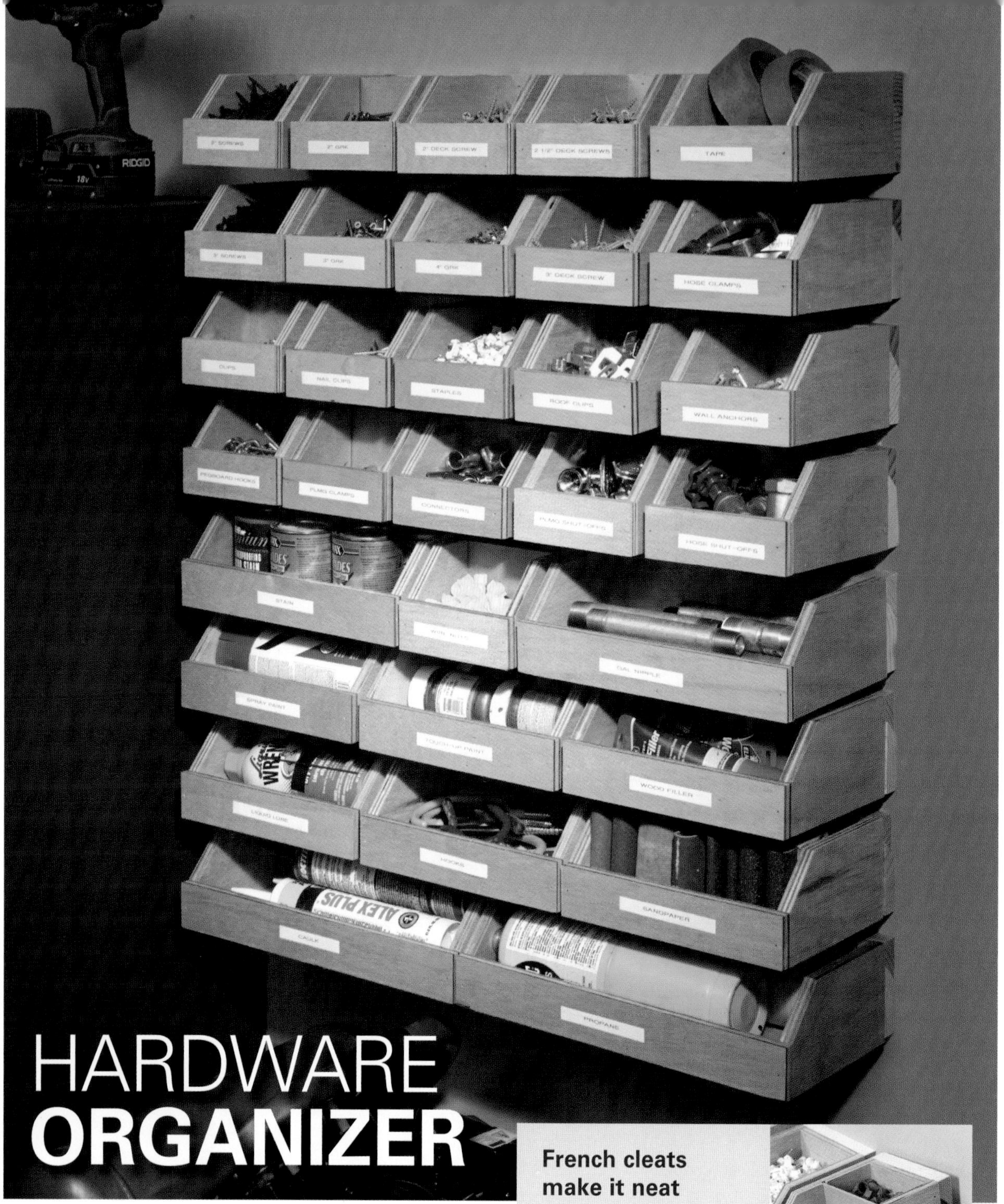

HARDWARE ORGANIZER

Flexible, portable—and possibly free!

by **Gary Wentz, Senior Editor**

French cleats make it neat

This simple hanging system—made from a 1x4 cut at a 45-degree bevel—lets you grab a bin and take it to the job, or rearrange bins instantly as your needs change.

DIY isn't just about building and fixing things. It's also about inventory management: maintaining a supply of the stuff you need and knowing where to find it. This simple bin system is the perfect project to get you organized. It's modeled on the systems used in cabinet shops, plumbers' vans and mechanics' garages.

The materials cost for the bins shown here is $30 to $55, depending on the type of plywood you choose. A store-bought light-duty system would cost just a few bucks more, but these homemade bins offer two big advantages: They're far tougher than plastic bins, and you can customize them to suit your stuff. Plus, they make the perfect scrap-wood project because all the parts are small. We built these bins from leftovers and didn't spend a dime.

Figure A
Basic bin

Inside dimensions: 4" wide x 6" long x 3" deep

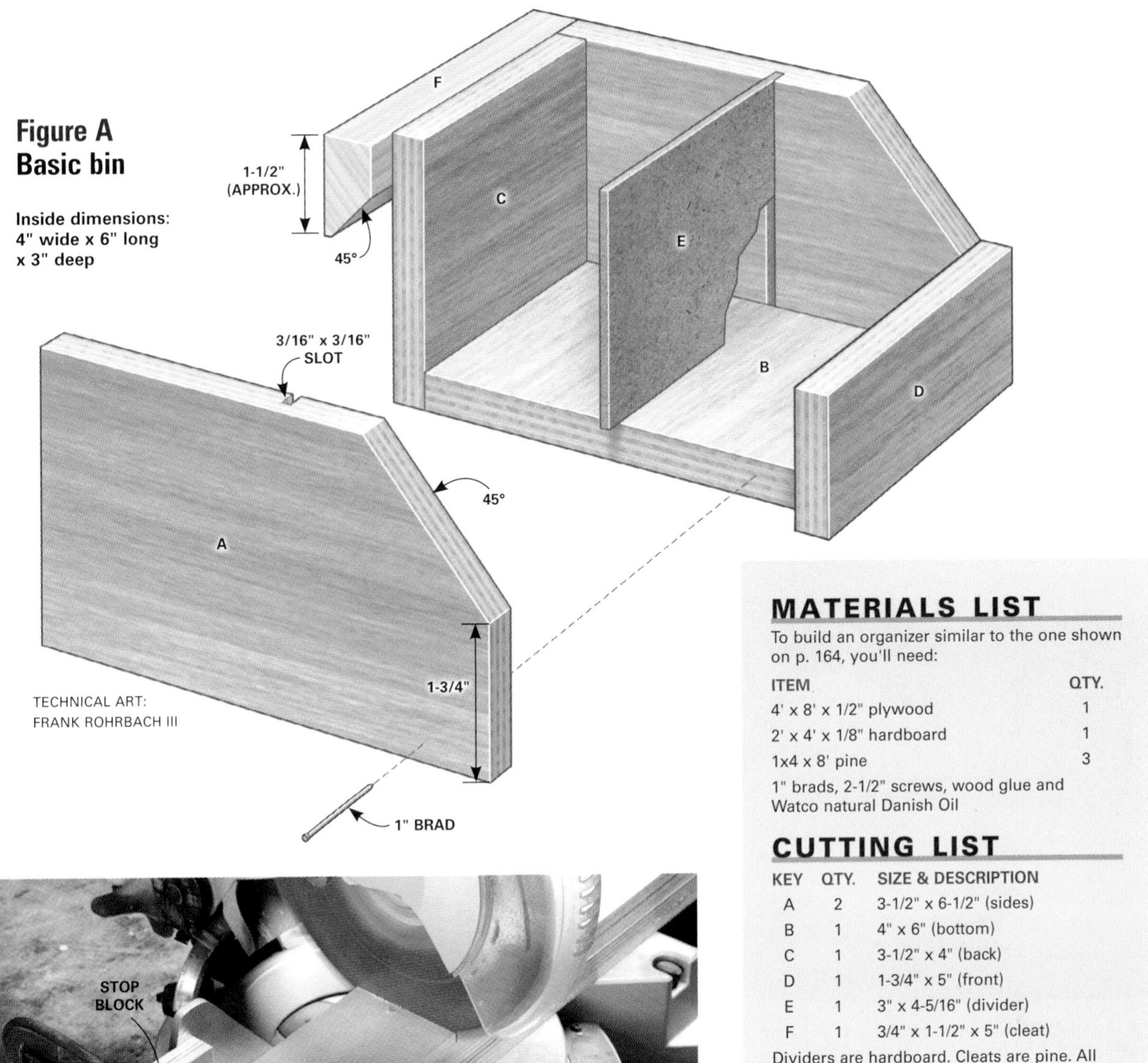

TECHNICAL ART:
FRANK ROHRBACH III

MATERIALS LIST

To build an organizer similar to the one shown on p. 164, you'll need:

ITEM	QTY.
4' x 8' x 1/2" plywood	1
2' x 4' x 1/8" hardboard	1
1x4 x 8' pine	3
1" brads, 2-1/2" screws, wood glue and Watco natural Danish Oil	

CUTTING LIST

KEY	QTY.	SIZE & DESCRIPTION
A	2	3-1/2" x 6-1/2" (sides)
B	1	4" x 6" (bottom)
C	1	3-1/2" x 4" (back)
D	1	1-3/4" x 5" (front)
E	1	3" x 4-5/16" (divider)
F	1	3/4" x 1-1/2" x 5" (cleat)

Dividers are hardboard. Cleats are pine. All other parts are plywood.

1 Cut the parts. Rip strips of plywood to width on a table saw, then cut them to length with a miter saw. Clamp a scrap of plywood to the saw's fence to act as a stop block. That lets you cut identical lengths from several strips with one chop.

Mass-produce parts

Begin by measuring the items you want to store. We found that the basic bin (see **Figure A** above) was just right for most stuff: nuts and bolts, construction screws, plumbing and electrical parts. For larger items, we made a few bins wider, but didn't change the bin sides (A). That approach is the most efficient because the sides are the most complex parts and changing them requires more fuss.

Once you've determined the sizes you want, fire up your table saw and rip plywood into strips. If you're following our plan, you'll need strips 1-3/4, 3-1/2 and 6 in. wide. Then cut the strips to length, making parts for one box only. Test-assemble the box to check the fit of the parts. **Note:** "Half-inch" plywood is slightly less than 1/2 in. thick, so the bin bottom (B) needs to be slightly longer than 6 in. Start at 6-1/8 in., then trim as needed. When you've confirmed that all the parts are the right size, mass-produce them by chopping the strips to length (**Photo 1**).

What it takes

TIME: 4 hours

COST: $55 or less

SKILL LEVEL: Beginner

TOOLS: Table saw, miter saw, brad nailer

2 Cut divider slots. Mount a fence on your saw's miter gauge and position a stop block on the fence. Run the bin side across the blade. Then rotate the side 180 degrees and make a second pass to widen the slot. **Caution:** You have to remove the guard for this step. Be extra careful!

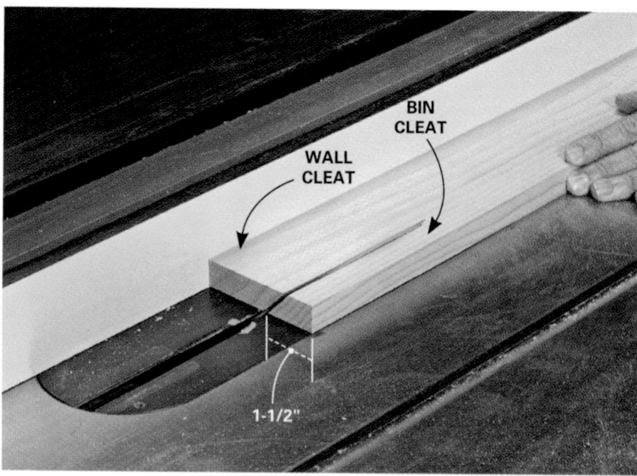

3 Cut the cleats. Tilt the blade to 45 degrees and set the fence so that the bin cleat is 1-1/2 in. wide. Getting the fence positioned may take some trial and error, so cut a test scrap first. **Note:** Our guard was removed for photo clarity. Use yours!

4 Assemble the bins. Join the parts with glue and brads. The glue will provide plenty of strength, so drive only as many brads as needed to hold the parts together while the glue sets.

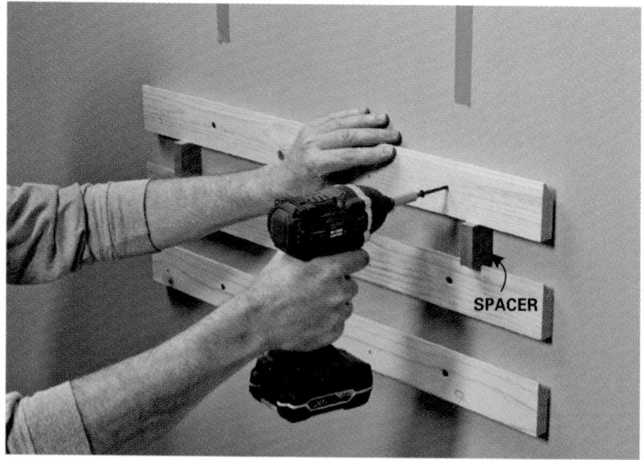

5 Mount the wall cleats. Mark the stud locations with tape and screw on the lowest cleat. Then work your way up the wall, using spacers to position each cleat.

If you want dividers (E) in any of the bins, your next step is to cut the divider slots. Set your table saw blade to a height of 3/16 in. Screw a long fence to your miter gauge and run the fence across the blade to cut a notch on the fence. Position a stop block 3-1/4 in. from the center of the notch. Place a side (A) against the block, run it across the blade, rotate it and cut again (**Photo 2**). Check the fit of a divider in the slot and reposition the block slightly to adjust the width of the slot. It may take two or three tries before you get the width right.

When you're done cutting slots, it's time to clip off one corner of each side. Set your miter saw 45 degrees to the right. Clamp on a stop block and "gang-cut" sides just as you did when cutting parts to length (similar to **Photo 1**). Remember this: Slotted sides require left/right pairs. For every side that you cut with the slot facing up, cut another with the slot down.

Next, cut the cleats (**Photo 3**). The 45-degree bevel cuts will leave sharp, splintery edges, so crank the table saw blade back to zero degrees and shave 1/8 in. off each cleat before cutting them to length.

Assemble them and hang them up

Assembly is fast and easy with glue and an 18-gauge brad nailer. First, tack the back (C) to the bottom (B), then add the sides (A), the front (D) and finally the cleat (F). After assembly, we wiped on two coats of Watco Danish Oil to keep the wood from absorbing greasy fingerprints and oils from hardware.

When mounting the wall cleats, start at the bottom. Make sure the bottom cleat is level and straight. Then cut spacers at least 1-3/4 in. tall and use them to position the remaining wall cleats (**Photo 5**). Larger cleats will create more space between rows of bins, making it easier to reach in and grab stuff. Bins filled with hardware put a heavy load on the cleats, so drive a screw into every wall stud.

TOGGLE CLAMP

SUPPORT

10 SIMPLE WOODWORKING JIGS

Built-in accuracy yields better results

by **Tom Caspar**

For a woodworker, good jigs are golden. They ensure that cuts are straight, holes are plumb and parts are square—among many other things. Sure, they take extra time to make, but they're worth it because you'll use them over and over again for years.

I've built lots of jigs over my 35 years as a cabinetmaker. Many, I regret to say, have been ridiculously complex, but these days I try to adhere to the KISS principle: Keep it simple, stupid! Here are 10 of the jigs I use most often.

MEET AN EXPERT

Tom Caspar's passion for woodworking goes way back. He's been a professional cabinetmaker since 1978 and recently retired as editor of *American Woodworker Magazine.*

Table saw guide box (photo above)

When I have to stand boards on end to machine them on my table saw, I pull out this simple box. It steadies the wood so I get a straight cut. The box is made of melamine and measures 8 in. square and 5-1/2 in. deep. It's screwed to two optional runners that are 12 in. long.

Here, I'm cutting slots into the ends of each part of a picture frame so I can join them with spline (thin pieces of solid wood). I couldn't do this using the table saw's fence alone because the fence doesn't offer enough support—it's not tall enough. Using this box, I'm sure to get an absolutely straight cut.

My picture frame piece is supported by a block that's screwed to the box. If I need to support pieces at 90 degrees—for cutting tenons, for example—I just remove the 45-degree support and screw on another.

To ensure a straight cut, I clamp the workpiece to the box. I use a toggle clamp to hold the frame's lower end because it's difficult to get a regular clamp down there. The table saw's fence gets in the way. You can buy a toggle clamp at a woodworking store or online for less than $10.

Drill press table

I love my drill press, but its table is way too small because it was designed for metalworking. In addition, the table doesn't have a fence or an insert to back up holes drilled all the way through a piece of wood. This jig solves all three problems.

I made the table from three layers of 1/2-in. medium-density fiberboard glued together. It's fastened to the machine's table from underneath with four lag screws.

The table's top layer is composed of three pieces. The outer pieces are glued to the table, while the center piece—the insert—is loose. The insert is 1/8 in. narrower than the gap between the two outer pieces. I installed three flat-head screws in the side of the insert and adjusted them so the insert fits snug in the gap (see detail, below left). When I need a fresh surface to drill into, I slide the insert in or out, flip it around or flip it over. I also made a few extra inserts so I can toss one away when it starts looking like Swiss cheese.

The fence is just a plain board clamped to the table.

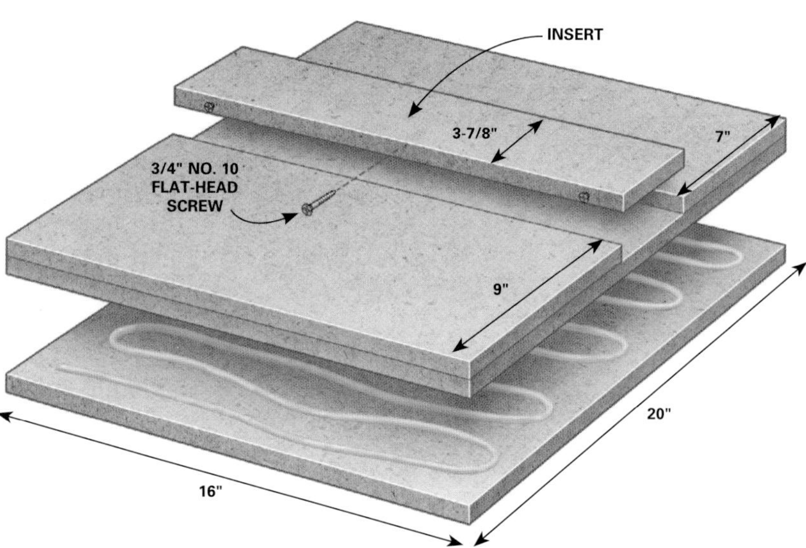

Squaring blocks

A cabinet that's out of square is like a house built on a foundation that's not level. Good luck getting doors to hang right! When I glue and clamp up a case, I often use a couple of "squaring blocks" to make sure the case has 90-degree corners. I clamp the blocks to the case before putting the final squeeze on the case's clamps.

This type of squaring block is very easy to make. First, cut a piece of plywood about 8 in. square. (Make sure the inside corner is truly square by testing it with a combination square.) Next, screw two 3/4-in. x 2-3/4-in. x 7-in. lips to adjacent sides of the block for clamping. Leave a gap at the inside corner of the block so you can remove glue that squeezes out of the joint.

1 Perfect dadoes made easy. Use this jig to rout a dado that perfectly fits any piece of 3/4-in. plywood. Take two passes with a 1/2-in. top-bearing bit.

Jig for routing dadoes

When I build a cabinet, I often use dadoes to ensure that shelves and partitions are spaced correctly. To make a strong joint, the width of the dadoes must exactly match the thickness of the plywood. That can be a challenge because few pieces of plywood are precisely 3/4 in. thick. They're usually 1/32 in. or so less than the "nominal" thickness. I designed this jig to rout perfect-fitting dadoes for any piece of 3/4-in. plywood regardless of its actual thickness.

I use a special top-bearing trim router bit (below) with the jig. The bit is 1/2 in. wide, 1/2 in. long and has a bearing mounted above the cutter. The bearing is flush with the bit's cutting edges.

TOP-BEARING BIT

The routing jig has two long, parallel guides made from 1/2-in. MDF. When I rout the dado, I ride the bearing along one guide, then make a second, return pass and ride the bearing along the second guide. This way, the space between the guides determines the width of the dado.

Setting up the guides is easy. One guide is fixed to the jig's 3/4-in. cross members; the other is loose and adjustable. I take two small pieces of the plywood I'm using and place them against the fixed guide. Then I slide the adjustable guide against the pieces and clamp the guide to the cross members. Done!

2 Goof-proof setup. Set up the jig using scrap pieces of your plywood to space the guides. It's foolproof!

Boost your holding power

When you clamp a board using only one side of your vise, have you noticed that the board often slips or rotates if you push down on it? That's because the vise's jaws don't stay parallel when the vise is tightened. Your board is getting pinched only along one edge. Even the best vises "rack" like this.

Fixing the problem is quite simple. You just need to place a spacer on the opposite side of the vise. The spacer should be the same thickness as your workpiece—a scrap offcut works well. Drive a screw into one end of the spacer or pinch it with a spring clamp so you don't have to hold on to the spacer while tightening the vise.

Sacrificial fence

When I have to adjust my table saw's fence so it sits right next to the blade, I put a "sacrificial" fence on the saw. Using a sacrificial fence avoids accidentally cutting into the real fence, which would be really bad news.

My sacrificial fence is made of four thicknesses of 1/2-in. MDF glued together. (Three-quarter-inch plywood would work just as well.) I cut the middle pieces into thirds in order to create holes for clamping. The holes ensure that the clamp's heads won't get in my way when I'm making a cut.

The beauty of this system is that you can use all sides of the fence until it wears out—but it's easy to make another!

Extra-large sander table

When I bought a benchtop disc sander a few years ago, I asked the clerk, "What's with the small table? I'm not just making dollhouse furniture, you know."

Well, of course the clerk couldn't make the table larger, but I sure could. I made a new one and clamped it to the original table. At first I thought I would add the extra-large table only when I needed it, but once I put it on, I never took it off! This jig is far fancier than it has to be—a plain piece of melamine would suffice.

My favorite materials for jigs

You can build a good jig from just about anything, but I usually turn to three different materials: MDF, Baltic birch plywood and melamine. Each has its own advantages—and disadvantages.

- MDF (medium-density fiberboard) is inexpensive and dead flat. It's not very strong, however, and will sag if left unsupported.
- Baltic birch—or equivalent plywood made from multiple veneers of equal thickness—is much stronger and stiffer than MDF. It also holds screws much better. Large pieces may or may not be flat. The best material comes in awkward-to-transport 5 x 5-ft. sheets.
- Melamine has two slick faces. If you need parts to slide past each other, this stuff is great. However, melamine usually has a chipboard core, which doesn't hold small screws very well.

No-wiggle crosscuts

If your miter gauge's bar wiggles in the saw's miter slot, you'll have a hard time getting an absolutely straight crosscut. Here's a way to fix that: Use two miter gauges connected by a fence.

An extra miter gauge isn't very expensive, but you can cut the cost to zero by making one yourself. Glue two pieces of Baltic birch plywood together to form an L-shape body, then carefully cut a bar to fit snugly into your saw's miter slot.

I used a piece of maple to make the bar, but 1/4-in. tempered hardboard is also a good choice. Glue the bar to the body using spring clamps, so you can easily adjust the bar to be exactly 90 degrees to the body before the glue sets. Install screws later.

You probably won't be able to use your saw's guard with this setup, so it's smart to add a plastic shield to the fence. The shield will remind you to keep your fingers away from the blade and will keep sawdust out of your eyes.

Three-layer hole spacer

OK, I know you've seen this trick before—using a piece of pegboard to drill evenly spaced holes for shelf pins. But here's my take on it: Make the jig from three layers of pegboard.

A thick jig has a couple of advantages. First, the holes won't wear out as fast (holes in a single layer of pegboard tend to become oval quickly). Second, the additional thickness will help keep your drill perpendicular to the panel.

When using the jig, I tape over the holes I don't need so I don't make a dumb mistake. I also slide a wood block onto the drill bit to limit the hole depth.

So, how do you keep the holes aligned when gluing the pieces together? It's really quite simple. Insert a couple of 1/4-in. machine bolts through opposite ends of the glue-up, then add washers and nuts. Tightening the nuts will force the pieces into alignment and keep them there. Trim the edges of the jig after the glue dries.

Accurate miter saw cuts

I clamp this small Baltic birch table to my miter saw when I want to cut a few short pieces to an exact length. The slot in the table's fence shows me precisely where the blade will cut—I just mark my piece with a pencil and line up the mark with the slot.

The slot has "zero clearance," meaning there's no gap on either side of the blade. The slot in the table is zero clearance too. Zero-clearance slots reduce tear-out to an absolute minimum, eliminating splintered edges.

When I made the table, the fence was one long piece of wood. I screwed cleats to the table's ends to lock the table in place, then lowered the saw to cut the slot in the fence. Note that the table must be wider than your saw's turntable—the uncut portion of the table is what holds it together!

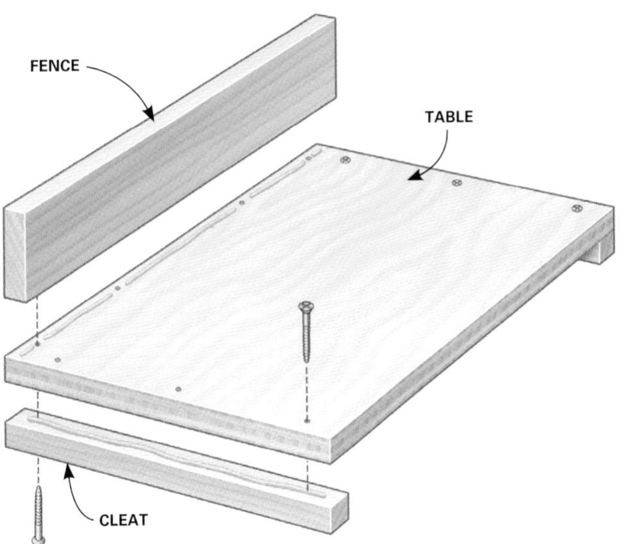

WOODWORKING & WORKSHOP PROJECTS & TIPS

GET **CREATIVE** WITH **TOOLS**

We've all done it: When the right tool for the job isn't nearby—or doesn't exist—we do the best we can with what we've got. Here are examples of creativity at its finest.

by **Gary Wentz, Senior Editor**

Cut with a drill

If you need to shorten a bolt, let your drill do the hard work. Spin two nuts onto the bolt, tightening them against each other. Then chuck the bolt into the drill and hold a hacksaw blade against the spinning bolt. The nuts help to steady the blade and clean off burrs when you unscrew them.

Shape stone with a router

Special routers made just for shaping stone spin big, water-cooled bits. But you don't need that expensive setup for small profiles. Instead, just chuck a diamond-grit bit into your wood router. Works great, even on hard granite. Like other diamond bits, it leaves a pretty rough surface. You can shine up a routed edge with diamond polishing pads. This granite tile edge was rubbed down with a 150-grit pad, followed by 400 and 800 grits. Diamond bits and pads are available online. Prices vary but you can find them for about $20 each.

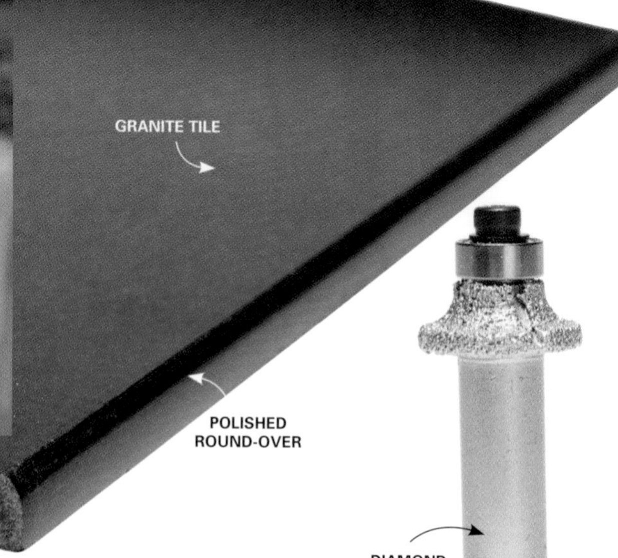

Flatten a board with a router

This is a slow, crude method. But if you don't have a planer—or the board is too wide for a planer—it may be the only way. First, replace the router's base plate with an oversize plate made from 1/4-in.-thick acrylic (available at home centers). Attach stretchers to the plate, lock a straight bit into the router and set up rails to support the stretchers. To lock the board into place, drive a couple screws deep enough so that the router bit can't hit them. Make shallow cuts, lowering the bit again and again until the board is flat. Then flip the board over and flatten the other side.

Uncork with a screw

When you can't find a corkscrew, a screw will do. You may work up a thirst while yanking out the cork—it takes some muscle—but refreshment awaits. Be sure to use a screw with coarse threads.

Drive spikes with a demo hammer

Mauls and sledgehammers are the usual tools for driving huge nails. But a demolition hammer is a lot easier on your arms. To make it work, you need a ground rod driver, which is designed to ram electrical ground rods deep into soil. With a smaller demo hammer like the one shown here, you'll still have to drill holes before you drive. You can rent a demo hammer for about $50 per day. Some rental centers also have ground rod drivers, or you can buy one online for about $55. Be careful which one you buy; the driver and the demo hammer must use the same locking system.

DEMO HAMMER

GROUND ROD DRIVER

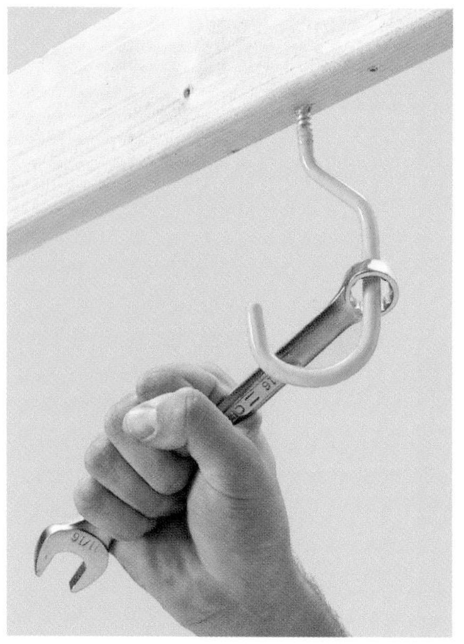

Drive hooks with a wrench

Screwing in a big storage hook requires strong hands or pliers (which wreck the plastic coating). Or you can use a wrench. Start by screwing in the hook by hand, then slip the wrench onto the hook. The wrench will catch the front of the hook and drive it home.

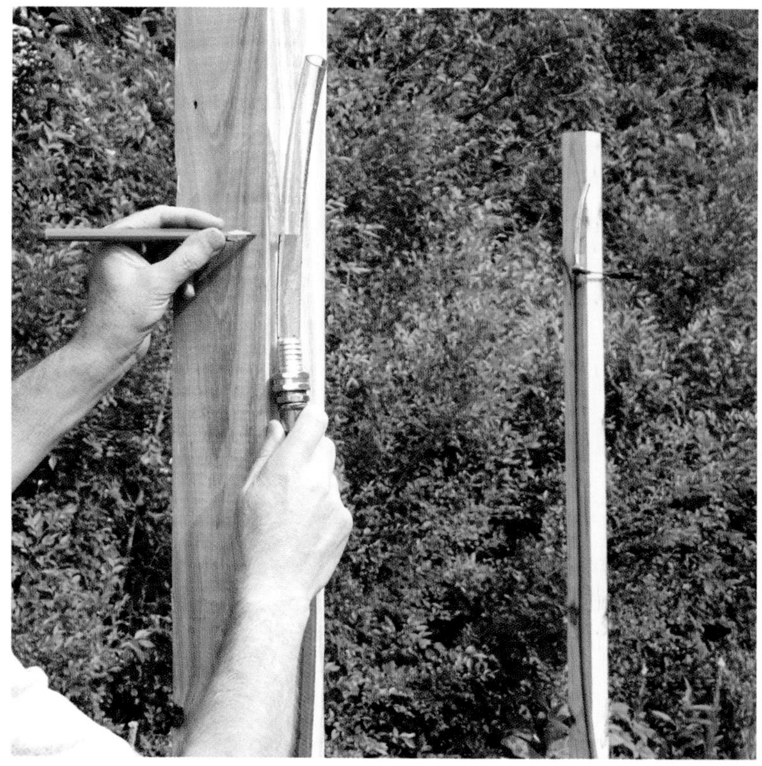

Level with a garden hose

When you need to level over long distances, around obstacles, even around corners, nothing beats a water level. You can buy one online, but you'll pay $35—or more. For $15 or less, you can rig up your own with parts found at any home center. The version shown here is made from male and female barbed hose fittings and 5/8-in. clear tubing.

Mark angles with a miter gauge

A table saw's miter gauge makes a great protractor for marking angles accurately.

Brush with a drill

Got a big scrubbing job on your list? Chuck a brush into your drill and save the elbow grease. You'll find drill-ready brushes for all kinds of scrubbing at drillbrush.com for $10 to $30 each.

Buff a finish with a sander

A classic way to shine up a dull finish—whether it's been sanded or is just worn—is to "rub it out" with very fine steel wool. But here's a faster way: Set your random orbit sander on an abrasive pad. This tabletop got three coats of polyurethane, followed by wet sanding with 600-grit sandpaper. An 800-grit pad then brought back a satin luster. Very-fine abrasive pads are available online and at some auto parts stores.

Lube with a pencil

It's not the perfect lubricant for most jobs, but the graphite from your pencil is slippery stuff, and it's always right there in your tool belt. Just rub the part to make it slick.

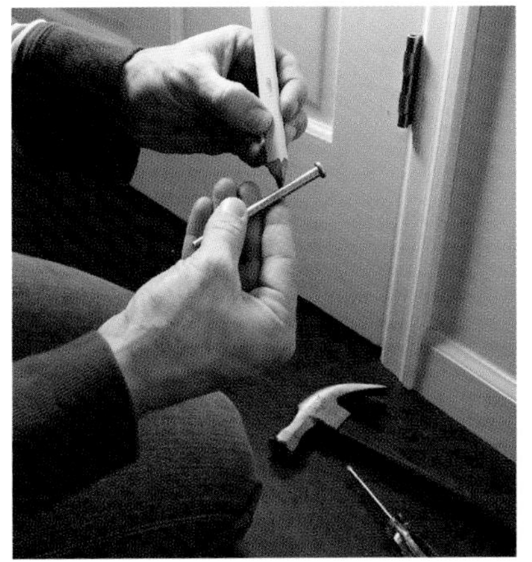

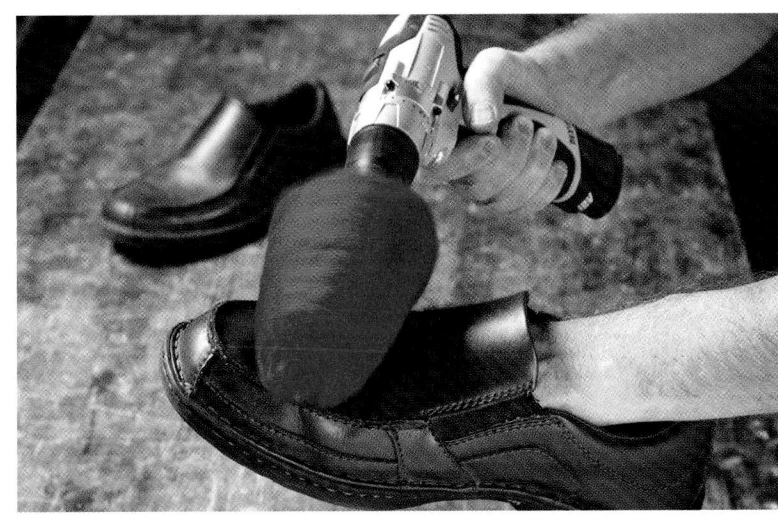

Shine shoes with a drill

Thirty seconds with a drill-powered buffer does wonders for dull shoes. For a glossier shine, apply polish before buffing. You can get a drill buffer for about $20 online. Search for "drill shine shoes."

Lift with a clamp

Whether you're raising plywood to the roof or lugging a sheet of MDF across your shop, a C-clamp gives you something to grab on to.

Inject glue with a compressor

Ever tried to work glue into a crack with a toothpick? It kinda works, but it's slow and sloppy. A blast of air, on the other hand, drives the glue in deep, evenly and fast. Don't have an air compressor? Hold your shop vacuum nozzle under the crack so it can suck glue deep into the crack.

SPECIAL SECTION

Work Smarter

LADDER CADDY

When I was hanging suspended grid for ceiling tiles, I was constantly switching between two drills—one to drill pilot holes, the other to drive screws. Tired of changing back and forth and running up and down the ladder, I thought there must be a better way. I found a scrap of 3/4-in. plywood (10 in. x 24 in.) and cut an opening in it to fit over the stepladder (7 in. x 14 in.). Then I made cutouts to hold my drill and my driver. I wedged a scrap piece of 2x4 between the ladder top and the holder to stabilize it when one tool was in use. This seat-of-the-pants solution saved me a lot of time and labor. I now use it for a variety of ladder-related tasks.

—Ron Brewer

CUFFS FOR CLEANLINESS

I use rubber gloves for all types of tasks involving solvents, chemicals, grease, paint, stain, bleach and especially motor oil. To keep whatever liquid you're using from dripping down your arm, fold a cuff at the end of the glove. It'll catch the drips before they find their way to your armpit.

—Mike Cutini

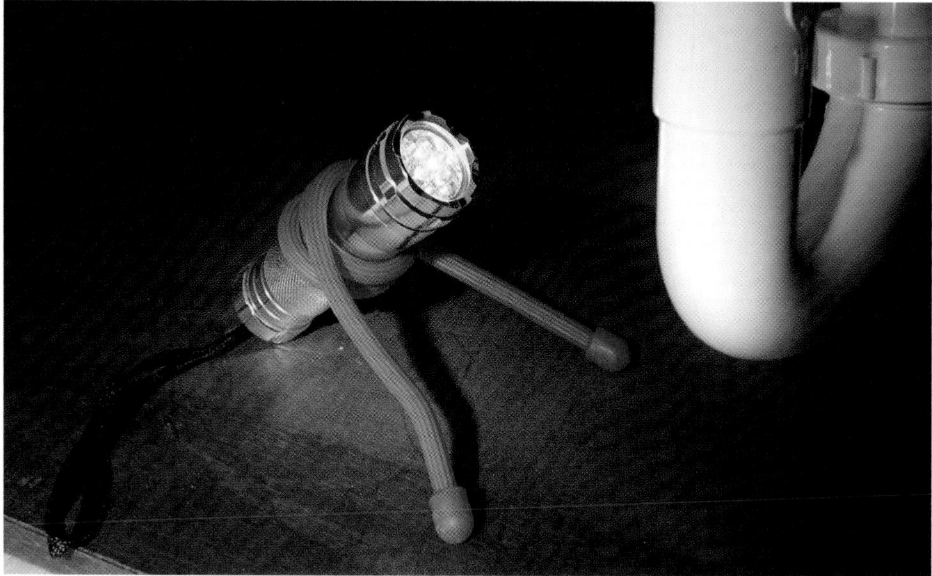

GEAR STAND

I bought a couple of flexible gear ties at my local hardware store for twisting together trim and holding skis to my car rack. Now I keep one with my portable flashlight for setting it up at just the right angle when I'm working in dark corners. You just bend the ties and they hold that shape until you're ready to change it. They cost about about $5 a pair.

—Mike Grimm

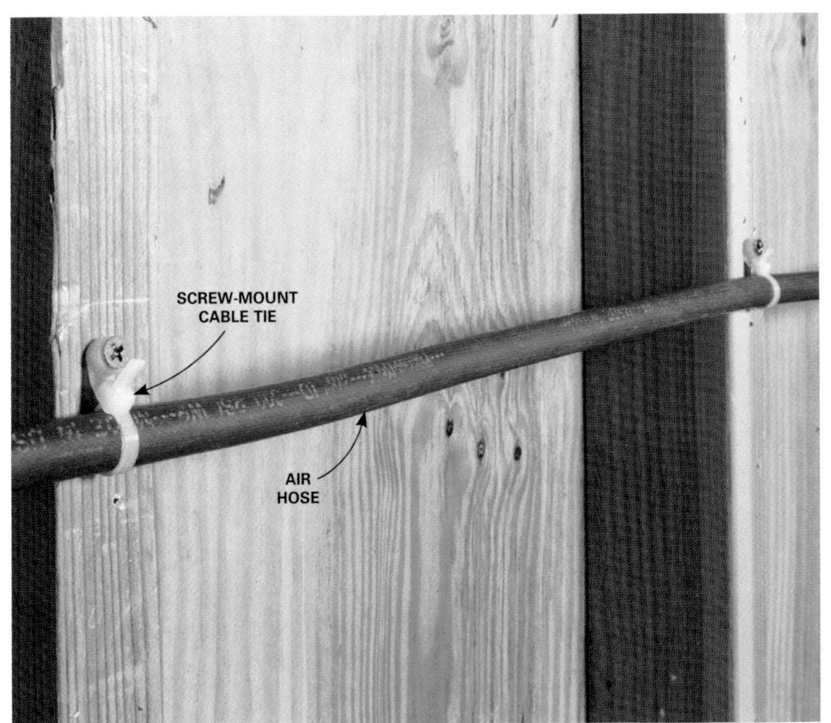

SCREW-MOUNT CABLE TIE

I use my air compressor a lot, but it's as loud as a freight train, and is always interrupting the ball game on the radio. So I moved it out of my shop and into a storage room. Instead of running an expensive copper air line from the compressor to my shop, I just hung a regular air hose on the wall with screw-mount cable ties. A bag of 50 ties cost me less than $10, and it took me about 15 minutes to hang the air hose.

Travis Larson,
Senior Editor

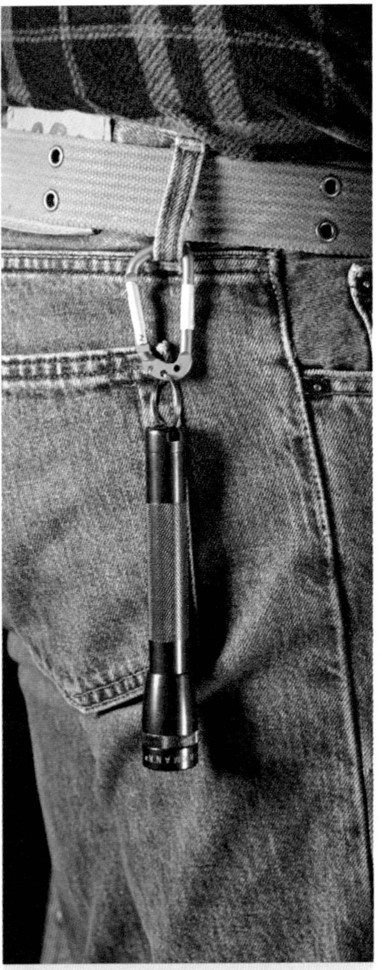

"FLASHY" BELT ACCESSORY

When I had to climb a ladder to get into a dark attic space, I needed to find a safe way to carry a flashlight and tools with me. So I fastened a small flashlight to a key ring and then clipped it to a carabiner that I got from the key-making department at the home center. Now I can hang my flashlight from a belt loop and safely climb and navigate hands-free. Once I'm in the attic, I can either hold the light in my hand or use the carabiner to hang it from a nail in the rafters.

—Robbie Keman

Work Smarter

NITRILE-PALM GLOVES

If you don't already know about nitrile-palm gloves, go out and get some today. They are that good. There are many styles, but our favorites have a stretchy and breathable fabric on the back, and a textured nitrile foam coating on the palm.

What makes them so great? One, they are unbelievably tough. Electricians use them, plumbers use them, bricklayers use them, carpenters use them—all pros who handle sharp, abrasive and caustic stuff. Two, the fabric breathes, so your hands won't feel clammy. And three, they give you great dexterity. You can pick up a finish nail while wearing these gloves, something that's hard to do wearing leather gloves.

You'll find lots of brands, including Atlas and Ansell. Ansell makes the gloves in numeric sizes (rather than S, M, etc.) to help you get a precise fit. These gloves cost about $3 to $10 a pair and are even cheaper by the dozen. Buy them online, at home centers or at pro tool outlets.

GreatGoofs®

Doggone helper!

Because of a recent insurance inspection, I was forced to finish building our back porch and steps quickly. It was raining at the time, so I did all the cutting under the cover of the front porch and hauled the pieces into the backyard to install. In the meantime, our dachshund, Beavis, was very interested in the excavation part of the project. He spent the day digging inside the area where I was building.

When the final board was screwed into place, my "helper" was nowhere to be found. Then I heard whining under the steps and realized what I had done. While I was working on the front porch, Beavis's exploring had led him under the porch for a snooze. Of course, removing one board wasn't enough to get him out. I had to remove several and crawl in there to fetch him! Next time I'll screen my helpers more carefully.

Gerald (Gary) Price

KICK UP A DUST STORM

Most blow guns have a pinhole-size opening. That's fine for blowing away small wood or metal chips. But these Typhoon variable-flow blow guns have multiple openings and a tapered tip that develops 2.1 lbs. of thrust. Use one to blow your entire work area or even blast the water off your freshly washed car. It's the most powerful blow gun we've ever seen. And the trigger is a true variable-volume design, not just full on or full off.

Buy the traditional gun (about $15) for workbench use or the 12-in.-long version (about $20) to gain some distance between you and the dust cloud you'll kick up. Find them at air tool sellers or online.

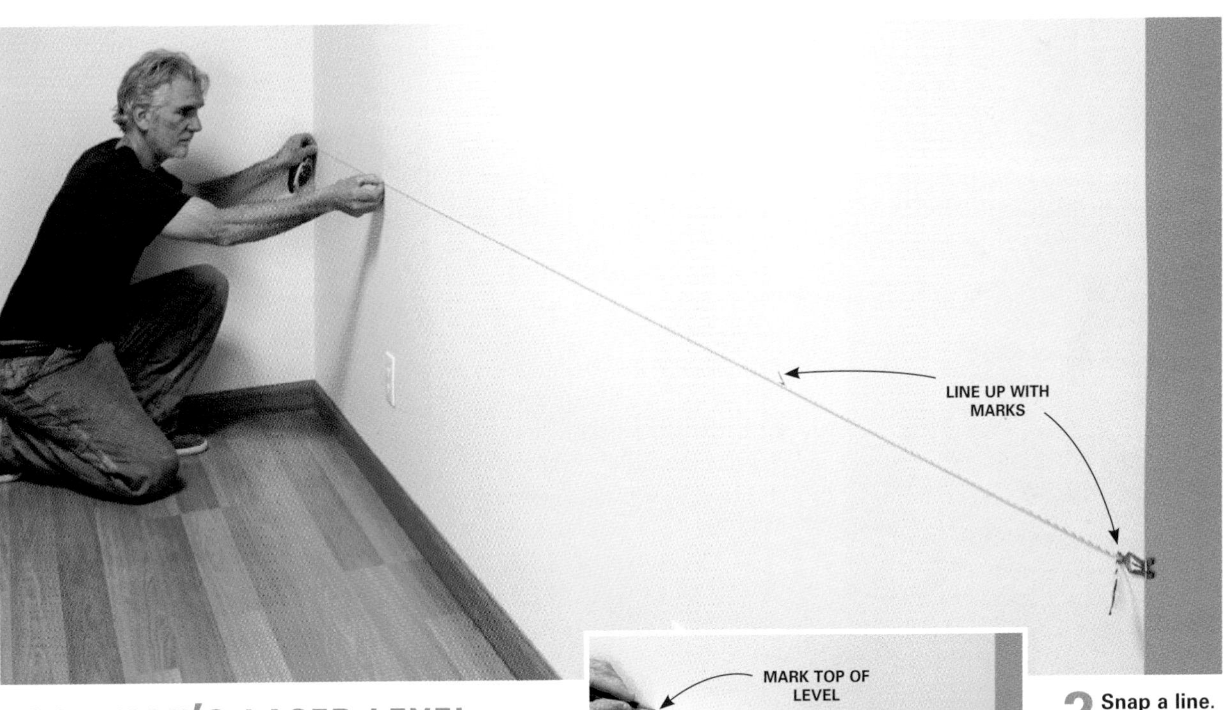

2 Snap a line. Line up a chalk line with the two marks and snap a line.

1 Make a level mark. Align the top of the level with your mark and center the bubble. Mark the opposite end.

POOR MAN'S LASER LEVEL

If you need to make a long, level line and don't own a laser, try this method. Mark the desired height of your line on the wall. Hold your level at the mark and adjust it until the bubble is centered. Then make a mark at the opposite end of the level (Photo 1). Extend the line by stretching a chalk line and aligning it with both marks (Photo 2). If you're working indoors, use dust-off marking chalk, which is easy to erase. Stretch the chalk line and snap it to create a perfectly level line across the wall.

Work Smarter

1 Rest the level against a corner. The bubble on this level is lined up with the right-hand line.

CHECK OLD LEVELS BEFORE YOU USE THEM

When levels get beaten up like this one, it's likely that some or all of the vials will be out of whack. And if you have a super cheap and/or older one, don't trust it! Before you do any more leveling, test the vials for level (horizontal) and for plumb (vertical). Check the leveling vials by placing your level on a flat surface and piling playing cards under one end until the bubble is centered. Now lift the level and rotate it 180 degrees, end for end, and rest it on the cards in the same location. The bubble should still be centered. If it's not, your leveling vial is inaccurate.

To check for accurate plumb vials, rest your level against a wall and note the location of the bubble between the lines (Photo 1). Then rotate the level 180 degrees, edge to edge, keeping the same end facing up (Photo 2). The bubble should be in the same spot. If not, your plumb vial is off. Levels like the one shown can be adjusted, but many levels can't. In some cases, one set of vials will be good, and you can simply cross out the bad set with a permanent marker to avoid using it. Or toss a bad level and buy a new one.

2 Put the opposite edge against the corner. Now the bubble on this level is lined up with the left-hand line, indicating a bad plumb vial. Adjust the level or mark this vial as bad with a permanent marker.

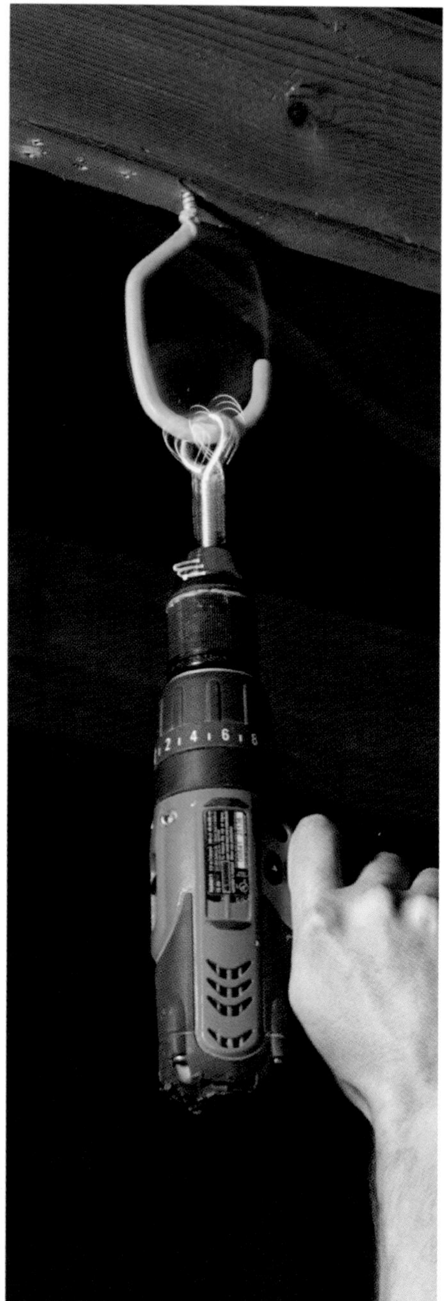

FAST HANGER HOOK INSTALLATION

The job of screwing hanger hooks into the ceiling is a lot easier when you chuck the hook into a power drill. I simply slip the eyebolt over the hook and turn on the drill. This goes a lot quicker than using a hand screwdriver and is a lot easier on your wrists!

Larry Dobbs

PAINTING TOOL DRYING CAGE

An inverted tomato cage makes a great drying rack for rollers, brushes, pads, rags and whatever is wet after painting clean-up. The stuff dries quickly outdoors, and there's room for everything!

—Tom Anderson

BATTERY I.D.

I got extra batteries for my cordless tools, but I could never remember which battery was newly charged and which was run down. Now I can easily tell them apart because I painted a number on each battery with my kid's white nail polish. It dries fast and is—you got it—"tough as nails."

—Tom Baker

COLOR-CODED TOOLBOXES

I have different toolboxes for different jobs around the house. Occasionally I'd grab a tool out of one box and then put it away in another. Eventually all my flat-head screwdrivers would end up in one toolbox. To solve the problem, I now mark the handles of the tools and the corresponding toolbox with a band of colored electrical tape. Now all the tools are in the box where they belong.

—Kim Litkenhaus Marino

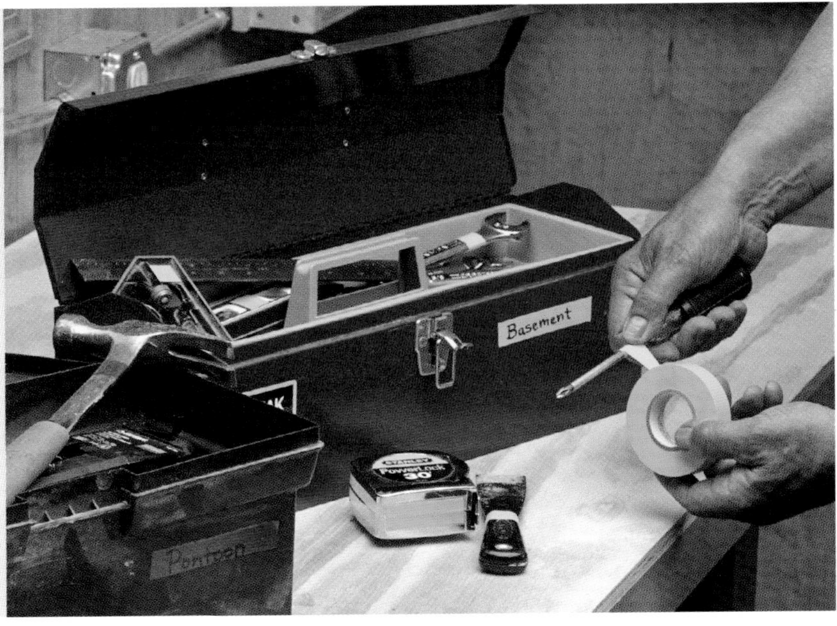

Work Smarter

EXTEND YOUR LEVEL

You could use a plumb bob to transfer layout marks from the floor to the ceiling, but extending your level with a straight board works much faster. Just remember to mark on the correct side of the level.

ADJUSTABLE TABLE HEIGHT

When I'm working on projects in the shop, I often have my laptop close by so I can refer to an article or take notes. The craft table I'd been using was too low, so I got some pieces of 1-1/4-in. PVC pipe to slip over the legs. I measured the height so it was just right—no more aching back! The pipe pieces are easy to slip off when we need the table for another use.

—Donna M. Courie

A WELL-LIT TOOLBOX

When I was at the hardware store, I saw this nifty battery-operated light. It attaches to a cooler lid and turns on when the lid is lifted. I thought it would be a great addition to my black toolbox. The light mounts with double-stick tape to any smooth surface. It worked so well that I put one on my truck toolbox too. The light stays on for about 20 seconds (long enough if your toolbox is organized) then shuts off. Coghlan's Cooler Light is available for about $7 at sporting goods stores, hardware stores and online.

—Brian Thomton

5 Exterior Repairs & Improvements

IN THIS CHAPTER

Home Care & Repair.................................184
Fix a driveway apron, touch up a vinyl-clad fence and patch hairline cracks in concrete

How to Roof a House................................187

Great Goofs..195
Hookin' ladder

Exterior Spray Painting.............................196

Tips for Reviving a Wood Deck.................. 200

FIX A DRIVEWAY APRON

It's normal for asphalt driveways to sink a bit over time. But when your driveway has sunk to the point where it's 4 or 5 in. lower than your garage floor, it's time to fix it. If you don't, water will pool in the depression, seep into the soil below, and eventually destroy the driveway.

Asphalt companies charge about $1,000 to dig out the old portion and install a new apron. Concrete contractors charge even more. But you can rebuild your asphalt driveway apron yourself. The entire job takes a full day and it's not much fun. But the materials and tools only cost about $250, so the savings is worth it.

You'll need a diamond blade for your circular saw, a tamper, a pry bar and a short square-blade shovel. Plus, you'll need enough cold patch material to fill in the trench you make (one choice is Quikrete Asphalt Cold Patch, $10 a bag). To figure out how many bags you'll need, refer to the depth and width tables on the bag. Finally, you'll need mineral spirits and rags for cleanup. Here's how to make the repair.

First check the weather

Cold patch cures by solvent evaporation, and it takes about 30 days to reach a full cure. So the best time to do the project is during an extended warm, dry spell. You can do it in spring or fall, but cold weather and rain will greatly extend the cure time.

Wear old clothes and protect your carpet

This is a messy job, and no matter how careful you are, you're going to get tar on your clothes and shoes. You can't wash off the tar with soap and water. So wear old clothes and shoes that you can toss into the trash when you're done. If you have to go into the house during the project, leave your shoes outside so you don't track tar into the house.

Cut out the sunken area

Cold patch works only when it's compacted and "keyed" into at least two vertical surfaces. So don't think you can build up the driveway height by pouring cold patch on top of the old sunken asphalt—the patching material will just break off in chunks. Instead, you'll have to cut out the sunken asphalt (**Photo 1**). After it's cut, lay a block of wood on the soil at the edge of the driveway, shove a pry bar under the old asphalt, and pry against the wood block. The old asphalt will lift up and break off in sections. Remove all the cut asphalt and scrape off any caulking material sticking to the edge of the garage floor.

Next, build a starter row of patch material (**Photo 2**). Once the starter row is in place and tamped, apply additional patch material in 1-in. layers (**Photo 3**). Resist the temptation to completely fill the area and compact it in

1 Cut out the sunken asphalt. Slap a diamond blade into your circular saw and set it to its maximum cutting depth. Then snap a chalk line out from the garage floor to a maximum distance of 24 in. Wear an N95 respirator and safety glasses and cut out the old asphalt.

2 Put in the bottom layer. Pour in a small amount of cold patch material and level it with a square-blade shovel. Tamp down a test section and measure the depth. The bottom layer should only be 1/2 in. thick when compacted. Add or remove cold patch material and then tamp down the entire starter row.

3 Build additional layers. Add and compact the cold patch in 1-in. layers until you reach the garage floor. Then overfill with an additional 1/2 in. of material and tamp to get a smooth surface.

4 Drive over it to compact. Cut a piece of plywood slightly wider than the trench. Lay it over the patch material and cover it with 2x4s. Then drive over it several times with your vehicle until the patch is level with the garage floor.

one fell swoop. You simply can't exert enough compaction force with a tamper to properly key it into the vertical surfaces—the patch material will just creep out the sides when you drive on it.

Once your tamped layers are level with the garage floor, add a final topping layer. Then lay down wood scraps and use your vehicle to do a final compaction (Photo 4). Clean all your tools with mineral spirits and dispose of the rags properly to prevent spontaneous combustion.

The instructions say you can drive over the patch immediately. But tires may still make slight depressions in the asphalt until it's fully cured, which takes 30 days. So leave the plywood in place for a few weeks at least.

HomeCare&Repair

TOUCH UP A VINYL-CLAD FENCE

Vinyl-clad chain-link fence keeps its appearance for a long time. But the vinyl can get scuffed and worn where the gate latch locks onto the post. The repair is a little tricky because you're trying to paint over vinyl and metal. If you use a spray paint formulated for metal, it won't bond well to the vinyl. Instead, coat the damaged area with paint formulated for plastic (Krylon Fusion is one choice).

Start by cleaning the damaged area and beyond with a household spray cleaner. Then rough up the surface (Photo 1). Finish the repair with special plastic paint (Photo 2). Let the repair dry at least 24 hours before operating the gate latch mechanism.

1 Sand the area. Lightly scuff the vinyl and metal with 120-grit sandpaper. Then wipe with a tack cloth.

2 Coat with paint. Apply a first coat of plastic paint and allow it to set up the recommended time shown on the label. Then apply a finish coat.

PATCH HAIRLINE CRACKS IN CONCRETE

It's easy to ignore hairline cracks in your sidewalk or concrete patio. But patching them early is the key to preventing them from growing into larger and uglier cracks. The type of sealant you use is critical to a long-lasting repair. Don't use a traditional vinyl or latex concrete patching product—it will dislodge as soon as the slab moves. Instead, use a self-leveling flexible urethane sealer (two choices are Quikrete Polyurethane Self-Leveling Sealant and DAP Concrete Waterproof Filler and Sealant).

Blow loose sand and debris out of the crack with compressed air. Cut the tube nozzle slightly smaller than the crack width and inject the sealer (Photo 1). Allow a few minutes for the surface bead to self-level. Clean up the excess with a rag and mineral spirits (Photo 2).

1 Use urethane sealant. Hold the tube upright and force the sealant deep into the crack until it oozes up around the nozzle tip.

2 Wipe off the excess. Wet a clean rag with mineral spirits and wipe across the crack to remove excess sealer.

HOW TO
ROOF A HOUSE

Our pros show you how to do it right—and save thousands!

by **Mark Petersen, Contributing Editor**

There's no question that roofing your own house is a big undertaking, but if you have a strong back, a couple of buddies who "owe" you and a week of vacation time, you could save yourself thousands of dollars. The cost of pro installation varies a great deal, but in most regions you can expect to save about $150 per 100 sq. ft. of roof—that's about $3,600 for a typical house!

A DIY project like this won't be nearly as intimidating once you know the basics, and it doesn't require a lot of expensive tools. And if you do it right, you won't have to worry about it for another 25 years. If you need a new roof but are planning to hire it out, read on anyway to learn all the steps your crew should take for a first-class roofing job.

What it takes

TIME: Four days for a crew of three to do a simple roof

COST: $150 to $175 per 100 sq. ft. for materials

SKILL LEVEL: Intermediate

TOOLS: Ladder, hammer, staple tacker, chalk line, tin snips, utility knife with hook blades, caulking gun, roofing gun, air compressor, scaffolding for steep roofs, safety equipment

CONSULTANT: INTELLIGENT DESIGN CORP.

1 Stick on the underlayment. Protect the roof against ice dams and windblown rain with self-stick ice-and-water underlayment. Peel off the top half of the plastic backing as you unroll the underlayment.

2 Peel off the bottom backing. Make sure the underlayment lies smooth before you nail the top edge. Then pull off the lower half of the backing.

3 Add the second course of underlayment. Install the second course just like the first, using the guidelines on the underlayment to get the correct overlap.

It's been awhile, but I've worked on dozens of roofs in my carpentry career. I thought I knew all there was to know. But after recently spending a day with a full-time professional roofing crew, I learned that a lot has changed since my last job ... and all for the better! Metal flashing techniques have improved. Self-stick underlayment is more widely used. And more attention is paid to proper attic ventilation. I also have to admit that these guys are a heck of a lot faster than I ever was.

Can you do it yourself?

Make no bones about it—roofing is hard work. There's no hiding from the elements. You can't be afraid of heights and you need to be pretty fit. Before committing to this project, try this: Get out a ladder and climb up onto your roof. If you can't walk around on it comfortably, hire a pro. If you passed this first test, go to the lumberyard or home center and throw a bundle of shingles onto your shoulder. Imagine yourself carrying that load up a ladder ... many, many times.

If you're still feeling positive at this point, why not give it a shot? You can skip a lot of heavy lifting by having your roofing supplier hoist the shingles onto the roof. Be sure you spread the load evenly across the length of the roof's peak. However, don't have the shingles delivered to the roof if you have two layers of old shingles yet to tear off—it could be too much weight for your trusses.

Tear off the old

It's impossible to properly install new flashing and underlayment if you don't tear off the old roof beforehand. When tearing off the existing shingles, be sure to remove all the old nails or pound them flat. Protruding nails will tear holes in your new shingles. If you have movable items near your house and you're worried they might get damaged, relocate them. Invest in a few large tarps to protect your plants and landscaping and to catch the thousands of nails that will rain down off the roof. It can be downright impossible to remove old self-stick ice-and-water underlayment, but it's OK if you have to leave it in place. And if at all possible, have the rented trash bin parked close to the house so you can toss in the old shingles right from the roof. For more information, search for "roof tear off" at familyhandyman.com.

Install the drip edge

Metal drip edge isn't usually required (check with a local building official), but it gives roof edges a nice finished look, prevents shingles from curling over the edge, and keeps water from running directly down your fascia boards.

Before you install the underlayment, fasten the drip edge that covers the fascia on the eaves. The whole length of the fascia is probably not perfectly straight, so don't snap a line; just hold the drip edge snug against the fascia and fasten it through the top into the decking with roofing nails. Nail it every couple of feet.

Install the drip edge on the gable ends of the roof after you finish installing your underlayment. Start at the bottom side of the gable, and overlap the sections of drip edge a few inches as you work your way up the roof (see **Figure A**, p. 190). Use a tin snips to cut the drip edge to size.

Roll out the self-stick underlayment

When an ice dam forms on a roof (usually caused by poor attic insulation/ventilation), ice and water can work their way up under the shingles and leak back into the house. Also, strong winds can blow rainwater under shingles. Self-stick roofing underlayment (often called "ice-and-water" underlayment) can prevent this because it sticks to the roof decking to seal out water. It also seals around nails, which keeps water from leaking through nail holes.

Rolls of self-stick underlayment have a plastic backing so the material won't stick to itself. The backing is separated down the middle. Line up the lower edge of the roll with the outside of the drip edge. Peel back part of the uppermost backing on the roll, and nail the top corner of the underlayment to the decking. Start pulling the roll across the decking using the backing, making sure the material is lying as flat and as straight as possible as you pull.

You'll be able to roll out long sections at a time if you have a low-pitched roof, but the underlayment may slip off the eaves on steeper roofs, so roll out no more than 10 ft. there (**Photo 1**). It's important to make sure all your underlayment lies flat before you fasten it to the decking. Ripples and lumps can telegraph through the shingles and may be noticeable from the ground.

On warm days, self-stick underlayment will stick to clean decking without any fasteners. Fasten it to the roof with staples or nails on colder days, but only fasten the top part of the underlayment until you go back and peel off the bottom half of the plastic backing (**Photo 2**). The higher the temperature outside, the stickier the adhesive on the rolls gets. This ice-and-water underlayment is tricky to work with on super-hot days; keep that in mind when you plan your project.

Many severe climate areas require self-stick underlayment to be installed at least 2 ft. in from exterior walls. This means you'll need two rows if you have 2-ft. eaves. Any two sections of underlayment on the same row should overlap a

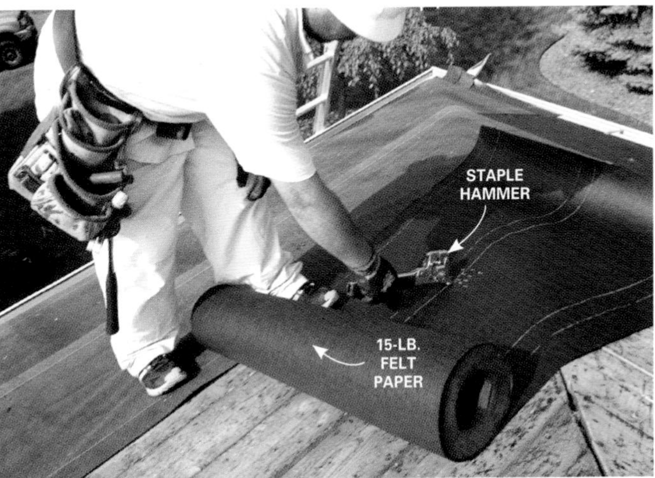

4 Roll on the felt paper. Cover the roof above the underlayment with roofing felt paper. To start each course, drive a dozen staples grouped close together. Then unroll the felt and straighten out the row before you add more staples.

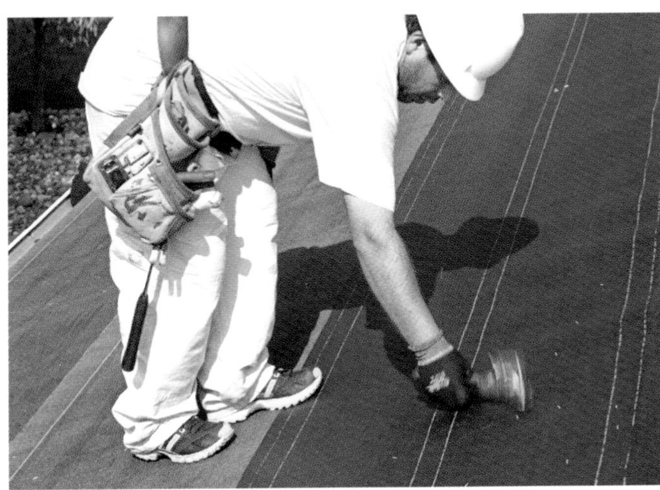

5 Don't skimp on staples. Place staples no more than 12 in. apart. Paper with too few staples will tear out under your feet and could cause a fall.

6 Overlap the ridge. Run the felt paper over the peak and overlap it onto the other side. Do the same when you reach the peak from the other side of the roof.

Figure A
Roofing overview

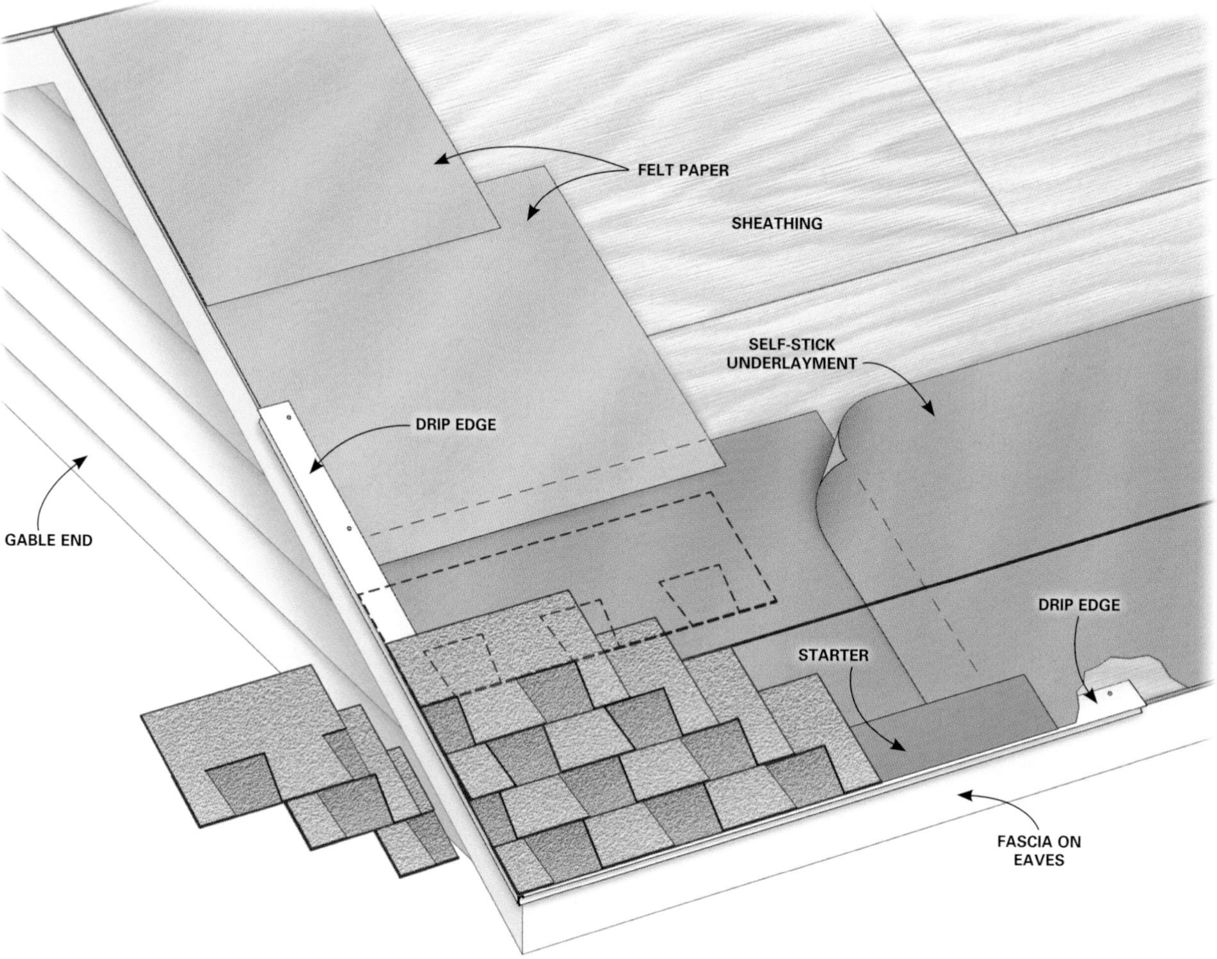

Stay safe

When it comes to roofs, even the best safety equipment is no substitute for common sense and good judgment. Here are some tips for working safely on a roof:

- Leave steep and/or high roof work to the pros. No amount of money you could save is worth the risk of death or a lifelong disability from a fall.
- A fall protection kit (harness, rope and hook) costs about $100 at home centers.
- Wet roofs are slippery. Wear shoes with soft rubber soles for extra traction.
- Keep the roof swept clean of dirt and debris.
- Everyone on the ground should wear a hard hat—even the most careful worker can drop a tool off the roof.
- Always look and call out before tossing anything down.
- Carefully position ropes and extension cords so they're not underfoot.
- Check the weight rating on your ladder—it needs to hold you plus 80 lbs.
- Extend the top of the ladder at least 3 ft. above the roof edge so you'll have something to hang on to as you step onto and off the roof.
- Never step on any of the ladder rungs above the roof.
- Set up scaffolding to install the drip edge and first few courses.

Figure B
Step and dormer flashing

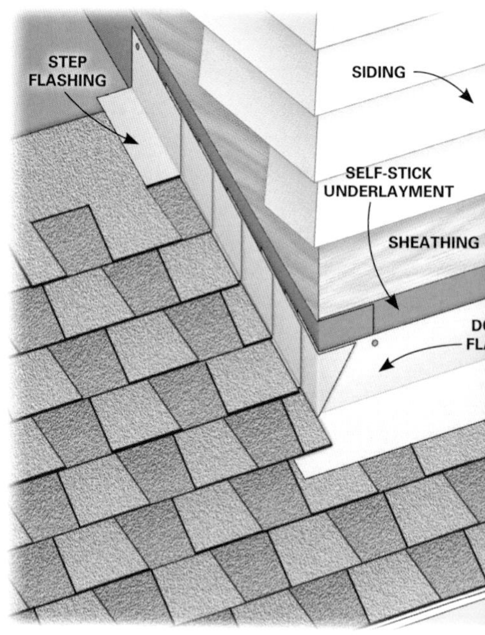

Rent or buy?

Unless your roof is tiny, you're going to want to get your hands on a pneumatic roofing nailer. Prices range from about $100 to over $300. Renting one costs about $35 a day or $90 a week, so if you own a compressor, you might as well buy rather than rent. A compressor rents for about the same as the nailer. If you don't own a compressor and know you're going to finish your house in less than a week, then renting is probably the way to go.

If you do buy a roofing nailer and you know you'll only use it for one job, a cheaper model will work just fine. It just won't be as durable as the high-end models the pros use. But don't tell anyone you bought it. If the word spreads that you're a roofing gun owner, you run the risk of being recruited by a whole bunch of friends and neighbors to help work on their roofs.

minimum of 6 in., and each course should cover at least 2 in. of the one below it (Photo 3). These rules can vary, so always consult your local building official.

Cover the roof with felt paper

Felt paper, also called tar paper or builder's paper, helps shed water that gets under the shingles, protects the asphalt shingles from the resins in the wood decking, increases a roof's fire rating and helps keep your house dry if it rains during the job. Most roofing suppliers carry 15-lb. and 30-lb. rolls of felt. For most applications, 15-lb. felt works just fine. Install 30-lb. felt if you plan to leave the paper exposed for more than a couple of days because it wrinkles less then 15-lb. And 30-lb. felt doesn't tear as easily, so it's safer to walk on when you're working on steeper pitches.

Start a row by rolling out a short section of paper and securing it with a dozen staples grouped together near the center of the paper (Photo 4). That way you'll then be able to roll out a long section and swing it back and forth until your overlap is even. Each row of paper should overlap the one below it at least 2 in. There will be overlap lines printed on the paper to guide you. Overlap seams on the same row 6 in.

Practice on a couple of 10-ft. sections until you get the hang of it, and don't roll out a 25-ft. section of paper on a steep roof or when it's windy. If you're fastening the paper with a staple hammer, try to get a staple in every square foot of the paper (Photo 5). That may seem like a lot, but insufficiently stapled paper can tear out under your feet, which could result in a fall. Don't walk on any paper that isn't completely stapled down. Fasten the felt with cap staples/nails if you're working on a windy day or are working on a roof with a pitch steeper than 6/12.

When you reach the top of the roof, run your last row long (Photo 6), and drape the paper over the peak (top ridge) onto the other side. When you reach the top on the other side of the roof, run that paper up and over as well. That way you'll end up with a watertight ridge. Your local building official may want to come out to inspect your roof

7 Flash the valleys. Install self-stick underlayment under the metal flashing. If you need more than one flashing in your valley, lay them both in place and make sure they're straight before nailing them down.

8 Fold flashing over the peak. Cut the flashing back to the peak along each crease. Then fold the flashing over the peak and cover the cut ends with self-stick underlayment.

at this point, but sometimes you can get by with snapping a few photos. Ask about the inspection schedule when you pick up your permit.

Waterproof your valleys

Roof valleys channel a lot of water, so they need extra protection. Start by installing self-stick underlayment on the decking. This process is much easier with two people. Cut the underlayment to size (or in sections for long valleys), and peel off the entire plastic backer. With a person on each end, fold the underlayment in on itself, sticky side out. Then lay it into the valley and unfold it. Try to push it down into the crease of the valley as tightly as possible. If this self-stick ice-and-water underlayment bridges both sides of the decking, leaving a gap underneath, it could tear once you install the metal valley flashing. Run the underlayment past the drip edge at the eaves, and trim off the extra with a utility knife. Once it's smooth, nail it down on the outside edges.

Finish installing felt paper on the rest of the roof, overlapping the self-stick underlayment. Be careful when you trim back the felt paper so you don't slice into the underlayment. Photo 7 shows the underlayment covering the felt on one side. That's because one side of the valley

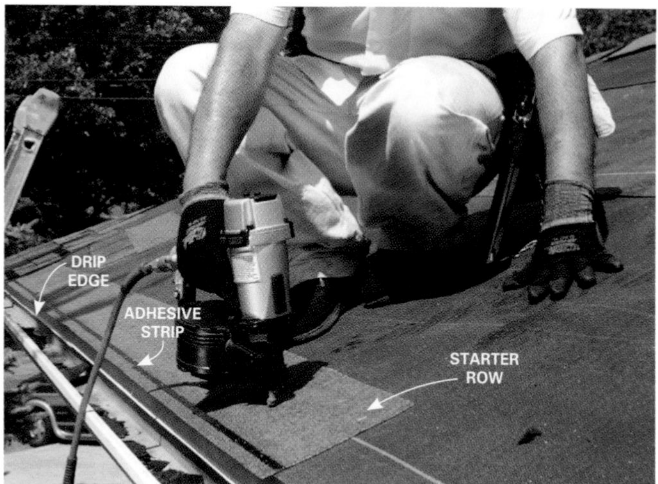

9 Install starter shingles. Run the row of starter shingles 1/2 in. past the drip edge. Position them so the adhesive strip is toward the bottom and facing up. Place nails 2 to 3 in. up from the bottom of the eave.

10 Nail on shingles. Following the manufacturer's nailing instructions is critical; improper nailing is the biggest cause of roof failures in storms. Where and how often you nail your shingles will depend on wind speeds in your area and the pitch of your roof.

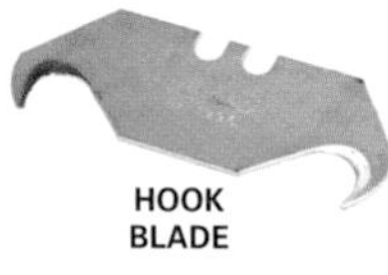

11 Run shingles long, then trim them off. For nice straight lines, run shingles over the edge of the roof. Then snap a chalk line and trim them off with a hook blade in your utility knife. If the overhang is more than a foot, cut some off and use the remainder elsewhere.

Avoid extreme temperatures

Avoid roofing your house in below-freezing temperatures. The shingles won't stick together, which makes them prone to wind damage. A couple of cold days won't cause trouble, but after weeks and months, the adhesive strips on the shingles can attract dust and fail to seal even when the weather does warm up. And try to avoid working on sunny days when the temperature is above 90 degrees F. The ice-and-water underlayment gets overly sticky and difficult to work with, and the shingles get soft and are easily scuffed by feet and tools.

is relatively small, and our crew felt this method would provide better protection. There'll be judgment calls like this on most roofs, so do as the pros say when there's a unique situation: "Think like a drop of water."

Set your first section of the metal valley flashing in place at the bottom, and run it past the drip edge. Before you nail it into place, set the one above it (if necessary) in place. Overlap the flashing at least 4 in. Not all valleys are built perfectly straight, so you may have to cheat your flashing a bit one way or the other. Crooked valley flashing will be very noticeable from the ground. With all the flashing in place, use a string or sight down the length of the valley to make sure the flashing is straight. There's only so much that can be done with valleys built severely out of whack, because the flashing does need to fit snugly into the decking. Once you're satisfied with the position of the flashing, nail it to the decking every several feet. Nail the outside edges only.

Run the top of the flashing up past the peak of the house 4 to 6 in. Cut it back to the peak at every crease in the flashing (Photo 8), and then fold it over the peak and nail it down. Cover the end cuts with a small sheet of self-stick underlayment.

Trim the bottom of the flashing with a tin snips. Cut the outside edges of the valley flashing flush with the drip edge, but angle your cut so the middle portion of the flashing extends past the drip edge a couple of inches. This will keep water farther away from the inside corner of the fascia. You can extend the center out even more but not so far that water overshoots your gutters if you have them.

Be careful not to nail your shingles any closer than 8 in. from the center of the valley. Once all the shingles are installed, snap lines as guides to trim them off. There should be 6 in. of the valley exposed on top (3 in. on each side), and each side of the valley should widen 1/8 in. for every linear foot of the valley run. So, if you have a valley run of 16 ft., your valley exposure would be 6 in. on the top and 10 in. on the bottom.

Another way of dealing with valleys is to use the "weave" method, which we don't cover in this story. The shingles are woven together from both sides of the valley. The benefit of a woven valley is that it doesn't leave an exposed flashing, which results in a cleaner look. The downfall is that leaves and twigs don't get washed away as easily, which can cause little water dams. This is especially true for roofs with low pitches.

Begin with starter shingles

Water can get in the seams between any two shingles, but that's OK because shingles overlap and the seams are staggered. But if you don't use starter shingles, water will run in between the seams on the first row and right onto the underlayment, increasing the odds of a leak. The starter row shingles are only half as wide as a full shingle. If they were full size, the top half of the first row would have three layers of shingles instead of the two the rest of the roof has, causing a visible hump.

Don't bother snapping lines for the starter shingles; just overlap them 3/4 in. past the drip edge. Fasten them down with five nails about 2 to 3 in. up from the bottom of the eave. Position the starter shingles so the adhesive strip is toward the bottom and facing up (Photo 9). The adhesive strip bonds to the shingle above it, creating a nice tight seal, reducing the chance of wind damage and water infiltration.

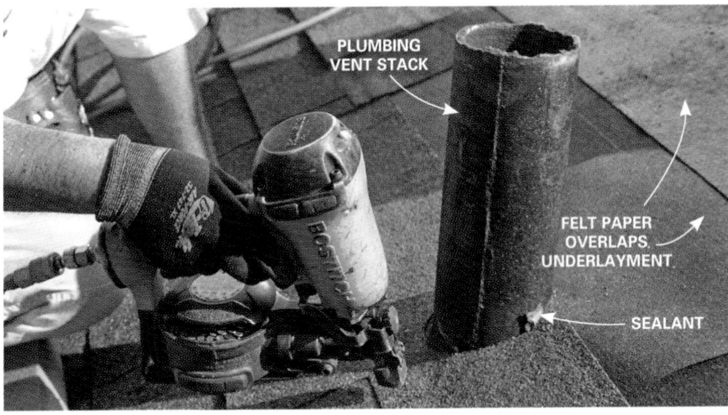

12 **Make plumbing vents leak proof.** Install a layer of underlayment around vent pipes and caulk with roof sealant before shingling. Run shingles halfway past vents before installing vent flashing.

13 **Add the vent flashing.** Drive three nails along the top edge of the flashing and one at each of the lower corners.

Some pro roofers install starter shingles on the gable ends as well. It's not usually required, but it provides a cleaner look. Hang gable-end starter shingles 1/2 in. past the drip edge, and make sure you overlap the starter shingle on the eave by 2 to 3 in.

Install the shingles

Laying shingles isn't easy, but it's probably the simplest part of roofing a house. Line up the bottom of the first row of shingles with the bottom edge of the starter row, making sure the seams are staggered. With that row complete, you'll need to figure out the reveal (the portion of the shingle that isn't covered by the one above it). Standard reveals vary between 5 and 6-1/2 in. Whatever the reveal is supposed to be, snap a horizontal line that distance from the top of the first row of shingles (see Figure A, p. 190).

Your roofing gun should have an adjustable guide to help keep the rows straight. If it doesn't, cut a block of wood the same size as your reveal and use that as a gauge. Slightly wavy rows won't be noticeable from the ground, so only snap lines every several rows to straighten things out. It's easier to work from right to left if you're right-handed. Stagger each row so the seams don't line up. Follow the stagger pattern recommended by the manufacturer of your shingles. Use partial shingles to start subsequent rows.

No one will notice if the last rows are not the same size on both sides of the ridge, but it can be very noticeable if the row that meets the ridge has a 4-in. reveal on one side and a 1-in. reveal on the other. Once you get within 8 ft. of the ridge, measure down to your shingles at each end of the row. If one side is closer to the peak than the other, snap lines for all the remaining rows, making the reveal on one side progressively larger until you make up the difference. Don't adjust any row by more than 3/16 in.

Every shingle brand has its own nailing pattern requirement. The pitch of your roof and the wind conditions in your area also affect how many nails to use and where. Most shingles require four to six nails, about 1 in. in from each side and placed so they get covered at least 1 in. by the shingle above them. The nails should penetrate the decking at least 3/4 in. Most pros use 1-1/4-in. zinc-coated roofing nails.

Nail straight into the shingle, and adjust the setting on your gun or the pressure on your compressor so the nails pull the shingle tight to the decking but stay flush with the surface. Keep a hammer close at hand to take care of nails that get only partially driven in. And never use staples!

14 **Shingle over the vent flashing.** Seal the nail heads, and trim around the stack flashing with a utility knife fitted with hook blades.

Even if a buddy has an old roofing stapler with free staples, politely decline. Staples don't have the holding power of nails; they tend to rust out before the shingles go bad; and most manufacturers don't allow staples, so you'll void the warranty.

When you reach the ridge, use the same technique as you did with the felt paper: Wrap the first side over the top, and then wrap the second side over the first. Cut the shingles to size with a utility knife fitted with hook blades. Run the shingles long over hip ridges and rakes, and in the valleys. When you're all done installing the shingles, snap lines and trim the shingles to the line (**Photo 11**).

Install step and dormer flashing

It's possible to reuse existing step flashing and dormer flashing, but the best way to get a watertight seal is to tear off the siding in those areas and install new flashing. Start by running self-stick underlayment at least 6 in. up onto the walls. This provides an additional barrier if water does get past the flashing. Cover the front wall first and then work your way up the side wall. Overlap the sidewall underlayment around the corner onto the front wall about 1 in. or so.

Install the shingles right up to the front wall. Cut a couple of inches off the vertical portion of the dormer flashing, and run the horizontal portion past the side wall that same distance. Nail the dormer flashing to both the wall and the shingles.

Make a 1- to 2-in. cut with a tin snips at the bend in the first step flashing. Run a bead of sealant on the corner edge of the dormer flashing, and then run that step flashing past the dormer flashing the same distance you made your cut. Bend the step flashing around the corner onto the dormer flashing with your hammer.

Install your next row of shingles over that first step flashing, then cover that row with a step flashing, and so on. Nail the step flashing to the wall toward the top of the flashing at the end that's closer to the peak, so the next step flashing in line will cover the nail. Don't nail them down through the shingles. For information about flashing around chimneys, search "install chimney flashing" at familyhandyman.com.

Working around vents and stacks

Installing shingles around attic vents, plumbing vent stacks and furnace stacks is basically the same process. The main difference is that you'll install a piece of self-stick underlayment around all the stacks, but you just need to roll the felt paper over the vent holes and cut out the holes. When installing the felt paper over a stack, it's OK to make an oversize hole. But before you roll out the row of paper above the stack, cut a 2- or 3-ft. section of self-stick underlayment, cut a hole in it slightly smaller than the diameter of the stack, and slide it over the stack. Make sure the piece is large enough so that the next row of felt paper overlaps the top at least a couple of inches (**Photo 12**). Caulk around the pipe when you're done.

Install the shingles up and halfway past the vent hole or stack. Next, install your vent or stack flashing over that row of shingles (**Photo 13**). Nail it down with your roofing gun, top and bottom.

Seal the top nail holes and continue on up with your shingles. Trim the shingles with your utility knife (**Photo 14**). Some vent and stack flashing is covered in protective plastic, which will have to be removed.

If you're installing the type of stack flashing with a rubber boot that seals around the pipe, spray-paint the pipe a similar color as your roof. You can also paint electrical masts and other projections (before installing shingles). This simple step adds a lot to the finished look of your roof.

Architectural vs. three-tab shingles

The shingles shown here are commonly called "architectural." Some architectural shingles are partially laminated (two layers), and others are fully laminated, which gives them more of a textured look, similar to wood shakes. Because of the extra material, architectural shingles are heavier. Some can handle winds up to 150 mph, which is twice the wind rating of many three-tab shingles.

Architectural shingles are easier to install because you don't have to worry about lining up the tabs vertically. The life span depends on the quality of the shingle. Both styles are available with 25-year and 30-year warranties. Expect to pay about 15 to 20 percent more for standard architectural shingles than for standard three-tabs.

Whichever you choose, make sure all the bundles have the same "lot" number on the packaging. That means they were all made in the same batch or run. Shingle color can vary noticeably from one batch to another.

To find out if you have proper attic ventilation, go online and search "attic ventilation calculator." Just type in the dimensions of your attic to learn how many vents you need. If you don't have adequate ventilation, cut in more holes with a circular saw (**Photo 15**).

Cap the ridge

Once all your shingles are installed, you'll need to cover (cap) the ridge (and hip ridges if you have a hip roof). The top ridge cap shingles will overlap the hip ridge cap, so start with the hips. Snap a couple of guide lines just a little inside the perimeter of the ridge so the lines get covered up when you're done. Nail each shingle on both sides about 1 in. above the overlap seam (**Photo 16**). Store-bought architectural-style ridge caps are often two layers thick, to match the look of the shingles. You may need longer nails to fasten the ridge because of all the extra layers of shingles.

Install the top ridge cap so the prevailing winds blow over the overlaps rather than into them. If wind isn't an issue, start at either side, or start at both sides and end in the middle. Rip the top half off the last ridge cap shingle, and nail through the face of it with two nails on the ends of each side.

15 Add ventilation. If you need more ventilation, cut additional vent holes in the decking with a circular saw and install vent flashing.

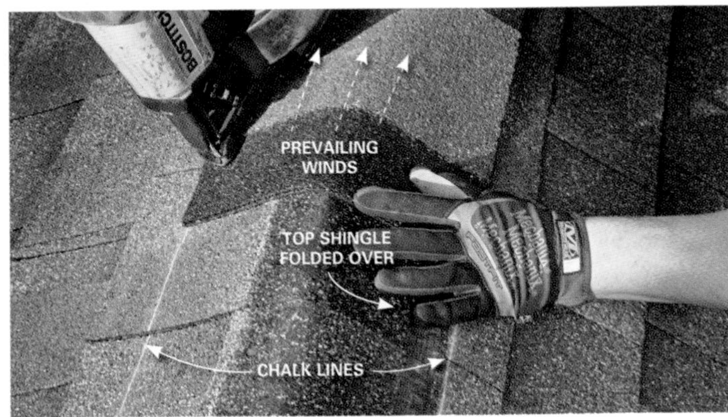

16 Cap the ridge. Snap chalk lines to help keep the row of ridge cap shingles straight. Install the ridge cap so the prevailing winds blow over the overlap seams, not into them.

Seal it up

Before you put your ladder away, sweep all the debris off the roof, and then seal all the exposed nails on your vents and stack flashing. If you used stack flashing that has the rubber boot, seal the area where rubber meets the pipe. Avoid silicone (it won't hold up) and asphalt-based sealants (they tend to dry out when exposed to direct sunlight). Our roofers prefer a product called Lexel. It's clear like silicone, sticky as model glue and lasts for years. And remember, these areas you sealed require maintenance—they should be inspected every few years.

GreatGoofs®

Hookin' ladder

About three or four times a year, my wife and I climb up on the roof of our house to blow off the leaves and pine needles that have accumulated, and as long as we're up there, clean our skylights. I usually place the ladder and go up first, blowing off debris while she rakes and cleans below. Then she joins me with a garden hose and cleaning supplies for the skylights and we work as a team.

The last time we were up there, the hose tangled with the ladder and sent it to the ground. The skylights were sealed, we had no cell phone and there were no neighbors within earshot. I had an idea: Lasso the ladder with the hose and pull it up! After several unsuccessful attempts, I hooked one of the ladder rungs with the handle of the hose sprayer and was able to gently pull the ladder back safely. We still work as a team, but from now on, it's one up and one down!

—Dan Brown & Kellie Hogan

EXTERIOR SPRAY PAINTING

Sprayers do a great job—if you follow these tips from a painting pro

by **Mark Petersen, Contributing Editor**

Every professional painter owns an airless paint sprayer. There's just no more efficient way to deliver paint onto a surface, and for most pros, every minute saved is money in the bank. And the smooth, even finish that sprayers deliver just can't be matched with a brush or roller.

Working with a paint sprayer may seem intimidating, but it only takes a few minutes to get the hang of the proper technique. We visited the training/testing facility at Schoenfelder Renovations in Hopkins, MN, where Daryl Becker showed us the basics. He also shared some extra gems you won't read about in the operator's manual for your paint sprayer. In this story, we'll focus on exterior painting, but most of these tips apply to any painting job that involves a sprayer.

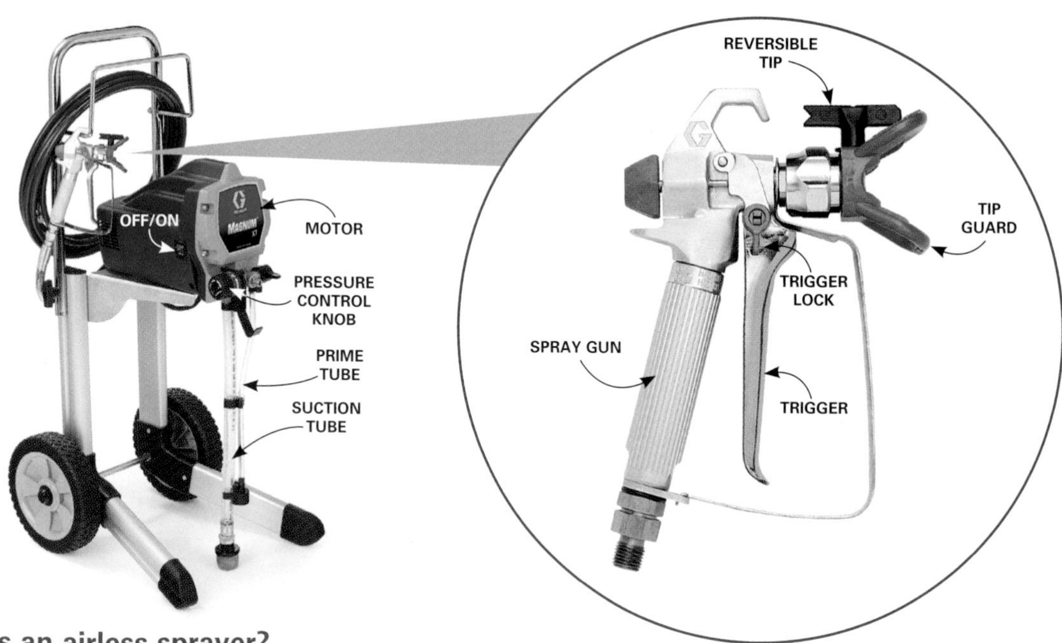

What's an airless sprayer?

Airless sprayers work by pumping paint at very high pressures (up to 3,000 psi). They can suck paint from a large bucket (fewer refills), and the gun is lighter because it's not attached to the paint reservoir, as is the case with many air sprayers. Airless sprayers can spray both paint and finishes. There are different tips for different materials.

An entry-level model will cost about $250. The Graco X7 model shown retails for about $370 at home centers. Pros use models that range from $500 up to several thousand dollars. The basic operations of the machines are the same; what you get for your extra dollars is mostly durability. You can rent an airless sprayer for about $85 a day.

Pay attention to the weather

Our expert told us that one of the most common mistakes newbies make is ignoring the weather. Painting a wall in direct sunlight on a really hot day is next to impossible—the paint dries before there's time to back-brush and back-roll (see p. 199). If you can, pay attention to where the sun shines on the house at different times of the day. Plan your painting day so you can stay on the shady side. And make sure you don't get rained on. Most paint containers specify the length of time the paint must be dry before being exposed to water.

Reverse the tip to purge clogs

Most spray tips have an arrow on them because they're reversible. A forward pointing arrow means you're ready to paint. If you start to get an uneven spray pattern, you probably have a clog in the tip. To purge the debris, turn the tip 180 degrees and spray some paint onto a piece of cardboard or rosin paper for a couple seconds. Then turn the tip back around and continue painting. If you still aren't getting good results, you may need to clean the tip or one or more of the inline filters. These filters are located in various places depending on the sprayer.

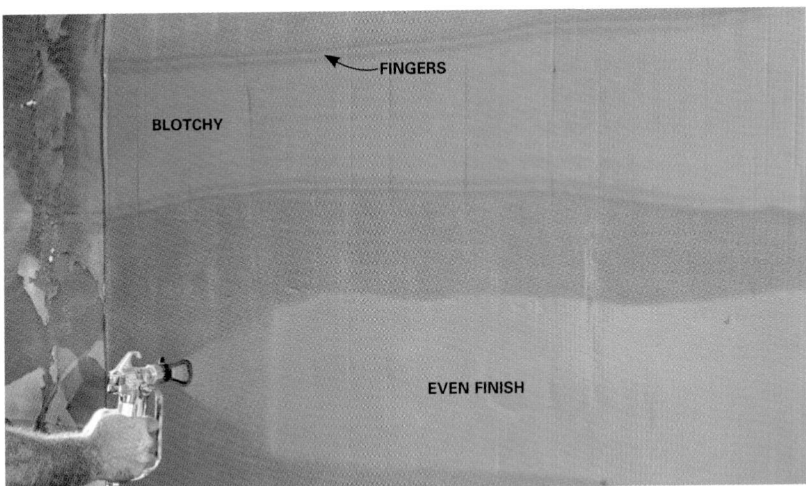

Adjust the sprayer, starting with low pressure

The thickness of the paint will determine the proper pressure setting on the sprayer. Start with the pressure on low and make a pass on a scrap piece of cardboard or rosin paper. If the pressure is too low, the spray pattern will be uneven and there'll be "fingers" on the edges. Keep upping the pressure until you get a nice, even spray pattern with a consistent edge. If the pressure is all the way up and the pattern is still weak, you may have to go up one tip size.

Avoid overspray messes

Even a finely tuned spray pattern will create some overspray. Wind and high humidity will cause the overspray to travel farther. Make sure you cover plants, decks and walkways, and move cars and any other items you don't want paint on.

Tape off windows and doors

Before you crack open that first bucket of paint, tape off your windows and doors. We prefer the dispensers that roll out the tape and plastic at the same time. You can buy a high-end dispenser like the 3M M3000K shown for about $60 at paint stores. More basic models can be purchased at home centers for $20. Only the face of the trim needs to be protected (see "Spray the edge of the trim the same color as the wall," p. 198).

Use a shield to get closer

If you plan to spray your soffits, do that first. When it comes time to paint the walls, use a shield to protect the soffits from overspray. The pros use shields like this one, but you could get by with a sturdy piece of cardboard. The same trick works with the foundation, electric meters or whatever else you don't want to mess up with overspray. And the shield doesn't have to be precisely positioned; you can come back and clean up the line with your brush.

Keep a lid on it

Always keep the lid on the bucket. Just remove the small cap and stick the intake tube into the smaller hole. This will keep debris out of the paint and prevent clogs. Plus, an open bucket dries out faster, and dried clumps of paint can also clog the works. Always use a 5-gallon bucket. If your project only requires 3 gallons, pour that amount into an empty 5-gallon bucket and draw your paint from that.

Spray the edge of the trim the same color as the wall

Tape off only the face of the windows and doors, then spray the edges of the trim at the same time as the walls. After the walls are done, come back and roll on the trim color. Eliminating the laborious task of cutting in the edge of the trim around each and every lap in the siding may seem like cheating, but it's not. First, no one will ever notice. Second, the caulking between the trim and the siding is rarely perfect, and trying to cut in paint over blobs of caulking rarely results in a nice clean line.

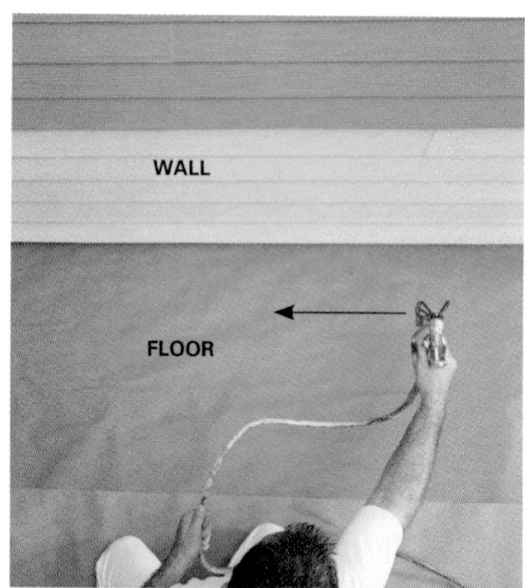

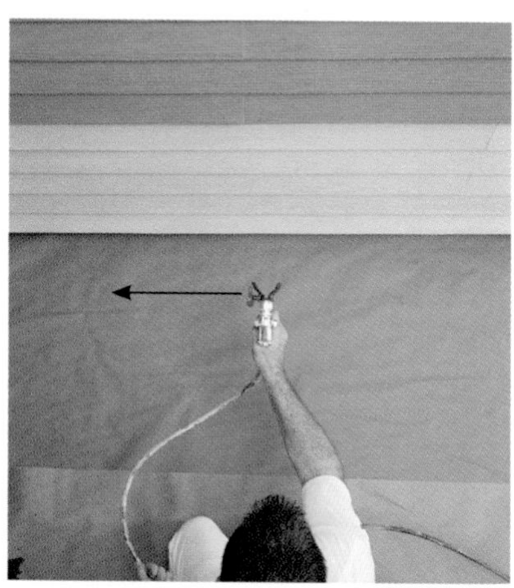

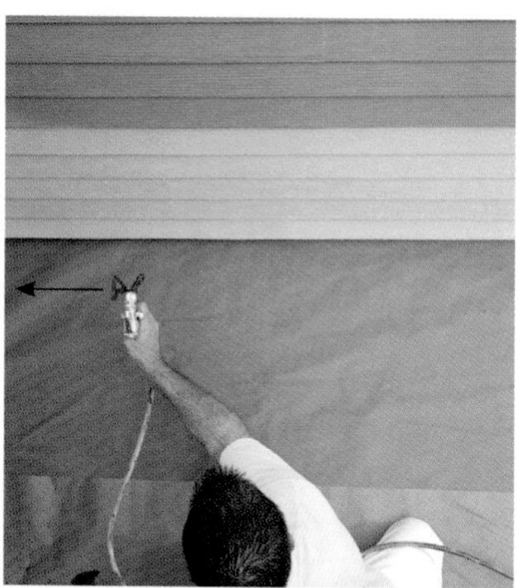

Keep the gun perpendicular to the wall

To achieve a consistent layer of paint, the tip of the sprayer should be held about 12 in. from the surface and the gun should always remain perpendicular to the wall. This technique is the foundation for a professional finish. It seems tricky at first, but after only a few passes you'll be painting like a pro. Practice on a low-visibility wall until you get the hang of it.

Overlap 50 percent and keep the gun moving

Overlap the pattern about 50 percent. Release the trigger at the end of each pass. Start the gun in motion before pulling the trigger. If you start spraying with a stationary gun, you'll get a glob of paint. When spraying under lap siding or the side of trim boards, angle the tip upward so you get enough paint on the bottom portion of the board. Always start at the top of the wall and work your way down.

Back-brush the nooks and crannies

If you thought you could just blast the wall with a sprayer and call it a day, I've got bad news for you. The paint sprayer is only a paint *delivery* system. In order to achieve a coating that will last for years, you need to push the paint into every crack and crevice and underneath every lap with a brush. It seems like a tedious extra step, but it's absolutely necessary.

Back-roll, then recoat

After you back-brush, it's time to back-roll. Don't spray an area so large that the paint dries before you can roll it out (drying times vary greatly depending on the weather). A roller with a thicker nap is better at reaching the uneven surfaces. Many pros use a roller with a 3/4-in. nap because it gets up into more of the recessed areas. And while it's tempting to roll lap siding horizontally, always roll in an up-and-down motion. It's hard to stop the paint from dripping off the bottom of the laps if you roll horizontally.

One coat may be enough if you're just freshening up the paint with a new coat of the same color. But if you're working with new siding or changing colors, a second coat will be needed. But no back-brushing or back-rolling is necessary on the final coat, so it goes fast, and the final coat hides many of the smaller brush and roller marks.

CAUTION: Houses built before 1978 may contain lead paint. Before disturbing any surface, get a lab analysis of paint chips from it. Contact your local public health department for information on how to collect samples and where to send them.

TIPS FOR REVIVING A WOOD DECK

Don't be ashamed of your deck—rejuvenate it!

by **Travis Larson, Senior Editor**

If you have a wood deck that's dirty, stained and covered with mildew and mold, read on. It's easier than you might think to rejuvenate it. Here are some tips to make your deck attractive and ready to enjoy again.

Sometimes decks need stripping

If a thoroughly cleaned deck has leftover finishes, especially solid stains, you'll have to get busy with a deck stripper. It's not as arduous as it sounds. Stripper typically dries in about 15 minutes, so work in sections, spreading a heavy coat over a small area that you can scrub before it dries. Then rinse it off and recoat any areas that have stubborn spots. You may have to use a stripping disc in an angle grinder to knock off really rough areas.

STRIPPING DISC

Clean out the cracks

Don't leave all that organic stuff in the cracks between the boards. You can make your own crack cleaner by screwing a utility hook into the end of any broom handle or board that fits your hand, and use it to plow out all that junk. We used a grinder to make the hook thinner so it would fit into tighter cracks.

Apply deck stain fast with a paint pad

Before you begin, cover anything beneath the decking that you want to protect from stain drips. Start your stain application by cutting in around posts and areas next to the siding with a brush. Stain the adjoining deck areas before the cut-in stain dries. You can spray or roll on the finish on the main deck section, then back-brush it to even it out. Or use a paint pad on an extension handle. Always overlap the previous board and maintain a wet edge as you go. The goal is to prevent lap marks. Avoid staining on hot days, and never apply stain when the deck is in direct sunlight.

Tape off and cover fascia and trim boards, even if you plan to stain them; any drip marks will show up noticeably darker. Each additional row of stain should be applied while the previous row is still wet to blend the finishes. Gauging the open work time before the stain dries will take some experimenting. You'll have to take into account how much cut-in work you're doing, the weather conditions and the particular product you're using.

A power wash will work wonders

You could scrub with a deck brush, but it's far smarter to rent, borrow or buy a pressure washer. You'll need to spray with at least 2,000 psi, and that usually calls for a gas-powered unit—few electric ones possess the power. Choose the 15-degree spray tip and then experiment. The trick is to hold the wand just far enough away to avoid tearing up the wood but close enough to remove all of the ugliness. You'll get the feel pretty quickly, but it's best to start in an inconspicuous area. If your washer is capable of distributing detergent, you can use it to speed things up.

Cleaners and brighteners

If your deck has black or green stains, choose a cleaner that's formulated to remove mildew. If you just want to brighten a dull finish, try a simple deck brightener, which will remove a thin layer of aged wood fibers. You can apply either product with a plastic pump sprayer. Scrub the deck while the brightener or mildew remover is still wet, then rinse the residue immediately. Experiment, though—sometimes a pressure washer can handle both the scrubbing and the rinsing.

Read product directions!

When you're using liquid restoration or finishing products on decks, be sure to read the label at least twice. Some products need diluting, some are very sensitive to temperature, and some require completely dry wood. All that labor you're putting into this project can go to waste because of a simple application mistake. So remember: Study the directions carefully, then *follow* them!

Choosing a stain

You have to balance how much traffic your deck gets, the condition of your deck, and how much maintenance you can stand. Here are the choices:

■ **Transparent:** It goes on easy as pie, but you'll see every little flaw on an old deck since it has less pigment than semi or solid stains. Transparent stains don't wear as well either, so you'll be down to bare wood in a year or two and have to reapply it if you want a fresh finish. You'll need to clean it again, but that and the recoat go pretty doggone fast.

■ **Semitransparent:** Because there's more pigment in semitransparent stains than in transparent ones, they last longer and wear better under foot traffic. Semitransparent stains also offer more UV protection. Depending on how long you wait to recoat it, you may have to use a stripper first.

■ **Solid stains:** If you want a finish that lasts three to four years, a solid stain may be the best choice—but there is a dark side. If you're not meticulous with the prep work or your deck gets lots of foot traffic, solid stains can start to peel, which means extra work. Peeling, which is typical of a failing solid stain but not of the other two, is especially unsightly and obvious as it exposes the bare wood beneath the finish.

Still, solid stains mask flaws well and blend in any newer wood you've installed to replace bad deck boards. Choose a solid stain if hiding surface flaws is what matters most to you, there's little foot traffic and you're willing to do extra work when it's time to refinish your deck.

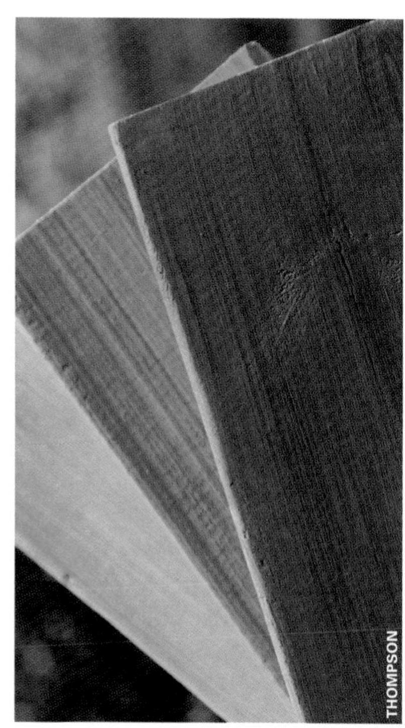
THOMPSON

SPECIAL SECTION

Dealing with Old Man Winter

SNOW BLOWER SMARTS

Running a snow blower seems like a skill you could master in two minutes. But we wondered: If it's really that simple, why are there 6,000 blower-related injuries in the United States every year? And why do repair shops get overwhelmed after a big storm?

To get answers, we talked with experts at all the major manufacturers—as well as the guys who fix blowers. It turns out that operator error is the No. 1 cause of clogs and breakdowns, and improper clearing of clogs is the most common cause of injuries. The experts shared some great tips on how to avoid both. So even if you're an experienced snow blower operator, read on.

Dealing with Old Man Winter

Don't wait for it to stop

If you're in for a huge snowfall, start clearing the snow before it reaches 6 in. Sure, you'll spend more time snow-blowing, but your machine won't have to work as hard, and it'll throw the snow farther. That'll reduce the height of the snowbanks flanking your driveway.

Get your property ready for snow

Before the snow flies, take a few minutes to inspect your property. Remove rocks, dog tie-out cable, extension cords, holiday light cords and garden hoses. Then stake out paths that run near gardens so you don't accidentally suck up rocks and garden edging. Mark your walk and driveway perimeters by pounding in driveway markers. If the ground is frozen, just drill a hole using a masonry bit and your battery-powered drill.

Start with fresh fuel

Stale gas is the No. 1 cause of hard starting. So don't use what's left in the lawn mower can. It's better to dump that summer blend into your car's tank, then refill the can with winter blend, which is more volatile and provides better starting.

Throw it far

Avoid throwing snow only partway off the driveway and then throwing it a second time. That just creates a heavier load for the blower. There are four ways to get the maximum throw: Take smaller bites of snow (see p. 205), run the blower at full rpm but at a slower ground speed, adjust the chute diverter to its full raised position and blow with the wind.

Don't swallow the newspaper

A frozen newspaper is the leading cause of machine jams. It can break shear pins or belts and damage expensive auger and impeller components. A fresh layer of snow over newspapers makes them hard to see, and they're easy to forget (**photo above**). So protect your machine by scouting the area before you hit it. If you do suck up a newspaper, shut down the engine and remove it with a broom or shovel handle—never with your hands. If you can't remove the paper, take your machine to a pro, who will charge a whole lot less than even the cheapest surgeon.

Cool off, then gas up

If your snow blower runs out of gas halfway through a tough job, you'll be tempted to refill it right away. But think about this: The engine is hot and the gas tank sits right on top of that hot engine. Even worse, you're standing right over the machine holding a gallon of gas. If you spilled gas on the engine or overfilled the tank, you could instantly turn your snow-blowing adventure into a painful burn-unit experience. Even if you managed to escape injury, you could still wind up with a freshly toasted snow blower.

Snow-blower fires happen often enough that the manufacturers strongly recommend that you let the engine cool for at least 10 minutes before refilling. Take that opportunity to grab a cuppa joe or hot chocolate and warm up your fingers and toes. Then, once your personal tank is refilled, refill your snow blower and carry on.

Take smaller bites to prevent clogs

When you get blasted with wet, heavy snow and you're in a hurry, it's tempting to crank up the speed and plow right through it. That's the single best way to clog your machine and wear out (or break) the drive belts. And when you consider how long it takes to constantly stop and unclog the chute, ramming at full speed doesn't actually save any time.

Worse yet, improperly clearing a clogged chute is dangerous, and the most common cause of snow blower–related injuries. Instead of making a full-width pass through the snow, manufacturers recommend taking smaller bites—about one-third to one-half the width of the machine. It's faster than slogging through a full path of heavy snow and it's easier on the machine. Another reason it's a better snow-blowing technique is that it allows the machine to throw the snow farther.

Switch to synthetic oil for easier starting

Small engines typically have to reach at least 400 rpm before they'll fire up. But traditional motor oil thickens when cold, making it much harder to reach that 400-rpm threshold. Synthetic oil allows the engine to spin faster when you yank the cord, so it starts with fewer pulls.

Add stabilizer to the fresh fuel

Follow the stabilizer dosing recommendations on the bottle label. Add the stabilizer to the gas can right at the gas station so it'll mix up on the way home. Or, add a premeasured packet to the gas can before filling it with gas.

Dealing with Old Man Winter

Pre-season snow blower maintenance

Get your snow blower ready for action by installing a new spark plug, changing the oil and checking the condition of the belts. Replace the belts if you see cracks, fraying or glazing or notice that chunks are missing.

Next, sand any rusted areas and repaint. Once the paint cures, apply a high-quality polymeric car wax (such as Meguiar's Ultimate Liquid Wax, about $20 from any auto parts store) to all painted surfaces. The wax will shed the snow and water and protect the paint. And, wax the inside of the chute to help prevent clogs.

Then consult your owner's manual to find the lubrication points and the recommended lube. If the type of lube isn't listed, here's some general guidance: Use motor oil on metal linkage joints, gears and cables, but dry PTFE lube on plastic parts (knobs, gears and chute). Spray the auger, second-stage impeller and chute with silicone spray to prevent snow from sticking.

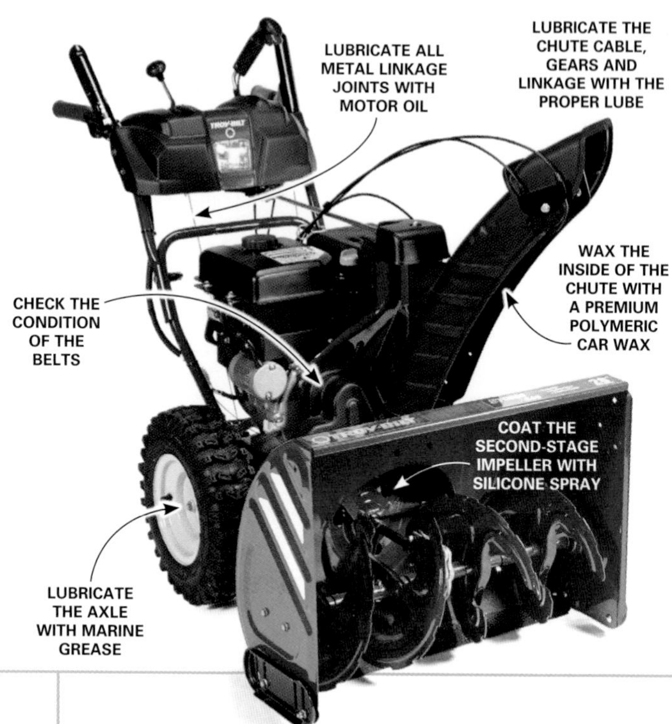

Prevent major auger damage

The drive shaft applies torque to the shear pin, which then applies it to the auger. However, if the auger rusts to the drive shaft, they'll become one and the shear pin will never break. If that happens, the auger clog can cause major damage to the machine. Lubricate the drive shaft to prevent it from rusting to the auger.

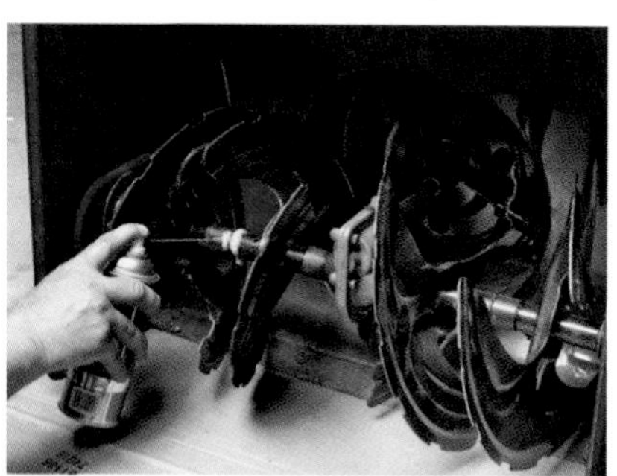

Lube and spin Remove shear pins and lubricate the drive shaft with lubricating oil.

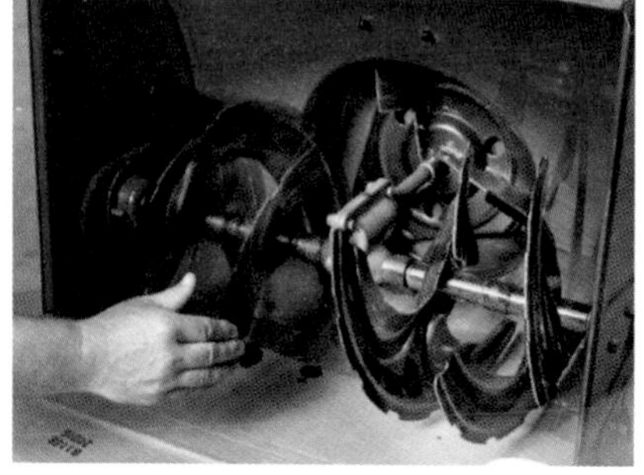

Then spin the auger to spread the oil along the length of the shaft. Reinstall shear pins.

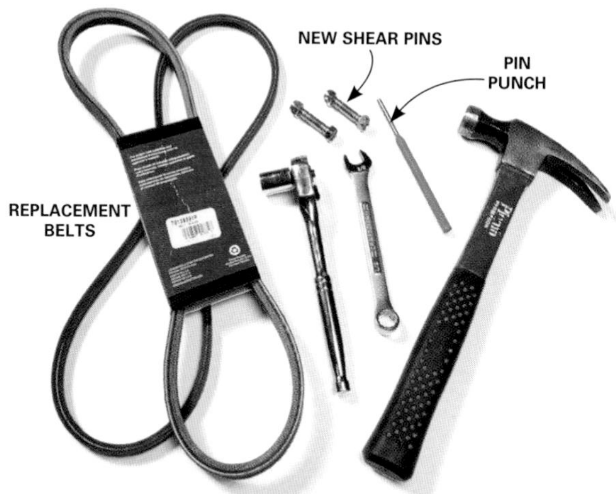

Buy parts before you need them

Belts and shear pins always break on a Sunday night in the middle of a blizzard. So buy replacement parts at the start of the season when everyone has them in stock. If you break a shear pin and try to improvise using the wrong shear pin—or worse yet, an ordinary bolt—you risk major damage that can easily cost you $200. A set of belts and a few extra shear pins will cost about $25. Also make sure you have the right size of wrenches and sockets and the correct size pin punch to drive out the broken pin. Then assemble a parts and tool kit.

THE CASE FOR WINTER TIRES

GETTY IMAGES/DANIEL LOISSELLE

Winter tires are supposedly much better than even the best all-season tires for winter driving. We wondered if that was true and if they were worth the extra cost and hassle. So we contacted four large tire manufacturers—Goodyear, Michelin, Bridgestone and Cooper Tire—to find out exactly what drivers get for their money.

The manufacturers pointed us to independent tests showing how winter tires compare to all-season tires. The test results were impressive. But the out-of-pocket expenses are equally as impressive. So we crunched the numbers to find out exactly how much they cost per year. Here's what we found.

Not just for snow

Winter tires perform much better than the "snow" tires you may remember (if you're old enough). They work better in snow, ice, slush and mud and on cold, dry pavement. The rubber compounds are entirely new. Most manufacturers include silica, and some spruce up the formula with traction bits and hollow "cells" that squeegee and suction water off the road. Tread designs are far more aggressive to provide better acceleration and shorter stopping distances (see "Tread that saws and pumps," below).

Increased performance on snow

Since snow-on-snow contact creates far more traction than rubber on snow, winter tires are designed to grip and hold more snow. That means better (and faster) acceleration and shorter stopping distances. An independent test by Tirerack.com shows a 33 percent improvement in acceleration over all-season tires (and that's with an AWD vehicle). Plus, the test tires stopped 30 ft. shorter than the all-seasons (**Figure A**, p. 208). That's a huge difference—enough to avoid a serious accident or a fender bender.

Tread that saws and pumps. Winter tires have more sipes (cuts in the tread) than all-season tires to squeegee more water off the road. Saw-tooth sipes provide more surface area and cut into snow and slush better than straight sipes. The "micro pump" holes in the tread act like plungers to suck water off the road and then spit it out as the tire rolls.

Better performance on ice

All-season rubber compounds literally skate on ice. But winter tires are made with softer rubber compounds and added silica to give them more flexibility and grip on ice. And the special tread removes more water from the ice. The test results show that winter tires outperform all-season tires on ice, too.

Tirerack.com used an indoor ice rink and timed the acceleration from a dead stop and measured stopping distances from 10 mph (**Figure B**, p. 208). Winter tires accelerated faster. When taking a 90-degree turn at 10 mph, the car with winter tires stayed within the marked driving lane, while the car with all-season tires skidded out. That kind of cornering performance can mean the difference between avoiding an accident and causing one.

Cost vs. benefits

A set of four winter tires costs $600 or more, depending on your wheel size. If you have the tires mounted on your existing wheels, you'll have to pay a shop to swap them each spring and fall. Most shops charge about $18 apiece to demount your all-season tires, mount the winter tires, balance and install them. However, if you buy an extra set of wheels and tire pressure sensors ($480 per set), you'll save at least $50 on each changeover. Don't think you can skip the tire pressure sensors—the shop can't legally install wheels without tire pressure sensors if your vehicle was already equipped with them.

Sure, winter tires cost a lot. But consider that you're getting a lot for your money. When you factor in the better stopping distance and handling in turns, it's easy to see how winter tires could prevent an "at-fault" accident. If your collision deductible is in the $500 to $1,000 range, winter tires could actually pay for themselves in a single season if they keep you out of an accident.

Dealing with Old Man Winter

Figure A: Winter tires stop sooner on snow
In one test, vehicles accelerated to 30 mph, and both drivers slammed on their ABS brakes at a marked spot. The car equipped with winter tires stopped 66 percent faster (30 ft. shorter) than the vehicle equipped with all-season tires.

Figure B: Winter tires grip better, too
In the same test, the car with winter tires accelerated 44 percent faster and stopped 48 percent faster (18 ft. 8 in. shorter) than the car with all-season tires.

Buy extra wheels. It's more cost effective to mount winter tires on a set of extra wheels (including pressure sensors). You'll save time and money on the twice-yearly tire swapping.

Here's another way to analyze the costs. Winter tires last about five years or 35,000 miles. Those are miles you won't be putting on your all-season tires. So if you go all the way and buy new wheels, the true cost of winter tires comes out to about $150 per year for the first five years. Then if you buy a second set for those same wheels, the cost drops to just $65 per year. We think it's worth the relatively small annual cost to get the extra stopping power and better handling that can help you avoid an accident.

Tire manufacturers make multiple winter tire models for specific winter conditions. So get expert advice from your local tire dealer to match the tire to your vehicle, your climate and your driving habits.

Save money on the changeovers

Mounting winter tires on a second set of wheels saves money over swapping tires on a single set of wheels. But you can save even more if you negotiate a package deal with the tire shop. Get a price for the tires, wheels, sensors and free seasonal mounting. If your shop offers a "Tire Hotel" service to store your off-season tires, ask them to throw that into the package as well. That way you won't have to haul the off-season tires back and forth or store them in your garage.

GreatGoofs®

Drip irritation

Not long ago my husband read an article in a gardening magazine that showed a unique way to water foundation plantings. The idea was to drill holes in the gutters so that water could drip down and irrigate the plants. Well, this seemed like a great idea until we got our first ice storm of the year. At all the hole locations, we had icicles so big that they nearly touched the ground. It looked unattractive, and the extra weight was starting to pull the gutters out of shape. Guess we have some gutter patching to do in the spring!

—Donna Stewart

6 Outdoor Structures, Landscaping & Gardening

IN THIS CHAPTER

Home Care & Repair 210
Make your gas grill look like new

Avoid the Top 4 Fertilizer Blunders 212

Deck a Patio 216

Mark's Mini Shed.......................................221

Handy Hints 228
Skunk spray antidote, mowing in comfort, twig pickup on the go and more

North Woods Bench 232

Roof Under a Deck 236

MAKE YOUR GAS GRILL LOOK LIKE NEW

If your gas grill is looking old and gray and the cart is starting to rust, you're probably thinking it's time for a new grill. Sure, it would be cool to own one of those shiny new stainless steel models—if you're willing to spend $500 or more. But if the cart, base and cover of your current grill are still sound, you can whip it into like-new shape in less than a day.

You just need special paint, some new accessories and elbow grease. The paint and supplies cost less than $50 at home centers. And you can pick up new handles, knobs, emblems and a new thermometer for about $25 from a local appliance parts store or online (grillparts.com is one source). You'll have to wait at least 24 hours for the paint to cure, but then you can get back to burger-flipping. Here's how to do the job.

Buy supplies

Stop at any home center and buy a bottle of heavy-duty degreaser, nitrile gloves, a respirator, a stiff-bristle scrub brush and a wire brush. Also pick up 80-grit and 120-grit sandpaper, brush-on or spray-on rust converter, primer for rusty metal and a few cans of heat-resistant paint (one choice is Krylon High Heat Max; under $15). You'll also need disposable plastic sheeting, a shop vacuum, a palm sander, a bucket and a garden hose.

Clean and sand and prime

Cleaning a greasy gas grill creates quite a mess. And the last thing you want is to move the grease from the grill to your driveway or garage floor. So do the project outdoors and tarp off the entire work area. Start the job by removing the burners, grates and grease cup. Use your shop vacuum to suck up all the loose crud from the bottom of the grill and any dirt and rust from the propane tank shelf. Next, remove the knobs, emblems and thermometer (if equipped). Mix up a strong solution of degreaser using the dilution ratios listed on the label. Then grab your scrub brush and gloves and wash the entire grill (**Photo 1**). If you have a power washer, soak the grill with degreaser and then blast off the grease and loose paint. Rinse it with water and let it dry in the sun.

Next, mask off the wheels, gas valves, warning labels, manufacturer's nameplate and any other parts that won't be painted. Then grab your respirator and palm sander and sand the exterior (**Photo 2**). Pretreat the worst rust spots with a rust converter product. Once that dries, prime the rusty areas and bare metal with a primer for rusty metal (**Photo 3**). Let the primer dry.

Paint the grill and install the new parts

Wipe the entire grill with a tack cloth, then spray-paint it (**Photo 4**). Finish up by installing the new accessories (**Photo 5**). Remove the masking and let the paint dry for the recommended time. Then install the burners and grates and get grilling.

1 **Degrease the entire grill.** Spread degreaser inside the cover and burner area and over the entire exterior. Then scrub the entire grill with a brush. Make sure you remove grease from all the crevices.

2 **Sand and wire brush.** Sand pitted and corroded areas with 80-grit sandpaper. Use a wire brush in the crevices to remove surface rust and chipping paint. Then switch to 120-grit sandpaper and sand the entire grill and cart.

3 **Spray on primer.** Apply rust converter, then spray primer over the converted rust and bare metal areas. Let it "flash" for the recommended time. Then apply a second coat.

4 **Apply the finish coat.** Paint the top of the grill lid first. Then spray down each side all the way to the bottom of the cart. Paint the front of the grill last. Apply a second coat after waiting the recommended time.

5 **Install new parts.** Attach the new cover lift handle or knobs. Snap on the new emblems. Screw in the new thermometer.

AVOID THE TOP 4 FERTILIZER BLUNDERS

Save money, get greener grass and fewer weeds

by **Joe Churchill, Contributing Editor**

When you're fertilizing your lawn, mistakes are easy to make. I know, because I've been in the grass business for a very long time. And I can tell you that professional turf managers and homeowners tend to make the same four mistakes when they feed their grass.

Read along, avoid these blunders and you'll be thrilled with your lawn and get the most for your buck.

MEET AN EXPERT

Joe Churchill has worked in the professional turf industry for more than 30 years. He is a branch manager for Reinders, a major turf supply and equipment distributor in the Midwest.

1 Failure to test the soil

When I'm asked to help bring a homeowner's lawn back to life, the first thing I do is to make sure they have their soil professionally tested. Think of it as a checkup for your lawn. The results will provide important information that will help determine what type of fertilizer you should use and how often you should apply it.

You can collect your own samples by randomly pulling 10 to 12 individual soil samples from your lawn to a depth of 3 to 4 in. Make sure there is no vegetation or excessive root mass in the soil sample. Mix together the soil samples and put about a cup of this mix in a plastic bag. Write your name on the bag and send it off for testing.

Most often, a soil test will focus on measuring major nutrients like phosphorus (required for good root development) and potassium (needed to remedy environmental stresses). If your soils are lacking in these major building blocks, your lawn will suffer.

Another important piece of information received from a soil test is your soil's pH. Most lawn grasses like a soil pH in the range of 6.5 to 7.0. If your lawn's soil pH is too low or too high, the fertilizer you use may not work very well. Soils with a low pH, like 5.5 or 6.0, will require applications of lime to "sweeten" the soil. Soil pH values above 7.5 will require soil sulfur or a fertilizer containing sulfur to bring the pH down.

If your soil test results recommend adjustments to correct nutrient or pH issues, it's wise to test annually until the problems are corrected. If your soil test does not reveal any issues, test about every three years to monitor the health of your soil.

The best time to test your soil is early spring just before your lawn comes out of dormancy. Don't collect samples after fertilizing. This will skew the results. And don't use do-it-yourself kits! They may be less expensive, but they aren't very accurate. Your county extension office, reputable garden center or local university can help you test your soil accurately, interpret the results and then offer solid recommendations for fixing any soil problems.

OUTDOOR STRUCTURES, LANDSCAPING & GARDENING

Too much fertilizer

Many retailers promote a four-step fertilizer program for homeowners. Fertilizing more than four times a year is overkill. In fact, most homeowners could get by with two every year. You can cut back on the amount of fertilizer you need by making sure you apply it at the right time of the year. More on that later.

If you apply too much fertilizer, especially in sandy soils, a good share of it will leach through the soil and make its way into our precious groundwater, lakes, streams and wetlands. Lawn grasses only need a certain amount of food. More isn't always better.

Unlike us humans, lawn grasses don't know how to stop eating when they're full! This luxury consumption of nitrogen, phosphorus and potassium actually makes the lawn grasses weak and more susceptible to disease. Excessive fertilizer will create too much thatch, which will ultimately choke out your lawn. Too much fertilizer also means you'll be mowing far more often than necessary. Too much mowing means excessive soil compaction, exhaust and noise pollution and excessive wear and tear on your mower.

More than four fertilizer applications a year is a waste. Save time and money by being more judicious in your use of fertilizer.

More even application

Dial back the rate of application to 1/2, then make two passes with your spreader at right angles.

Fertilizing at the wrong time

If you fertilize just once a year, apply it around Labor Day. That's when your lawn is the hungriest and when it will respond best to the nutrients it receives. Fertilizing at this time will help replenish food reserves after a long, stressful year of growing and before the harshness of winter sets in.

If you fertilize twice, apply the second application about the middle of October. This acts like a "second helping" of much needed food going into winter. A third application can be added in mid to late spring and can be combined with your crabgrass preventer. A fourth application, if you feel the need, can be added mid-summer. Watch the weather when applying midsummer fertilizers. Fertilizing during hot, humid weather can harm your lawn. An exception would be using an organic fertilizer. They are much more lawn friendly during the dog days of summer.

In the spring, apply just enough fertilizer to help green up your lawn. About half the normal amount will do. Even without fertilizer, your lawn naturally grows quickly as soon as temperatures become consistently higher. Have you ever noticed that grass grows fastest in the late spring and early summer? Why promote even more growth at this time by fertilizing?

"Many lawn owners don't follow a schedule. They fertilize when they think their lawn needs it, when they have time or when the stuff is on sale."

My take on organic fertilizers

Organic fertilizers are becoming more popular with lawn owners because of the idea that they are more environmentally friendly. Quality organic fertilizers will contain meal-based nutrients (bone meal, feather meal, blood meal, fish meal) or some may contain poultry litter. A complete natural organic lawn food will have low NPK (nitrogen, phosphorus, potassium) numbers, most always below 10. It's best to apply these fertilizers during the warmer growing months, from May through September, depending where you live. Organics help feed your lawn by stimulating microbial activity in your soil, creating a healthier medium in which your grass can grow.

They are safer to use and will not harm your lawn like some conventional fertilizers will, especially during the hot summer months. They work a bit slower, however, so you'll need to be patient.

You'll also discover they are much more expensive. All that said, give them a try!

4 Getting careless

As much as fertilizer can be a valuable tool to keep a lawn healthy, dense and great looking, it can also create environmental concerns if not used responsibly. Too often I see people not paying attention when fertilizing. They're in a hurry or just don't care. They think the little bit of fertilizer that gets washed off your lawn and into the street doesn't matter. But what if all your neighbors thought this? Or worse yet, every lawn owner in your town? Not only can we help our environment by using less fertilizer, we can do even more by making sure it stays where it's intended.

Never apply any type of fertilizer close to wetlands, rivers, streams, lakes and ponds. We're trying to grow lawn grasses, not aquatic weeds. Heavy nutrient loads in these types of water features will create excessive weed growth and algae blooms. Nobody wants that. Stay at least 6 to 8 ft. away from water when applying fertilizer.

After you're done fertilizing, sweep up and collect what remains on hard surfaces, such as your driveway, sidewalk or street. If fertilizer is left on these surfaces, rains will eventually wash it into water features and storm sewers.

Never apply fertilizer to frozen ground. This can easily happen in the spring if you're anxious to apply your crabgrass preventer. If the ground is still frozen, it's too early to apply crabgrass preventer anyway. In short, be a good environmental steward.

"It's not the use of phosphorus and other nutrients that are creating environmental issues; it's the misuse of them."

DO:

- Test your soil first.
- Use test results to choose the right fertilizer.
- Spend time accurately measuring the size of your lawn.
- Try an organic during the hot summer months.
- Buy a quality spreader that best fits your needs.
- Accurately calibrate your spreader to make sure you apply the right amount.
- Keep your spreader well maintained.
- Keep records of what and how much you apply and when you apply it.

DON'T:

- Test your soil after you have fertilized.
- Guess on how much fertilizer you need and what setting you use.
- Apply fertilizer in hot, humid weather.
- Apply fertilizer near water features, on hard surfaces or on frozen ground.
- Use phosphorus unless your soil test indicates a deficiency.
- Apply more than four times a year.
- Use liquid fertilizers on your lawn.
- Use a drop spreader in big lawns.
- Bag your clippings.

DECK A **PATIO**

The ultimate solution for a hopeless slab

by **Gary Wentz, Senior Editor**

This was the ultimate bad patio: severely cracked and cratered, some areas raised by frost, others sunken after 50 years of settling. Originally, it was tiled, then the tile was chiseled off and the pockmarked surface got a coat of paint.

A slab with this much damage can't be fixed. But it can be covered up—and this article will show you how. The final project looks just like a deck, but it is much easier and less expensive than building a deck from scratch. In most cases, this project is also less expensive than a new patio installed by

Before!

a contractor. Local contractors estimated costs of $7 to $10 per sq. ft. to remove this patio and pour a new slab. You could probably replace your patio yourself for less than the cost of this project, but DIY demolition and concrete pours are big, backbreaking jobs.

Will it work on your patio?

Even if your patio is in terrible shape, you can deck over it. Cracks, craters and seasonal movement along cracks are no problem. But beware of these three situations:

- If an area is badly cracked and sinks noticeably year after year, any decking you put over it will also sink and develop a low spot. In most cases, settling concrete stops sinking eventually, so delay this project until it does.
- This project raises the level of your patio by 2-1/2 to 3-1/2 in. (depending on the thickness of your decking and whether or not you put spacers under the sleepers). So any door thresholds adjoining the patio must be at least that far above the concrete. If not, this project won't work for you. If you live in a climate where the ground freezes, allow an extra 1/2 in. so that seasonal "frost heave" can raise the slab without damaging the threshold.
- Stairs connected to the patio can complicate this project. To keep step heights equal, you'll have to raise the treads by the same distance you raise the patio (2-1/2 to 3-1/2 in.). On concrete steps, that's a straightforward job: You can treat them just like the patio, screwing sleepers to the treads and risers and decking over them.

Time, money and tools

Covering a patio with decking typically takes a weekend or two. This patio took much more time—five long days. That's partly because it's a big one (14 x 28 ft.). The grid pattern formed with different-colored decking also added a few hours to the job. But the biggest time factor was the unevenness of the patio surface. All those ridges and sunken spots meant hours of tedious shimming under the sleepers to form a flat surface for the decking (see Photo 3).

The cost of this project depends mostly on the decking you choose. Decking ranges from about $1.50 per sq. ft. for treated wood to more than $10 per sq. ft. for a top-grade manufactured product. The other materials for this project add up to about $1.50 per sq. ft., so your total cost could be anywhere from $3 to $12 per sq. ft. For looks and durability, we chose AZEK XLM decking ($7 to $9 per sq. ft.), which is made from PVC. We used Harvest Bronze, with Walnut Grove as the accent color.

MATERIALS LIST

Aside from the decking, here's an estimate of what you'll need to cover 100 sq. ft. of patio. Exact quantities depend on the shape of your patio and the layout of the decking.

- 90 linear ft. of treated 2x4
- 90 linear ft. of flashing tape
- Sixty 3/16" x 3-1/4" concrete screws
- 1/2"-thick PVC trim or deck fascia (for spacers), plastic shims, 3/16-in. masonry drill bits (minimum drilling depth of 3-1/2 in.)

Aside from standard carpentry tools, you'll need a hammer drill for this project. You can get a hammer drill for less than $50 that will do the job. But consider spending $100 or more. Even a very small patio will require more than 50 holes, and a more powerful drill will make that chore a lot easier. Also consider buying an impact driver. Impact drivers pack a lot more torque than standard drills or drivers and will drive concrete screws much better. Most models are cordless, but you can get a corded model for less than $50 online.

What it takes

TIME: One to two weekends
COST: $3 to $12 per sq. ft.
SKILL LEVEL: Intermediate
TOOLS: Circular saw, hammer drill, drill/driver

Figure A
Deck over a patio

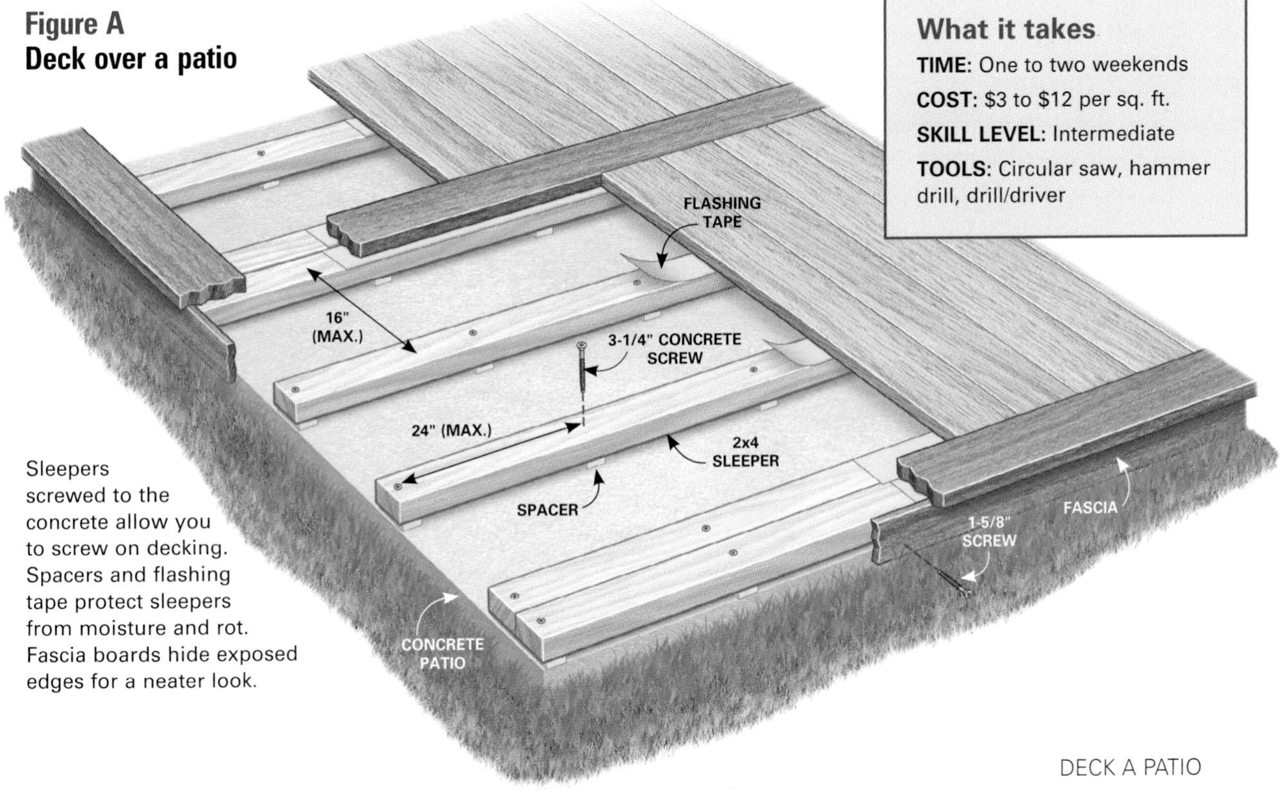

Sleepers screwed to the concrete allow you to screw on decking. Spacers and flashing tape protect sleepers from moisture and rot. Fascia boards hide exposed edges for a neater look.

OUTDOOR STRUCTURES, LANDSCAPING & GARDENING

1 Start with a layout. Mark the sleeper locations on the patio. Don't forget about extra sleepers to support stairs or railings.

2 Predrill for concrete screws. Drill through sleepers, spacers and into the concrete with a hammer drill, then drive in concrete screws. Overhang the sleepers along one edge of the patio and trim them to exact length later.

3 Screw down and flatten the sleepers. Check for flatness with a straightedge. Raise low spots with shims. At high spots, skip the spacer; stack up shims instead.

4 Lay the decking. Install the deck boards just as you would on a standard deck. When you reach the end of the patio, position the last board, mark the overhanging sleepers and trim off the excess.

Plan the layout

The layout of your sleepers will depend on the layout of your decking. If you want a standard decking design—all the deck boards running one direction—all you need are rows of parallel sleepers. If you want a more complicated decking pattern, like the one shown here, you'll need doubled sleepers to support any boards that run perpendicular to the others (see Figure A, p. 217). We also installed sleepers to support the steps we later added to the concrete stoop (see Photo 1).

Lay the sleepers

The sleepers don't have to be level—they can follow the slope of your patio. But they do need to form a flat plane.

Keeping it simple

If you're a beginning DIYer, don't let all the details on our deck scare you away. Your project can be a whole lot easier if you choose a simple decking design like the one at right. With all the deck boards running in the same direction, all you need are sleepers centered 16 in. apart. You won't need to do the careful measuring required by our design, or make angled miters and other fussy cuts. A simple deck design makes this project almost impossible to get wrong. If you have a badly uneven patio like ours, flattening the sleepers with shims (Photo 3) may take hours. It's tedious but not complicated.

You can slash the cost by using treated wood deck boards instead of manufactured decking. And if you live in a drier climate where the sleepers won't stay damp, you can skip the spacers and flashing tape.

Solve water problems first

This corner of the patio had settled by more than 2 in. over the years. That meant a big reservoir after rain—and water in the basement. So we filled the reservoir with exterior-grade self-leveling compound. After the first batch hardened, we poured on a thin coat and gave it a slight slope so water would run away from the house.

Self-leveling compound hardens fast, so you can get on with the project. But it's also expensive (about $30 per bag). If you're not in a rush, you can get similar results for less than one-third the cost with concrete topping mix such as Sakrete Top 'n Bond or Quikrete Sand/Topping Mix.

We also took a couple of other water-fighting steps. To prevent water from seeping down along the foundation, we caulked the gap between the patio and the house. At the other end of the patio, a corner of the slab had sunk slightly below the level of the soil and rainwater pooled there. To correct that, we shaved off the sod with a spade, dug out a couple of inches of soil and replaced the sod.

Why use spacers?

You could lay your sleepers directly on the concrete, but we bought a 1/2-in.-thick PVC trim board and cut spacer blocks from it. Here's why:

- Spacers let you run sleepers parallel to the house so decking can run perpendicular to the house (if that's what you prefer). A patio typically slopes away from the house so that water runs off. If you run sleepers parallel to the house and set them directly on the concrete, each sleeper will block runoff. But with spacers, water can run under the sleepers.
- Spacers allow for longer decking screws. We wanted to use Cortex screws, which come with cover plugs made from the same material as the decking. They're easy to use and almost invisible. But they're 2-3/4 in. long; that's too long to sink into our decking if we use sleepers only.
- Spacers let the sleepers dry out. If kept damp, common grades of treated wood will eventually rot. Spacers keep the sleepers off the damp concrete so they can dry.

If your patio is in good shape, you'll get a flat plane automatically. If your patio has ridges and sunken areas, you'll spend lots of time fussing with shims.

To preview the situation, lay a straight board across the patio in a few spots. Look for the highest hump in the patio and fasten your first sleeper there. Then work outward from the high spot, adding sleepers and checking for flatness along each sleeper and across them. Add shims to raise low spots.

Screwing down sleepers with concrete screws (Photo 2) is simple, but there are some things to keep in mind:

- Screws should penetrate the concrete by *at least* 1 in., so 3-1/4-in. screws are perfect. In low spots, where we had to stack up shims, we switched to 3-3/4-in. screws.
- As you drill, dust compresses around the drill bit. That slows you down, strains your drill and overheats the bit. To clear the dust, pull the bit completely out of the hole once or twice while drilling each hole.
- Drill the holes 1/4 to 1/2 in. deeper than the screw will reach. Extra depth provides a space for dust and grit, so screws are easier to drive.
- Have extra drill bits on hand. As a bit wears, it doesn't just drill more slowly; it also bores a slightly smaller hole and screws become harder to drive. We replaced each bit after about 40 holes.

When all the sleepers are screwed down, take a few minutes to double-check for flatness. Set a 4-ft. straightedge on each sleeper, both across it and along it. If you find spots that are 1/16 in. or more out-of-plane, back out the screw and add or remove shims (Photo 3).

Install the decking

Before decking, we covered the sleepers with flashing tape. Without it, water soaks the tops of the sleepers and the decking prevents the wood from drying. Common grades of treated lumber will rot if kept permanently damp, and flashing tape is the best insurance against that.

Installing deck boards over sleepers is just like installing them over standard deck framing (Photo 4). We began with the darker "accent" boards, screwing them into place temporarily to act as guides for the "field" boards. When we reached the end of the deck, we removed the center divider board and cut it to final length. Then we removed and mitered the border boards and trimmed the sleepers to final length.

To cover the ends of the sleepers, we used a deck "fascia" board made from 1/2-in.-thick PVC. We cut the fascia into strips and screwed them to the sleepers.

More ways to improve a patio

Whether your patio is in bad shape or just bland, there are many ways to revive it. But before you weigh your options, consider the "crack factor."

Cracks in your patio drastically limit your options. That's because cracks tend to move. Some grow wider over time, while others shrink and widen as the soil freezes and thaws. Some become uneven as one side of the crack sinks. Any movement happens so slowly that it's hard to detect. But if you know—or even think—that you have moving cracks, you have to choose a patio upgrade that can "float" over moving cracks without becoming damaged.

Cover-ups for a *cracked* patio

Along with the deck project shown on the previous pages, here are some other projects that can withstand moving cracks:

Bury it under pavers

A concrete slab provides a firm, stable base for pavers. Cover the patio with a thin layer of sand, lay pavers over it, and the results look like a standard paver patio. It's a fairly simple project and the cost is reasonable ($3 to $6 per sq. ft.), but expect a weekend or two of hard labor. For complete step-by-step instructions, go to familyhandyman.com and search for "cover patio."

GETTY IMAGES/TIM ABRAMOWITZ

Hide it under a rug

The quickest way to hide damaged concrete—or just add color—is with an outdoor area rug. They're available in a huge range of colors, designs and prices ($50 to $600). The largest rugs are typically 9 x 12 ft. That may not cover your entire patio, but just covering most of an ugly patio makes a huge difference. Shop online or visit a store that handles patio accessories.

Snap-together tiles

Interlocking plastic tiles simply snap together; no need to fasten them to the patio. Some versions are plastic only. Others are topped with wood, ceramic or stone. (Ceramic or stone tiles require a flat surface—they may crack if installed over ridges or depressions.) To browse online, search for "deck tile" or "patio tile." Plastic-only tiles start at less than $3 per sq. ft. Wood, ceramic or stone versions typically cost $8 to $15.

Projects for a *crack-free* patio

If your patio isn't cracked, you could choose any of the options at left, or one of these:

Stain it

A coat of stain followed by a coat of sealer transforms a patio in a weekend for less than $1 per sq. ft. But there are downsides: You'll have to reseal every one to three years and may eventually have to restain it. Also, stain won't hide damage, and any repairs will likely show through the stain. To see how to apply stain in multicolor patterns, go to familyhandyman.com and search for "stain patio."

Resurface it

With a coat of resurfacer, you can make an old patio look like new concrete in a day for less than $1 per sq. ft. Just mix the cement-based powder with water and spread it over the patio. You can repair cracks and resurface over them, but the cracks may return. Quikrete Concrete Resurfacer and Sakrete Flo-Coat are two common brands.

Tile it

A concrete patio is a great foundation for tile. And tile is a great way to turn a bland patio into a showpiece. The cost depends mostly on the tile you choose; the project could cost $4 per sq. ft. or three times that. Freezing water can destroy outdoor tile. So if you live in a climate that freezes, pay extra attention to the details. For the complete story, go to familyhandyman.com and search for "tile patio."

MARK'S **MINI SHED**

What it takes

TIME: Two weekends

COST: $350 to $450

SKILL LEVEL: Intermediate

TOOLS: Miter saw or circular saw, 18-gauge brad nailer, compressor, drill, hammer, stapler, level, caulking gun

A convenient storage locker for yard gear—and relief for your overstuffed garage

by **Mark Petersen, Contributing Editor**

My wife recently complained about having no space for her garden tools. It's true—our garage was overcrowded, and the yard shed was crammed full of stuff. The solution was a mini shed on the exterior wall of the garage just for her. Now my wife is happy to have a place for all her garden tools, and when she's happy, I'm happy.

I spent about $450, but you could save $100 if you used pressure-treated trim boards instead of cedar, and three-tab shingles instead of cedar shingles and felt paper. The project took me about 20 hours to build, a few hours at a time. I wanted to build as much of this project as I could in the comfort of my shop, so I made each section an individual unit. You can build two sections like this one or stack a whole bunch of them together. Ours is filled with garden tools, but it would also work great for pet supplies, grilling accessories, toys or whatever.

1 Assemble the boxes. Paint all the plywood components, then assemble them with self-tapping, trim head screws. Screw one side to the back, then add the shelves and finally the other side.

2 Trim the sides. Mount the boxes on their bases, then add trim and siding to the sides that will be exposed. Fasten the trim and siding with construction adhesive, plus a few brads to hold them in place while the adhesive sets.

Cut the box components

Start by cutting the sides (A) and backs (B) to the dimensions given in the Cutting List on p. 225. Clamp two sides together, and crosscut them to length at the same time with a circular saw. Crosscut one back at a time with your circular saw set to a 20-degree angle. This will match the angles you'll be cutting on the sides to achieve the slope of the roof. For all your cuts, make sure the surface of the plywood with the least flaws faces inside the locker. Measure down 6 in. from the top of one of the sides and mark the slope of the roof. Again, clamp two sides together and cut them at the same time.

Rip the three shelves (C) down to size and clamp them all together before crosscutting them. Rip the bottoms (D) to size and crosscut them together as well. The only plywood pieces left to cut are the top braces (F).

Cut the cedar parts that will be installed inside the boxes. These include the door stops (L), hinge supports (M) and the door latch blocks (N). Crosscut one of the 12-ft. cedar 1x6s in half, and then rip down the door stops and the hinge supports out of one of the 6-ft. halves. Always square up the factory edges before cutting any of the boards to length.

Sand and paint the inside parts

Paint all the interior parts of this project before assembling them. Fill any voids and holes in the plywood with wood filler. I spot-sanded the really rough spots with 80-grit paper but didn't sand any of the exterior surfaces.

Only the plywood surfaces that face the inside of the storage locker need painting. Paint all but one of the 3/4-in. sides on the door stops, hinge supports and door latch blocks. The plywood that forms the roof can be painted if you wish, but it really isn't noticeable, and the top braces (F) will be completely covered by trim, so there's no need to paint them. I rolled on a product that was a combination of exterior paint and primer. I was able to get full coverage with one thick coat.

Assemble the boxes

Set the sides next to each other and mark the location of the shelves with a framing square. Then mark a guideline for the screws on the exterior of the sides. I measured up from the bottom of the sides and marked the top line of the shelves at 22-3/4 in., 37-3/4 in. and 51-3/4. These measurements are based on some specific items I wanted to store. Make your shelves any height you wish, add more shelves, or eliminate them altogether.

Attach one of the sides to the back with 1-1/2-in. stainless or exterior-grade screws. Save time and buy self-drilling screws that don't require a predrilled hole. Space the screws about 16 in. apart. Once one of the sides is attached, transfer the shelf lines to the back with a framing square. Secure the bottom and the shelves with the same type of 1-1/2-in. screw (Photo 1). Install three screws per shelf side.

Flip the box on its side, and mark a screw guideline on the back of the back. Secure the bottom and shelves to the back with three screws in each. Flip the project on its back again and attach the other side to the back, and then finish securing the bottom and shelves.

The top braces create a solid surface to fasten the top front trim board to. Screw them to the boxes with one screw in the center of each end, and then go back and tack two more 1-1/4-in., 18-gauge brads, one above and one below the screw. Two screws would likely split the plywood.

The hinge supports add extra strength to the trim board that the hinges will be fastened to. Attach the hinge supports and the door stops by driving 1-1/2-in. screws every 16 in. through the plywood sides into the back of the cedar strips. Install the two door catch blocks with two screws driven through the back side. Space them about 6 in. down from the top and up from the bottom, on the back side of the door stop in the box that has no shelves. The door catches on the other side will be fastened to the shelves.

Build and install the base

Cedar is naturally resistant to rot, but it doesn't do so well in direct contact with the ground. That's why I decided to build the base out of pressure-treated wood and keep the cedar trim at the bottom 3/4 in. from the ground. Screw the base fronts, backs and sides (J and K) together with two 3-in. screws in each connection. Attach the boxes to the base with 2-in. exterior grade screws. Install two screws on each of the four sides of the box. Make sure all screws used with treated wood are compatible with treated lumber.

3 Add the front trim. Trim the front after the boxes are attached. Double-check that both door openings are the same size before you permanently attach the center trim board.

Storage locker on steroids!

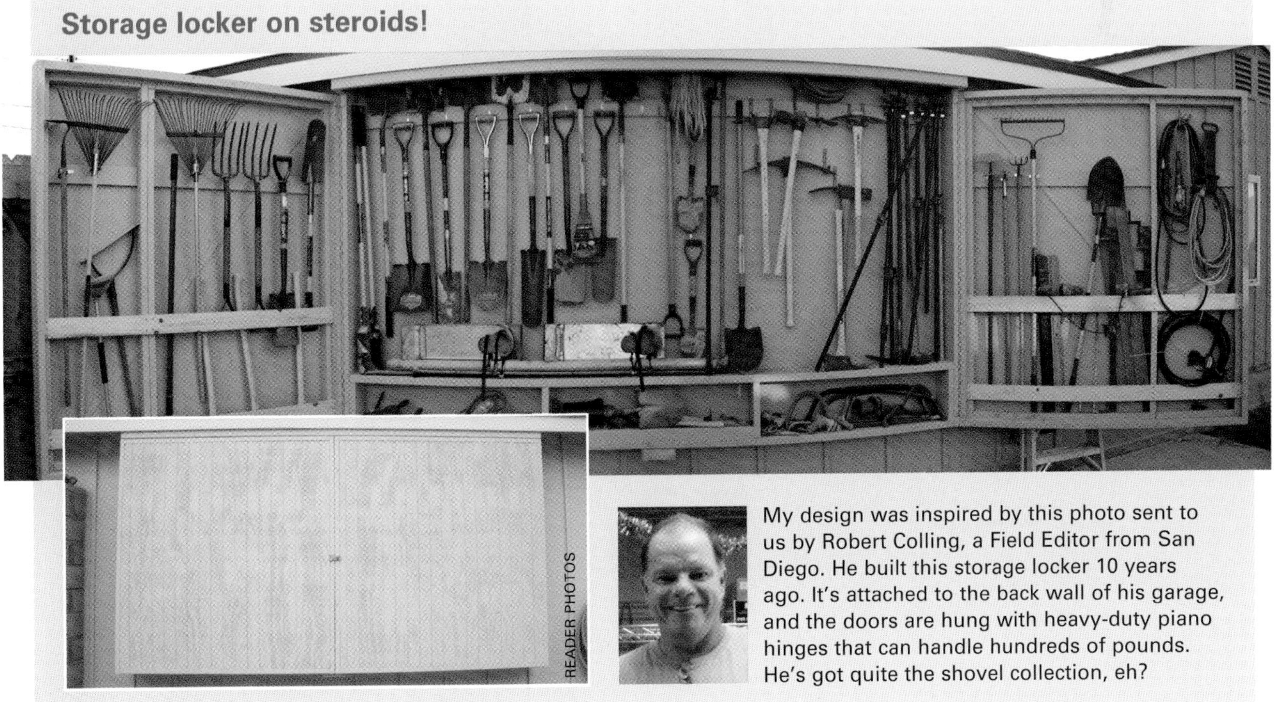

My design was inspired by this photo sent to us by Robert Colling, a Field Editor from San Diego. He built this storage locker 10 years ago. It's attached to the back wall of his garage, and the doors are hung with heavy-duty piano hinges that can handle hundreds of pounds. He's got quite the shovel collection, eh?

OUTDOOR STRUCTURES, LANDSCAPING & GARDENING

Figure A
Mini shed

Overall Dimensions:
Approx. 79" tall x 55" wide x 18" deep

Figure C
Door construction

Figure B: 3/4" plywood cutting diagram

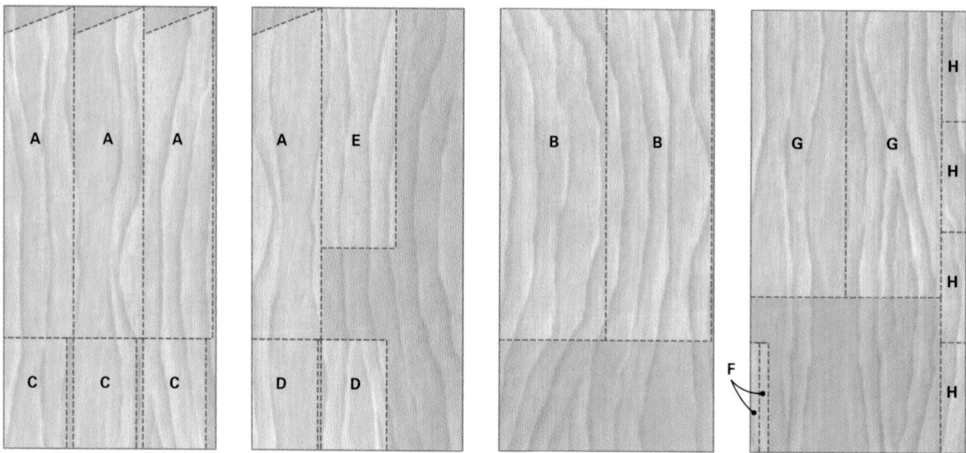

Install the trim and siding on the sides

Cut the side trim board (P) to length and install it with construction adhesive and 1-1/4-in., 18-gauge brads. The brads just hold the board in place while the adhesive dries, so you don't need more than one in each corner and one in the middle.

Create the smaller trim pieces by ripping the 12-ft. cedar (or treated) boards in half. Find the length of the two side trim boards (Q) by setting them on the side bottom trim board and marking the top angle on the back side of the board. Install them with adhesive and two brads every couple of feet. Make the side top trim board (R) by cutting one 20-degree angle and then marking the other angle in place. Install the side center trim board (S) so the top side is 42-3/4 in. off the ground.

For siding, I chose 1/4-in.-thick cedar planks often used as wainscoting (BB). Look for it at home centers near the paneling, not the lumber. If this product isn't available in your area, you could use pine paneling, vinyl siding, fiber cement panels, cedar shingles or whatever is available to you. Just make sure the siding profile is less than 3/4 in. or it will stick out past your trim boards. It just so happened that three of the cedar siding planks I bought fit in between the trim boards on the side without having to be ripped down. There was about a 3/16-in. gap on either side, which I caulked later.

Avoid a big mess by cutting all the siding planks to length and dry-fitting them before applying the adhesive. Tack them in place with 3/4-in. brads (**Photo 2**). Just shoot a couple of brads at the very end of the planks

MATERIALS LIST

ITEM	QTY.
4' x 8' x 3/4" sanded pine plywood	4
1x6 x 12' cedar	6
2x6 x 8' pressure-treated lumber	2
1/4" x 4" x 8' tongue-and-groove cedar paneling (six-pack)	3
Bundle of cedar shingles	1
1-1/4" exterior-grade trim head screws (100-pack)	1
1-1/2" exterior-grade trim head screws (100-pack)	1
2" exterior-grade screws (1-lb. box)	1
3" exterior-grade screws (1-lb. box)	1
1-1/4" 18-gauge brads (small box)	1
3/4" brads (small box)	1
1-1/4" 6d galvanized nails (1-lb. box)	1
Roll of 15-lb. felt paper	1
Construction adhesive (tube)	3
Polyurethane caulking (tube)	2
Composite shims (small bundle)	1
8" decorative T-hinges	4
Door handles	2
Roller door catches	4
1-1/2" fender washers	2
4" structural screws	2
Wood filler (small container)	1
Paint and/or exterior sealant	

4 Mount the door slabs. Screw the door slabs to temporary braces. This will let you build the doors in place for a perfect fit. Keep the screws at least 4 in. from the edge of the slab so they won't get covered up by the trim.

CUTTING LIST

KEY	DIMENSIONS	QTY.	NAME
3/4" BC sanded plywood:			
A	15-3/4" x 72"	4	Sides
B	23-3/4" x 72"	2	Backs
C	14-1/4" x 23-3/4"	3	Shelves
D	15" x 23-3/4"	2	Bottoms
E	17" x 52-1/8"	1	Top*
F	2" x 23-3/4"	2	Top braces
G	21-1/4" x 62-1/4"	2	Door slabs*
H	5-1/4" x 23-1/2"	4	Temporary door brace
*Cut to fit			
Pressure-treated lumber:			
J	1-1/2" x 5-1/2" x 25-1/4"	4	Base fronts and backs
K	1-1/2" x 5-1/2" x 12-3/4"	4	Base sides
Cedar (or pressure-treated):			
L	3/4" x 1-1/4"	2	Door stops*
M	3/4" x 3/4"	2	Hinge supports*
N	3/4" x 1-1/4" x 4"	2	Door latch blocks
P	3/4" x 5-1/2"	2	Side bottom trim boards*
Q	3/4" x 2-3/4"	4	Side trim boards*
R	3/4" x 2-3/4"	2	Side top trim boards*
S	3/4" x 2-3/4"	2	Side center trim boards*
T	3/4" x 2-3/4"	2	Front side trim boards*
U	3/4" x 5-1/2"	1	Front bottom trim board*
V	3/4" x 2-3/4"	1	Front top trim board*
W	3/4" x 2-3/4"	1	Front center trim board*
X	3/4" x 2-3/4"	4	Door side trim boards*
Y	3/4" x 5-1/2"	4	Door top and bottom trim boards*
Z	3/4" x 2-3/4"	2	Door center trim boards*
AA	3/4" x 1-1/8"	3	Drip edge*
BB	1/4" x 3/1/2"		Cedar planks*
*Cut to fit			

OUTDOOR STRUCTURES, LANDSCAPING & GARDENING

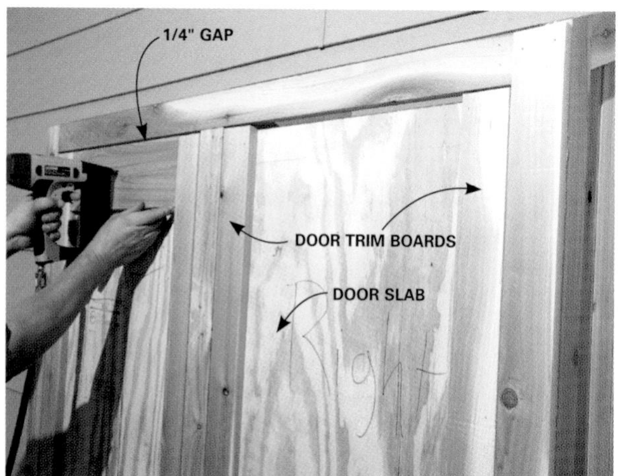

5 Build the doors in place. Nail and glue the trim to the slabs, leaving an even gap around the edges. Then screw on the hinges, remove the temporary screws in the slabs, and install the siding back in your garage.

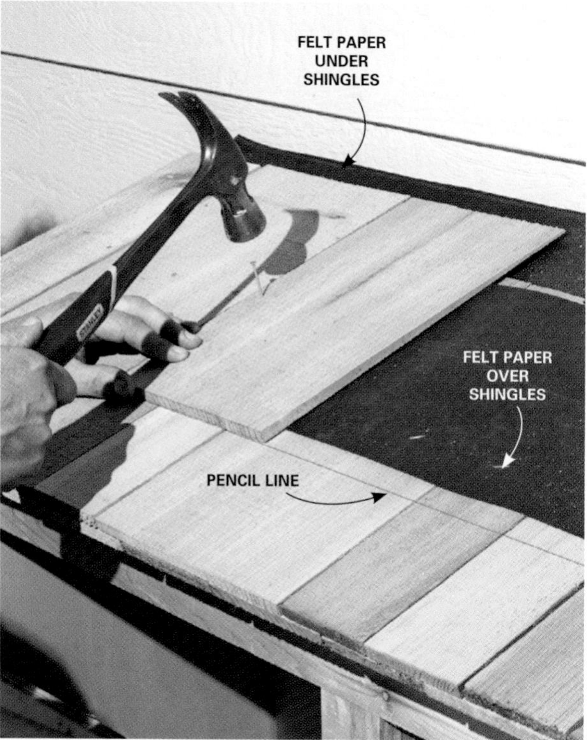

6 Shingle the roof. Cover the roof with felt paper. Prevent water from leaking between the shingles by covering every row with a strip of additional felt paper.

and a few on the edges. After they're all in, pound each plank flat with a rubber mallet or your fist and add one more brad in the center of each groove. The brads are only holding the siding in place until the adhesive sets up. Now repeat all these steps to build the other box.

Join the boxes

It's time to head outdoors. I pulled up some of my hostas and created a platform out of the same pavers I used as my edging. You could pour a small slab, tamp down some gravel or build a pressure-treated wooden platform. If you build a small platform, make sure it's level; larger patios should always slope away from the building.

Push the boxes into their permanent location and clamp the two sections together. Before fastening them, measure and cut the top plywood (E) so it's flush on all four sides. Temporarily set the top in place to see that it sits flat. Slip composite shims under one or both bases until the top is flat, the fronts are aligned and each side of the unit is relatively plumb. Secure the boxes to each other with eight 1-1/4-in. exterior grade screws, four through each side.

Trim the front

Install the two outside side trim boards (Q) first. Overlap them so they're flush with the trim boards on the sides. Keep them 3/4 in. off the ground like the trim on the sides. These trim boards will be shorter on top than the side trim to accommodate the slope of the roof. Find the length by holding a straightedge on the roof slope and measure up to that. The drip edge (AA) installed under the shingles will overlap all the top trim boards and cover any imperfections. Install the trim boards with 1-1/4-in. brads and construction adhesive.

Cut and install the front bottom trim board (U). It should be flush with the top of the plywood that makes up the bottom of the boxes. Cut and install the top trim board (V). After you cut the center trim board (W) to length, apply the adhesive. Then center it over the door stops and tack it on with just a couple of brads to hold it in place (Photo 3).

Build the doors

Start by cutting the four temporary braces (H) that will hold the door slabs in place while you install the trim. Attach the braces to the back of the door stops and hinge supports. One 1-1/4-in. screw through each side will be enough to temporarily hold the doors.

The door slabs (G) sit flush with the door stops and the hinge supports. Cut each door slab so there's at least a 1/4-in. gap around all sides. The gap can be a little bigger, but a smaller gap may cause the doors to bind. Screw the slabs into place with two screws into each temporary brace (Photo 4).

Now install the door trim with construction adhesive and 1-1/4-in. brads. Install the sides first (X), then the tops and bottoms (Y; Photo 5). Leave a 1/4-in. gap between the outside edge of the door trim and the trim on the face of the locker. Install the door center trim board (Z) so the top is 42-3/4 in. up from the ground, the same height as the center trim board on the sides.

Install the hinges before removing the doors. Cheap hinges tend to sag, which makes the doors a real challenge to hang, so buy good ones. These sturdy strap hinges cost $8 each. Center the hinge on the top and bottom door trim. These hinge screws required predrilled holes. I held the hinges in place and marked all the hole locations with a pencil. Punch a starter hole in each spot with a nail set before predrilling the holes with a 1/8-in. bit. Mark the depth on the drill bit with a little masking tape so you don't drill too deep.

Once the hinges are installed, take out the screws that hold the slab to the temporary braces, and make sure the doors open and close without binding. Now remove the hinges, and take the doors back to your garage. Doors take a lot of abuse, so I installed additional 1-1/4-in. screws through the plywood slab into the door trim for a little extra support. I spaced them every 16 in. or so.

Install the siding the same way you did on the sides. It looks best if the first and last siding planks are close to the same size. I had to rip about 1/4 in. off the first and last pieces to make them come out even. I'm not much of a math guy, so I just snapped a bunch of pieces of siding together, centered them over the opening and marked how much to take off each side.

Install the roof

There is a difference between cedar shakes and cedar shingles. I tried using shakes on my first attempt, but they looked too gnarly on such a small surface. Fasten the top plywood with two 1-1/2-in. screws along the outside edges and middle, and four more along both the back and the front edges.

Cover the whole roof with 15-lb. felt paper. Install the first row of shingles so they overhang 1-1/2 in. past the trim on the front and sides. Drive in two 1-1/2-in. galvanized 4d nails per shingle about 3/4 in. from each edge and about 1-1/2 in. above the exposure line. Lay down a layer of felt paper about 8 in. wide and cover the whole first row almost to the bottom of the shingles. Install the second row directly over the first, staggering the seams as you go. Install another 8-in. strip of felt paper over this second row about 5-3/4 in. up from the bottom of the shingles. That's an inch higher than the exposure line. In this case, each of the four rows will have a 4-3/4-in. exposure. I used a straightedge and a pencil line to mark each row as I went (**Photo 6**).

Overlap the rest of the rows with felt paper in the same manner. You'll need to trim the back side of the shingles on the last two rows. It's easier to do this if you pull the locker away from the wall and mark each shingle as you go. The exposed nail heads on the last row will get sealed later on.

Install the drip edge (AA) under the shingles. Install the sides first, then the front. Secure them with construction adhesive and 1-1/4-in. brads spaced every 8 in.

Seal the exterior

Seal the exterior before you push the storage locker back up against the wall and reinstall the doors. Start with a polyurethane caulk similar to the final color of your project. Seal all the areas where the siding meets the trim. Fill any knotholes or voids in the siding and trim, and don't forget to cover the exposed nails on the shingles. Let the caulk dry overnight before applying the finish.

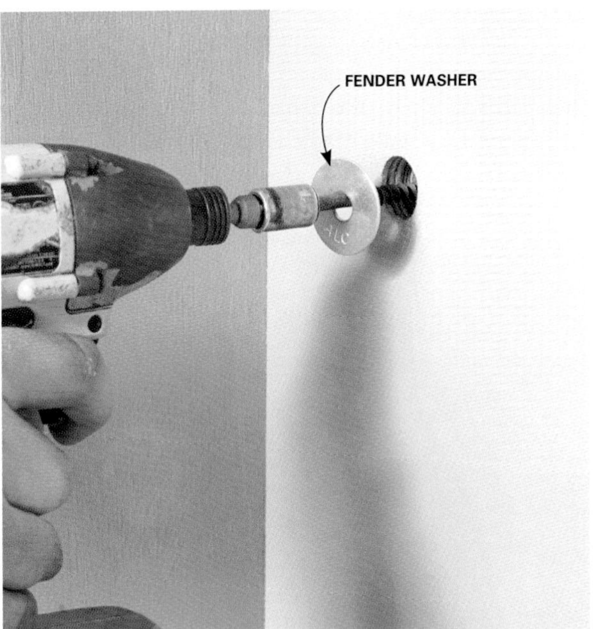

7 Prevent tipping! This shallow locker can tip forward easily, so once you've applied your finish to the exterior, fasten the locker to wall studs with a couple of screws. An oversize hole and a fender washer on your screws will allow the locker to move up or down slightly with ground movement.

I coated my storage locker with a wood finish made by Sikkens, which darkened the wood just a bit. This product holds up well, but it's also really stinky. Wear a respirator and finish the doors outside. I laid it down with a roller and back-brushed it. Force a little extra sealant into the holes made by the brads. If you don't want your shingles to turn a weathered gray, cover them with sealant as well (I left mine alone). I applied one coat and will add another coat next year.

Finish it up

The profile of this storage locker is tall and thin, so secure the locker to the wall to prevent it from tipping over. Push it back into place and reinstall the shims so it's tight up against the wall and the sides are plumb. Soil can rise and fall in cold climate regions because of the freeze/thaw cycle. To give the unit a little wiggle room, drill a 3/4-in. hole through the back and secure the locker to your garage wall with two 4-in. screws and 1-1/2-in. fender washers (**Photo 7**), one on each side. An easy way to find the studs in the garage wall is to locate the nails in the siding.

Reinstall the doors and install the door catches. Install them where you attached the support blocks. On the other side, install one underneath the top and bottom shelves. All that's left is to trim off the shims, attach the handles and fill up your locker.

HandyHints®

FROM OUR READERS

CLEAR LEAF BAGS FOR STORAGE

I had a few clear leaf bags left over from fall, so I decided to put them to good use. Because they're large, I can cover lawn chairs, cushions, space heaters, fans and other items to keep them dust-free in the rafters or on shelving in the garage. The best part is that I can easily find items at a glance because the bags are transparent—a feature my old black garbage bags lacked!

—Frank Normoyle

SKUNK SPRAY ANTIDOTE

Humans rarely get sprayed by skunks, but for dogs it's almost a rite of passage. If (or when) Fido gets sprayed, leave him outside for a while—the smell will subside dramatically in 24 hours and you won't stink up your whole house the way you would if you brought him in right away. It takes a lot longer than that for the smell to disappear completely, so you'll eventually want to wash the stink out. But before you spend a bunch of money on expensive shampoos, take a tip from the Humane Society: "Mix a quart of 3 percent hydrogen peroxide with 1/4 cup of baking soda and a teaspoon of liquid dish soap. Bathe the dog in it and rinse." Wear gloves to avoid smelling like a skunk yourself.

MOWING IN COMFORT

My mower is now a pleasure to use thanks to the pipe insulation taped to the handle. I used to get numb hands and blisters (we have a big yard!) from the bare metal handle. Make sure the insulation doesn't interfere with your auto-shutoff bar, if you have one.

—Joe Eisenbraun

STAY-CLOSED PATIO UMBRELLA

One day I was playing with my dog on the backyard patio and saw the table umbrella being tossed and partially opened as the wind picked up. Thinking fast, I removed the dog's quick-release collar and wrapped it around the umbrella. Perfect fit! Later in the day when the wind had subsided, I gave the collar back to my dog and got a shiny new one for the umbrella for about $4 at a local pet store.

—Richard Stith

SMARTER LEAF COLLECTION

I have lots of leaves to gather every fall and haul to the local compost site. Rather than buy and fill a bunch of plastic leaf bags, I save lots of time and effort by raking leaves into a Bagster bag that I bought at a home center. I can pull the full bag into my trailer, transport the leaves and store the bag for the next season.

—Tom Hayden

FLY-TRAP HAT

I use this trick to keep those pesky flies from biting. They go for the high spot and find their way onto the trap, which keeps them off my neck! The Mini Reel Fly Tape Kit by Revenge is available online.

—John Wojnas

HandyHints

SEED LIBRARY

Now that CDs are being replaced with smartphones and other devices, I use my old CD case to organize and store my seed packets. It works great to store them by seed type or even alphabetically. It's a convenient reference to have for the following year. I write notes on the packets to remember which seed variety worked and which didn't.

—Lisa Vice

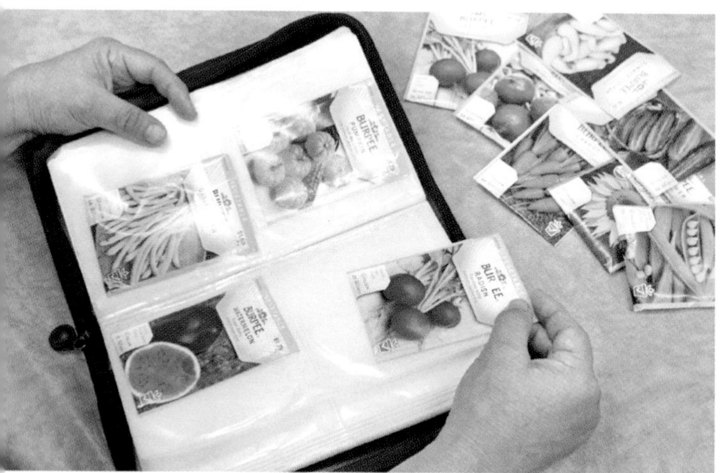

TWIG PICKUP ON THE GO

Before I mow, I usually go around and pick up fallen twigs and other debris. Inevitably, I miss some and have to stop and pick it up. To solve the problem, I attached a wastebasket to my mower. Now when wrappers, cans and sticks suddenly appear, I can stuff them into my basket and keep moving.

—Jared Reiners

READER PHOTO

TRAILER LINER

I use a 4 x 8-ft. trailer to haul mulch and dirt to the house. It's extremely handy except when it comes to cleaning out the cracks and corners after each load. I discovered that a Bagster from the local home center could serve as a great trailer liner. The bag is not only the same size as my trailer but also tall enough to fold over my load and strap down so that I don't blow the contents on the drivers behind me. The bag is tough enough to stand up against shovel strikes and pulling along the ground, and it also works great for sand, dirt and gravel.

—Joel Eisenbraun

BETTER TREE WATERING

I got tired of hauling buckets of water to my distant trees and dumping the water at the base of the tree only to see it quickly run off. I took some old 5-gallon buckets and drilled a 1/4-in. hole near the bottom of each one. After plugging the holes with dowels, I fill the buckets and haul them in my wheelbarrow to the trees. Once I unplug the holes, it takes several minutes for the buckets to drain, allowing the soil to soak up every drop.

—David Radtke

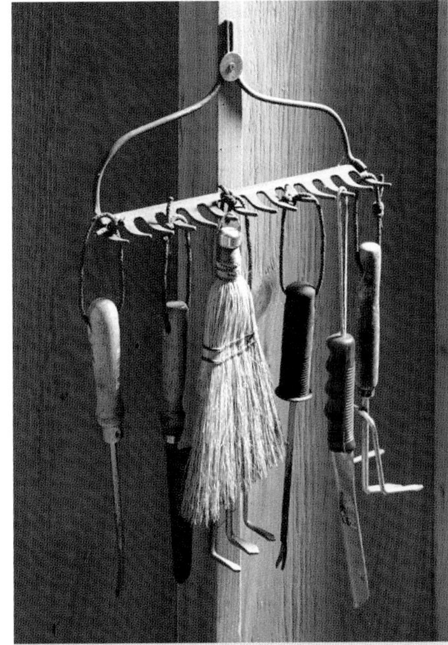

RAKE RACK

Don't throw away that old rake. When the handle broke on our old rake, I decided to repurpose it for use as a rack to store my garden hand tools. It fits the gardening theme and keeps what I need in plain sight!

—Judy G. Todd

HOLEY WEED BUCKET

Don't throw away the plastic pots from potted plants. With a rope handle attached, they make great weed buckets to carry with you as you tend the flower beds or vegetable garden.

Glen Weller

NORTH WOODS BENCH

An inexpensive, easy-to-build classic

by **Jeff Gorton, Associate Editor**

While visiting a cabin in the woods of northern Wisconsin, I saw the cute red stool shown at the top of the facing page. Made by an anonymous carpenter, it was simplicity itself: pine boards, nailed together. And it had an interesting and ingenious design detail: a cloverleaf, clearly made with three overlapping drill holes. It was just the kind of little bench I needed for the backyard, so I went into the shop and made this modern version. A little longer and a little stronger than the original, but the same folk art detail. And since it's made from lumberyard pine, the price can't be beat. Here's how to make one.

This bench is simple enough to build with a few hand tools, but to speed things up, we chose to take advantage of the power tools in our shop. We used a miter saw to cut the stretchers to length and to cut the 10-degree angles on the ends of the center stretcher, and a circular saw for all the other cuts. If you don't own a miter saw, you can use a circular saw or jigsaw for all the cuts.

To make the holes for the clover shapes, you'll need a 1-in. hole saw mounted in a corded drill, or a powerful cordless drill.

We used No. 2 knotty pine to build this bench. You'll need one 6-ft. 1x12 and one 10-ft. 1x4. Select boards that are straight and flat, with solid, not loose, knots. We assembled the bench with countersunk 2-in. trim screws and then filled the holes with wood filler. If the bench is going outdoors, be sure to use corrosion-resistant screws.

Cut out the parts

Using the Cutting List on p. 234 as a guide, cut the two legs and the top from the 1x12 (**Photo 1**). The legs require a 10-degree bevel on the top and bottom. Be careful to keep both bevels angled the same direction. Then cut the stretcher and aprons to length. The stretcher has a 10-degree angle on each end.

> **What it takes**
>
> **TIME:** Half day
>
> **COST:** $12 to $20 (depending on the finish)
>
> **SKILL LEVEL:** Beginner to intermediate
>
> **TOOLS:** Tape measure, square, circular saw or jigsaw, drill, 1-in. hole saw

1 Cut the leg blanks. Set the saw to cut a 10-degree bevel. Mark the 1x12 and align the saw with the mark. Then use a large square to help guide the cut.

2 Drill out the clover shape. Mark out a grid with lines spaced 1/2 in. apart. The centers of the holes are on four of the intersections. Drill all four holes halfway through the board. Then flip the board over and drill from the other side to complete the holes.

3 Cut the leg angles. Mark the "V" in the center and the two outside angles on the legs. Then cut along the lines with a circular saw. Accurate cutting is easier if you clamp the leg to the workbench.

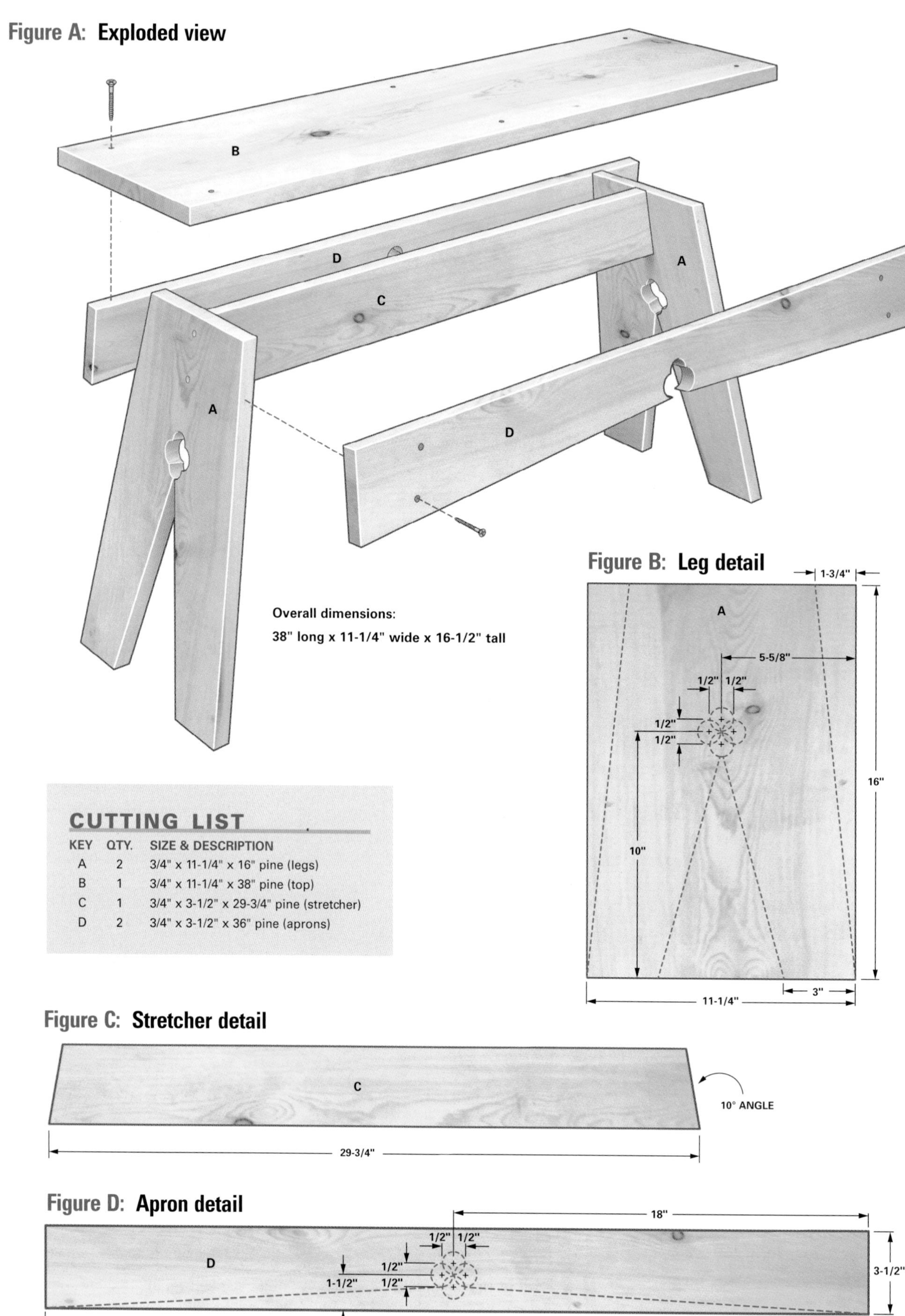

CUTTING LIST

KEY	QTY.	SIZE & DESCRIPTION
A	2	3/4" x 11-1/4" x 16" pine (legs)
B	1	3/4" x 11-1/4" x 38" pine (top)
C	1	3/4" x 3-1/2" x 29-3/4" pine (stretcher)
D	2	3/4" x 3-1/2" x 36" pine (aprons)

Next, mark the legs and aprons for drilling and cutting, using the dimensions in **Figures B and C** as a guide. Draw the grid layout as shown in **Photo 2** to locate the holes. Use a nail or a punch to make starting holes for the hole saw at the correct intersections.

Drill the 1-in. holes halfway through the boards (**Photo 2**). Make sure the pilot bit on the hole saw goes through the board so you can use the hole to guide the hole saw from the opposite side. Then flip the boards over to complete the holes.

Make the remaining cuts on the legs and aprons with a circular saw (**Photo 3**). Finish up by sanding the parts. We wrapped 80-grit sandpaper around a 1-in. dowel to sand the inside of the holes. Sand off the saw marks and round all the sharp edges slightly with sandpaper. If you plan to paint the bench, you can save time by painting the parts before assembly.

Build the bench

Start by marking the location of the stretcher on the legs. Arrange the legs so the bevels are oriented correctly, and screw through them into the stretcher. Next screw the two aprons to the legs (**Photo 4**).

The only thing left is to screw the top to the aprons. It'll be easier to place the screws accurately if you first mark the apron locations on the underside of the top and drill pilot holes for the screws (**Photo 5**). Stand the bench upright and align the top by looking underneath and lining up the apron marks. Then attach the top with six trim screws.

We finished this bench with old-fashioned milk paint. You can find milk paint online and at some paint stores. If the bench is going outdoors, rub some exterior glue on the bottom ends of the legs. That will prevent the end grain from soaking up moisture and rotting.

4 Screw the aprons to the legs. Drive trim screws through the legs into the stretcher. Then attach the outside aprons with trim screws.

5 Position the seat screws. Here's a goof-proof way to position the screws that fasten the seat to the bench frame. Center the frame on the seat and trace around the aprons. Then drill pilot holes through the seat to mark screw locations. Drive screws through the seat and into the aprons.

ROOF UNDER A DECK

Inexpensive roof panels keep it dry down below

by **Jeff Gorton, Associate Editor**

What it takes

TIME: A weekend or two depending on the size of your deck

COST: About $2.50 per sq. ft.

SKILL LEVEL: Intermediate

TOOLS: Standard carpentry hand tools, drill, circular saw

MEET THE HOMEOWNER

Rune Eriksen is a retired electrician who has spent the past 20 years building his dream lakeshore cabin, garage and shop.

One of our readers, Rune Eriksen, sent us photos of his design for a home-built deck drainage system, and we were impressed enough to check it out. His low-cost, easy-to-build system catches the water that drips through the deck boards and redirects it to the outside of the deck. Now Rune can use the area under the deck as a covered patio, where he can enjoy warm summer rainstorms without getting wet.

Several commercial systems are available to create a dry space under a deck (see p. 238), but Rune's seems to be just as effective. And it's inexpensive and easy to build using materials found at any home center. Here are the details in case you'd like to build your own version. Thanks, Rune!

Round up the materials

Rune bought corrugated fiberglass panels at a home center to use for his under-deck roof. The panels he used are 26 in. wide and 12 ft. long and cost about $34 each. He attached the panels with special roofing screws that have hex heads and neoprene washers for sealing. You'll find these screws where steel or fiberglass roofing is sold. You could also use galvanized steel or plastic roofing panels and install them the same way. Rune screwed treated 2x4 purlins to spacer blocks to support the panels and provide the necessary slope (**Figure A**, p. 238).

Gutters aren't required, especially if the water drains onto your lawn. But if the water falls onto the patio, gutters can prevent splashing. Rune chose PVC gutters because they're inexpensive and easy to cut and install. If you decide to install gutters, you'll need lengths of gutter, gutter straps, end caps, a downspout outlet, downspouts and special glue to join the sections.

1 Hang the purlins. Rune screwed the 2x4 purlins to spacer blocks. The blocks are incrementally thicker as they approach the outside edge of the deck so the new roof will drain toward the outside.

2 Attach the fiberglass panels. Rune attached the fiberglass panels with special screws that have a neoprene washer under the head to seal the holes. The panels overlap at the seams.

3 Finish up with a gutter. To keep rainwater from splashing onto the floor, Rune installed gutters along the beams. The gutters slope to a downspout at the end.

Figure A: Roof details

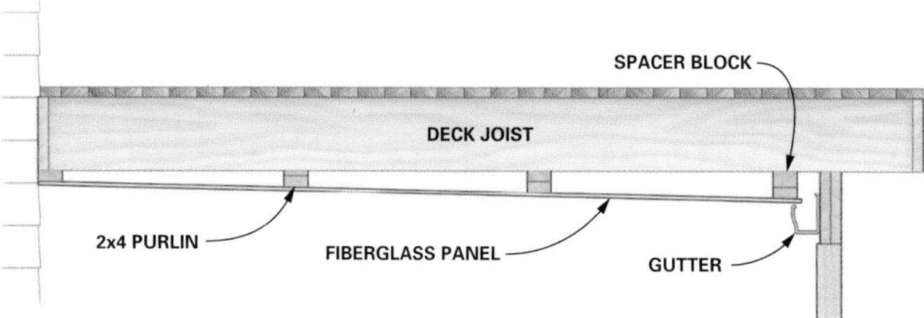

3 ways to keep dry under your deck

If you want to buy a manufactured system rather than build your own as we show here, you have a lot of choices.

1. One option is to cover the deck boards with a watertight membrane. DeckRite makes a deck floor covering that has the added advantage of creating a dry space below the deck. For more information, visit deckrite.com.

2. If you're building a new deck or replacing your deck boards, you can use a system like Trex RainEscape, which installs in the joist spaces before you install the decking. The advantage of this system is that it allows you to easily add lighting or other wiring in the joists, and cover the bottom of the joists with bead board or any attractive ceiling finish you choose. Learn more at trexrainescape.com.

3. If your deck is already built, you can cover the bottom of the joists with a system like TimberTech's DrySpace (photo left). One advantage these systems have over simply screwing roof panels to the bottom of the joists is that you can remove a section to gain access to the joists if necessary. To learn more, visit timbertech.com/products/finishing-touches/dryspace-drainage-system.

These are just a few examples of what's available. Search online or visit your local lumberyard or home center to find other options.

Attach the purlins

Plan to space the 2x4 purlins parallel to the house and 3 ft. on center. To provide drainage, the panels should slope toward the outside edge of the deck about 1/4 in. per foot. If the span under your deck is 12 ft., for example, the purlin at the outer end of the deck should be 3 in. lower than the purlin along the house (12 x 1/4 = 3).

First, mark all the purlin locations on the deck joists. Install the purlin along the house and the outer purlin. Then stretch a string between them. Measure down from the deck joists to the string at the other purlin locations. Those measurements (minus the thickness of the purlins) will give you the widths of the spacer blocks.

Cut the spacer blocks and screw them to the bottom of the joists at the marks. Then attach the remaining 2x4 purlins by screwing them to the spacers (Photo 1).

Screw the panels to the purlins

Starting at one end, attach the first fiberglass panel to the purlin with the roofing screws (Photo 2). Place the screws in every other valley. Snug the screws enough to compress the washer slightly. Overlap the next panel onto the one you just installed and attach it the same way. When you get to the end, the last panel may be too long. You can just overlap it a bit more or cut it to fit. It's simple to cut panels to length or width with a circular saw and a carbide blade.

Install gutters and downspouts

If you want to install gutters, plan ahead and leave space for them. You may have to get creative to come up with an attachment method, depending on how your deck is built. Since the in-stock 12-ft. panels didn't quite reach the beams on Rune's deck, he nailed vertical 2x4s to every other joist to provide an attachment point for the gutters. Then he screwed the gutter hangers to the 2x4s. Slope the gutters toward the downspout for drainage.

7 Vehicles & Garages

IN THIS CHAPTER

Car Care & Repair 240
Patch a tear in leather or vinyl, clean your car ducts, homemade rust penetrant and more

Replace Your Car's Seat Covers 242

Replace a Serpentine Belt 246

Roll On a Truck Bed Liner 249

Pro Tips for Detailing a Motorcycle.........252

Advanced Garage Door Repairs 255

Great Goofs...261
Adding oil one drop at a time

Don't Just Polish—Rejuvenate! 262

Spray-On Paint Protection 265

Great Goofs...267
Clean—and scratched!

Refinish Wheels & Wheel Covers 268

Great Goofs...271
Special delivery, hot-melt mystery

Small-Engine Gas Tips 272

Handy Hints 274
Bike gear to go, stuck receiver hitches, luggage rack protector and more

Motor Oil Smarts......................................277

Handy Hints 281

Car Care & Repair

REBUILD A BOOSTER PACK

Using a battery-powered booster pack is the safest way to jump-start a car because it eliminates the possibility of sparks and alternator damage. But the lead-acid battery inside the pack doesn't last forever. When the battery inside your booster pack stops working, you can rebuild the pack yourself for a fraction of the price of a new one.

You'll need a 6-in. Phillips or star bit, a drill and a 1/4-in.-drive socket or nut driver set. Once you open the case, remove the battery and match it up at a local auto parts or battery store. If you want to order a replacement online, measure the battery's overall size and note the terminal style and amp-hour rating. Our replacement battery cost just $35 online.

To replace your battery, start by removing the decorative trim pieces and screws (Photo 1). Then separate the case and swap the batteries (Photo 2). Reassemble the case and charge the battery until the charge light turns green.

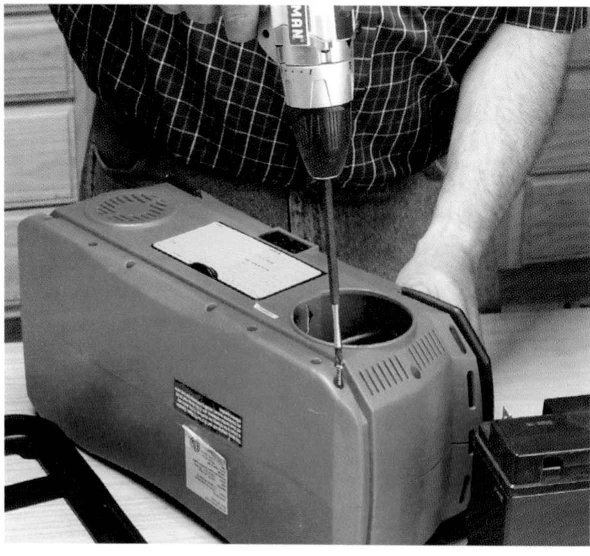

1 Remove the case screws. Pry off the plastic and rubber trim pieces to access the screw holes. Plunge a 6-in. driver bit deep into the holes to remove the screws. Keep track of their locations so you can put them back into place.

2 Swap out the battery. Remove the cables from the negative battery terminal, noting the locations of the lock washers and the placement of any other wires. Do the same at the positive terminal. Then swap in the new battery, making sure the positive and negative terminals are near the correct cables.

CLEAN YOUR CAR DUCTS

Neutralize smoke and other smells in your car with an aerosol can of automotive duct cleaner. Most products require you to spray the cleaner into the vents and the blower motor intake. One way to find your blower motor intake opening is to turn the system on defrost and hold a tissue under the dash. You can buy a can at auto parts stores for $8 to $13. One brand is Clean Air, which has an instructional video at cleanairauto.com.

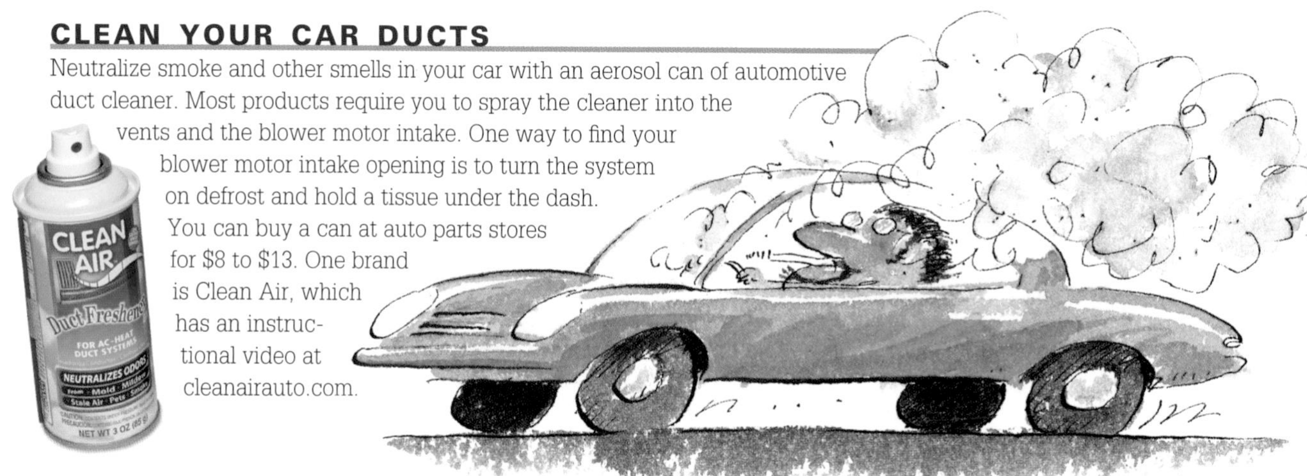

PATCH A TEAR/HOLE IN LEATHER OR VINYL

If you walk around with tools in your pockets, don't be surprised if you tear a hole in your car seat, sofa or easy chair. If a perfect repair is important, call a pro to fix it (about $150). But if you just want to prevent further tearing, you can fix it yourself with a leather/vinyl repair kit. The kit costs about $15, and the repair takes only an hour. But don't expect perfection. You'll still see the tear, and you probably won't get a perfect color match. However, this fix will contain the tear and look better than a gaping hole.

Buy a kit at any hardware store, home center or auto parts store (one choice is the 3M 08579 Leather and Vinyl Repair Kit, about $15). Follow the cleaning instructions in the kit and trim the damaged area to remove any frayed edges. Then cut the backing fabric so it extends under the tear by at least 1/2 in. Glue it in place (**Photo 1**) and let it dry for the recommended time.

Then mix the heat-set colored filler. This is the hardest and most frustrating part of the repair. But take your time and get as close to the color as you can. Apply just enough colorant to fill in the tear. Then cover it with the textured mat and apply heat (**Photo 2**). Let it cool and remove the mat (**Photo 3**).

1 Glue in the reinforcement fabric. Tuck the backing under the damaged area to form a patch. Then apply adhesive around the edges and the middle. Let it dry before adding colorant.

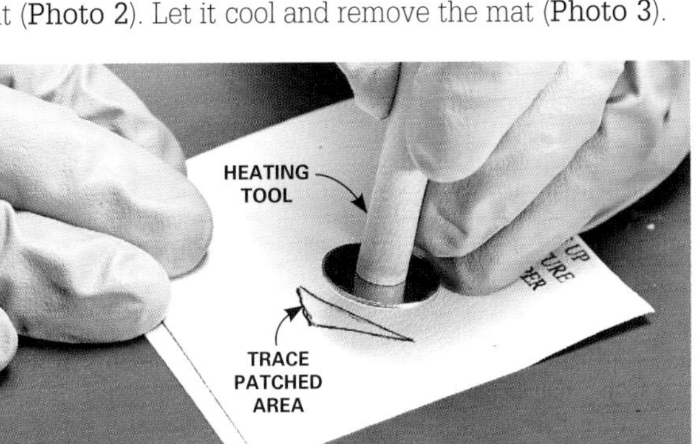

2 Cure the patch with heat. Touch the heating tool (included with the kit) to the face of a hot clothes iron. Then press the hot tool onto the textured mat and hold it in place.

3 Check out the results. The patch won't be perfect. But it sure beats the look of a tear or burn.

HOMEMADE RUST PENETRANT

Rust penetrant manufacturers are constantly working to improve their products. The latest formulations work better than previous brews. So if you're still using a 10-year-old can of penetrant, you might want to upgrade to the latest formulas from Liquid Wrench or the Specialist Rust Release Penetrant from WD-40.

As great as those new products are, occasionally you can get by with a home brew—a 50/50 mixture of acetone and automatic transmission fluid. It has a strong smell and is far more flammable than commercial products, so make sure you use it outdoors and away from flames. It doesn't work as fast as the commercial products, but if you need rust penetrant in a hurry, it will work.

DRIVING THROUGH PUDDLES

You may have heard that driving through puddles is bad because the brakes will get wet. Disc brakes, however, spin the water off, and wet brakes are the least of your worries. What you really need to worry about is damaging your engine. Most late-model cars pull in combustion air from the lowest part of the engine compartment. That ensures the engine gets the coldest, most dense air. If you plow through a puddle and splash water into the intake, it could get sucked up into your air filter. That'll restrict engine breathing and damage the filter. And, if the "puddle" is really deep, you can suck in enough water to fill the cylinders and cause hydro-lock and destroy your engine. It happens far more often than you would think. So why risk $3,000 in engine damage just to save a few minutes? Find a drier route.

REPLACE YOUR CAR'S **SEAT COVERS**

Spruce up the interior of an older car with snazzy custom-fit covers

by **Rick Muscoplat, Associate Editor**

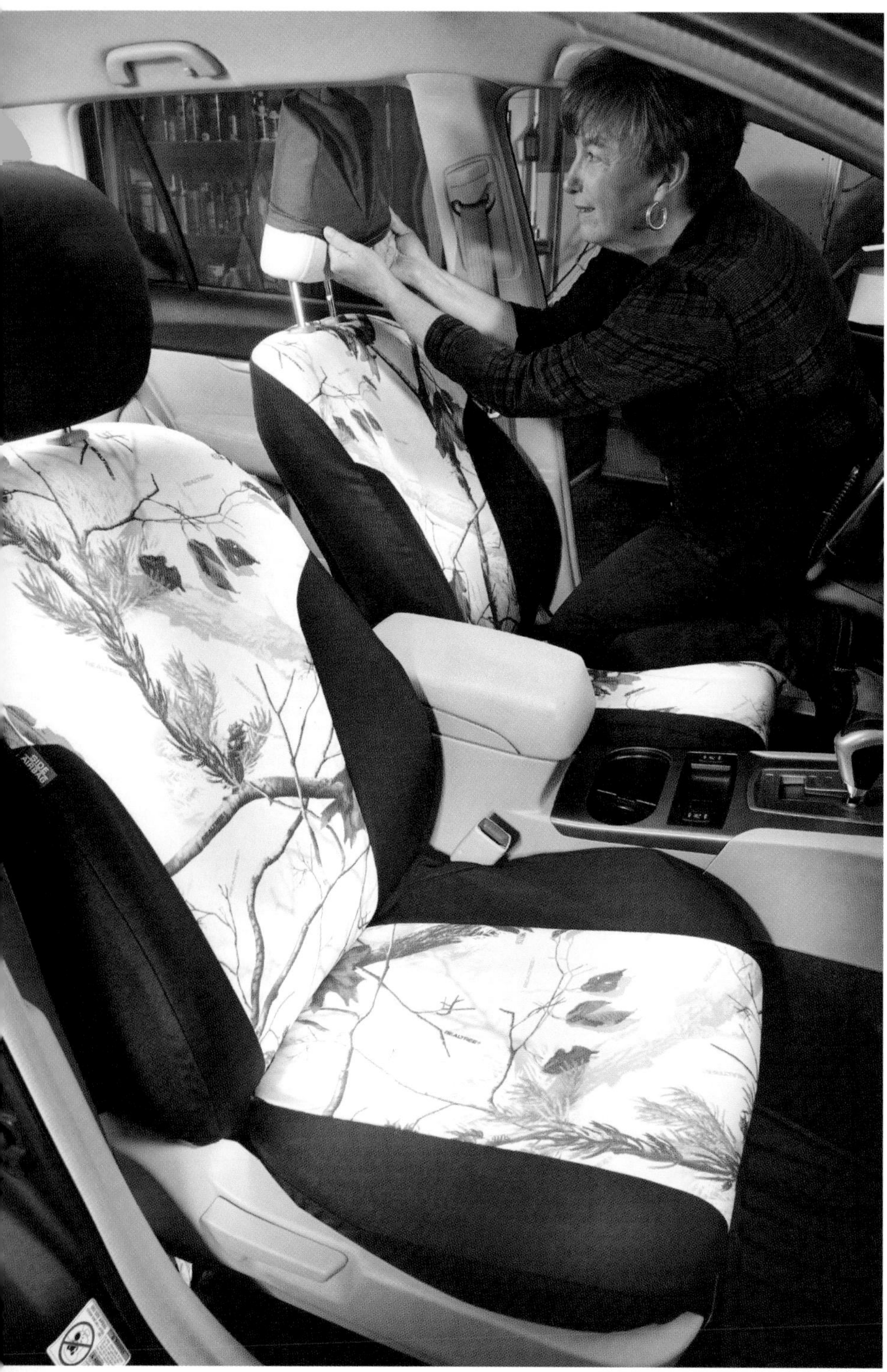

Whether you fill your vehicle with construction materials, haul kids and grandkids around or just spill lots of coffee, you know how easy it is for factory seat covers to get grungy. If they're beyond rescuing with an upholstery cleaner and you want to spruce up your vehicle's interior, you have only three options: Pay a professional automotive upholsterer to reupholster your seats (well over $1,000), buy used seats from a junkyard, or buy and install seat covers yourself.

Aftermarket seat covers cost as little as $50 per seat for a universal-fit style or about $150 per seat for top-of-the-line custom-fit covers. We'll show you how to order and install custom-fit seat covers. The installation is similar across makes and models. The job takes about two hours for front and rear seats. The only tools you'll need are a wire coat hanger and some tape to fish the straps under plastic trim pieces (if equipped). Everything else is included with the seat covers.

How to buy seat covers

Seat covers come in two styles: universal and custom-fit. You can buy universal seat covers right off the shelf at an auto parts store or order them online. Custom-fit seat covers must be ordered to fit your exact year, make, model and seat style. They're far more expensive than universal-fit seat covers. But they fit like a glove, stay put when you slide in and out, and are more comfortable. Plus, custom-fit seat covers include breakaway stitching so the air bag can deploy properly if your vehicle has side bolster air bags.

NOTE: We couldn't show you the trim disconnect and seat cover attachment points with the seat still in the vehicle. So we bought a junkyard Subaru seat to show how everything fits together.

To get around the air bag issue and keep costs down, universal seat covers simply eliminate the fabric that would normally cover the seat air bags. Then, to reduce slipping, the manufacturers coat the underside of the fabric with an anti-skid rubber. That makes them a bit more uncomfortable to sit on for long periods. And they will inevitably slip out of place and wrinkle because they're not an exact fit for your seats.

For some strange reason we don't understand, officially licensed designer camouflage and sports patterns are the most popular seat cover fabrics these days. Since the fabric designers get a royalty on every sale, you'll pay more for those patterns. If you want to keep the cost down, skip the trendy camo and sports fabrics and choose a solid color.

If you order custom-fit seat covers, you'll have the option of also ordering matching armrest and headrest covers, console covers, seat back storage and map pockets.

Buy custom-fit and universal seat covers from retail and online auto parts stores (search for "auto seat covers"), or directly from the manufacturer.

We bought the custom-fit seat covers for this 2010 Subaru Outback at nwseatcovers.com. We bucked up and picked the trendy Bill Jordan Realtree AP Snow camo pattern and added headrest covers. The front seat covers cost $341 and the rears, $331. Here's how they install.

Install new seat covers

You don't have to remove the seats from the vehicle to install new seat covers (although we show them removed; see the note above). And since most seats are made the same way, these instructions will work with the majority of makes and models. However, if the seat cover manufacturers' instructions differ from ours, follow theirs instead.

1 Release the bib panel. Follow the bib panel straps and unclip them from the springs or pull the elastic straps out from under the springs. Then lift the bib panel up to access the gap between the back and the bottom cushion.

2 Thread the straps through the gap. Push the bottom cushion straps through the gap between the seat back and the bottom cushion. Then pull the straps completely through until the seat cover is taut.

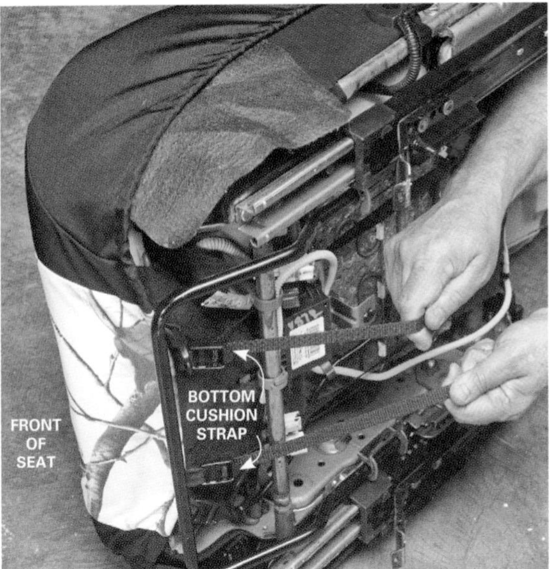

3 Buckle the seat cushion straps. Route the bottom cushion straps toward the front of the seat, making sure the straps don't interfere with the seat adjuster mechanism. Thread the strap into the buckle and cinch it tight to remove wrinkles in the seat cover.

VEHICLES & GARAGES

4 Tighten and connect the bungee cords. Pull the bungee cords to cinch the skirt on the bottom seat cover. Then connect the ends using the supplied S-hook.

5 Install the seatback cover. Pull the cover down until it reaches the side bolsters (cushions). Then compress the bolster while you pull the fabric down to the bottom.

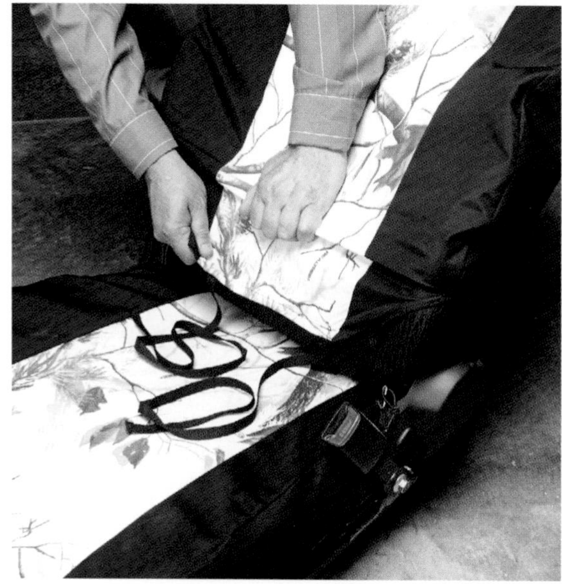

6 Install the headrest covers. Stretch the elastic edges around the headrest and pull it down. Tug at the cover fabric until it fits smoothly on the contour of the headrest.

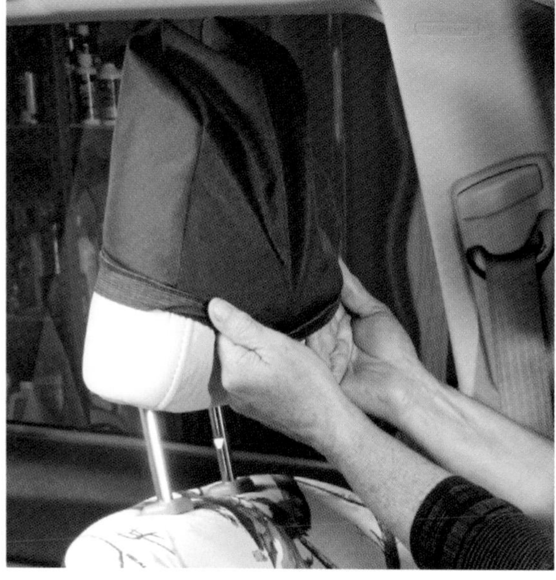

Start with the front seat covers

The bottom seat cushion covers usually attach to the seat with straps, buckles and S-hooks. You'll have to thread bottom cushion straps through the gap between the seat back and the bottom cushions (where the back reclines). That's easy in older vehicles. But the gap in newer vehicles is usually covered with a "bib" panel. Don't worry. The bib is easy to disconnect. It's connected to the seat springs with either clips or an elastic strap. Just reach under the seat and disconnect the straps (**Photo 1**). Then lift the bib to access the gap.

Next, fit the seat cover onto the bottom cushion and thread the rear straps through the gap (**Photo 2**). Route the straps toward the front buckles and tighten (**Photo 3**). Then connect the bungee cords (**Photo 4**). Tuck the puckered seat cover "skirt" behind the plastic trim panels (if equipped).

Remove the headrests. Then slide the cover over the seat back cushion (**Photo 5**). Push the bottom straps through the gap and into the buckles just like you did on the bottom cushion (refer to **Photo 3**). Reconnect the bib panel and pull down on the rear portion of the seat back cover to remove wrinkles. Then stick the hook-loop edge to the bib to secure it. Stretch the headrest covers onto the headrest (**Photo 6**) and reinstall them on the seats.

Then move to the backseats

If your vehicle has 60/40 rear bench seats, remove the bottom cushion first. If you have bucket seats in the rear, install them just like you did on the front seats.

To remove a bench seat bottom cushion, run your hand along the front edge to locate the latch points. Try jerking straight up at the latch points. If the cushion doesn't release, push it straight back as you lift up to release it from the hook latches. Then remove the entire bottom cushion from the vehicle and set it on a bench. Install the bottom cushion seat cover with straps and S-hooks (**Photo 7**).

Remove the rear headrests and slide the rear seat back covers onto the rear seats. Secure with the attached hook-and-loop fasteners. Add headrest covers and replace the headrests. You're done.

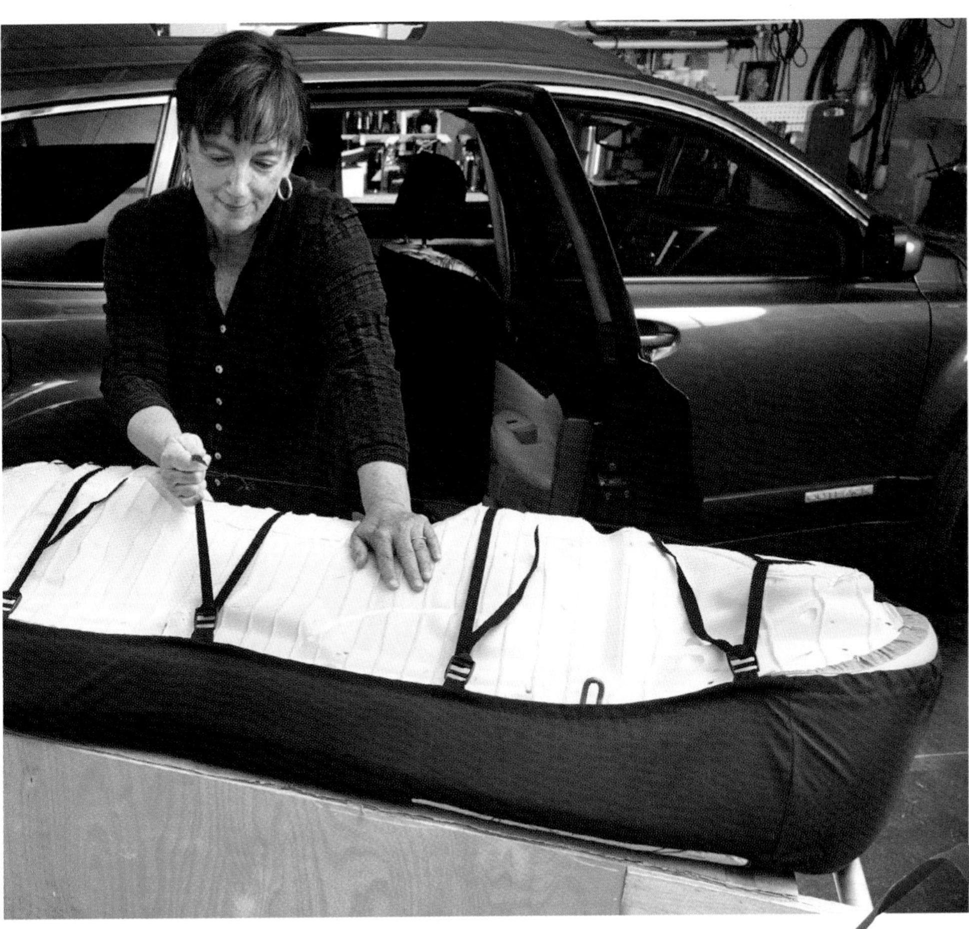

7 Install rear bench seat cover. Fit the cover onto the bench seat and thread the straps into the buckles. Tighten until snug. Check the fit and adjust. Then tighten the buckles, secure the bungee cords and connect the remaining straps to the springs with S-hooks.

Add a bun warmer and lumbar support

If your vehicle didn't come with seat heaters, now's the time to add them. Add-on electric seat heaters fit between your existing seat cushions and the new seat covers and secure with elastic bands and straps. The seat heater control connects to a cigarette lighter or power outlet. The model we show here (the ProHeat pad and controller; $84 from nwseatcovers.com) has an adjustable heat setting and automatic shutoff to prevent battery drain (in case you forget to turn it off).

And, if you want lumbar support, slide this inflatable unit ($66 at nwseatcovers.com) under the seat back cover before strapping it in place. Route the pump and tube out to the side. Once the seat covers are fully installed, adjust the firmness with the pump.

REPLACE A **SERPENTINE BELT**

It's much easier than you might think to replace this all-important belt

by **Rick Muscoplat, Associate Editor**

In the past, carmakers used several belts to drive alternators, water pumps, power steering pumps and AC. But now those components are all driven by just one—the serpentine belt. So if that single belt fails, there's no limping home—you're stranded. In the meantime, if the oil change guy wants to install a new belt, resist the sales pitch, at least for now. You may be charged up to $125 for a job you can do yourself for as little as $30, in less than an hour.

Before you begin, pop the hood and take a good look. You'll see the belt at the front or side of the engine. It's the one running around all the pulleys. If the belt is exposed and looks like it'll slip free relatively easily, and you can access the belt tensioner bolt without disconnecting anything, you can do this job yourself. But if access is blocked or there's very little room, you may want to hire this one out. Here's what you need to know.

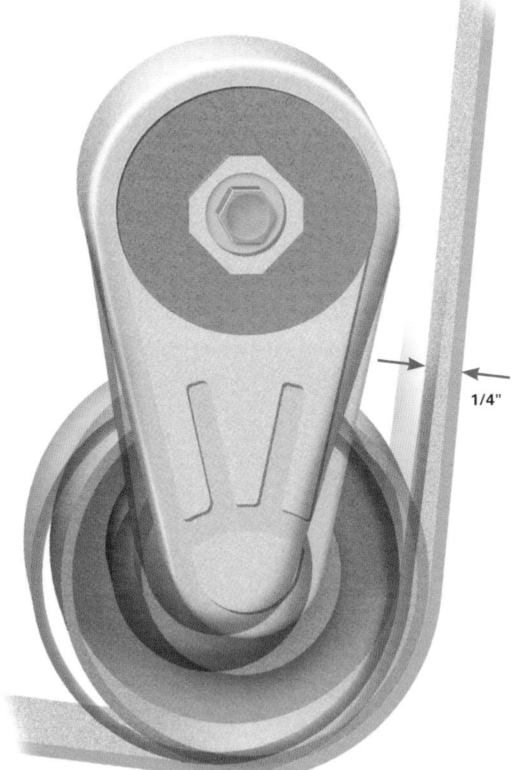

1 Check for excessive movement. A "good" tensioner arm should exhibit just a slight vibration with about 1/32 in. or less of arm movement. And the belt should run smoothly with no visible vibration. If the tensioner arm exhibits a jerky vibrating motion, the belt vibrates, or the tensioning arm moves 1/4 in., the tensioner is bad.

Check the tensioner first

If your tensioner is bad and it's one of the more difficult styles to replace, you won't want to waste your time changing the belt. The shop would just have to remove the belt again to replace the tensioner. So check the tensioner first with these three tests.

The first test is a visual inspection with the engine running to assess the dampening feature of the tensioner. Pop the hood, start the engine and turn on the AC. Then shine a light on the belt tensioner and observe the tensioner arm roller for excessive movement (Photo 1). If it passes the visual test, move on to the "crank" test (Photo 2). The tensioner arm should rotate smoothly during crank and release with no binding. If the travel isn't smooth, replace the entire tensioner. Next, check the condition of the tensioner arm pulley/roller (Photo 3). If the pulley or roller exhibits any roughness, binding or noise, that is also cause to replace the entire tensioner.

How to replace the tensioner

Many tensioners are readily accessible and attach to the engine with a single bolt. To replace that style, simply remove the belt and then the retaining bolt. Pull off the old tensioner, noting the location of the locking pin on the back. Then slide the new unit into place, lining up the locking pin with the hole in the engine. Hand-tighten the bolt and then tighten it with a torque wrench to the factory specifications shown in your shop manual.

2 Check for smooth rotation. Snap a long-handled ratchet into the square 1/2-in.-drive or 3/8-in.-drive opening. Or use a socket on the hex-shaped protruding nut. Slowly rotate the tensioner arm as far as it will turn. Then release the tension. Feel for binding and creaking in both directions.

3 Check the pulley/roller. Rotate the tensioner and slide the belt off the pulley/roller. Then turn the pulley/roller and feel for resistance, binding and roughness. Then spin it and listen for rumbling. If it doesn't spin smoothly or has a rough surface, replace it.

How to replace the serpentine belt

Before you even think about removing the old belt, find the belt-routing diagram (**Photo 4**). If the diagram is missing, sketch one yourself. Trust us, if you don't have a diagram, you'll spend far more time trying to figure out how the new one installs than it takes to make a sketch ahead of time.

Remove the belt by releasing the tension (see **Photo 5**) and sliding the belt off any smooth pulley. Then release the belt tensioner and remove the old belt. To install the new belt, wrap the belt onto the pulleys as far as you can and then rotate the tensioner to allow the rest of the belt to go on (**Photo 6**). If you can't get the belt onto the last pulley, that's a sign it isn't seated properly on a preceding pulley. Don't force it on. Recheck your work to make sure all the ribs are properly seated on each grooved pulley.

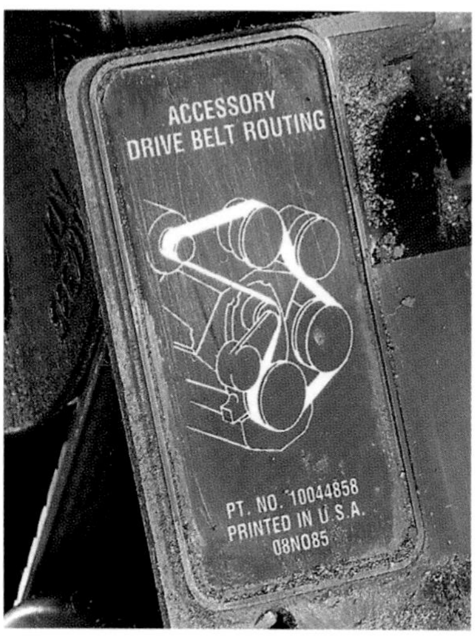

4 Find the under-hood diagram. Search for the factory belt-routing diagram. It's located near the serpentine belt, on the radiator support or strut tower or on a label affixed to the underside of the hood.

5 Remove the old belt. Rotate the tensioner and slide the belt off any smooth pulley. Then release the tensioner and finish removing the old belt.

6 Begin with the grooved pulleys. Wrap the new belt around the crankshaft pulley, then around the grooved pulleys. Finish the job by sliding the belt onto a rounded, non-grooved pulley.

How to tell if you need a new serpentine belt

First-generation serpentine belts were made from a nitrile compound that cracked with use. If your belt has cracks in three or more adjacent ribs within a 1-in. span, or has four or more cracks per inch on a single rib, it's time to replace it. You also need a new belt if you notice any of these conditions: chunks missing from the rib area, torn or frayed fabric, glazing on the belt's back side or debris trapped in the ribs.

Starting with the 2000 models, carmakers switched from nitrile to ethylene propylene diene monomer (EPDM) belts. EPDM belts last much longer and don't crack or lose chunks the way nitrile belts do. But they do wear, and that wear is much harder to detect. You can measure EPDM belt wear with a gauge or a smartphone app. Both products are available for free from Gates Corp. (go to gatesprograms.com/beltwear and click on either tool).

In most cases, you'll want to use the plastic gauge to measure your belt, as shown below left. However, if you have a smartphone and enough maneuvering room to shoot a close-up photo (engine off), let technology do the work for you. The app (photo below right) works by analyzing the width of the ribs compared with the width of the grooves.

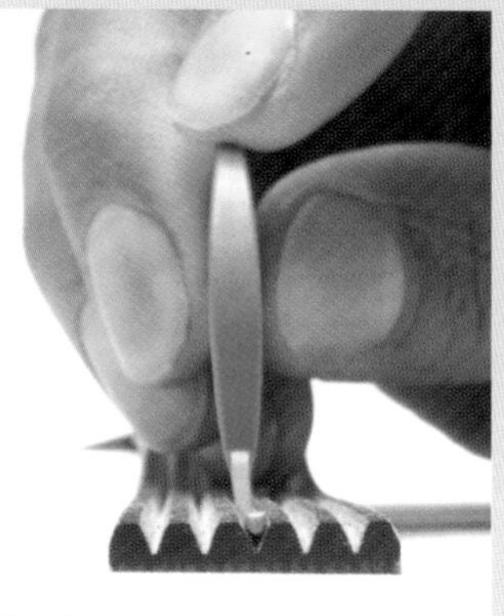

Measure wear with a gauge
Press the gauge into a belt groove. As long as the gauge sits above the ribs, the belt is good. If it slides down so it's even with the rib, the belt is worn and must be replaced.

Measure wear with an app
Draw a line on the belt ribs with a silver permanent marker. Then shoot a photo with your smartphone. The app will tell you if the belt is good or bad.

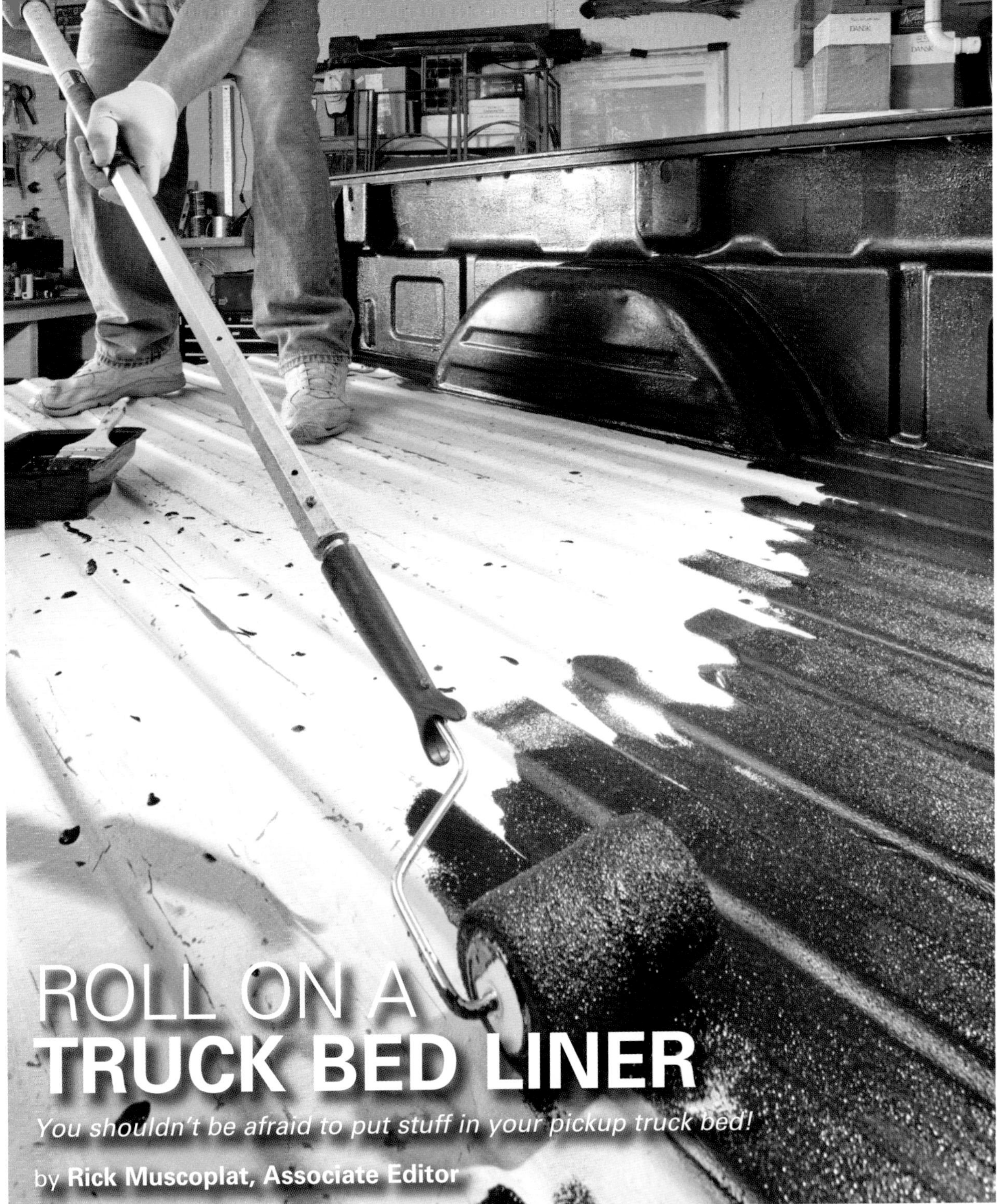

ROLL ON A TRUCK BED LINER

You shouldn't be afraid to put stuff in your pickup truck bed!

by **Rick Muscoplat, Associate Editor**

You bought a pickup truck because you needed to haul things. But what can you haul in a pickup bed that's not going to destroy the finish and eventually rust out the bed? Pillows? Precisely. That's why you need bed protection. Your choices are a preformed hard plastic drop-in liner, professionally applied epoxy coating or a DIY roll-on coating. The best preformed liners cost about $500. That's about the same cost as for a professionally applied epoxy liner. (See "Other Bed Liner Options," p. 251). However, you can roll on a fairly high-quality bed liner yourself for about $150. That's the path we're going to take you down.

Choosing a roll-on product

Herculiner, Dupli-Color and Rust-Oleum are the most popular retail brands. You can find them at most auto parts stores. However, you can also find many other brands online. Just search for "roll-on bed liner."

The products come in three types: water-based, solvent-based single-stage and solvent-based two-part formulas. Prices range from $70 to $120 per gallon for water-based and single-stage products, to $150 and up per gallon for two-stage formulas. One gallon is enough to apply two coats to most truck beds. The preparation work is the same for all three formulas.

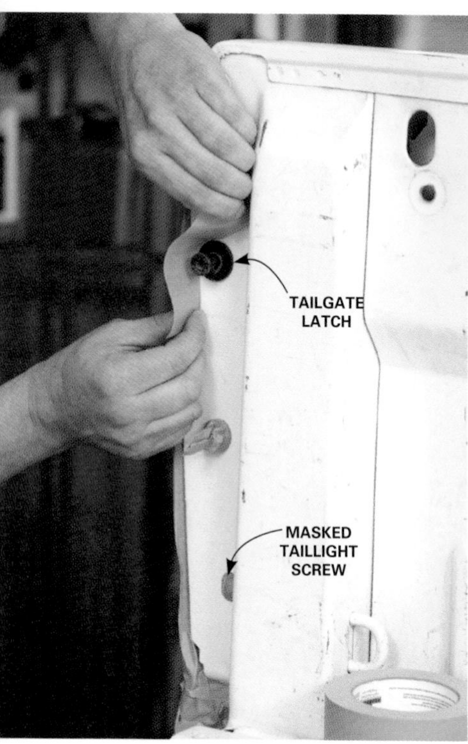

1 Mask off operational components. Butt the tape against the painted edge and stretch it around latches and lights. Cover small taillight retaining screws with tape and cut off the excess with a razor blade.

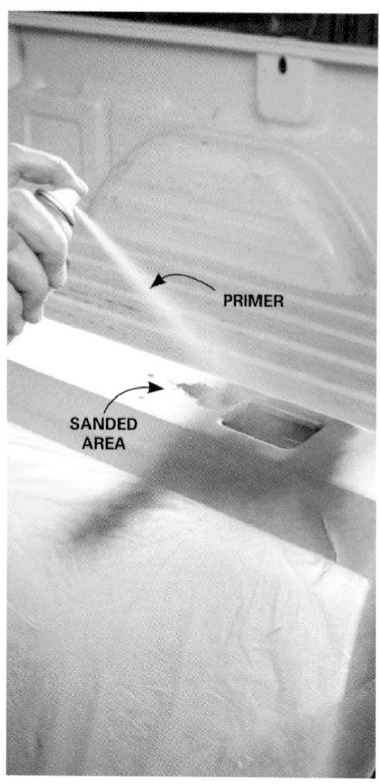

2 Treat rusty areas. Spray primer or rust converter over the sanded areas. Allow the first coat to "flash" the recommended time. Then apply a second coat and let it dry.

3 Mix the bed liner in a box. It will contain any mess. Throw the box into the truck bed before you even pop the lid of the bed liner product. Leave the gallon can inside the box and add the activator. Then mix with a drill and a stirring paddle until the product is smooth.

All DIY bed liner products contain a gritty material for skid resistance. However, some of the higher-priced versions also include rubberized bits for added impact resistance.

You'll have to brush the product into corners and seams. You may choose to brush it onto the bed itself. But we recommend buying the manufacturer's optional application kit and applying the product with its special roller. If you opt to brush it on, at least back-roll it to achieve a more uniform texture.

If cost is your most important consideration, buy the water-based or single-stage product. However, if you want a bed liner that's closest in durability to a professionally sprayed-on product (see "Other Bed Liner Options," p. 251), spend the extra dough and buy a two-part bed liner. We chose the two-part Rust-Oleum Professional Grade Truck Bed Liner Kit for this story.

Just like painting, it's all about the prep

No bed liner is going to stick to the factory paint if you haven't done the recommended prep work. It's awful work and there are no shortcuts. First remove any grease stains, dried paint, caulk or adhesive with chemical removers and a scraper. Then wash the entire bed with car wash soap. Rinse and let dry.

Next, remove any remaining car wax using wax remover (from any auto parts store) or acetone. **Caution:** When you're using these chemicals or applying the bed liner, work in a well-ventilated area and wear a respirator with a charcoal filter. Make sure you're far away from open flames and sparks.

Use the scuff pad provided in the bed liner kit and scuff every square inch of the bed (we told you it was awful work). Sand off any surface rust and feather the edges. Wash the bed a second time with car soap and water and let it dry. Always follow the directions on the product label, especially if they differ from ours.

Mask the truck and tarp the floor

This is an incredibly messy project, and there's no way you can "cut" around lights and latches without getting the goop on them. So mask off any part you don't want covered with bed liner (Photo 1).

If you want to coat the bed rails (the ledges at the top of the bed), mark off the flat portion of the bed rail and mask along it with a painter's tape that prevents paint bleed. Then cover the fenders with a drop cloth. Cover the back and roof of the cab as well. Protect the floor or driveway with drop cloths under the truck and along the sides. Shove a drop cloth under the gaps between the bed and the cab and under the tailgate. Or, remove the tailgate and set it on sawhorses. Once the vehicle is masked and tarped, prime the sanded areas with a "rusty metal" primer. If the areas were heavily rusted, use a "rust converter" product instead (Photo 2).

Mix, cut in and apply

You'll find all the traction grit/rubber particles settled into a heavy glob at the bottom of the can, so plan to take the time to mix the product thoroughly. Some kits include a plastic mixing paddle for your drill. The paddle in our kit broke right away. So do yourself a favor and buy a mixing paddle made of metal at the hardware store before you start. Then mix the product (Photo 3). Next, cut in with a brush around the truck bed box (Photo 4).

Coat the front and sides of the box with the roller. Then coat the floor (Photo 6). Allow the first coat to dry the recommended time, then apply a second coat.

4 Cut in with a brush. Apply a heavy coat of bed liner into the corners, around the wheel wells and under the bed rail—all the areas that are hard to reach with a roller.

5 Brush the tailgate. Brush an extra-heavy coat of bed liner onto the tailgate. Then use the roller to texture it. Allow additional drying time and then apply a second heavy coat.

6 Do the floor last. Working from front to back, roll a liberal coating of the bed liner onto the corrugated flooring. Back-roll to get an even texture, but don't spread the product too thin.

Other bed liner options

Custom-molded drop-in bed liners

Prices: $250 to $500, depending on the bed size, material choice and thickness

PROS:

- Best impact protection
- Easiest to clean because the liners don't have sharp corners or seams

CONS:

- Cracks must be repaired immediately to prevent water leaks between the liner and the bed
- The surface will be slippery unless you pay more for a nonskid texture
- Even if the liner stays intact, water and moisture eventually cause the bed to rust prematurely

Professionally installed spray-on two-part bed liners

Prices: $500 to $1,000

PROS:

- Excellent scratch and gouge protection
- More impact protection than roll-on but less than custom-molded liner
- Watertight

CONS:

- Must return to installer to get material match for deep gouges

CONSULTANT: RENNY DOYLE, OWNER OF ATTENTION TO DETAILS, DETAILINGSUCCESS.COM

PRO TIPS FOR **DETAILING A MOTORCYCLE**

Learn how a pro detailer does the job

by **Rick Muscoplat, Associate Editor**

Getting your bike professionally detailed can cost a bundle, from $200 all the way up to $600 for a complete job with the optional protectant package. So it makes sense that you'd want to do it yourself to save the dough.

To learn the right way to detail a bike, we consulted Renny Doyle, owner of Attention To Details, a school for professional detailers. Renny walked us through his step-by-step method for detailing a motorcycle. His technique may seem like overkill, especially his recommendation for multiple rinse/dry cycles, but that's how he achieves perfection. He can detail a bike in less than four hours. But you'd better plan on a full day. And, you probably won't save any money on the first round because of the investment in cleaners and tools. But after that, you'll detail like the pros and save money every time.

The products we show are Renny's personal favorites, but other major brands of motorcycle cleaners work just as well. Find these products and tools at auto parts stores and online (detailing.com is one online source).

Remove the leather and start with a light wash

Work in a shaded area and don't start cleaning until the engine is cool to the touch. Remove the seat and leather saddlebags and set them aside. Then cover the battery with plastic sheeting and seal off the exhaust pipe (or pipes) with plastic wrap and a rubber band.

MEET AN EXPERT

Renny Doyle owns a detailing business and runs a school for professional detailers. He even wrote a book on it titled *How to Start a Home-Based Car Detailing Business.* And he was a member of a select team chosen to restore the first 707 Air Force One.

Next, do a prerinse with plain water to remove surface dust and grit. A fireman's-style garden hose nozzle works great because you can dial in a different spray pattern for each area of the bike. You can also use a pressure washer to rinse the bike, but dial down the pressure to its lowest setting and maintain a healthy distance from the bike to avoid damaging the softer metal and plastic parts. Use a gentle stream around wheel hubs to avoid forcing water into the bearings.

Follow the rinse with a prewash (**Photo 1**). Use a gentle car wash soap (Meguiar's Gold Class Car Wash Shampoo & Conditioner is one choice), a microfiber wash mitt, and separate soap and rinse buckets. The prewash is just to remove the light road dirt and mud. So don't go scrubbing the really dirty and greasy areas with your mitt. Save those for the special cleaners you'll use later on. Rinse off the suds and dry the bike right away to prevent water spots. Rather than hand-wiping the entire bike, use a power blower (such as the Metro SK-1 Motorcycle Dryer; $75 at homedepot.com) or compressed air, keeping the pressure under 70 psi. Wipe off any remaining water with a waffle-weave microfiber towel.

Next, clean the tires, wheels and spokes with an "aluminum-safe" cleaner like Sonax Full Effect Wheel Cleaner (**Photo 2**).

Move up to the dash and clean it with a gentle cleaner like Leather Therapy Wash or Meguiars D180 Leather Cleaner & Conditioner. Then polish the dash with Meguiar's M205 Ultra Finishing Polish (**Photo 3**). Use the same polish on the windshield.

Next, clean the engine, transmission, chain or driveshaft housing with a spray cleaner like S100 Total Cycle Cleaner and brushes (**Photo 4**). If the S100 product isn't strong enough to remove caked-on grease, dilute a heavy-duty degreaser 4 to 1 with water, or cut a mild degreaser like Simple Green 50/50 with water. Apply the diluted degreaser and

1 Prewash with a damp mitt and suds. Dip the mitt into soapy water and wring out the excess. Then wipe the damp mitt over the entire bike. Avoid soaking the dash gauges, buttons and switches.

2 Clean the wheels. Spray the wheels and spokes with wheel cleaner and let it soak for about 30 seconds. Then brush the rim and spokes with a boar-bristle brush. Rinse everything with water and dry with the blower and towel.

3 Clean and polish the dash. Squirt a small dollop of polish onto a microfiber towel and work it into the dash using a random circular motion. Continue wiping until the haze is almost gone. Then wipe off the remaining product with a clean towel.

4 Clean the engine and drivetrain. Spray cleaner on all engine and drivetrain components and let it penetrate for about one minute. Brush the greasy areas with a boar-bristle brush. Rinse off the cleaner. Blow dry. Repeat if necessary.

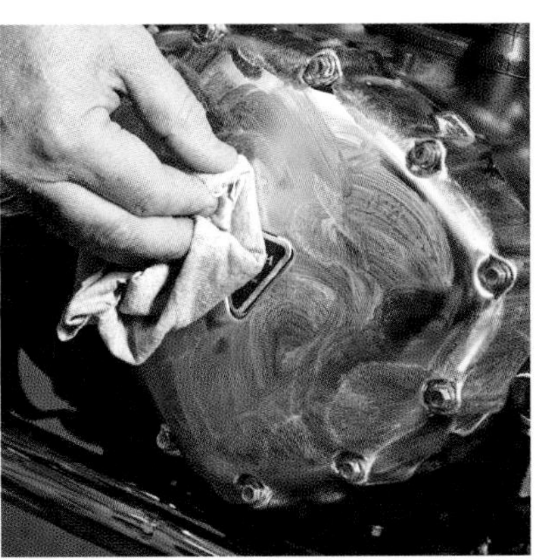

5 Shine up the chrome. Apply polish to a cotton rag and polish the chrome until the haze almost disappears. Wipe off any remaining haze with a clean section of the rag.

Removing dried wax

The best way to remove old dried-on wax is to apply new wax and let it soften the old. But if it's still stuck in crevices, use a household steam cleaner and direct the steam right onto the dried wax. Then wipe it clean with a rag.

Avoid these mistakes

- Never use full-strength automotive or household degreaser products. They can permanently stain aluminum and strip off paint. Also avoid dishwashing detergent and household spray cleaners.
- Never let cleaners sit on the parts for more than a few minutes, and always rinse the cleaned areas with water. Never allow cleaners, even diluted degreaser, to dry on the bike.
- Never use scrub pads or coarse wheel brushes anywhere on the bike.
- Work in the shade and dry each component after you rinse it to avoid water spotting.
- Never use tire dressing on your bike. The silicone in those products presents a slipping/safety hazard.

6 Clean and protect the leather. Apply the leather cleaner to a sponge and gently work it into the leather. Then wipe dry and apply the conditioner with a different sponge. Wipe with a rag and let dry.

7 Do a full rinse. Rinse again with water and blast off the final rinse with a blower or compressed air. Wipe off any remaining water drops to prevent spotting.

8 Blow it dry. Starting at the top, blow the water down and to the front and back. Use a compresser set to 70 psi or less, or use a power blower. The blower shown here costs about $75.

9 Apply paint sealant. Spray sealant onto the paint and spread evenly with a wax applicator sponge, working in small sections. Immediately buff the paint with a microfiber towel. Don't let the product dry before buffing.

expect to put some elbow grease into the job. Don't ever apply full-strength degreaser to your bike.

Before you polish the chrome, switch out your microfiber towel for a smooth 100 percent cotton rag. You can use an old T-shirt or dish towel as long as you cut off the seams first. Seams that are stitched with synthetic thread can scratch chrome, and the seams can retain grit. Then use the Meguiars M205 polish that you used on the dash (**Photo 5**).

Clean the leather seat and saddle bags with Leather Therapy Wash and Leather Therapy Restorer & Conditioner, or Meguiar's D180 (**Photo 6**). These products rejuvenate and condition the leather, and they don't contain any slick additives, so you won't slide off the seat.

Next, use a new batch of soapy water to remove any remaining traces of the cleaners. Then rinse and dry the bike completely (**Photos 7 and 8**).

Clean and treat rubber foot pegs/rests and pedals with 303 Aerospace Protectant. The product contains UV inhibitors to prevent rubber degradation and dries to a nonslip matte finish. Then seal painted areas with Sonax Polymer Net Shield (**Photo 9**).

Remove melted rubber from exhaust pipes

Use household oven cleaner to remove melted boot heel residue from hot exhaust pipes. Test it first on your bike by spraying it in an inconspicuous spot on the chrome. If it doesn't discolor the chrome, run the bike until the pipe is warm. Then spray the oven cleaner directly onto the melted rubber and let it soak in for a few minutes. Wipe it off with a cotton towel.

ADVANCED **GARAGE DOOR REPAIRS**

How to replace springs and cables—without ending up in the emergency room

by **Rick Muscoplat, Associate Editor**

Lots of things can go wrong with a garage door, and most are easy to fix. But problems involving the springs are more serious. The springs provide lifting force for the heavy door and are under tremendous tension—get careless, and they can hurt you. But if you use the correct tools and follow our instructions, you can rebuild the entire torsion spring system in just a few hours, without any side trips to the ER. We won't cover extension spring systems in this story. But we'll show you how to replace the more common torsion springs, the kind that mount on a bar above the garage door.

Before you do this yourself...

Depending on where you live, doing this job yourself might save you $200 or more. Then again, it might save you less than $50. So before you spend several hours fixing your garage door, it's a good idea to gather a few professional estimates.

Start by getting a rough measurement of your springs (length and diameter). Then measure the width and height of your door. Make sure the quote includes the trip charge, parts and labor. Then ask for a price based on 7x19 lift cables and double-life springs. Those items will give you more years of service and should only add about $65 to the price.

What it takes

TIME: Four hours

COST: $125 for two springs and new lift cables

SKILL LEVEL: Advanced

TOOLS: Winding bars ($25), C-clamps and locking pliers, wrenches, eye protection and leather gloves

Figure A: Garage door lift system

To help lift a heavy garage door, the springs apply twisting force to the torsion tube. Drums at the ends of the tube act as reels, winding up the cables connected to the door. The most common problems with this system are broken springs or cables. Smaller doors often have just one spring.

STATIONARY CONE
TORSION SPRING
CABLE DRUM
SIDE BEARING BRACKET
WINDING CONE
TORSION SPRING
LIFT CABLE
BEARING (INSIDE SPRING)
CENTER BRACKET
TORSION TUBE
LIFT CABLE

Play it super safe!

- NEVER use screwdrivers, pin punches or pliers handles to wind or unwind a torsion spring. Trust us: This is the best way to wind up in the hospital. Don't even think about doing this job without a proper set of winding bars. You can buy a set of professional hardened-steel winding bars for about $25 (from either of the online sources listed in "Buying Replacement Parts" on p. 258). Professional winding bars work with 1/2-in. and 7/16-in. winding cones. If your winding cones have 1/2-in. openings, you can make your own winding bars for about $10 by cutting a 36-in. length of 1/2-in.-diameter round bar stock in half (buy round bar stock from any hardware or home center). Just file a smooth bevel on each end so it slides into the winding cone holes more easily.
- Position your ladder to the side of the spring ends so you're never directly in front of the spring cones when they're winding or unwinding.
- Keep the garage door opener disconnected from power at all times, and lock the door in the lowered position, especially when you're winding the springs.
- Wear eye protection and leather gloves throughout the project.
- Step off the ladder and move it off to the side before unclamping the door and testing the balance. Never test a door while you're standing on the ladder.

CONSULTANT: TB SWEENEY REPAIR

1 Lock down the door. Clamp a locking pliers or a C-clamp to the track just above one of the rollers. This will prevent the door from shooting up and breaking your nose when you wind the new springs. Also yank the cord and unplug the garage door opener.

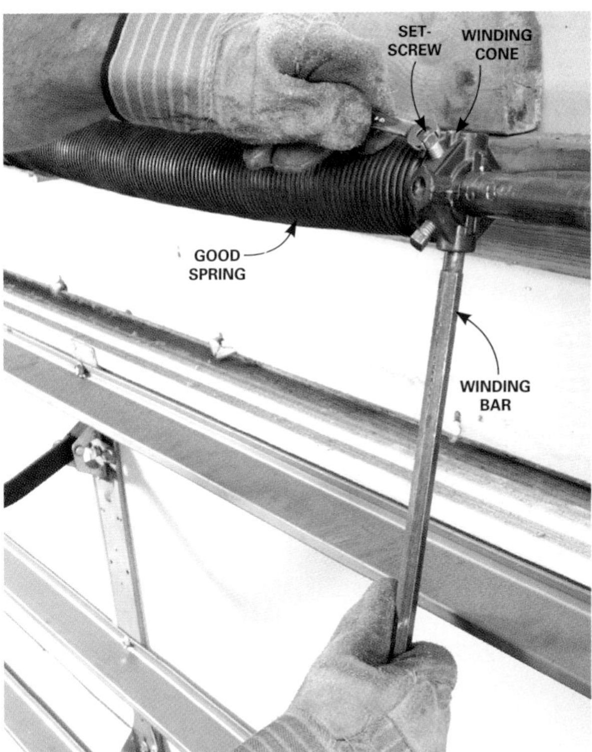

2 Loosen the unbroken spring. Shove a winding bar into a bottom hole of the winding cone of the good spring. Hold the bar in place while you loosen the two setscrews. Hang on tight; the spring will push with powerful torque as the screws release.

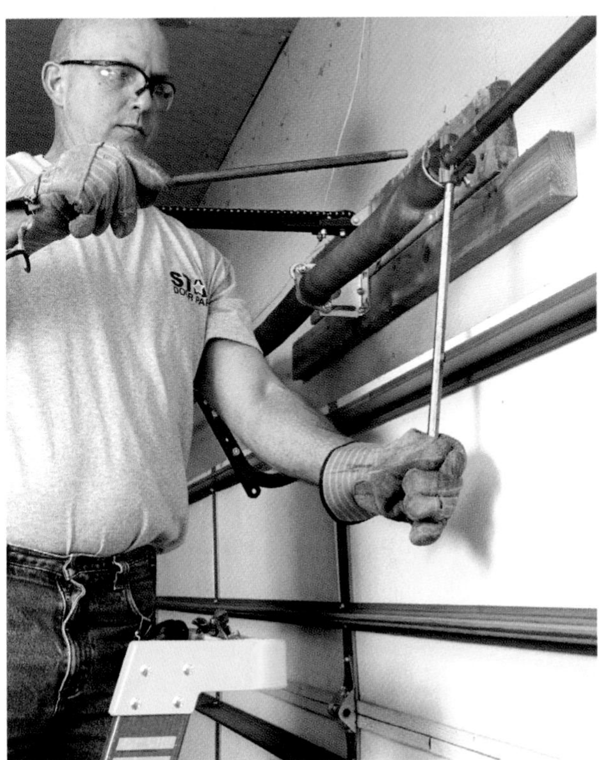

3 Unwind the unbroken spring. Insert the second winding bar into the hole at the 9:00 position. Remove the bottom bar and unwind the spring a quarter turn at a time, leapfrogging the winding bars with each turn.

4 Disconnect the springs from the center bracket. Remove the two nuts and bolts that fasten the stationary spring cones to the center bracket. Then slide the springs toward the end brackets.

Buying replacement parts

Most home centers don't carry all the replacement parts you'll need, and most garage door service companies won't sell you springs. So you may have to order the parts online and wait for the shipment to arrive. (Garagedoorpartsusa.com and stardoorparts.com are two online sources.) First, inspect the condition of your cables and brackets. If you see any frayed strands on the cables or rust on the bottom brackets, replace them now before they fail. Bottom brackets cost about $15 per set. Premium-quality cables (listed as "7x19") last much longer than economy cables and cost only about $4 more. So it's smart to buy the better cables for about $12 per set.

Standard torsion springs (about $40 each) have a service life of 7,000 to 10,000 open/close cycles. However, you can buy double-life (25,000 cycles) replacement springs for about $65 per spring. If you have a two-spring setup and one spring breaks, the second spring will break soon. So replace them both at the same time. To get the right springs for your door, you'll have to provide the supplier some details. Here's how:

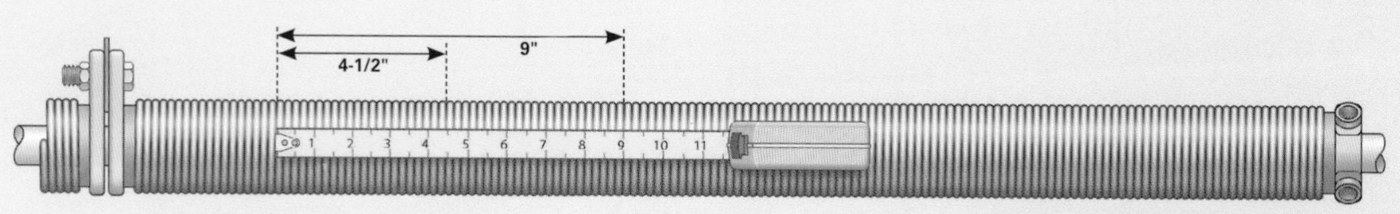

Calculate the wire diameter

Grab a tape measure and press the hook between two spring coils and note the length of 20 coils. Then measure 40 coils. Convert the measurements to a decimal (4-1/2 in. to 4.5 in., or 4-1/8 to 4.125, for example). Divide the two measurements by 20 and 40 to obtain the spring's wire diameter. Here's an example:
4.50 divided by 20 = .225-in. wire diameter
9.0 divided by 40 = .225-in. wire diameter
If the two results match, you've measured correctly.

Determine the "hand" of the springs

View the end of each spring to determine its wind direction, or "hand." If the end of the spring is pointing up on the right, it's a right-hand wind. If the end is pointing up on the left, it's a left-hand wind. Doors with two springs will always have a left- and a right-hand spring.

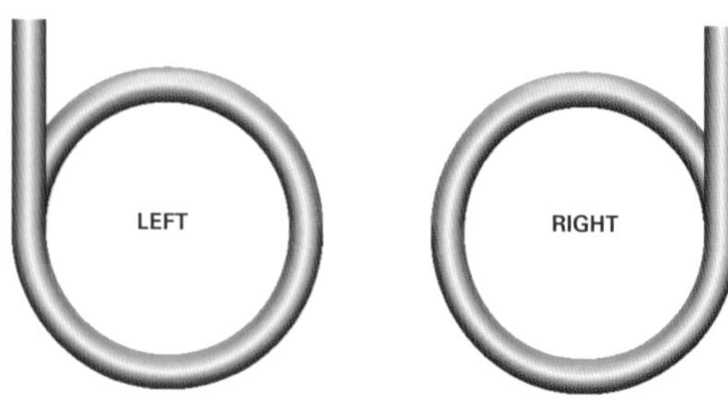

Measure the inner diameter and length

Measure the inner diameter of the broken spring as shown. Loosen the setscrews on the broken spring and slide the broken portion over to meet the stationary section. Measure the overall length of the springs (not including the cones).

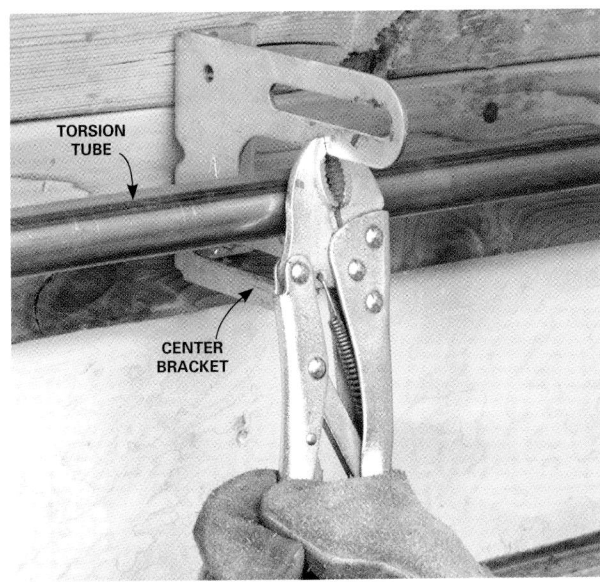

5 Secure the torsion tube. Snap a locking pliers or a C-clamp onto the center bracket to hold the torsion tube in the bracket. Then loosen the setscrews on the left and right lift cable drums and disconnect the lift cables.

6 Remove the old spring. Starting on the left side of the door, slide the torsion tube to the right so you can remove the cable drum. Then slide the old spring off the tube.

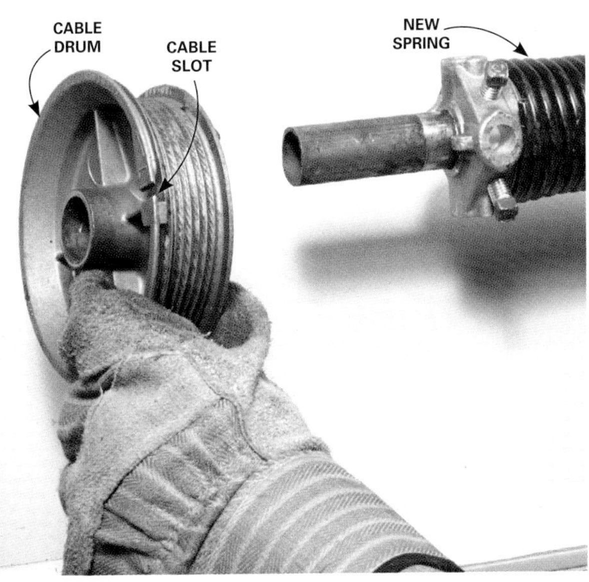

7 Install the left spring. Slide the new spring onto the torsion tube with the stationary cone facing the center bracket. Then reinstall the cable drum. Reinsert the torsion bar into the left-side bearing bracket.

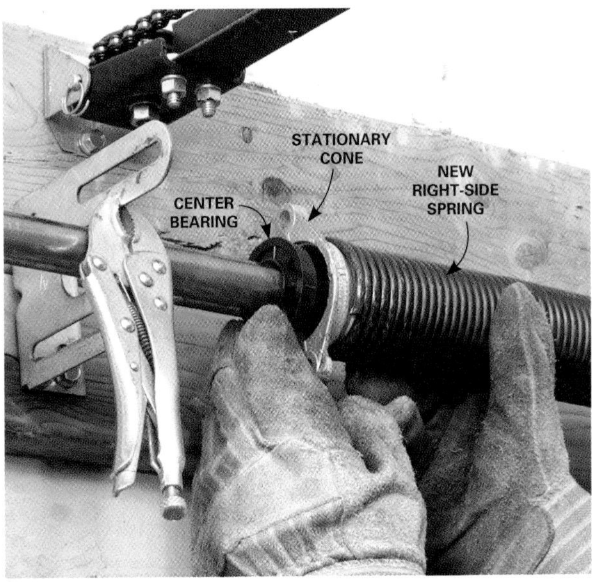

8 Install a new center bearing. Shove the torsion bar to the left, then slide on the center bearing. Install the right spring and push the bearing into the stationary cone. Reinstall the drum as shown in Photo 7. Connect both stationary cones to the center bracket.

If your car is trapped...

If a spring or cable breaks while your cars are parked inside, the garage door won't open and you'll be stranded. Getting emergency evening or weekend service from a garage door professional can easily cost $400. However, if you can get your vehicles out of the garage, you can postpone the repair to get normal weekday repair rates.

If you want to do the repair yourself, get several phone estimates first, because rates vary widely among service companies (see "Before You Do This Yourself...," p. 256). Most garage doors are heavy (200 to 300 lbs.), so call in three strong friends to help you lift the door and hold it open while you lock it in the full raised position with a locking pliers. Then move your vehicles and have your friends help you lower the door.

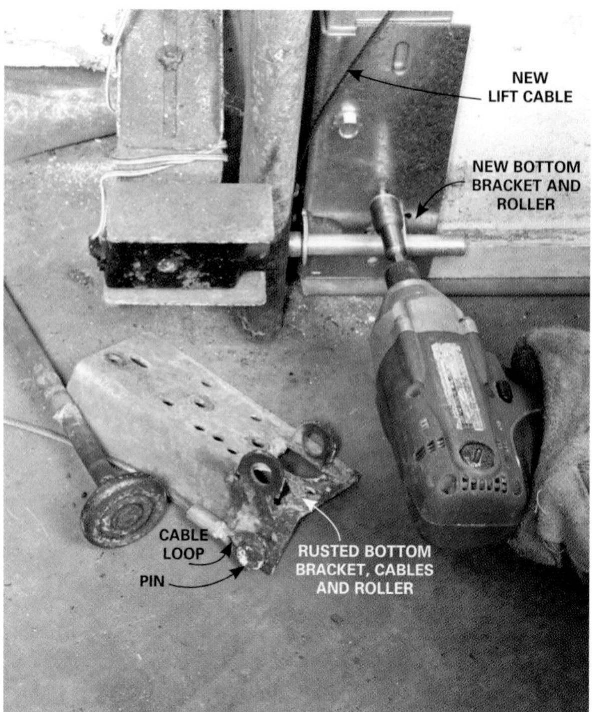

9 Replace the bottom brackets, rollers and lift cables. Snap the lift cable loop over the pin on the new bottom bracket. Insert the new roller. Then swap in the new bottom brackets and cables.

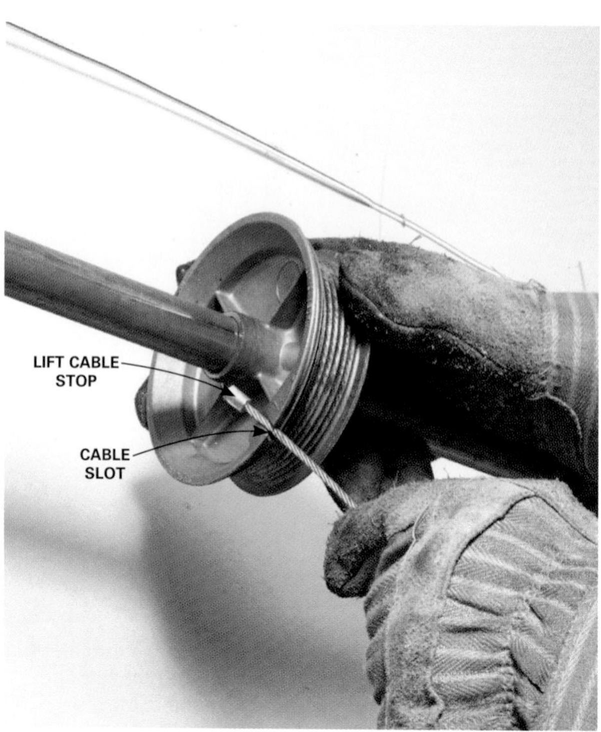

10 Thread the lift cables. Run the lift cables straight up between the rollers and the doorjamb. Slide the lift cable stop through the slot on the drum.

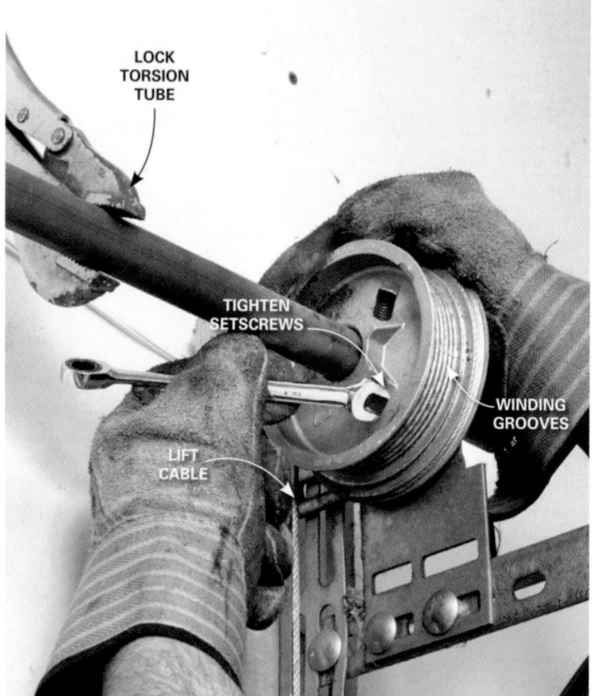

11 Tighten the drums. Snap a locking pliers onto the torsion tube to lock it into place while you tighten the drums. Rotate the drum to wind the cable into the winding grooves. Pull the cable as tight as possible before tightening the setscrews. Leave the locking pliers in place and repeat the tightening procedure on the other side. You want equal tension on both sides. Otherwise, the door will open unevenly.

12 Wind the springs. Slide a winding bar into the cone and wind toward the ceiling. Turn the spring a quarter turn at a time, leapfrogging the winding bars as you go. Follow the spring supplier's recommendations for the total number of turns. If you didn't get a recommendation, perform 30 quarter turns for a 7-ft.-tall door and 36 quarter turns for an 8-ft.-tall door.

13 Stretch the springs. With the spring fully wound, tap the winding bar to stretch the spring out from the center about 1/4 in. before tightening the setscrews. Rotate the setscrews until they contact the torsion tube. Then tighten the screws a one-half to three-quarters turn. Tightening the screws beyond that point can puncture or distort the torsion tube.

14 Lubricate the spring. Slide a piece of cardboard or paper grocery bag between the spring and the wall. Then saturate the spring with garage door lube spray. Wipe off the excess.

Finish with a test

Remove the clamps and pliers from the torsion tube and track, and lift the door about 3 ft. by hand. If the door springs are properly adjusted, the door should stay in place when you let go. If the door falls when you let go, add a quarter turn to each spring. Repeat if necessary. If the door continues to open on its own, release spring tension in quarter-turn increments until the door stays in place when you let go. Then reconnect the opener.

MEET AN EXPERT

Tim Sweeney, owner of TB Sweeney Repair, has 22 years of experience installing and repairing residential and commercial garage doors.

GreatGoofs®

One drop at a time

I promised my 15-year-old son that I'd help him buy a car when he turned 16 if he first learned a few auto maintenance jobs. Mom's car needed an oil change, so we agreed that hers would be a good one to start with. That day I came home to find oil running down the driveway! I immediately went to my son and asked about the oil. He said, "Dad, it's hard to get all the oil into that little tube." He thought you had to refill the oil tank through the dipstick tube!

Bill Pritchard

VEHICLES & GARAGES

DON'T JUST POLISH— REJUVENATE!

Invest in some supplies and keep your car in showroom condition

by **Rick Muscoplat, Associate Editor**

CONSULTANT: JOEY KASPER

You can rejuvenate your car's finish yourself and get it pretty darn close to the factory shine. But it takes more than a simple wax job. The process starts with a good wash, followed by scratch repair, polishing and a protective wax finish. A pro would charge upward of $200 for this. But after a one-time $200 investment for a polisher and supplies, you'll be able to make your whole fleet look like new. Our expert, Joey Kasper, can do the job in four hours. Your first attempt will take a whole day.

All about polishers, pads and compounds

You can't polish a car with a $25 wax applicator/buffer, so don't waste your money on one. And avoid professional high-speed rotary polishers. In unskilled hands, those babies can burn the paint off your car in three seconds flat. Instead, buy a dual action (DA) polisher with changeable foam polishing pads. (Two choices are the Porter-Cable No. 7424XP, $130, and Meguiar's No. G110v2, $180, available at various online sources.) Or, if you want to try your hand at polishing smaller areas but don't want to spend big bucks, try a drill-mounted DA unit (such as Meguiar's G3500, about $50 online).

When it comes to foam pads, each manufacturer has its own color code to denote foam density and pore size. So check the seller's application chart to get the right pad for each type of job. To remove oxidized lacquer or enamel

MEET AN EXPERT

Joey Kasper has been an auto detailer for more than 20 years. He specializes in luxury and collector cars as well as cars used for corporate events and advertising. His van is fully equipped with water tanks, a power washer and a generator so he can perform a complete detail job on-site.

paint from older vehicles, use a "cutting pad" made from stiffer foam with larger pores. To remove fine scratches and polish the clear coat on newer cars, use a medium-density foam pad with smaller pores. Then use a soft foam pad with fine pores to apply wax and paint sealant.

Rubbing and polishing compounds are two very different products, and DIYers often confuse the two. Rubbing compound removes heavy oxidation and deep scratches. Think of it as coarse sandpaper. Because this compound is designed to remove more material, never apply it with a polisher. Apply it only by hand with just enough pressure to remove the scratch.

If you have an old container of rubbing compound lying around your garage, toss it. Those older compounds aren't compatible with the clear coats used on late-model vehicles. If you need to remove a scratch from the clear coat, find a rubbing compound that's clear-coat-safe and contains a "diminishing abrasive." It'll have smaller particles to remove scratches without adding more.

Polishing compound, on the other hand, is like fine-grit sandpaper you'd use to get the smoothest finish on wood. Use it with your DA polisher to remove light scratches and swirls and to bring the finish to a uniform gloss.

Start with a thorough wash

Mix up a bucket of sudsy water (**Photo 1**). Our expert prefers Meguiar's Gold Class Car Wash Shampoo & Conditioner. He uses a wash mitt with two buckets—one for soapy water and one with clear rinse water. Both buckets have dirt traps to prevent dirt and grit from getting back onto the mitt. (Grit Guard, about $9 at auto parts stores, is one choice.)

Start with a clear water rinse (**Photo 2**). Scrub the bugs and tar off the grille, hood, bumper and side mirrors (**Photo 3**). Wash the roof and windows (**Photo 4**). Then rinse the entire car again so you're not wiping gritty roof and window suds over the hood, doors and trunk. Finish

1 Prepare the wash bucket. Drop a dirt trap into each 5-gallon bucket and fill with water. Then pour the car wash soap into the wash bucket and stir with your wash mitt.

2 Scrub the wheels. Spray the wheels with an aluminum-safe alloy wheel cleaner and scrub with a wheel-cleaning brush. Rinse the wheels and clean any areas you missed. Then do a final wheel rinse.

3 Remove bug splatter. Put soap on the dried bugs and let it soak. Then scrub lightly with a nylon bug sponge. Rinse with clear water.

4 Start with the roof. Apply suds to the roof and wipe small sections. Rinse the mitt frequently and grab fresh suds for each new section.

5 Dry the vehicle. Swipe the water off with a water blade squeegee. It will dry the surface faster than a chamois.

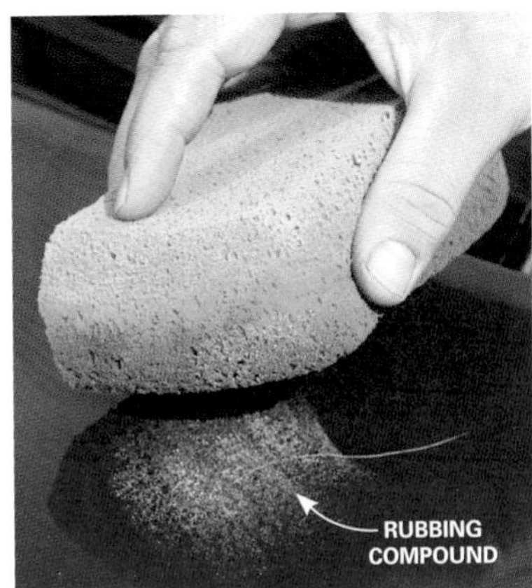

6 Feather a deep scratch. Apply rubbing compound on a sponge and wipe it into the scratch. Use a circular motion to feather the edges. Wipe with a microfiber cloth to check your progress.

7 Accent the wheels. Spray the tires and the wheel wells with tire dressing to give them a dark, factory-fresh look. If you skip the wheel wells, their gray look will detract from the dark tires and shiny paint.

8 Apply the polish. Swirl the polish onto a small section of the car using a sponge. Don't coat the polishing pad with polish and then hit the trigger. The polish will just fling off and make a mess.

9 Work in the polish. Run the DA polisher front to back, then from top to bottom, overlapping each row. Then reverse, going back to front and bottom to top, again overlapping each row.

10 Polish until shiny. Run the polisher until the haze disappears and the paint glistens. Then wipe off the excess polish with a clean, dry microfiber towel.

washing the rest of the car and then do a final rinse. Dry the car with a silicone water blade (Photo 5). Wipe off any remaining wet spots with a microfiber towel. To get the finish even smoother, consider clay-barring the entire car (to learn how to use a clay bar, search "car cleaning tips and tricks" at familyhandyman.com).

Assess and treat any scratches

To determine whether you can remove a deep scratch, rub your fingernail across it. If it doesn't catch your fingernail, you can usually remove it with polishing compound and your polisher. If it catches your nail but doesn't go all the way through to the metal, you can try feathering it with rubbing compound (Photo 6). However, if the scratch goes all the way down to the metal, forget about rubbing compound—you'll have to fill it with touch-up paint. After you fix the scratches, spray the wheel wells and tires with tire dressing (Photo 7).

Polish the finish

Apply the polish to a small section of the car using a soft sponge and a circular motion (Photo 8). Then attach a polishing pad to your DA polisher and work in the polish (Photo 9). Polish until the haze disappears (Photo 10). Move on to the next section and repeat the procedure until the entire car is polished.

Protect with wax or paint sealant

Remove the polishing pad and attach a waxing pad. Apply the wax or paint sealant to the car with a sponge or the manufacturer's applicator. Then buff the wax using the DA polisher and the same procedure you used with the polish. Finish the job by cleaning the windows with a spray cleaner.

SPRAY-ON
PAINT PROTECTION

Keep the front edge of your car's hood in great shape with this easy process

by **Rick Muscoplat, Associate Editor**

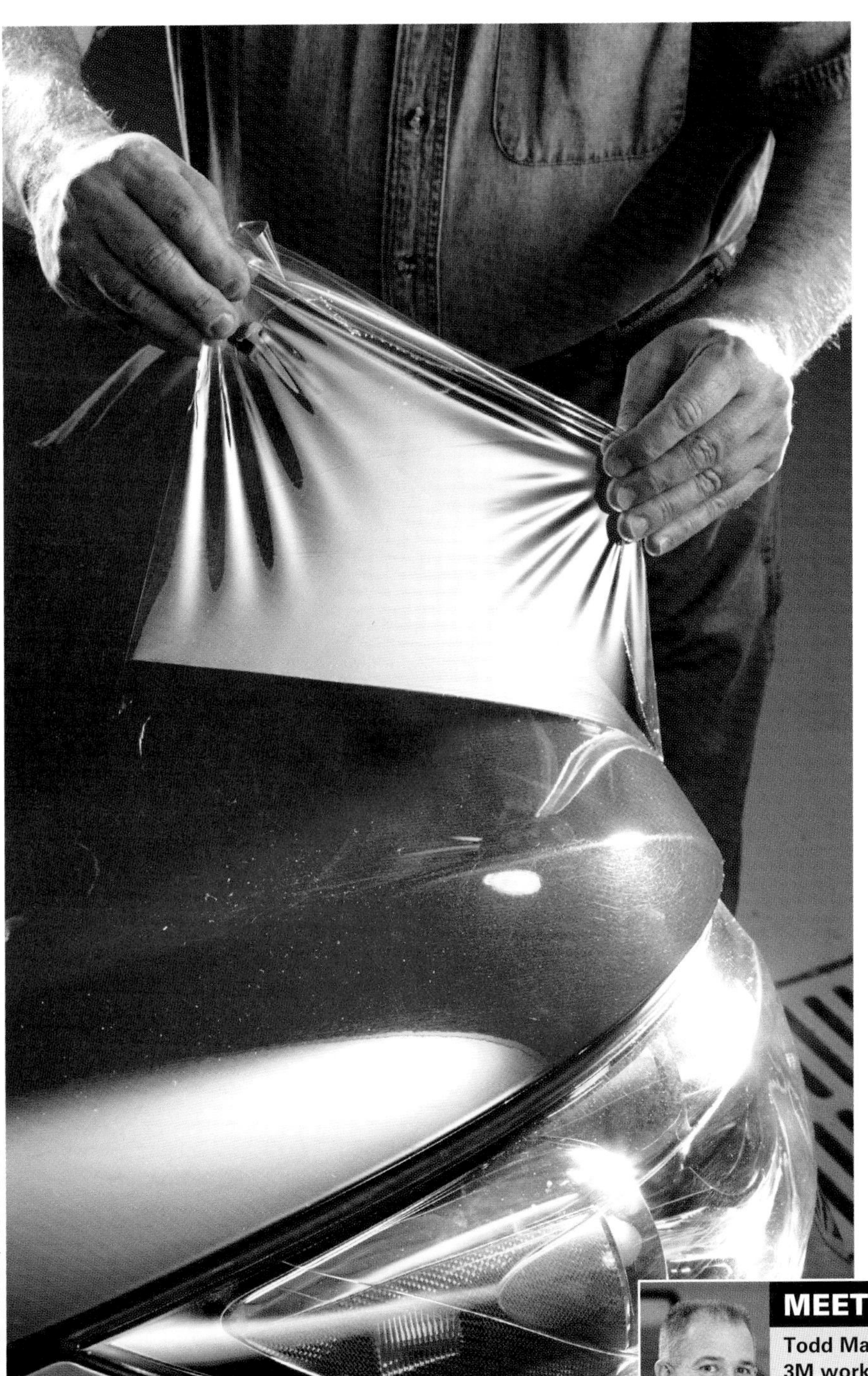

CONSULTANT: TODD MATHES, TECHNICAL SERVICES SPECIALIST, 3M

The paint on the leading edge of car hoods is on the front line for gravel and sand damage. Until recently, you only had two ways to protect the hood: install a "bra" or apply paint protection film. Bras are not only ugly but also lower gas mileage and trap road grit, which damages the paint. Paint protection film looks and works much better, but professional installation costs about $500. Now there's a product that DIYers can apply to protect against paint chips—spray-on/peel-off paint protection film.

Several companies make this paint film, but we chose the 3M Paint Defender product for this story because it lasts up to a year. It costs about $25 and contains enough material to coat the bottom third of your hood. Find it at any auto parts store or online. We asked 3M product expert Todd Mathes to walk us through the prep and application process.

You'll also need car-washing supplies, poly sheeting to cover the entire car and ground, clean-edge masking tape and a microfiber cloth. Or buy the optional installation kit and a spray trigger for about $20. The entire job takes less than two hours. Here's how it's done.

MEET AN EXPERT

Todd Mathes has 25 years of experience at 3M working with masking, abrasives and vehicle appearance products for both body shops and retail customers.

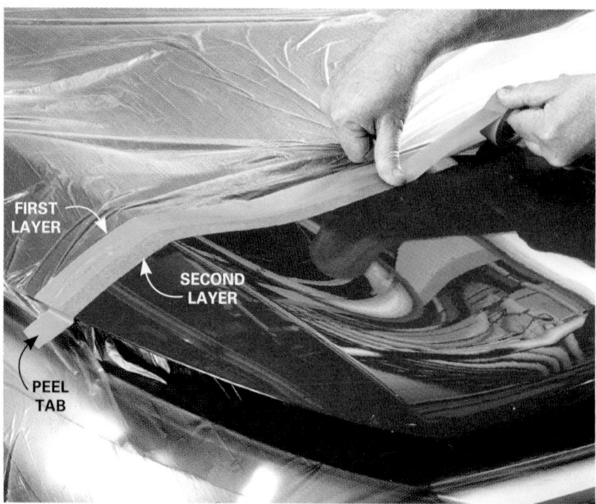

1 Tape the poly sheeting to the hood. Carefully apply the first layer and then the second layer directly below it. Make the second tape line as straight as possible, and press down along the edge to seal it to the hood as you apply. Double over one end of the tape to make a peel tab.

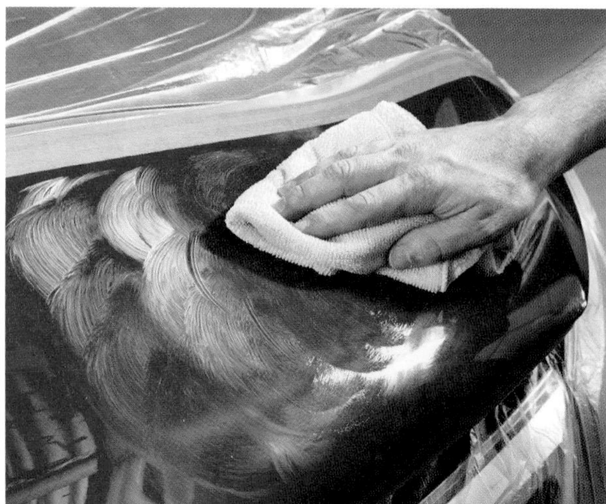

2 Wax the exposed hood area. Squirt a dollop of wax onto the hood and work it in with a microfiber towel. Continue wiping until the surface is free of haze.

Prep the vehicle

The engine and hood must be cool when you apply the product. A hot engine will heat the hood and force-dry the spray between coats, defeating its self-leveling feature. So check the weather report and pick a time when it'll be cool, dry and calm. The night before, park the car in an area that will be shaded the next day.

Start the project by washing the car with car wash soap. Make sure you remove all traces of bug splatter and tar. Then rinse and dry completely. Next, pop the hood and prop it open about 4 in. with a roll of paper towels or a block of wood.

Tarp, tape and wax

Spread a poly sheet over the entire vehicle. Then spread sheeting on the ground to catch any overspray. Starting at the grille, use a scissors to cut straight up the center of the poly, stopping about 18 in. from the bottom edge of the hood. Then cut right and left out to the fenders until you have formed a "T" cutout. Tuck the flaps under the hood and tape them inside the engine compartment to prevent them from moving while you spray. Secure the rest of the sheeting to the car and floor with tape to prevent it from blowing onto the wet finish.

Next, tape the top of the "T" to the hood. Apply another layer of tape to form the clean edge between the spray film and the rest of the hood (Photo 1). Once the poly is in place, apply the synthetic wax included with the product (Photo 2). Waxing is an important step to make removal easier a year from now. So even if you've recently waxed the car, do it again using the wax included with the product.

Apply the coating

Shake the can for a full minute before applying. Then hold the nozzle 6 to 8 in. from the hood and apply three coats to one-half of the hood (Photo 3). Spray all three coats in one continuous motion (don't stop and start at the ends of each row or coat). Move the can at the rate of six seconds per pass. Continue spraying onto the fender, over and above the tape line, and below the bottom edge of the hood to get a uniform film thickness at the edges. A proper application should have an "orange peel" texture and a slightly milky look. Don't worry—the product self-levels and dries clear. Then spray the second half of the hood. When you're done, remove the clean-edge tape while the spray is still wet (Photo 4).

Park the car in the sun and let it dry for two to four hours. The film cures fully in one to four days, depending on the air temperature and humidity.

Troubleshooting

- If bugs or leaves land on the wet spray, pluck them off immediately with a pair of tweezers.
- If the spray is solid white, has lumps or develops sags, you've applied too much. Stop spraying and let the product dry. Then peel it off and start over, moving a bit faster and applying less product.
- If the wet spray has a "dry" look or you've missed areas or pinholes, you can apply more product. But do it quickly. You only have a 10-minute window. If you wait too long the product loses its self-leveling quality and you can wind up with a textured look.

A year from now

Our expert says that the film can last a bit longer than one year but may yellow from UV exposure. However, the longer you wait, the harder it is to remove, so don't push your luck. Pop the hood and peel the film loose around all three edges using your fingernail. Then remove all the film (Photo 5).

3 Spray the hood with protectant. Starting at the tape line and spraying down to the bottom edge of the hood, spray the product continuously in alternating left to right rows at the rate of two seconds per foot. Overlap each row slightly. Immediately spray a second layer, moving up and down over the same section. Then apply a third coat in the side-to-side pattern.

4 Remove the tape while the spray is wet. Grab the doubled-over peel tab and pull the clean-edge tape up and away from the wet edge.

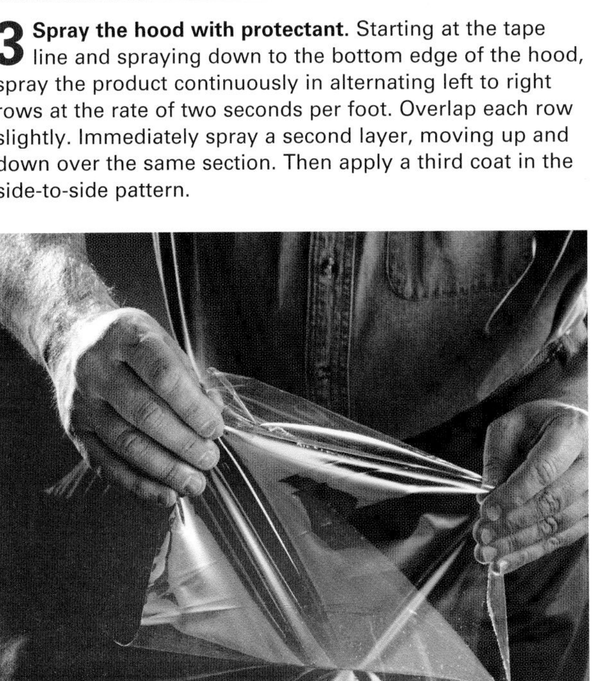

5 After a year, peel off the film. Lift up a top corner and pull the film down toward the bottom of the hood to release as large a piece as possible. Then use both hands to pull the old film up and across the hood. Wipe the excess off the edges with a rag. Apply a fresh layer of protection film following the steps shown.

GreatGoofs®

Clean—and scratched!

On a nice summer day one year, I decided to wash my motorcycle out in the front yard. I wheeled it into the grass and hosed it down and started washing it. After a thorough wash and rinse, I wiped all the water spots off with a chamois. It looked great! I left for a few minutes to rinse out the wash bucket and hang the chamois on the line to dry.

When I came back out to the front yard, my motorcycle was lying against the retaining wall. After investigating what had happened, I realized that all the water had softened the ground and the kickstand had sunk into the yard. That caused the bike to fall into the wall, which scratched the tank. I've since made up a more adventurous tale to explain the scratches on the tank!

—John Nussmeier

REFINISH WHEELS & WHEEL COVERS

Give your older ride a facelift!

by **Rick Muscoplat, Associate Editor**

BEFORE

AFTER

Sometimes a middle-aged car can still look fine except for wear and tear on the wheels and wheel covers. Fortunately, you can fix this yourself for very little cash. Removing the rust and painting your wheels take a full day. (Don't panic—mostly you're waiting for paint to dry.) Then the wheels must dry for 24 more hours after painting before you remount them. So make other arrangements for transportation for a day. The supplies cost about $50 from any auto parts store. Here's how to do the job.

Get all the supplies ahead of time

Besides the primer and paint, you'll need masking tape, plastic sheeting, a drill and a wire wheel. If the wheels are really rusty and the rust has pitted the metal, use "rusty-metal" primer. However, if they're only lightly rusted, buy self-etching primer instead. It'll prime any bare metal and bite into the old paint around the rest of the wheel.

Next, buy spray paint formulated for wheels. (Rust-Oleum, Dupli-Color and VHT are three well-known brands carried by most auto parts stores.) Wheel paint has higher pigment content, is more chip- and wear-resistant, handles higher temperatures and repels brake dust better than ordinary household spray paint. Then buy clear coat spray (gloss or satin) to further extend the life of the paint. Two cans each of primer, paint and clear coat is usually enough to paint the outer face of four wheels. Double the amounts if you plan to paint the inside of the wheels too.

If you want to refinish the wheel covers, buy three cans of plastic-rated metallic spray paint.

Remove and wash the wheels and set up a work area

Jack up the car and support it with jack stands. Then remove the wheels and scrub them with heavy-duty spray cleaner, a brush and water. Rinse off all the crud and blow the wheels dry with compressed air or a leaf blower.

Select a well-ventilated area to spray the wheels. Cover the floor with a tarp to catch the overspray. Then set out two sawhorses and lay down three 2x4s. Set the dry wheels face up on the 2x4s.

Remove the wheel weights and clean off the rust

If you paint over the wheel weights, you'll see the old paint spots the next time the shop rebalances your wheels or you change tires. So take the time to remove them before you start painting (**Photo 1**). Next, don an N95 paint respirator and protective eyewear and remove the rust with a drill and a wire wheel (**Photo 2**). Blow off the dust with a leaf blower—not compressed air from an oiled compressor. (Oiled compressors often spit out oil

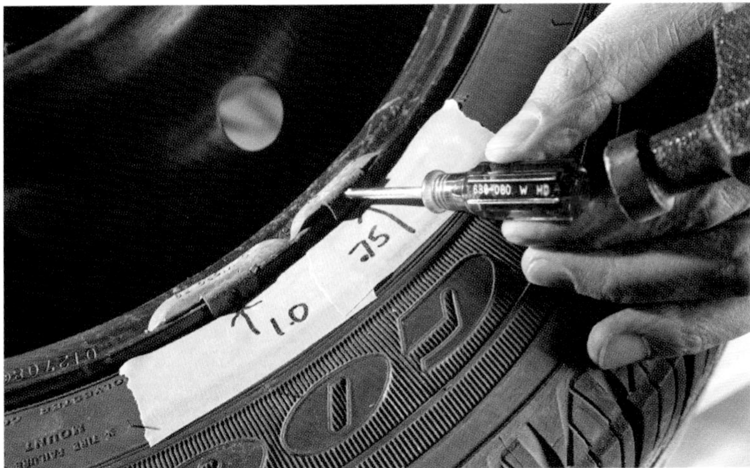

1 Mark and remove the weights. Apply masking tape to the tire and draw an arrow pointing to the center of the weight. Write the weight markings on the tape so you can get them back in the same place. Then insert a small Phillips screwdriver into the circular opening and tap the screwdriver until the weight pops off.

2 Wire-brush the entire wheel. Wire-brush the rusted areas down to the bare metal. Then lightly scuff all the painted areas around the entire wheel, including areas near the tire bead and lug nuts. Slow down around the valve stem so you don't damage it.

3 Prime the surface. Apply two coats of primer, letting each dry for the time recommended on the can.

droplets, which can cause fish-eyes in the paint. Trust me on this—I've done it and ruined paint jobs.) Then wipe down each wheel with a tack cloth.

Mask and refinish

Mask all around the wheel using small sections of masking tape (this is really tedious). Next, lay plastic sheeting over the wheels and cut out the center wheel portion with scissors. Tape the sheeting onto the first layer of masking tape. Then mask off the valve stem.

Read the can labels to find the recommended wait times between coats. Then apply two coats of primer (Photo 3), three coats of paint and two coats of clear coat (Photo 4). Let the wheels dry for 24 hours. Then remove the sheeting and tape. Reinstall the wheel weights and remount the wheels.

4 Paint and protect. Apply the color and protect it with clear coat spray. We painted our wheels a glossy black, and in this photo we're spraying on the first of two coats of clear coat.

Refurbish old wheel covers too

Most plastic wheel covers are painted. After a while, the paint peels and all those curb kisses gouge the plastic. You don't have to buy new wheel covers. Just refinish the old ones.

Start by scraping the peeled areas. Then feather the peeled edges with 120-grit sandpaper. Sand down high ridges on the gouges until they're level with the rest of the wheel cover. Then wash the wheel cover with heavy-duty cleaner and a scrub brush. Rinse and dry. Then paint the entire wheel cover with a metallic spray paint rated for plastic.

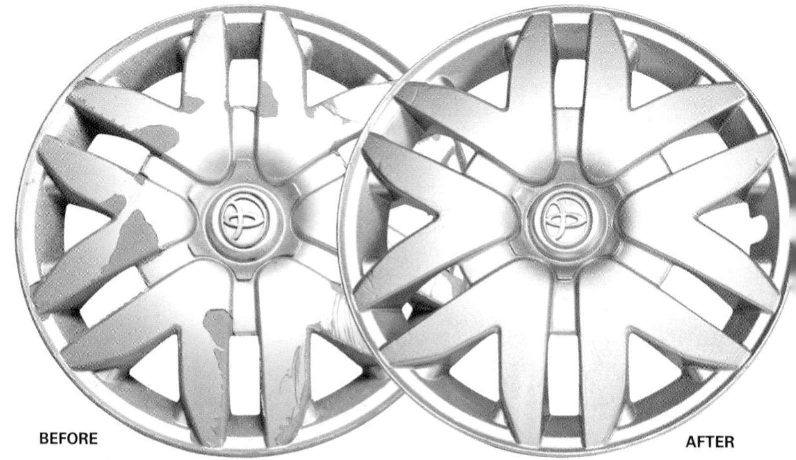

Add pizzazz with bright-colored peelable paint

Peelable paint is the latest craze. Car buffs use it to protect their wheel covers and rocker panels over the winter months or to give their rides a shot of color. Peelable paint is a spray-on rubbery coating that peels off when you're done with it. If you scratch it, you can simply recoat it. Use it on any smooth surface indoors or out.

When you use peelable paint outdoors, it should be removed after three months. You can leave it on longer, but it'll be harder (or impossible) to remove. But indoors, it's removable for nearly a year.

Peelable paint is available at auto parts stores, home centers and craft stores. Rust-Oleum, Dupli-Color and Plasti Dip are three well-known brands of peelable paint.

GreatGoofs®

Special delivery

I was helping a friend build a three-rail fence around his horse pasture. Since the local home improvement store was only about a mile from his house, we decided there was no need to rent a flatbed truck or have the wood delivered. It would only take a few trips.

Jennifer Johnson

On the first trip, we loaded about thirty 16-ft. 2x6s into the back of his pickup. We "anchored" the ends of the boards under his toolbox and let the boards rest on his closed tailgate. We got about a block from his house when we hit a pothole, the boards bounced, and BAM! The tailgate broke, the toolbox catapulted into the air and crashed back down into the truck bed, and wood spilled all over the road. Needless to say, the other drivers were not very pleased, and we ended up having to go and rent that flatbed truck after all.

Hot-melt mystery

Like many others who pull a camper trailer, I have a cable for my trailer lights installed inside my car's trunk that I connect when it's time to tow. When we came home from a recent camping vacation, I noticed the connectors were nearly melted together. But all the lights were still working!

I couldn't find any damaged wires and scratched my head for a week trying to figure out what had happened. When I had the oil changed on the car, I asked the mechanic to check it out. He asked to see exactly how the cable came out of the rear hatch. Within a few seconds he pointed out that the two connectors were dangling right in front of the tailpipe!

Tom Bigelow

SMALL-ENGINE **GAS TIPS**

Stale gas is the #1 killer of small engines

by **Rick Muscoplat, Associate Editor**

Small-engine mechanics tell us that stale gas is what keeps them employed and busy. It causes the vast majority of starting problems, which usually lead to a carburetor rebuild or replacement ($100). But if you follow a few simple rules, you can avoid hard-starting hassles and repair costs. Here's how.

Use the right kind of gas

Never use E-85 or E-15 gas in your small engine. Those fuels can cause catastrophic damage.

Most small engines operate best with 87-octane fuel (85-octane in high altitudes). Unless specifically recommended by the manufacturer, never use a higher octane fuel in your small engine.

Buy smaller quantities

As with any product that has a limited shelf life, you should buy only what you need for the near future. If you buy ethanol (oxygenated) gas, buy only enough gas to last for 30 days. If you buy non-oxygenated gas, limit your purchase to a 60-day supply. To find a source for non-oxygenated gas near you, go to pure-gas.org.

With either type of gas, use a container that's sized for the amount you'll buy. Storing 2 gallons in a 5-gallon container leaves you with 3 gallons of air, causing the gas to spoil faster—even if it's been treated with fuel stabilizer. Add the old gas in small quantities to your car or take it to the recycling center.

SMALLER GAS CAN

Add stabilizer every time you fill

Many people add gasoline stabilizer when they put the mower away for the winter. That's a good idea, but that's not the only time you should use stabilizer. Stabilizer works best when it's added to fresh gas right at the pump. That way it can start working immediately to prevent trouble. And, since small-engine gas tanks are vented, adding pre-stabilized gas to the tank can reduce the effects of water accumulation and slow the loss of volatile vapors. Look for a stabilizer product that includes antioxidant protection, corrosion inhibitors, detergent and metal deactivators. (Briggs & Stratton Advanced Formula Fuel Treatment & Stabilizer and STA-BIL are two examples.) If you have a two-stroke engine, buy oil with built-in stabilizer.

Get a new gas container

If your gas container doesn't seal properly, you're going to have gas problems. As the air temperature rises and falls, a poorly sealed container emits gas vapors and pulls in moisture. So you lose the most volatile ingredients in the gas—the ones you need most to start a cold engine. Also, the humidity that gets sucked in condenses on the container walls and falls to the bottom. As you reach the gas at the bottom, you're literally pouring in a blend of old gas and water. If your old container is missing caps, buy a new one. A plastic container costs about $15; a deluxe metal version like the Justrite model shown at right costs about $55 online.

Choose long-life gas for occasional use

If you use less than a gallon of gas during a season, long-life gas in quart cans may be your best option. It's non-oxygenated gas with stabilizer and specially formulated to keep its volatility and fire up right away, even after two years. Long-life gas is pricey (about $5 per qt.) but worth it if it saves you just one repair bill. It's available at most home centers and small-engine shops.

Filling and storage tips

Let the engine cool after use and then refill the tank to 90 percent. That will reduce moisture condensation and oxidation.

Consult your owner's manual for off-season storage recommendations. Most manuals specify "dry storage," which involves draining the tank and running the engine until it dies. Then pull the cord until you get no signs of life from the engine. If the manual recommends "wet" storage, fill the tank to 90 percent with fresh stabilized gas.

Is ethanol why your engine won't start?

Everybody blames oxygenated fuel (gas with ethanol) for carburetor failures. But guess what caused the problems before we started adding ethanol? Yup—stale gas. We're not saying that gas with ethanol is the perfect fuel. It's not. But the truth is, whether you buy oxygenated or non-oxygenated gas, operator error is really the root cause of carburetor corrosion and gunk buildup. Gasoline simply goes bad, and it goes bad faster if it's improperly handled and stored. You can avoid all gasoline-related starting problems by following the simple buying, storing and usage tips mentioned on these two pages.

HandyHints®

FROM OUR READERS

TANGLE PREVENTION

I like to store a lot of gear under the backseat of my truck. It can get pretty cluttered under there, but stretch wrap helps to restore order. It's perfect for bundling items that would otherwise turn into one big frustrating tangled mess. I also wrap my tow strap, tie-downs, jumper cables, raincoat, extension cord, bungees and extra pairs of gloves. I'm kinda addicted to the stuff, but for about $10 for a 1,000-ft. roll, it's one habit I can afford.

Mark Petersen, Contributing Editor

LUGGAGE RACK PROTECTOR

I needed to pick up a ladder from a friend. To keep the luggage rack on my new SUV from getting scratched, I covered the bars with swim noodles. I just slit them down the side with a utility knife and taped them on. The cushion of foam also kept the ladder from rattling. Don't forget to strap down your cargo before you go!

—Gerald Ruppert

BIKE GEAR TO GO

I got tired of hunting down all my biking gear when I wanted to go for a ride. I'm trying to be more organized, so I picked up this plastic crate at a garage sale to solve the problem. I simply screwed some 2x4 pieces to the back of the crate (use fender washers with the screws to better grip the plastic). Then I screwed through the studs into the 2x4s. Next I screwed a 25-in.-long 2x4 to the front of the top and added a pair of rubber-coated bike hooks. I keep biking shoes, a helmet, gloves, a tire pump and my water bottles within reach so I spend more time biking and less time looking in closets!

—Jay Norman

READER PHOTOS (2)

HOOK-AND-LADDER TRUCK

Here's how to easily carry long items on a truck. Attach a pair of flip-up tool or bicycle brackets to 2x2 wood posts that fit inside your truck bed pockets. My brackets are attached with drywall screws, but they could be bolted on for added strength. Just make sure to set the height of the brackets so they don't interfere with your side mirror. They install in seconds, store behind the seat in your truck cab, and allow you to carry long items like extension ladders, PVC, gutters and lumber.

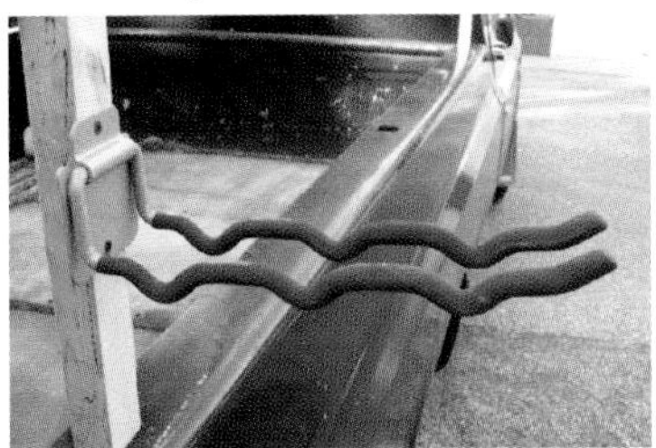

Stay within the weight limits of the brackets, and make sure your cargo is strapped tightly. This Everbilt Flip-Up Heavy Duty Tool Holder (part No. 01192) is available for $6 at Home Depot.

—Brian Zoeller

TRUCK-BED LINER EXTENSION

I haul a lot of landscaping materials in my truck. I used to get annoyed when dirt, leaves and rocks got caught between the tailgate and the bed liner. Now when I unload, I tuck a piece of thin plywood under the bed to span the gap. I can store it under the mat when I'm not using it. Plastic or a thin rubber runner would also work.

—Denny Badertscher

FREE STUCK WHEELS WITH A WHACK

I wanted to replace the rear brakes on my F-150, but the wheels were fused to the rotors and simply wouldn't bust free. I called Bobby, my diesel-mechanic brother-in-law. "Grab the biggest sledgehammer you have and pound on the bottom of the tire. In 35 years, I've never had a wheel that didn't fall free."

After I talked with him I thought, Would the sidewall get wrecked? What if I destroy the alloy rim with a bad swing? I jacked up the truck, loosened the lugs and propped a 2x10 against the tire and pounded away. After three swings, the wheel popped right off. But if you wait until you have a flat on the side of the road, you won't have a sledge to free up a stuck wheel. So before you head out on that road trip, maybe you should rotate those tires and make sure your wheels aren't stuck, especially if you have an older car with some rust.

—Travis Larson, Senior Editor

STUCK RECEIVER HITCHES

A ball mount that's been in the receiver hitch too long can rust in place. Here's the trick for freeing it up. Use an air chisel (about $30 at any home center or auto parts store) and a special 1-in. hammer impact chisel. (We used the Grey Pneumatic No. GRECH1177, which can be found online for about $15.)

After saturating the receiver hitch with penetrant, hold the hammer alongside the receiver tube and pull the trigger. Let the air chisel chatter away at the hitch for a minute or so. Then repeat on the other side of the hitch and try sliding the shaft out. You may have to try a few times and give the hitch a few whacks with a maul, but eventually it'll come out. Before slipping it back in, coat the shaft with water-resistant marine grease so it won't get stuck again.

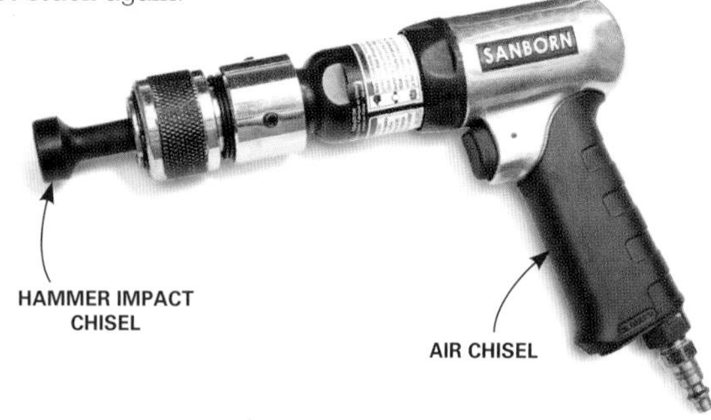

HOIST YOUR BIKE OUT OF THE WAY

Kevin Lind, Field Editor

When it comes to garages, there's no such thing as enough space. One product I found useful to free up some floor space is a bicycle hoist. It's easy to install and very easy to use. When shopping for a hoist, beware of models that have undersized ropes. They can slip off the pulley wheels and jam. Look for one with a good, hefty rope. I bought this one at a home center for $20.

BE GENTLE WITH SPARK PLUGS

Rick Muscoplat, the in-house mechanic at *The Family Handyman*, has this to say about extracting a stuck spark plug: "If you snap off a spark plug or strip the threads, you'll have a real nightmare on your hands. So if a plug shows any sign of seizing, stop and spray on rust penetrant. Let it sit for at least 30 minutes and try to loosen it just a one-eighth turn. Don't get greedy and keep turning. Add more penetrant and turn the plug in and out slightly to work penetrant down into the threads. Saturate with penetrant and tighten/loosen only an eighth of a turn at a time. Eventually, it'll start turning freely and you'll be able to back it out."

MOTOR OIL **SMARTS**

Buckle up; it's time to get smart about oil

by **Rick Muscoplat, Associate Editor**

Motor oil has gotten much better over the years. And, with oil-life indicators on newer cars, drivers don't have to guess when to change their oil. Yet even with better oil and oil change reminder lights, repair shops are reporting a shocking increase in the number of engines damaged by wear and sludge buildup.

It turns out that many DIYers and even some oil change shops are using the wrong oil, and drivers are simply going too long between oil changes. Just as troubling, many drivers have almost completely abandoned the job of checking their oil level when gassing up, and many more are causing engine damage by driving with low oil levels. Too many drivers seem to follow their own ideas about which oil they can use and how long they can run it in their engine. But that leads to trouble. Whether you change your own oil or take your vehicle to a shop, read on to get factual information right from the experts.

1 **Find the engine-specific oil.** The label under the hood of this VW says to use only oil that complies with VW specification 502.00. To find oil that meets that standard, look for the specification on the oil bottle label.

UNDER-HOOD LABEL

Engine Oil Huile moteur

Use only oil that expressly complies with VW 502 00.

Utilisez uniquement de l'huile qui satisfait expressément à VW50200

For a list of approved oils:
Pour une liste d'huiles approuvées:
> 1-800-822-8987
> www.vw.com
> www.vw.ca

07K 010 706 T

OIL BOTTLE LABEL

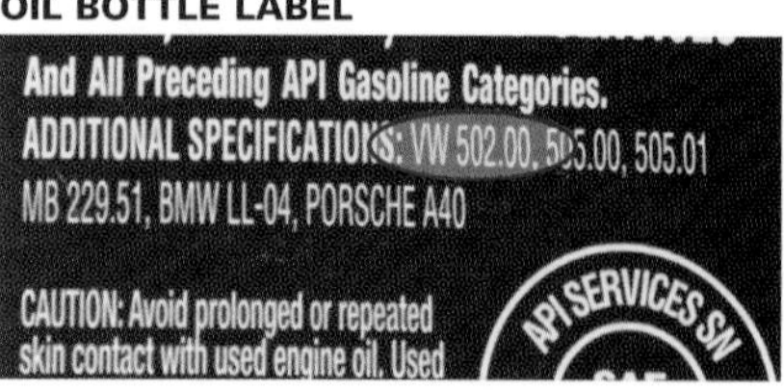

It's more than just viscosity

Every owner's manual lists the recommended oil viscosity for the engine. But knowing the correct viscosity is just the starting point. Your car may also require synthetic oil or oil that meets a specific industry service rating (API and ILSAC are two examples). The most recent ratings are API-SN and ILSAC GF-5. Both are backwards-compatible, so if your manual shows a lower rating, you can safely substitute the newer oil.

But not all carmakers use those two industry rating services. European carmakers may require a regular ACEA-rated oil in some engines and a different oil that meets more rigid specifications in another engine. Manufacturer-specific and engine-specific oil is a growing trend, and when a carmaker specifies a particular oil for an engine, that's the only oil you can use (**Photo 1**).

It really comes down to this: Engine designers know more than you or your buddies. If you use the wrong oil, you can destroy your engine. The damage won't be covered by the factory powertrain warranty or your extended warranty, even if the oil changes have been done by a pro.

If you use a shop for oil changes, make sure it has the correct oil on hand. The shop may charge more for the special oil, but it'll keep your engine running longer. When changing your own oil, you may have trouble finding the proper oil at big box stores, but you can always get it (or order it) at any auto parts store.

Should you use synthetic oil?

If your car doesn't require synthetic oil, here's why you should switch to it anyway. Synthetic oil is made from natural gas or crude-oil feed stocks that go through a chemical reaction that results in uniformly sized molecules. The uniform size reduces friction, heat and wear in your engine. Name-brand synthetic oil has higher-quality and longer-lasting additives that keep your engine cleaner. And, since it doesn't contain paraffin (wax) like conventional oil, it flows faster and builds pressure faster on cold starts. Sure, it costs a couple bucks more per quart, but it's a far better lubricant. It's worth the extra cost, especially if you love your car and/or plan to keep it for years to come.

2 **Older engines need stronger medicine.** Fill older engines with high-mileage synthetic oil to keep them running cleaner and provide maximum protection against wear.

CONSULTANTS: THOM SMITH, V.P. LUBRICATION TECHNOLOGIES, VALVOLINE; CHRIS BARKER, TECHNICAL MANAGER, ROYAL PURPLE; AIMEE CRONFELL, BRAND MANAGER, PENNZOIL

What about oil for older cars?

You can argue that your old car racked up 100,000 miles just fine with conventional oil. Great. But now it has some wear on the piston rings, and it's generating more "blow-by" (combustion gas slipping by the piston rings). That increase in blow-by means more acid, soot, corrosion, varnish and sludge formation throughout the engine. That's precisely why switching to synthetic oil makes so much sense for older cars. The more robust additive package is especially well suited to keeping an older engine cleaner and running longer. If you change your own oil, switching to synthetic costs only about $10 per change. We think it's well worth the extra cost.

How to protect your warranty

If you do your own oil changes and want to maintain your factory or aftermarket warranty, you'll have to prove you changed your oil on time. That's easy to document.

If you have a shop do your oil changes, make sure the receipt shows the oil viscosity and service rating.

Buy the right filter

Select an oil filter that's designed to last as long as your oil change interval. Economy oil filters last about 3,000 miles. So if your change interval is 7,000 miles, it won't do its job for the last 4,000 miles. To get a filter that'll last as long as your oil, plan to spend at least $6. Look for terms like "extended performance" or "extended life" on the box.

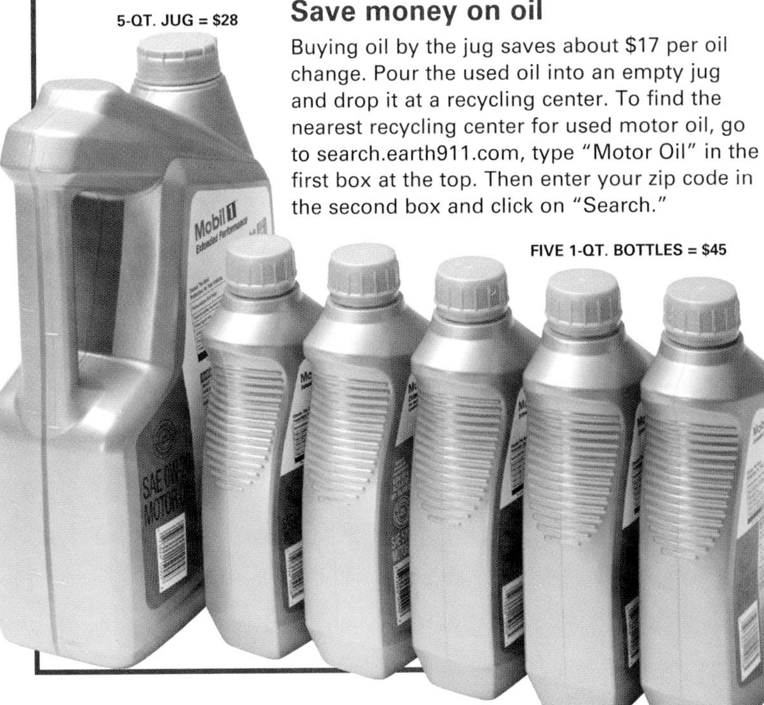

Save money on oil

Buying oil by the jug saves about $17 per oil change. Pour the used oil into an empty jug and drop it at a recycling center. To find the nearest recycling center for used motor oil, go to search.earth911.com, type "Motor Oil" in the first box at the top. Then enter your zip code in the second box and click on "Search."

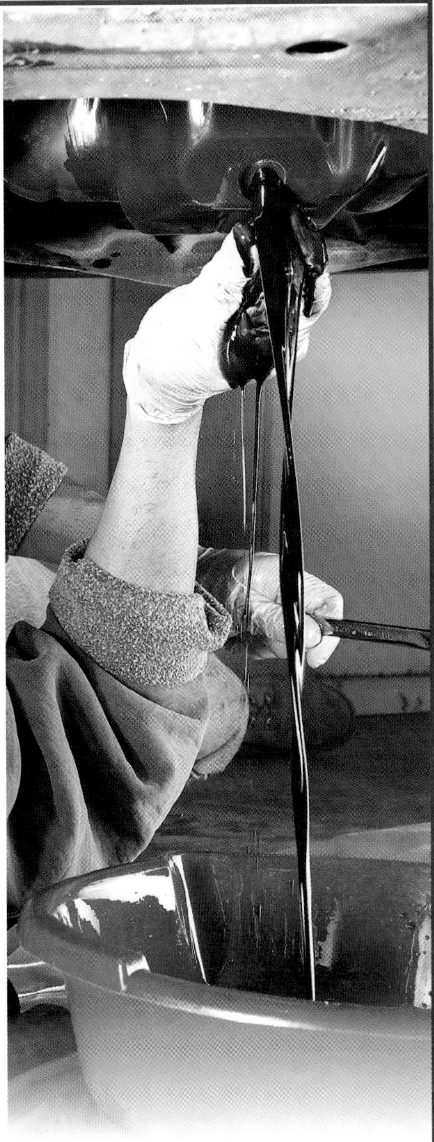

Oil-changing tips

- If the engine is cold, start it and let it run for five minutes to warm the oil. If it's hot, wait at least 30 minutes to avoid getting burned.
- Never use an adjustable wrench or socket on the drain plug. Use the proper size box-end wrench, usually metric, for the plug.
- Always use jack stands. Never work under a car that's supported by a jack only.
- Use new oil to coat the oil filter gasket before spinning it on.
- Always hand-tighten the filter. Never use a filter wrench.
- Recycle your oil at an oil recycling center near you (see "Save Money on Oil," left).
- Line up all the oil bottles you'll need for the fill so you don't lose count as you pour.

Are you a "severe driver"?

Believe it or not, most people fall into the severe driving classification. The Center for Auto Safety says this:

Extended oil change intervals of 7,500 or 10,000 miles or more are based on ideal operating conditions, not the type of short-trip, stop-and-go driving that is typical for many motorists. Consequently, most drivers should follow a "severe" service maintenance schedule rather than a "normal" one to protect their engines.

Severe driving includes:

- Most trips are less than 4 miles.
- Most trips are less than 10 miles when outside temperatures remain below freezing.
- Prolonged high-speed driving during hot weather.
- Idling for extended periods and continued low-speed operation (as when driving in stop-and-go traffic).
- Towing a trailer.
- Driving in dusty or heavily polluted areas.

Some engines, such as diesels, suffer more blow-by than others and typically require more frequent oil and filter changes. For most passenger cars and light-truck diesels, the oil should be changed every 3,000 miles without exception—especially in turbo diesels.

Turbocharged gasoline engines also require more frequent oil changes because of the high temperatures inside the turbo, which can oxidize oil. A 3,000-mile oil change interval is also recommended for all turbocharged gasoline engines.

GETTY IMAGES/MITCH DIAMOND

Internet lore advises performing an engine flush before switching to synthetic. That's a horrible idea. Just drain the old oil and pour in synthetic. Then pop on a premium filter and you're done. And it's time to discontinue the age-old practice of adding a higher-viscosity oil to combat low oil pressure. Higher-viscosity oil actually increases friction and reduces flow rate, causing the oil (and engine) to run hotter. So you wind up with lower gas mileage, more wear and sludge buildup.

High-mileage synthetic oil contains film-strengthening additives to improve ring sealing and oil pressure. Many brands also include seal conditioners to soften stiff seals, as well as extra anti-oxidant, anticorrosion, antiwear and detergent additives to handle the crud in the crankcase. So, if you have more than 100,000 miles on your engine, switch to a high-mileage oil. It costs only about $1 per quart more than regular synthetic.

When should you change oil?

Everybody's full of advice about how long you can go between oil changes. But unless they know your driving habits, that advice is just hot air. Frequent cold starts, short trips (less than 4 miles), stop-and-go driving, hauling heavy loads and lead-foot starts are incredibly hard on oil and deplete the additives quickly. Your owner's manual lists a different oil change schedule for this kind of severe driving, a category that includes most drivers. Unfortunately, those same drivers change their oil according to the optimistic "normal" schedule. So follow the oil change schedule that applies to your driving style. Or, if you have a newer vehicle with an oil-life monitor, rely on that.

Trust the oil change light if you have one

Some vehicles have an oil change reminder light that turns on when you've reached a set mileage. Those systems don't take your driving habits into account. So you have to adjust your oil change intervals according to how you drive. However, oil-life monitoring systems do track your driving habits. The computer records the number of cold

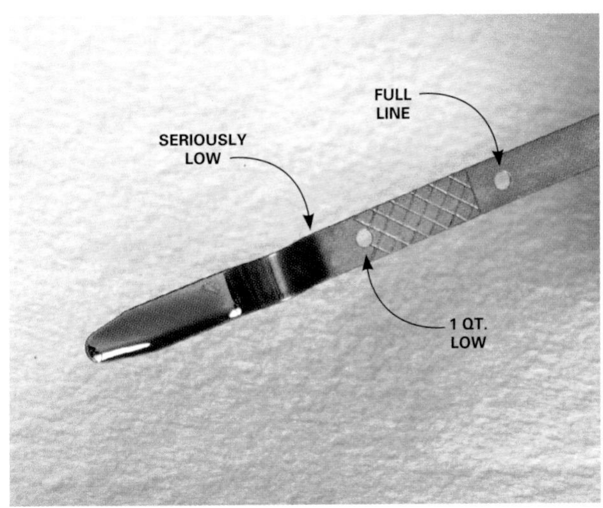

3 Check the oil level every 500 miles. Add more oil to bring the level up to the FULL line, even if the dipstick shows the oil is down only a half quart. This will prevent rapid oil degradation.

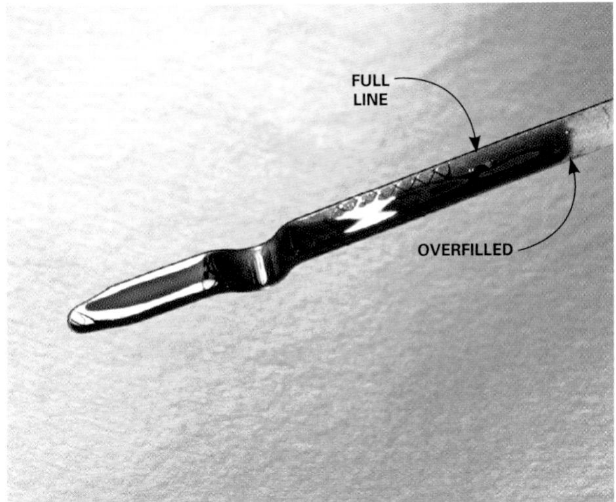

4 Overfilling damages the oil and engine. Overfilling creates foam, which rapidly degrades the oil and causes additional engine wear. Foam doesn't remove heat as efficiently as liquid oil, so the engine and the oil get much hotter. The extra heat and air rapidly degrade the oil.

starts, ambient and engine temperatures during startup, driving time between starts, engine load and whether the miles are highway or stop-and-go. It runs that data through an algorithm to estimate the remaining oil life. If you do a lot of short-trip city driving, the light will come on sooner than if you make long commutes.

You can trust the carmakers' oil-life monitoring systems only if you use the recommended oil and don't use any aftermarket additives. Pour in some miracle oil stabilizer and all bets are off.

What about those long-distance oils?

What about those claims that certain oils can go 15,000 or 25,000 miles between changes? Is there really an oil that comes with a 300,000-mile engine guarantee? Because severe driving degrades oil additives faster, oil manufacturers often qualify their oil change recommendations in the fine print. In some cases, your driving habits may require you to reduce the advertised mileage interval by as much as half. So don't assume you qualify for the best-case scenario: Read the instructions and the warranty terms. And no matter what the companies' promises are, if you skip the carmakers' recommended change intervals, your factory or extended warranty will be void. So you'd have to depend on the oil manufacturer to pay for repairs.

Check your oil level

Unless you own a luxury vehicle equipped with an oil level sensor, your vehicle won't tell you when it's low on oil because its warning light only indicates oil pressure. By the time the warning light comes on, you're already dangerously low on (or completely out of) oil.

Here's the bottom line: All engines burn oil. And with longer intervals between oil changes, you can count on losing up to a full quart before it's time for your next oil change. Driving a quart low puts tremendous stress on the remaining oil, dramatically reducing its useful life. So get into the habit of checking the dipstick every other fill-up. Add oil to raise the level to the full mark, even if it's down just a half quart (**Photo 3**). But don't overfill (**Photo 4**).

HandyHints®

FROM OUR READERS

Make a list to keep track of oil changes

With three different vehicles to keep track of and the time lapse between oil changes, I've got to write things down to keep them straight.

When I change the oil, I tear off the flap of the box that identifies the filter number, and then I write down the size of the drain plug and the type of filter wrench I use for each vehicle on the flap. I keep the info inside the car. When it's time for the next change, I pull out the tab to see which filter to buy and which tools to use. I don't waste time crawling under the car several times to get the right wrench.

—Daniel Oberholtzer

BONUS SECTION

GreatGoofs®

Be careful!

Up in smoke

We had recently bought an outdoor electric smoker/cooker and were excited to try it. The instructions recommended changing out the wood chips every two hours during smoking. It was Sunday and we decided to do the first chip rotation before leaving for church. I carefully opened the door of the smoker and removed the hot metal container of smoking wood chips. Looking around for a place to dump the charred wood, I focused on our old whiskey/wine barrel planter. I dumped it in and we left for church. Returning home, we could see smoke rising over the tops of the pine trees by our driveway. I raced to the planter and saw that the hot coals I'd dumped had ignited the dried peat in the barrel. Luckily, the barrel wasn't near the house.

—Steve Petersen

Thar she blows!

While shredding old checks and other documents, I decided my sluggish paper shredder needed lubricating. I happened to have a spray can of silicone lubricant, so I sprayed the shredding mechanism liberally as it sat on top of the catcher basket. When I pushed the switch to "on," I was surprised by a small explosion. A spark had ignited the accumulated vapors in the enclosed area of the shredder.

After taking a few minutes to calm down, I looked in the mirror and noticed my singed eyebrows and hair. Next time the shredder needs lubricating, I'll do it outside and let it dry before mounting it onto the basket!

—Robert S. Messer

Hoodwinked

Our new house had a very old kitchen, and our first project was to replace the nasty, greasy range hood. Simple enough, I thought—it would only take a few minutes.

To protect the cooktop, I covered it with cardboard. The old hood came out easily, but while I was putting in the new hood, the clamp I used to hold it in position slipped. The hood fell onto the cooktop and then down onto my shoeless foot. I picked up the new hood, set it back onto the cooktop and proceeded to hop on one foot into the next room to assess my injury.

When I hobbled back into the kitchen, there were flames shooting up from the cooktop. I threw the hood and the cardboard out the door onto the driveway. Apparently when the hood fell, it knocked one of the burner knobs, which started the fire. I bought another new hood, removed the burner knobs and had a successful second attempt without burning down our new home.

Steve Berzins

A close call

In the double garage of our first home, we had a one-piece swing-up garage door, also known as a "kick-out" garage door. The door pivots up instead of rolling on tracks. I decided to replace the springs one day, and I opened the door and propped it with a 2x4 to secure it while I did the job. The old springs were stretched out and not too hard to remove. I soon discovered that I couldn't stretch the new springs enough with the door in the open position, so I reached for the 2x4 to let the door down.

John Gray

Yiiiiiikes! The door was so heavy that it came down with a crash and sent me sliding on my keister halfway across the garage floor. Fortunately, I only had some bruises on my backside and scraped elbows. When my wits came back, I realized how lucky I was not to be in the back of an ambulance. I now leave garage door spring replacement to the pros!

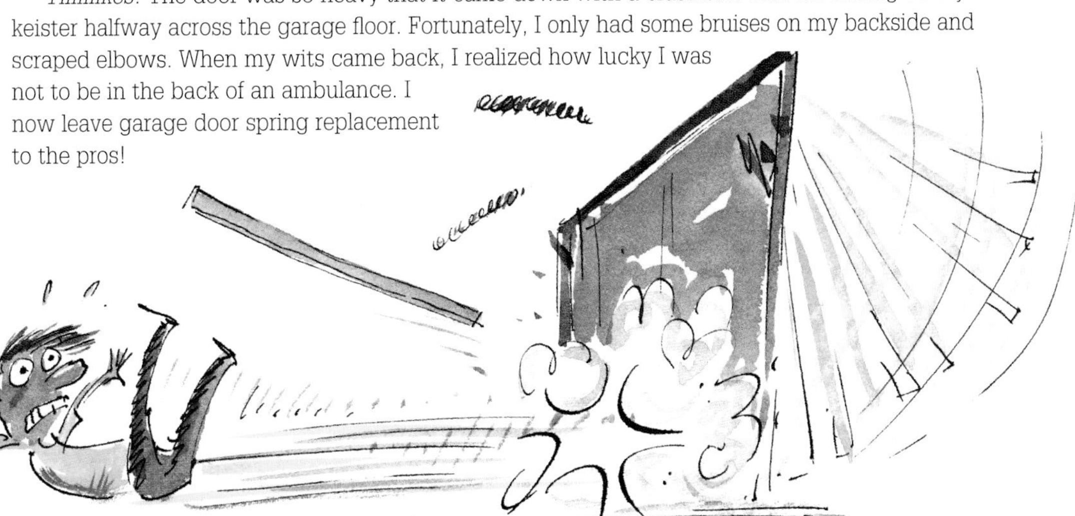

INDEX

Visit **familyhandyman.com** *for hundreds of home improvement articles.*

A

Adhesives, 39
Aerators, faucet, 108
AFCI (arc-fault circuit interrupter) outlets, 80
Air compressors, 175, 177
Air conditioner repairs, 98–101
Airless paint sprayers, 57, 196
Air returns, hiding place for valuables, 27
Alarm systems, 51
Aluminum wiring, 5
Appliances
  computerized touch pad and control board repair, 67
  leveling, 89
See also specific appliances
Asbestos, 5
Asphalt driveway apron repair, 184–185
Automobiles
  booster pack rebuild, 240
  duct cleaner, 240
  hood protection treatment, 265–267
  leather/vinyl repair, 241
  luggage rack protector, 274
  motor oil options, 277–281
  polishing, 262–264
  puddle navigation tips, 241
  rust penetrant, 241
  seat covers, 242–245
  seat heaters, 245
  serpentine belt replacement, 246–248
  snow tires, 207–208
  stuck receiver hitches, 276
  stuck spark plugs, 276
  stuck wheels, 275
  tensioner replacement, 247
  wheel and wheel cover refinishing, 268–270
  See also Pickup trucks
Axes, sharpening, 138

B

Backup sump pump systems, 95–97
Bagster bags, 229, 230
Baking soda, 12
Baltic birch plywood, 170
Baseboards. *See* Trimwork
Basements
  remodeling projects, 39–43
  sump pump options, 94–97
Basin wrench, 106
Bathtub installation, 105
Batteries
  booster pack replacement, 240
  cordless tool battery identification, 181
  lithium batteries, 66, 79
  smoke detector options, 66
  sump pump backup systems, 95
Bell boxes, 75
Belt sanders, 139
Bench project, 232–235
Bikes, 274, 276
Biscuit joiner tool, 119
Biscuits, 119, 124
Blade guards, 128
Blow guns, 179
Boards
  lengthening tip, 127
  straightening crooked, 130, 173
  See also Woodworking and workshops
Books, hiding place for valuables, 27
Booster pack rebuild, 240
Brick, drilling, 43
Bronze faucets, 103
Buckets
  safe storage, 5
  tree watering, 231
  weed pickup, 231
Buffing, 175
Bumper balls, 70
Burglary prevention, 49–51. *See also* Security
Buried cable repair, 64–65

C

Cabinets
  clothes cabinet project, 14–22
  face frame style, 148–151
  hiding places for valuables, 29
  hinge face-lift, 37
  marking for easy assembly, 133
  toe-kicks, 151
Cables
  buried cable repair, 64–65
  "running," 68–71, 84–86
Cable ties, 177
CA (cyanocacrylate) glue, 122, 127
Calculator protector, 161
Capacitors, A/C, 100
Carbide router bits, 139
Carbon monoxide (CO), 5
Carpet, pre-leveling of doorjambs before installation, 13
Cars. *See* Automobiles
Cat litter box tips, 36
Caulk
  faucet installation, 108
  organizer, 163
C-clamp lifting tool, 175
Ceiling painting tips, 52
Cement, hydraulic, 43
Central air conditioner repairs, 98–101
Chairs, caster repair, 12
Child-proof outlets, 80
Chisels
  flattening, 137
  sharpening, 138
Chrome faucets, 103
Cinch clamps, 91
Clamps and clamping
  board alignment tips, 121, 123
  C-clamp lifting tool, 175
  corner clamps, 125, 127
  hands as, 125
  holders, 132
  right-angle jig, 135
  T-bars, 134
  vises, 169
  wax paper to prevent dark spots on wood, 121
Cleaning
  air conditioner condenser coils, 99
  car air ducts, 240
  jars, 38
  litter boxes, 36
  metal shavings, 160
  tabletops, 159
Clothes cabinet project, 14–22
Clothing, dust control tip, 161
Concrete
  crack patches, 186
  fastening, 39–43
Concrete screws, 40
Condenser coils, cleaning, 99
Conduit, 71, 72–75, 86
Contractors, A/C, 100
Cookbook clamp, 35
Cooler light, 182
Cord control clips, 79
Cordless tool battery identification, 181
Cork removal tip, 173
Countersink bits, 141
Countersink tool, 135
Countertops, laminate installation, 130
Crack-repair spray, 23
Crosscuts, 130, 170
Cutting-in painting technique, 58–59

D

Dado blade, 129
Dadoes, 169
Decks
  installation over patio, 216–220
  lag screws, 142
  rejuvenation, 200–202
  roof panel, installation under, 236–238
Delta EZ Anchor system, 104
Demolition hammers, 173
Detailing
  automobiles, 262–264
  motorcycles, 252–254

Diamond paddles, 139
Dogs, skunk spray antidote, 228
Doors
hiding place for valuables, 30
hinge repair, 13
paint protection, 197
painting tips, 53–57
pre-leveling doorjambs, 12
reinforcement of exterior doors, 49
Dowel joints, 133, 134
Drain assembly replacement, 10–11
Drain deodorizer, 36
Drawers, sticking problem fix, 34
Drill Doctor, 138
Drill press table, 168
Drills and drilling
countersink bits, 141
cutting with, 172
drill bit sharpening, 138
drill clutch settings, 142
dust catcher for, 35
flex bits, 68, 70
hook installation, 180
magnetic bit-tip holders, 141
scrubbing with, 174
self-centering bits, 142
shoe shining, 175
spade bits, 136
step bits, 162
stop for, 132
Driveway apron repair, 184–185
Driving tips, 241. *See also* Automobiles
Dryers, 105
Drywall
installation, 142
mud rings, 70
patching, 23–25, 160
taping, 44–47
Dust control
catcher when drilling, 35
wood finishing tips, 156, 157, 161

E

Ear syringe, as dust removal tool, 42
Electrical
aluminum wiring, 5
buried cable repair, 64–65
circuit breaker identification, 79
outdoor wiring, 72–75
wire fishing tips, 68–71
See also Lighting; Outlets
Electrical box size calculation, 80
Electronics
appliance repairs, 67
outlet strips, 78
recycling, 66
Wi-Fi, 76–77
Ethanol, 273
Exterior repairs and improvements
asphalt driveway apron repair, 184–185
concrete cracks, 186
covered patio, 236–238
outlet installation, 84–86
painting, 196–199
shed project, 221–227
vinyl-clad fence repair, 186
wiring tips, 72–75
See also Decks; Roofs
Eye protection, 5

F

Face frame cabinets, 148–151
Faucets
choosing, 102–103
installation, 104, 106–108
manuals, 108
Fence, vinyl-clad fence renewal, 186
Fertilizer application, 212–215
Finishes and finishing
final inspection before, 133
masking glue joints before, 120
polyurethane, 158
preparation, 156–157
samples, 157
sanding tips, 157–158, 159
stand for, 131
tabletops, 156–159
Flex bits, 68, 70
Flooding, sump pump installation, 94–97
Flux brushes, 121, 160
Fly trap, 229
Foam insulation, 39
Freezers. *See* Refrigerators and freezers
Fuel stabilizer, 205, 273

G

Garage door repairs, 255–261
Garages
bike storage, 274, 276
clear leaf bag storage, 228
Gardening. *See* Landscaping and gardening
Gas, small-engine tips, 272–273
Gas containers, 273
Gear ties, flexible, 176
Generator-powered sump pumps, 97
Gift wrap storage, 34
Gloves, 176, 178
Glow rods, 68, 71
Gluing wood
injection into cracks with air compressor, 175
miter joints, 125, 127
tips, 120–123
Goofs, 57, 79, 97, 105, 178, 195, 208, 261, 267, 271, 282–283
Grain filler, 158
Grass. *See* Lawn care
Grill covers, as tool protectors, 162
Grills, painting, 210–211
Grocery bags, improvement to make sturdier, 36

H

Hardware organizer project, 164–166
Hardwood floors, installation, 35
Hat, fly-trap, 229
Hatchets, sharpening, 138
Headlamps, 59
Hearing protection, 5
Heated seats, 245
Hiding places, 26–30
Hinges
doors, 13
kitchen cabinets, 37
Hole spacer jig, 171
Honing steels, 139
Hood protection treatment, 265–267
Hooks, installation tips, 174, 180
HVLP paint sprayers, 57
Hydraulic cement, 43

I

Impact drivers, 141
Inspection mirrors, 69

J

Jars, cleaning tip, 38
Jigs, 167–171
Jigsaw guide, 162

K

Keys, hiding place, 30
Kid's workbench, 147
Kitchen cabinets. *See* Cabinets
Knives, sharpening, 136–139

L

Labels
removal tip, 160
workshop drawers, 132
Ladder caddy, 176
Lag screws, 142
Laminate countertops, 130
Landscaping and gardening
bench project, 232–235
fly-trap hat, 229
seed library, 230
tool rack, 231
tree watering bucket, 231
weed bucket, 231
Laptops, port damage protectors, 78
Lawn care
fertilizer application, 212–215
leaf collection, 229
twig pickup, 230
Lawn mowers
gas options, 272–273
handle insulation, 228
Lead paint, 5, 199
Leaf collection, 229
Leaks
bottom-freezer refrigerators, 88
faucets, 108
Leather car interior repair, 241
Levels and leveling
accuracy checks, 180
extender for level, 182
garden hose level, 174
"poor man's" laser level, 179
Lightbulbs
changing tool, 34

lube to remove stuck, 78
Lighting
flexible stand for, 176
for detecting flaws in finishes, 133, 158
headlamps, 59
in toolboxes, 182
key ring flashlight holder, 177
recessed can lighting installation, 70
security, 50
Light switches
crooked, fix, 66
glow-in-the-dark treatment, 38
painted covers, 160
Lithium batteries, 66, 79
Litter box cleanup tips, 36
Locker project, 110–113
Locknuts, 75
Low-voltage connectors, 65
Lubricants
pencil lead, 175
saw blade, 153
spray tube holder, 37

M

Magazines, reference notes, 34
Magnetic bit-tip holders, 141
Marking gauges, 135
Masking tape
glue joints before pre-finishing, 120
old, softening, 36
paint preparation tips, 59, 60–62
Masonry, fastening, 39–43
MDF (medium-density fiberboard), 170
Melamine, 170
Metal shavings, cleanup tip, 160
Mice, trapping tips, 31–33
Mirrors, inspection, 69
Miter gauges, 130, 174
Miter joints, 114, 124–127
Miter saws, 114, 126, 127, 171
Moen M-PACT system, 104
Moldings. *See* Trimwork
Motion sensors, 50
Motorcycles, detailing tips, 252–254
Motor oil, 277–281
Mud rings, 70

N

Nails, driving, 173
Nickel faucets, 103
Nitrile-palm gloves, 178

O

Odors
baking soda deodorizer, 12
drains, 36
refrigerators, 89
work boot deodorizer, 163
Office chair caster repair, 12
Oil, motor, 277–281
Oil-based polyurethane, 158
Oil-changing tips, 279, 280–281
Oil filters, 279
"Old work" boxes, 82, 83
Orbital cutting, reciprocating saws, 155
Organic fertilizers, 214
Organization. *See* Storage and organization
Oscillating tool, 118
Outdoor projects. *See* Exterior repairs and improvements
Outdoor rugs, 220
Outlets
AFCI protection, 80
fixing crooked, 66
folding wires into box, 81
indoor installation, 82–83
outdoor installation, 84–86
power sources, 81
tamper-resistant outlets, 80
Outlet strips, 78
Oxygenated gas, 273

P

Paint and painting
cabinet hinges, 37
ceilings, 52
cutting-in technique, 58–59
disposal, 52
doors, 53–57
exterior tips, 196–199
goof cleanup method, 52
grills, 210–211
lead paint danger, 5, 199
masking tape prep, 59, 60–62
panel doors, 53–57
switch plate covers and screws, 160
tool drying cage, 181
wall patching, 23–25
water-based alkyds, 55
wheel covers, 270
See also Finishes and finishing
Paint cans, hiding place for valuables, 90
Paint sprayers, 57, 196–199
Parts bins, 133
Patio doors, security upgrades, 48
Patios
covered, 236–238
renewal of, 216–220
Patio umbrellas, 229
Paver patios, 220
Peelable paint, 270
Pencil lead, as lubricant, 175
Pest control, 31–33
PEX (cross-linked polyethylene) pipe, 90–93
Pickup trucks
bed liner extension, 275
bed liner protection, 249–251
long item brackets, 275
motor oil options, 277–281
stretch wrap bundling tip, 274
stuck receiver hitch, 276
stuck spark plugs, 276
stuck wheels, 275
wheel and wheel cover refinishing, 268–270
Pictures, hanging tips, 38
Plane blades
flattening, 137
sharpening, 138
Plants
hiding place for valuables, 27
pot liner, 37
Plastic, scratch removal, 12
Plastic tiles, installation over concrete patio, 220
Plumbing
faucets, 102–104, 106–108
PEX pipe installation, 90–93
PVC pipe cutting tips, 154
Plywood edging, 129
Pocket hole screws, 149
Polishers, auto, 262–264
Polyurethane, 158–159
Port damage protectors, 78
Powder-actuated tool (PAT), 41
Puddles, driving tips, 241
Putty knives, 160
PVC pipe
conduit for outdoor wiring, 72–75
cutting tips, 154
hiding place for valuables, 30

R

Rabbets, 151
Rags, disposal, 5
Raking light, 25
Range extenders, 77
Recessed lights, 70
Reciprocating saws, 152–155
Recycling, electronics, 66
Refrigerators and freezers
bottom-freezer refrigerator leaks, 88
deodorizer, 89
hiding place for valuables, 29
Remodel boxes, 82, 83
Roofs
cutting shingles, 154
installation, 187–199
safety precautions, 5
Routers (Wi-Fi), 76–77
Routers (woodworking)
fences, 135
flattening board with, 173
stone shaping, 172
use after mitering, 125
Rubber gloves, 176
Rust penetrant, 241

S

Safety
eye protection, 5
garage door repairs, 256
gloves, 176, 178
hazards, 5
lead paint, 5, 199
roofs, 5, 190
table saws, 128
Sanders
buffing with, 175
replacement pad, 163
Sander tables, 170
Sanding tips, 157–158, 159
Sandpaper, 134
Screws
concrete screws, 40
driving tips, 140–142
lag screws, 142
pocket hole screws, 149

Torx-head screws, 140
trim-head screws, 140
Scribing technique, 115, 150
Seat covers, 242–245
Seat heaters, 245
Security
alarm systems, 51
exterior door reinforcement, 49
hiding places for valuables, 26–30
lighting, 50
patio doors, 48
sump pump alarms and backup systems, 95–97
video surveillance, 50
windows, 48
Seed library, 230
Self-centering bits, 142
Serpentine belt replacement, 246–248
Serrated knives, sharpening, 137
Setting compound, 24
"Severe driver" category, 280
Sharpening tips, 136–139
Shed project, 221–227
Shingles, 193–194
Shoes
shining, with drill, 175
storage, 37
Shutoff valves, 106
Sink
installation, 107
stoppers, 104
strainer replacement, 10–11
Skunk spray antidote, 228
Slop can, 133
Small engines, gas tips, 272–273
Smartphones, port damage protectors, 78
Smoke detectors, 5, 66
Snow blowers
gas options, 272–273
tips, 203–206
Snow tires, 207–208
Soffits, painting tip, 198
Soil testing, 213
Spade bits, sharpening, 136
Splice kits, 64
Spray foam, 161
Squaring blocks, 168
Stabilizer, fuel, 205, 273
Stairs, hiding place for valuables, 26–30
Step bits, 162
Stone, shaping with router, 172
Storage and organization
bikes and bike gear, 274, 276
caulk tubes, 163
clear leaf bags, 228
clothes cabinet project, 14–22
cordless tool batteries, 181
faucet manuals, 108
gas, 273
gift wrap, 34
hardware organizer project, 164–166
rags, 132
seeds, 230
shoes, 37
tools, 181
workshop, 132, 133
Stud finders, 69
Sump pumps, 94–97
Superglue, 122, 127
Synthetic oil, 205, 278–280

T

Table height extenders, 182
Table legs, 132
Table saws
fence, 170
guide box, 167
paste wax treatment for top, 161
tips, 128–130, 150
Tabletops, finishing tips, 156–159
Tamper-resistant outlets, 80
Tape. *See* Masking tape
Tensioner replacement, 247
Textured ceilings, painting tips, 52
THHN wire, 72
Tile
cutting holes for outlet, 83
installation, 35
patios, 220
Tires, winter, 207–208
Toe-kicks, 151
Toolboxes
labeling, 181
light for, 182
Tool markings, easy-to-read, 163
Tools, sharpening, 136–139
Torx-head screws, 140
Trailer liner, 230
Tree watering bucket, 231
Trim-head screws, 140
Trimwork
baseboard gaps, 116, 117
baseboard tilting problem, 118
joint strengthening with biscuits, 119
miter gaps, 114
oscillating tool, 118
paint preparation, 59, 60–62
steep angles, 114
transition blocks, 116
uneven walls, 115
Trucks. *See* Pickup trucks
T-square router fence, 135

U

Utility lines, marking before digging, 5, 64

V

Vacuums, hiding place for valuables, 27
Valuables, hiding places, 26–30
Video surveillance, 50
Vinyl car interior repair, 241
Vinyl-clad fence renewal, 186
Vises, 169

W

Walls
paint protection tips, 61
spray on texture, 25
See also Drywall
Washing machines, broken agitator replacement, 89
Water-based polyurethane, 158
Water-powered sump pump backup systems, 96
WaterSense faucet label, 104
Water supply lines, 107
Wax treatment
automobiles, 264
motorcycles, 253
Weatherproof electrical boxes, 75
Weed bucket, 231
Wet sanding, 159
Wheels and wheel covers
freeing stuck wheel, 275
refinishing tips, 268–270
Wi-Fi systems, 76–77
Windows
paint preparation, 59, 62, 197
security upgrades, 48
Wiring. *See* Electrical
Wood glue. *See* Gluing wood
Wood grain, matching, 124
Woodworking and workshops
bench project, 232–235
calculator protector, 161
caulk tube organizer, 163
clothing, 161
countersink tool, 135
creative tool use, 172–175
dowel joints, 133, 134
drawer labels, 132
drill stop, 132
driving screws, 140–142
dust control, 156, 157, 161
face frame cabinets, 148–151
gluing tips, 120–123, 125, 127, 175
grill cover tool protection, 162
hardware organizer project, 164–166
jigs, 167–171
jigsaw guide, 162
ladder caddy, 176
locker project, 110–113
marking gauges, 135
metal shavings cleanup tip, 160
miter joints, 114, 124–127
rag storage, 132
reciprocating saw tips, 152–155
sander pad replacement, 163
sandpaper, 134
sharpening tips, 136–139
slop can, 133
spray foam application tube, 161
table legs, 132
table saw tips, 128–130, 150, 161, 167
tool marking enhancement, 163
workbench project, 143–147
See also Clamps and clamping; Finishes and finishing; Trimwork
Workbench project, 143–147
Work boots, freshener, 163

ACKNOWLEDGMENTS

FOR THE FAMILY HANDYMAN

Editor in Chief	Ken Collier
Senior Editors	Travis Larson
	Gary Wentz
Associate Editor	Jeff Gorton
Senior Copy Editor	Donna Bierbach
Art Directors	Vern Johnson
	Marcia Roepke
Photographer	Tom Fenenga
Production Artist	Mary Schwender
Office Administrative Manager	Alice Garrett
Production Manager	Amy Tuller

CONTRIBUTING EDITORS

Elisa Bernick
Spike Carlsen
Dave Munkittrick
Rick Muscoplat
Mark Petersen
David Radtke

CONTRIBUTING ART DIRECTOR

Ellen Thomson

CONTRIBUTING PHOTOGRAPHER

Paul Nelson

ILLUSTRATORS

Steve Björkman
David Radtke
Frank Rohrbach III

OTHER CONSULTANTS

Charles Avoles, plumbing
Myron Ferguson, drywall
Al Hildenbrand, electrical
Joe Jensen, Jon Jensen, carpentry
William Nunn, painting
Dean Sorem, tile
Costas Stavrou, appliance repair
John Williamson, electrical
Les Zell, plumbing

We welcome your ideas and opinions.
Write: The Editor, The Family Handyman
2915 Commers Drive, Suite 700
Eagan, MN 55121
Fax: (651) 994-2250
E-mail: editors@thefamilyhandyman.com